A REBEL AND A TRAITOR

ALSO BY RORY CARROLL

Comandante: Hugo Chávez's Venezuela
Killing Thatcher: The IRA, the Manhunt and the Long War on the Crown

RORY CARROLL

A REBEL AND A TRAITOR

A Fugitive,
the Manhunt and the
Birth of the IRA

Mudlark
HarperCollins*Publishers*
1 London Bridge Street
London SE1 9GF

www.harpercollins.co.uk

HarperCollins*Publishers*
Macken House, 39/40 Mayor Street Upper
Dublin 1, D01 C9W8, Ireland

First published by Mudlark 2026

1 3 5 7 9 10 8 6 4 2

© Rory Carroll 2026

Rory Carroll asserts the moral right to be identified as the author of this work

A catalogue record of this book is available from the British Library

HB ISBN 978-0-00-869693-1
PB ISBN 978-0-00-869694-8

Printed and bound in the UK using 100% renewable
electricity at CPI Group (UK) Ltd

All rights reserved. No part of this publication may be reproduced, stored in a retrieval system, or transmitted, in any form or by any means, electronic, mechanical, photocopying, recording or otherwise, without the prior written permission of the publishers.

Without limiting the exclusive rights of any author, contributor or the publisher of this publication, any unauthorised use of this publication to train generative artificial intelligence (AI) technologies is expressly prohibited. HarperCollins also exercise their rights under Article 4(3) of the Digital Single Market Directive 2019/790 and expressly reserve this publication from the text and data mining exception.

To my parents, Joe and Kathy

Contents

Author's Note	ix
Dramatis Personae	1
Map	5
Prologue	7

Part I | Dream of the Celt

1	Obedient Servant	13
2	Chieftains	25
3	Guns	36
4	England's Difficulty	48
5	Shark's Jaws	62
6	Open Treason	75

Part II | Shadowplay

7	Sayonara	93
8	Brotherhood	106
9	Love Your Enemies	118
10	The Fools, the Fools, the Fools	128
11	Blinker's Web	141
12	We Have Decided to Attack	153
13	Conjurer's Box	166
14	Calm Lies the Sea	178
15	Good Friday: In the Name of King George	195

Part III | Terrible Beauty

16	Holy Saturday: The Professor	213
17	Easter Sunday: This Festering Sore	224
18	Easter Monday: Left Turn, Charge	235
19	Easter Week: Don't Be Afraid	247
20	Into the Dark	262
21	The Other Thing	271
22	Trial	281
23	Erased	296
24	God Is Not an Englishman	311
	Epilogue	323
	Acknowledgements	329
	Picture Credits	333
	The Forgery Thesis	335
	Endnotes	337

Author's Note

I did not smell the sweat in *U-19*, or see Roger Casement march with the Irish Brigade, or eavesdrop on Reginald Hall's intrigues, but this is a work of non-fiction. It is based on official archives, police reports, court transcripts, memoirs, private letters and, of course, diaries to reconstruct the events in this story. Where there is dialogue there is a source that is identified with other sources in the endnotes. Newspapers from that time, including weather reports, provided context and colour. I also drew on the work of historians and biographers, who are cited in the acknowledgements and endnotes. Research trips to locations in Ireland, the UK and Germany, and interviews with descendants of some of the protagonists, helped to fill gaps. In cases where the historical record falters I have selected what seems to me the most credible version of events and outlined conflicting versions in the endnotes. In cases where it is difficult to fathom why people did what they did, I leave it to readers to decide for themselves.

Dramatis Personae

Irish

Gertrude Bannister: Casement's London-based cousin.
Roger Casement: British consul who became Irish nationalist and rebel.
Tom Clarke: Veteran rebel who revived the Irish Republican Brotherhood (IRB) and conceived the Easter rising.
Michael Collins: Aide to Joseph Plunkett and future rebel leader.
James Connolly: Socialist trade union leader who headed the Irish Citizen Army militia and joined the IRB's plot for a rising.
John Devoy: veteran rebel and exile who from New York headed Clan na Gael, sister organisation to the IRB, and ran the *Gaelic American* newspaper.
George Gavan Duffy: London-based solicitor who represented Casement.
Alice Stopford Green: London-based historian, author and friend of Casement.
Eoin MacNeill: history professor and Irish Volunteers chief-of-staff.

Robert Monteith: former British army soldier who trained Irish Volunteers and was sent by the IRB to Germany to help Casement.
Patrick Pearse: Schoolmaster, orator and IRB conspirator.
Joseph Plunkett: poet and IRB conspirator who visited Casement in Germany.

British

Augustine Birrell: Chief secretary for Ireland who headed the Dublin Castle administration.
Ernley Blackwell: chief legal adviser to the Home Office.
Winston Churchill: First Lord of the Admiralty – in effect minister of the navy – until May 1915.
Mansfeldt de Cardonnel Findlay: British legation chief – de facto ambassador – in Norway.
Reginald 'Blinker' Hall: battlecruiser captain-turned Admiralty director of naval intelligence.
Rufus Isaacs (Viscount Reading): Lord Chief Justice who presided at Casement's trial.
Matthew Nathan: Under-secretary for Ireland who served as Augustine Birrell's most senior official.
Frederick Edwin (F. E.) Smith: Conservative MP and attorney general who later became Lord Birkenhead.
Basil Thomson: assistant commissioner of Scotland Yard who worked closely with Reginald Hall.

Germans

Rudolf Nadolny: head of German military intelligence political section.
Karl Spindler: naval lieutenant who skippered the *Aud* gun-running mission.
Raimund Weisbach: U-boat officer who sank the *Lusitania* and escorted Casement to Ireland.

Arthur Zimmermann: Under-secretary and later minister of foreign affairs.

Others
Adler Christensen: Casement's Norwegian servant, fixer and lover.
Walter Page: US ambassador to Britain.

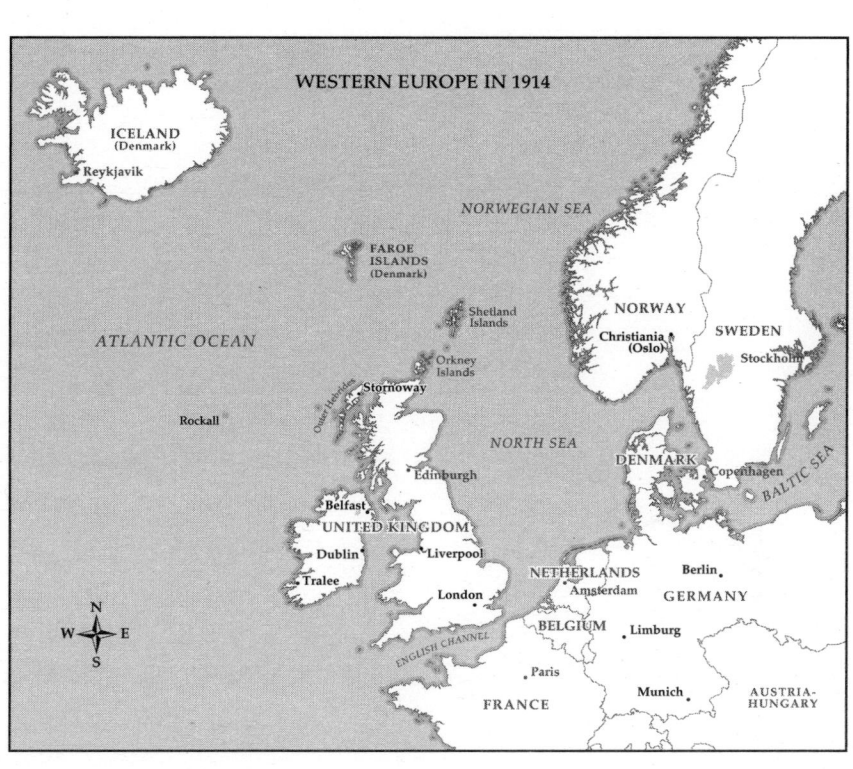

PROLOGUE

21 April 1916

The German submarine glided into Tralee Bay on the sea's surface, cloaked in darkness. Clouds veiled the stars and dimmed the moon. *U-19* cut its electric motors and slowed to a stop, rolling in a gentle swell. Two miles away, invisible in the blackness, lay Ireland.

It was 12.15 a.m. on Good Friday, 1916. The captain and his passengers stood in the conning tower, shivering in the chill, and scanned the bay. No lights or vessels were visible. The only sound was the slap of water against the hull. They raised their binoculars and did another sweep, 360 degrees. Nothing.

Somewhere in the inky void they were supposed to rendezvous with a cargo ship and a pilot boat that was to guide them to shore. The passengers were to disembark while comrades unloaded and transferred the weapons to a fleet of vehicles. But no signal lamps blinked in greeting. Nothing stirred.

Captain Raimund Weisbach peered into the night, uneasy. Was the plan cancelled? Or was it betrayed – was this an ambush? At any moment searchlights could blaze and light up the sub for hidden British gunners. He weighed his options. This was an important mission but maybe also a trap. The British had spies on land and at sea, and were refining ways to catch and destroy German submarines.

Entombed in a tin can as it plunged to the ocean floor, a submariner's death was not pleasant. Not that the trenches were much better; so many ways to die in the Great War. *U-19* had traversed the North Sea and rounded Scotland, evading mines and anti-submarine nets and Royal Navy patrols to deliver the three passengers to this Atlantic estuary. At times their leader had helped them all forget the danger and claustrophobia by singing ballads about his homeland. Weisbach preferred Schubert, but he appreciated these folk songs and the passengers' stories about previous uprisings when Spanish and French fleets had brought muskets and cannon to oust the English.

For the aristocratic Prussian it was the strangest thing: this tall, thin man with the rich baritone looked and spoke like an English gentleman. He had been knighted by the king. Now he sought to drive a dagger into the British empire.

But where were his comrades? An hour of prowling and still nothing but blackness and stillness, as if *U-19* were alone in the world. Weisbach did not know the fate of this latest rebellion and decided he was not going to linger in this eerie bay to find out. His passengers could row ashore in a dinghy to seek their comrades and start the revolution. One of the trio protested this plan as folly but the leader quietened him. 'Hush, it will be a greater adventure going ashore in this cockle shell.'

Under a rising moon the crew helped the men stow maps, revolvers and other kit, then lowered the dinghy from the deck into the sea. Moving stiffly in heavy coats and life-vests, the passengers murmured farewell. Weisbach asked if they needed anything else. The leader looked at him. 'Only my shroud.'

U-19 restarted its motors and slipped away, a grey ghost. The little boat bobbed in its wake. The two younger men rowed while the older man, at the stern, navigated with a steering oar. Through the gloom he spied a line of white foam and heard a thunder of breaking waves. The boat began to rock. 'Only two hundred yards more,' he said.

PART I

Dream of the Celt

CHAPTER ONE

Obedient Servant

Roger Casement stepped out into a damp, grey morning and a familiar tang of fish and old milk. The storm had passed, leaving a cold wind and a city of puddles. He would need to tread warily. There was a hole in his boot and the day had enough challenges without adding wet socks. Ebury Street woke early and so did its aromas. In a kinder world his boarding house would overlook the florists or fruit shops, but here it languished between a cheesemonger, a fishmonger and sour milk manufacturer.

Still, Casement favoured this terraced row of two-storey buildings and brightly painted doorways when visiting London. It had been good enough for a young Mozart, who composed his first symphony at number 180. Casement's digs at number 50 were cheap, respectable and central. And the landlord let him store his trunks there while travelling. With his long, swift strides Casement could make it to Whitehall in under half an hour.

The quickest route, once past Ebury's pungent wares, was right on Ecclestone Street, skirt the commuters spilling from Victoria station and gradually curve left, parallel to the river, until a proliferation of gothic spires, uniformed sentries and men with silk hats announced the administrative heart of Britain's empire.

The committee of grandees that had invited Casement to address the Royal Commission was possibly already gathered, awaiting him. The occasion called for Casement's best outfit of frock coat, starched collar and tie. He would be on stage, presenting the version of him they expected, giving his valedictory performance as a humble and obedient servant of the Crown.

It was Friday 8 May 1914, and the world's most populous city was launching into another day of aggravation and wonders. A pale sun hung in a leaden sky, casting feeble warmth. London's size and density astonished first-time visitors. Viewed from the eyries of St Paul's Cathedral it stretched in every direction, an endless vista of brick and spires. The Thames snaked through it all appearing timeless, but it had taken centuries of dredging to engineer it into a global waterway teeming with barges, tugs and steamers.

Everywhere, a ceaseless hustle. The earth itself vibrated with underground trains and tunnelling for new lines. Trams, motor cars and buses clogged streets in honking, swerving duels for supremacy while a rearguard of horse-drawn carts clip-clopped after them. Pedestrians had to gauge the speed of contraptions old and new before crossing streets. The previous day a bus had run over an errand boy named Cyril Ellis, who now lay dying in hospital. 'I will be brave,' he told doctors. 'I am a scout.'

Casement had been coming to London since he was a boy, but while he now edged towards his 50th birthday, the city of Dickens seemed younger, bigger, brasher. Derricks towered over scaffolding that birthed buildings taller and grander than what came before. The skeleton of a vast new county hall rose over Westminster Bridge, while at Knightsbridge Harrods prepared to metamorphose into a retail temple of unparalleled luxury. Even the *Titanic*'s collision with an iceberg two years earlier had not dented enthusiasm for record-breaking propulsion and technological marvels. 'Flying without wings,' the *Globe*'s front page declared over a report about an 'electro pulling magnet' that powered a model train to 300 miles per hour.

A restless, clamorous spirit reigned in what historians were to call the Edwardian era, after the late king. Suffragettes were smashing windows and detonating firebombs to demand votes for women, labour unions were striking for better wages and Ireland's demand for self-government was causing uproar.

Europe, at least, was at peace. There had been no war between the great powers in almost half a century. They had grown rich, made quantum leaps in scientific innovation and expanded colonies across Africa and Asia, making it a European world. But it was a tense calm. France pined for *revanche* – revenge to erase its humiliating defeat in the 1870–71 war with Prussia, which had paved the way for Germany's unification. The new nation yearned for a proper empire, a 'place in the sun', so built a fleet to challenge the Royal Navy, which induced Britain to build even bigger ships. Russia and the Austro-Hungarian empire glowered and bickered over the Balkans. Other nations nursed their own ambitions and grudges.

For years there had been talk of war yet it never came. Crises erupted, gunships sailed, then everyone backed down. There was too much to lose. Commerce bound the continent in tight embrace. So did kinship and affection. Royal families intermarried and people criss-crossed frontiers to study, work and play. Whenever a quarrel flared, diplomats lulled the continent back to somnolence.

Summer would usher in, as it always did, balls, regattas, polo, tennis, golf, concerts, seaside excursions and trips to the continent. The *Daily Mirror* fretted that Austria's aged emperor, Franz Joseph, had a bad night of coughing. 'But he felt fresher in the morning,' it reassured readers.

The Royal Opera House was rehearsing *Götterdämmerung*, the final opera of Wagner's *Ring* cycle that depicted war between gods and the burning of Valhalla, but nobody took it as a portent. This was the age of opulence and glitter. *The Dangerous Age* was the name of a comedy playing at the Vaudeville theatre.

Casement strode through this milieu with confidence. He knew London, knew its salons and chanceries, its boulevards and alleys, its lights and shadows. He would have known, too, that his visit here coincided with a royal funeral, and as he wove through the crowd of mourners and sightseers filing into Westminster he surely had heard the rumours about the man in the coffin.

The Duke of Argyll, a former governor general of Canada and son-in-law of Queen Victoria, had succumbed to pneumonia and was to receive a grand send-off. Pageantry preparations were well underway: an assemblage of horses with magnificently attired riders, guardsmen with drums and trumpets, bishops with fur cloaks. By the high altar a plumed hat and sword lay on a coffin draped in a union jack. At each corner stood a soldier, with rifle reversed. Wreaths of white blooms, mauve orchids, arum lilies and pink and red carnations scented the abbey.

The crowd was staking out vantage points to spot King George V, Queen Mary and other top-hatted and black-veiled royals, cabinet ministers, peers, ambassadors, admirals and field marshals in what would be England's most eminent gathering since George's coronation in 1911. The dead man's accomplishments were in truth meagre, but his rank demanded pomp.

And discretion. The duke's friendships with men known for unnatural vice had fuelled rumours of 'the love that dare not speak its name', a phrase famous since Oscar Wilde's gross indecency trial in 1895. Public shaming and prison broke the Irish writer, who died a wretch, but the duke would go to his grave eulogised and unsullied by the dread word. Homosexual.

Leaving the rubberneckers and courtiers to their business, Casement turned into Old Palace Yard, a secluded square tucked between the abbey and the palace of Westminster. A figure in bronze, holding a Bible in one hand, a sword in the other, gazed down from a pedestal.

Casement climbed the steps of Royal Commission House and entered a large room with besuited men seated amid documents and ink pots. Duty hung in the air. The Commission inquired into affairs of state and was currently examining Foreign Office management practices.

Hearings tended to dullness. Voices murmured, chairs creaked, papers rustled, the clock ticked towards lunch. But this day's expert witness was a famous hero. Roger Casement was an adornment, in every sense, of the British empire.

Roger Casement in a studio photo in London.

He was a striking physical presence, 6 ft 2 in., lithe, with deep-set blue-grey eyes and raven-black hair. Tropical sun had crinkled the forehead and some grey streaked the beard, but he still possessed a dark beauty that over the years had moved men and women to record it in memoirs. 'One of the finest-looking creatures I had ever seen,' wrote one. 'Magnificent-looking ... the gaze of all the tables was fastened on him,' gushed another. Casement resembled a Castilian aristocrat who had stepped from a Velázquez painting, said another. It wasn't just Europeans who swooned. Natives in Congo called him *Swami* (Woman's God) and *Monafuma* (Son of a King).

What gave the grandees most reason to sit straighter and adjust their collars was that Casement embodied imperial virtue. He had exposed villainy in dark corners of the globe and stirred a humanitarian response that reinforced Britain's sense of moral superiority.

It was all the more remarkable that Casement had reached such eminence the hard way via humble colonial outposts. He had sailed to Africa in 1883, aged 19, as a clerk for a Liverpool shipping line. Enchanted by the continent, he stayed. He surveyed railways, accompanied expeditions and ran supply bases for companies and missionaries in the Congo Free State, a vast, private fiefdom owned by Belgium's King Leopold II. While malaria felled other Europeans, Casement, for a time, seemed immune and criss-crossed jungles like a Victorian superman.

'There is a touch of the conquistador in him,' the writer Joseph Conrad, who met him at this time, later observed. 'I have seen him start off into an unspeakable wilderness swinging a crookhandled stick for all weapon, with two bulldogs at his heels and a Loanda boy carrying a bundle for all company. A few months afterwards it so happened that I saw him come out again, a little leaner, a little browner, with his stick, dogs, and Loanda boy, and quietly serene as though he had been for a stroll in the park.' Casement's accounts of his journeys, however, shook Conrad. 'He could tell you things! Things I have tried to forget, things I never did know.' The writer channelled some of this into his masterpiece *Heart of Darkness*.

In 1892 the Foreign Office hired Casement to work in a trading post in the Niger Oil Rivers Protectorate, the start of his long service for the Crown, and in 1895 sent him to Portuguese East Africa as part of the consular service. It was the poor cousin of the diplomatic corps. While ambassadors hobnobbed in palaces, consuls processed customs forms and sailors' grievances in mosquito-infested ports.

When the Boers rebelled in South Africa, Casement gathered intelligence for his Foreign Office masters and proposed a daring, though ultimately unsuccessful, commando raid. His judgement could be faulty, even histrionic. When malaria caught up with him, the start of recurring bouts of fever and ill-health, it also aggravated a tendency to hypochondria.

Nonetheless, in 1903 he accepted a new mission to investigate reports of abuses in Congo. With little more than a notebook, grit and guile, Casement ventured into forests and uncovered unspeakable vileness. King Leopold's soldiers, the *Force Publique*, were using whips, guns and terror to force tribes to harvest rubber trees that produced sap for European factories. Those who tried to flee or failed to reach quotas had limbs hacked off. The further Casement went up-river, the greater the horror – entire populations condemned to hunger, disease and brutality. The systematic plunder made Leopold immensely rich and would later be considered genocide.

When presented to the House of Commons, Casement's report – a model of meticulous evidence and controlled fury – created a sensation that eventually forced Belgium's monarch to give up the Congo and galvanised what became the modern humanitarian movement. In 1905 England's king appointed Casement a Companion of the Most Distinguished Order of St Michael and St George, an award for outstanding service in foreign affairs.

And then, incredibly, Casement did it again. He was consul general in Rio de Janeiro when reports emerged of abuses in Peru's Putumayo region. Casement took a steamer into the Amazon and discovered a system of bondage that was, if anything, worse than

Congo. The company responsible tried to conceal it, but Casement found survivors and perpetrators who recounted whippings, drownings, beheadings and shootings, all in the name of profit.

His 165-page report caused another sensation in 1911. Never before had voices of individual indigenous people – 'savages', as some still called them – so resounded in an official document. Casement briefed the US president, William Taft, and Pope Pius X issued an encyclical urging compassion for South America's Indians. Arrest warrants were issued, the rubber company went into liquidation and there were promises, not all kept, of kinder methods in the Amazon.

Plaudits rained down on the investigator. 'Roger Casement has deserved well of his countrymen and of mankind,' said *The Times*. 'A man of the highest character – truthful, unselfish, one who is deeply respected by all who know him,' said Arthur Conan Doyle, who modelled the dashing hero of his novel *The Lost World* on Casement. On 6 July 1911, in the throne room of St James's Palace, King George tapped a kneeling Casement on each shoulder with a sword, and when Casement rose he was a knight.

Little wonder, then, if the Royal Commission committee was star-struck. Sir Roger looked every inch the knight, and with his soft-spoken baritone and old-world courtliness sounded like one too, even if his testimony concerned Foreign Office minutiae. He recommended open competition for entry to the consular service and merging it with the diplomatic service. 'Nobody in the Foreign Office has ever been a consul, or knows anything about the duties of a consul,' he said.

This critique was duly transcribed. Whether the committee's final report would have any impact few outside Whitehall would ever care, but in helping to tweak Britain's bureaucratic machinery the esteemed visitor had shown he really was, in the formulaic terminology of Whitehall officials, a 'humble and obedient servant'.

Sir Roger spoke with the cadence of an English gentleman but the committee would have detected an Irish lilt. Sir Roger, after all, was from County Antrim on Ireland's northern tip and made no secret of his roots across the Irish Sea. In fact he had customised consul letterheads to specify he was a representative of Great Britain *and* Ireland. This was accurate – the two islands formed the United Kingdom – but idiosyncratic. No other consul seemed to bother with the appendage.

The grandees also knew Sir Roger favoured Home Rule, the term for devolved government in Ireland. He wrote letters to *The Times* about it. This did not dent his credentials. Transferring limited powers to an assembly in Dublin while London retained supreme control was government policy. Since the famine of the 1840s Ireland had stabilised and become somewhat prosperous, even cheery, and Home Rule seemed a way to heal old wounds while anchoring the Irish in the union.

Sir Roger, in any case, was the right type of Irishman: Protestant and verging on English. In Africa the explorer Henry Morton Stanley had called him 'a good specimen of the capable Englishman'. As the committee thanked its witness and showed him out, it was evident the Congolese had been on the right track. If not quite the son of a king, Sir Roger was the next best thing, a king's knight.

Casement stepped out into Old Palace Yard, his performance complete. He had not lied. The working conditions of consuls was a subject close to his heart. But he had his own reasons for accepting the invitation. The Royal Commission was covering his travel expenses. And he had indeed come to London for duty, just not the type they envisaged.

The day remained grey. The figure on the pedestal with the Bible wore a military tunic from another century and angled the sword downwards like a walking stick, the pose relaxed, almost jaunty. The expression was confident, composed. Etched on the white stone, a simple inscription: OLIVER CROMWELL. 1599–1658.

Such pride of place, here in front of parliament, for the general who led a Puritan revolution, established the Commonwealth of

England and unleashed ethnic and religious annihilation in Ireland, leaving a scorched wasteland and folk memory of terror. Ireland still shuddered at the name. The English knew this yet still honoured him with this statue.

For Casement, it was an abomination. In Antrim he had devoured the history and legends of Gaelic chiefs and written poems about their doomed efforts to save their land and culture. But as a young man he set aside such boyhood passions. In the 1880s Ireland was a settled part of the United Kingdom, and the horrors of the Great Hunger were fading. Public works had built roads and ports and fostered industry while agrarian reforms gave land to peasants. Emigration continued but most people stayed, and many became middle class. Ireland's grievances gathered dust.

When Casement moved to England to work for the shipping company he felt Irish *and* British. The young consul was diligent and proud to serve the empire. In South Africa he was all for giving the rebellious Boers a bloody nose. But as that grim war seeped across the velds, doubts seeped into Casement. His side was burning farmsteads and herding women and children into concentration camps. He could not bear to wear the medal they gave him. Memories of Irish legends stirred. In 1898 he began a poem, 'The Dream of the Celt', lamenting Ireland's subjugation by mercenaries in pay of an English king:

Stout Henry's purpose wrought with bastard blow;
The Celt too quick to trust . . .

He completed the poem in 1903, the same year Congo's desolation – wrought by another coloniser – led to epiphany. 'I had accepted imperialism,' he later wrote. 'British rule was to be accepted at all costs, because it was the best for everyone under the sun . . . well, the (Boer) war gave me qualms at the end. And finally when up in those lonely Congo forests where I found Leopold, I found also myself, the incorrigible Irishman. I realised I was looking at this tragedy with the eyes of another race, of a people once hunted themselves.'

Casement continued working for the Foreign Office for the salary – he had siblings to support – and masked a growing antipathy to his masters while moving from post to post. In the Amazon he identified a metaphor for England's impact on Ireland: *sipo matador* was a parasitic fig vine that attached itself to a tree and spread mould until the flow of sap ceased, leaving the vine clasping the lifeless and decaying body of its victim.

Visits to London reinforced this perception. In 60 years its population had more than doubled to 4.5 million while Ireland's had almost

Casement with Juan Tizon, head of the Peruvian Amazon Company, in the Putumayo region in 1912.

halved from 8.5 to 4.4 million. As the imperial capital filled, Ireland hollowed. On visits to Ireland, Casement supported attempts to revive the Irish language and ancient Gaelic sports and donated so much of his salary to schools, journals, festivals, street beggars and siblings that he was perpetually broke.

In 1913, citing malaria and other maladies, he took early retirement. He was no longer a government official but still confined public pronouncements to supporting Home Rule, which he considered a small but useful step towards Irish independence. He excoriated England's baleful influence in anonymous articles for Irish publications while, in public, remaining loyal to the Crown. But despite its promises, the government was now hesitating over granting even this limited form of self-government, hence Casement's trip to London. He planned to join a plot to *compel* the government to grant Home Rule. In 1606 the Gunpowder Plot conspirators were hanged, drawn and quartered in Old Palace Yard, but what Casement envisaged was not treason, merely illegal. He turned to go, leaving this place of execution.

Crowds still milled outside Westminster Abbey. The funeral service had been magnificent, the king himself joining a hymn for the Duke of Argyll:

Let thy mercy, O Lord, be upon us according as we hope in thee.
He will swallow up death in victory.

It was just over a mile to Grosvenor Road. Number 36 was a gaunt, narrow house overlooking the Thames. When Casement arrived a late spring mist shrouded the warehouses on the opposite bank and the tide was ebbing, leaving coal barges tilted on sleek mud. His friends were in a back room, discussing how to get guns.

CHAPTER TWO
―――

Chieftains

A Serbian melody filled the Golden Sturgeon cafe and Gavrilo Princip got up and swayed to the rhythm. He was 19, with a little moustache and a small, slight build. Too runty to be a soldier, the Serbian army told him, but he could dance. It was the music of Slavs, music no occupier could extinguish, and a way to pass the time until he got the opportunity to pull a trigger.

Princip was part of a militant group of young Serbs dedicated to uniting Slavs and expelling foreign overlords from the Balkans, and in spring 1914 he was haunting Belgrade cafes while mulling ways to hit the Austro-Hungarian empire, which held neighbouring Bosnia as a colony. His chosen method was assassination.

Spotting a friend, Princip forgot the music and fell into conversation. The friend showed him a newspaper cutting. It said Archduke Franz Ferdinand, heir to the Austro-Hungarian throne, was to visit Bosnia, and gave a date for the visit: late June.

. . .

There were days in May 1914 when it seemed the entire purpose of the oil painting on the ceiling of Dublin Castle was to mock the chief secretary for Ireland, Augustine Birrell. It loomed over St Patrick's Hall, a gilded ballroom used for ceremonies, and showed King Henry II receiving the submission of Irish chieftains. The monarch stood in the centre, all clanking armour and plumed helmet, and the chieftains huddled before him, paying homage. A cherub offered gifts. It was 1171 and England's conquest of Ireland was off to a good start.

The Romans who conquered Britain had steered clear of this sister island, which they called Hibernia, Land of Winter, but there was no stopping young Henry. He brought an army of knights and archers, got the Gaels to kneel, then sailed back to England.

Eight centuries later Birrell was tasked with managing the legacy of this royal foray. The days of homage were long gone. Henry's hubris had unleashed a chain of events that now charged at Birrell like an enraged boar.

Birrell's castle was not really a castle. It was a cobbled quadrangle in the centre of Dublin enclosed by offices and state apartments built over the ruins of a twelfth-century fortress. A sweeping staircase led to the Throne Room and St Patrick's Hall, where Queen Victoria had danced quadrilles. Previous viceroys eyed their successor from the portrait gallery. Charles Dickens, visiting in the 1860s, said these 'clever, and weak, and cunning faces' told the story of British control in Ireland. Some wore a diamond star and diamond badge, part of the Irish Crown Jewels. They were stolen in 1907, the year Birrell took this post. The chief secretary did not believe in portents but could recognise a metaphor.

A lawyer by training and writer by vocation, he was 64, with a capacious head and impressive sideburns, and had won acclaim for erudite essays spiced with a wit known as 'birrelling'.

When the Liberal party swept to power in 1906 and began laying the foundations of a welfare state, it sent Birrell to bring reforms to Ireland.

The actual viceroy was the Lord Lieutenant, who trotted around Dublin with brass-helmeted dragoons in velvet coats, but the chief secretary had the real power and a cabinet seat at Downing Street. This required regular crossings of the Irish Sea, which Birrell loathed, but Ireland he liked.

Taking up the post, briefing papers, historical tomes and dusty reports filled him in on events since Henry II. For a man disinclined to imperial adventure it was a sorry saga. England's Anglo-Norman mercenaries faced peril if they ventured beyond 'the Pale', a bastion around Dublin marked white on maps. Gradually the arrivals intermarried with the Gaels and formed a new class, the Anglo-Irish, which complicated England's effort to absorb this first colony, a template for its later global empire. The stakes escalated after Henry VIII turned England Protestant in 1534 and the indigenous Irish remained Catholic.

To subdue the rebellious northern province of Ulster the Crown expelled Gaels and gave their land to Protestant settlers from Scotland and England. Cromwell's army extinguished flickers of resistance and ushered in centuries of persecution of Catholics. Sporadic insurrections by Protestant radicals and the Catholic underclass all failed, even when England's enemies, Spain and France, sent ships to aid the rebels.

The 1800 Act of Union abolished Dublin's parliament – a final, rickety vestige of autonomy – and merged Ireland with Great Britain, which comprised England, Wales and Scotland, under the name of the United Kingdom of Great Britain and Ireland. Ireland's elected representatives henceforth sat in Westminster, but power still flowed through English officials in Dublin Castle.

When potato crops failed in the 1840s a million died and a million emigrated in coffin ships, a calamity the natives called *an Gorta Mór*, the Great Hunger. The government limited food aid to not encourage idleness in a race already deemed inferior and caricatured as apelike drinkers and brawlers. 'The real evil with which we have to contend is not the physical evil of the famine, but the moral evil of the selfish, perverse and turbulent character of the people,' said a Treasury mandarin in charge of famine relief. In the disaster's bitter aftermath, small, underground groups such as the Fenians and Irish Republican Brotherhood (IRB) staged sporadic bombings and assassinations.

For Birrell it all made for depressing reading, but after the 1880s optimism crept into the chronicles. Violence abated, public works extended ports, roads and railways, and improved education created a Catholic middle class.

The country embraced constitutional politics in the form of the Irish Parliamentary Party (IPP), which asserted Irish interests in Westminster debates on taxes and trade. As good Irish nationalists its MPs also stood up to request a devolved Dublin parliament – Home Rule – and as good parliamentarians they sat down again when told no. Back in Ireland the young drifted from politics to a revival of Gaelic arts, culture and sport. A country not quite humming but no longer weeping was Augustine Birrell's inheritance when he sailed into Dublin Bay in 1907.

Some proclaimed this provincial capital the 'second city of the empire' and from a distance it looked the part. Stately edifices with green domes lined the Liffey. Nelson's Pillar, a 134-foot granite tribute to England's greatest admiral, overlooked open-topped electric trams that rattled along Sackville Street, one of Europe's finest thoroughfares.

The site of the former parliament was now a bank with handsome porticos. Trinity College's Corinthian facade gave way to statues of Edmund Burke, Oliver Goldsmith and other Anglo-Irish scholars. There was a Royal College of Surgeons, a Royal Botanic Gardens, a Royal College of Science, a Royal Irish Academy, so many royals. A heroic-sized statue of Queen Victoria, with crown and sceptre, inhabited the Royal Dublin Society. Grafton Street's boutiques stocked the latest fashions, while in Stephen's Green picnickers fed ducks amid statues of royalty.

Dead nationalist heroes were not forgotten, but the more troublesome ones were tucked away. Wolfe Tone, who led a French military force in 1798, had only a flat stone inside a ring of iron posts. Robert Emmet, who led an 1803 rebellion, had not even that. 'When my country takes her place among the nations of the earth, then, and not till then, let my epitaph be written,' he said before execution, words the Irish could still quote, but there was no tombstone or even a body, which had disappeared.

Daniel O'Connell, who played by constitutional rules and won votes for Catholics in 1829, had a bridge named after him and a stone tower over his plot at Glasnevin cemetery. Charles Stewart Parnell, who led the campaign for Home Rule in the 1880s, got an obelisk inscribed with a Parnellism: 'No man has a right to fix the boundaries to the march of a nation.'

They had a way with words, these fellows, but epitaphs and boundaries did not trouble Birrell in his first few years in charge. He was an enlightened administrator and more urgent, prosaic concerns intruded, not least Dublin's stench and disease. Up close, elegant-looking houses turned out to be slums. Poverty herded almost a quarter of the city's 300,000 population into one-room tenements. Inadequate water and sanitation wafted a sickly-sweet aroma of filth that incubated tuberculosis, diarrhoea, whooping cough and one of Europe's worst child mortality rates.

It was not all because of British neglect. Members of Dublin corporation were slum landlords who profited from overcrowding, and local employers paid pittance wages. Many Dubliners escaped destitution by joining the British army, which offered wages and adventure, and earned honours across the empire. Belfast, a hundred miles north, throbbed with factories and the Harland & Wolff shipyard that built the *Titanic*, but it too had squalor.

Birrell did what he could for the slums, expanded university access and reinvigorated land reform. And then came the opportunity to do something truly historic. The Liberals had long favoured devolved government for Ireland but the Conservative-dominated upper chamber, the House of Lords, blocked Home Rule. Between 1909 and 1911 two things happened: the Lords blocked the government's budget, triggering a constitutional showdown that ended the Lords' veto power. And election results made the Liberals dependent on IPP votes at Westminster. Its price for supporting the government was a revived push for Home Rule that the Lords could no longer thwart.

The stars had aligned for a new era: a Dublin parliament to accommodate Irish distinctness while London retained overall control. After centuries of friction it had fallen to Augustine Birrell to apply the elusive balm – a belated atonement for the hubris of the monarch with the plumed helmet who gazed from the castle ceiling.

That's when the enraged boar charged.

It started as a faint, distant thud of hooves in 1911. Much of the Anglo-Irish elite, and almost all Ulster's Protestants, favoured preserving the existing union with Britain, which made them unionists. Home Rule risked free trade with Great Britain and Belfast's industrial pre-eminence. Worse, Catholics – the peasants, farmers, tradesmen and professionals that comprised almost three-quarters of the population – would be in charge. To play second fiddle to papists and descendants of rabble was an affront.

Two factors whipped unionists into a menacing charge. One was Sir Edward Carson, a Dublin-born Protestant barrister and MP of uncommon eloquence and resolve who vowed to destroy Home Rule. Protestants were thinly scattered across most of Ireland's 32 counties, but a strong majority existed in the four north-eastern counties, with the city of Belfast their beating heart. So Carson spearheaded resistance from here, aiming to keep Ulster, the historic province that encompassed nine northern counties, welded to Britain.

King Carson, as he was nicknamed, mobilised huge rallies and recruited a private army, the Ulster Volunteer Force. For Carson, loyalty to the Crown, in this upside-down crisis, required rebelling against His Majesty's government.

The other factor was Britain's Conservative and Unionist party. It viewed the Liberals as constitutional wreckers beholden to Irish nationalists, so it cheered the Irish unionist swerve into sedition. F. E. Smith, a party darling, became Carson's aide-de-camp, or 'galloper'. Chaos in Ireland was a means to sink Home Rule and the Liberals.

While Birrell wrung his hands, nationalists formed their own militia, the Irish Volunteers, as a counter-pressure to hold the government to its promise. So by 1914 Ireland had two opposing private armies, totalling about 200,000 men, that marched and drilled, though largely without weapons. Several times Birrell tried to quit, but the prime minister, Herbert Asquith, persuaded him to stay on.

The crisis escalated in March 1914 when army officers said they would ignore any order to crack down on the Ulstermen, a rupture of military discipline that became known as the 'Curragh mutiny'. Then, in a stunning move, Carson's militia obtained 25,000 rifles from a German arms dealer.

Irish nationalists gaped. They had no weapons and for generations had not even *thought* about weapons. They had embraced elections and parliamentary protocol, and here was the reward – unionists pointing guns at them and incipient civil war.

This was the backdrop to Casement's visit to London in May and the reason the tableau of homage to English rule on Dublin Castle's ceiling so mocked the chief secretary. What made it all even worse was German glee. In Berlin's calculus, England was too sunk in its Irish quagmire to wade across the Channel should any trouble arise on the continent.

. . .

On 28 May, as Birrell braced for another Irish Sea buffeting en route to Dublin, Gavrilo Princip and two comrades packed five Browning pistols and six grenades and sailed from Belgrade to the Sava river port of Šabac.

Since the newspaper clipping about the Archduke's pending visit to Bosnia, Princip had been busy recruiting helpers and sourcing funds and weapons for the mission. He was not thinking about the delicate equipoise between Europe's great powers. What mattered was he had a target and location and lacked only a precise date.

From Šabac the conspirators took a train to Koviljača, a spa town on the Serbian side of the Drina river, then evaded border guards by splashing across a shallow ford into Bosnia. They trekked over forested hills and took a train from Tuzla to Bosnia's capital, Sarajevo. A chatty fellow passenger turned out to be a policeman who mentioned when the Archduke was due in the city: 28 June.

. . .

It was a morning made for a parade. The sun beamed, the sea glistened and a light breeze ruffled the banners. The air tasted of salt. Roger Casement surveyed the gathering with satisfaction: more than a thousand men, all members of the Irish Volunteers, or soon to be signed up. At a shouted command the march began, pipers leading the way along a coast road to a rendezvous with history. It was Sunday 28 June.

Since his visit to London seven weeks earlier Casement had crisscrossed Ireland making recruiting speeches for the militia dedicated to Home Rule. He had addressed rallies in Cork, Limerick, Clare, Dublin, Tyrone, Monaghan and Derry, but this one would be special. It was in his native Antrim, so a homecoming, and coincided with a commemoration to honour a slain Gaelic chieftain. Plus the weather was glorious.

The Irish Volunteers, formed the previous year, now numbered more than 100,000 men who marched, drilled and sang. Irish nationalists had not openly organised like this in over a century. Having done nothing to impede the Ulster Volunteer Force's seditious swaggering against Home Rule, the government could hardly object to nationalists organising in *support* of government policy. Still, police officers monitored the rallies and noted Casement's speeches. He was not breaking the law, but his vehemence raised eyebrows among former colleagues in London.

The lack of modern weapons stung. While the UVF brandished rifles and even machine-guns, the nationalists made do with batons and hurley sticks. Casement fizzed with a secret. Soon, all going well, there would be rifles. His meeting in London had raised funds and set a plan in motion.

Meantime, arms swinging, long legs loping, he had a parade to lead.

. . .

Some 1,700 miles to the east, the sun also blazed down on Sarajevo, which awaited its own procession. The royal visit was going well. For two days Archduke Franz Ferdinand had reviewed military manoeuvres and feasted on trout, beef, pineapple and wines from across the empire.

This was the last day. Before returning to Vienna the royal party would make a ceremonial drive in an open car through central Sarajevo, giving the public a chance to see the heir to the Hapsburg throne and his wife Sophie. Imperial flags and crowds lined Appel Quay, a riverside boulevard. The procession was due at 10 a.m. Amid the throng, the conspirators waited.

. . .

Casement's procession wound its way up to a hilltop mound of stones that marked the reputed burial site of Shane O'Neill, a chieftain slain in June 1567. The splendour of Murlough Bay unfurled below them. This was the landscape of Casement's youth, the hills and glens and waters where he hiked and swam, imbibed stories and legends, and embarked on the great puzzle that was his life. Who was he, really?

Casement was born in Dublin in 1864, the youngest of four children, to parents ill-equipped for the role. His father, Roger senior, a scion of Protestant gentry, was an eccentric wanderer who served in the British cavalry in India and studied Hindu mysticism before riding to Europe in 1849 to help Hungarian rebels, which he did by delivering a crucial message, an improbable yarn that was actually true and entered family lore as romantic heroism.

In 1855 Casement senior married Anne Jephson, who converted to her husband's faith but secretly baptised her children as Catholics. They had two sons, Tom and Charlie, a daughter, Agnes, known as Nina, then Roger. Unable to settle or earn a regular income, the family hopscotched around the British Isles until landing in Antrim. When Roger junior was nine his mother died in an English boarding house of liver cirrhosis, suggesting alcoholism. His father left the children to be raised by relatives and lived in a hotel where he held seances, withered and died. Orphaned at the age of 12, Roger junior would spend the rest of his life idolising parents he never really knew.

Shuttled between relatives, the closest thing to home was Magherintemple, an uncle's dark, forbidding house on the Antrim coast. Casement's refuge was its library, a portal to poets, heroes and rebels. He never found a true home. When visiting England and Ireland between foreign postings the consul would stay at boarding houses or hotels or crash with friends. A nomad with no partner, no children, stranded somewhere between being Protestant and Catholic, British and Irish, serving yet scorning the Crown, it was a fractured identity. He had friends but was lonely and prone to depression, which turned to elation when a cause possessed him. That cause now was Ireland.

Shane O'Neill's burial mound was close to Magherintemple, but Casement was no longer welcome – his unionist relatives disapproved of Home Rule agitation. He mustered courage for a quite different reception from an old childhood friend. Ada McNeill was tall, smart, attractive and in love with him. It was excruciating. For years he had dodged her during her visits to Antrim. 'I wish, poor old soul, she would leave me alone,' he confided to a friend. 'I have very strong feelings of friendship for her, and goodwill, and brotherly Irish affection, but I wish she could leave other things out of the reckoning.' Still, he took time from the march to dutifully call into her home. She gave him a rose.

. . .

In Sarajevo, Gavrilo Princip stepped out of a crowd, aimed at the royal car and fired two shots.

Franz Ferdinand's wife slumped, fatally wounded. The Archduke swayed. There was a small puncture hole in the gilt trim of his collar. Blood trickled from his mouth. 'It is nothing,' he murmured, then closed his eyes and died.

. . .

At the top of the hill, Casement addressed the marchers. The voice hoarse, he appealed for unity. Ulster Volunteers or Irish Volunteers, all were Irishmen, and England must not divide them, he cried. Surveying the eager faces and sparkling bay, Casement must have felt a pang. The plot to get rifles was not his only secret. This speech was his last public appearance in Ireland before leaving on a quest for money, allies and more guns. While Europe slumbered through another summer, he was heading west, to America.

CHAPTER THREE

—

Guns

Captain Reginald Hall's watch said it was 10 p.m., but night refused to set over St Petersburg and his hosts did not want to say goodbye. Russians thronged the embankment along Pont Nicholas to give final cheers as the yacht slid from its moorings to ferry the English officers back to their ships. The news from Sarajevo had ricocheted around Europe hours earlier, jarring its holiday languor, but nothing could darken this moment of rapturous amity on the Neva river, where the sun would glow till midnight.

The goodwill visit of the Royal Navy's 1st Cruiser Squadron to Russia's Baltic ports had uncorked 10 days of champagne, vodka, caviar, gala balls and declarations of eternal friendship. Tsar Nicholas II had marvelled at the British Dreadnoughts and inspected their turrets while his daughters, the Romanov princesses, gambolled on deck. The British had admired his Winter Palace, banqueted till they burst and applauded a thousand Russian cavalrymen who charged and wheeled in perfect formation.

Now it was time for the visitors to start the long journey home. The yacht chugged past the yellow dome of St Isaac's Cathedral to the port of Kronstadt, where Hall and the other officers rejoined their four battlecruisers. The next morning, 29 June 1914, under azure skies, the squadron sailed to a coaling station at Bjorko Sound to fuel up for the journey home.

The *Queen Mary* was pride of the fleet, a newly minted model of firepower, armour and speed powered by 42 boilers, but to her 1,000-strong crew she was really impelled by the personality of her captain. Reginald Hall was small, 44 and looked older – bald dome, tufts of snowy hair over the ears, conspicuous false teeth and such pointed features it was said he could hold a piece of toast between his nose and chin. Pale blue eyes continuously blinked, a twitch possibly caused by dry-eye syndrome, yielding the nickname Blinker.

Reginald 'Blinker' Hall aboard his battlecruiser HMS Queen Mary in 1914, before being appointed director of naval intelligence.

Hall had the taut physique and swift movements of youth, dragon tattoos on his arms and an abrupt, incisive way of speaking that could boom into a parade ground command. And those eyes. Depending how he looked at you it could be the contemplation of a benevolent grandfather or the scrutiny of a peregrine falcon. 'Eyes of hypnotic force, dark, penetrating, index of an indomitable soul,' an awed newspaper interviewer wrote in 1911.

As the *Queen Mary* loaded supplies and 1,300 tonnes of coal, days of backbreaking, choking work, Austria-Hungary mourned the Archduke and eyed an opportunity. Whether or not Serbia was implicated in the assassination, the Hapsburg empire now had a pretext to throttle its uppity Slav neighbour.

'One day the great European War will come out of some damned foolish thing in the Balkans,' Otto von Bismarck, Germany's Iron Chancellor and sage, had reputedly warned, but that was in 1888, and the prophecy had gathered dust. No one yet envisaged a wider crisis, let alone calamity. After the initial shock of the assassination, Europe seemed to return to its siesta.

The long peace had dulled the combat instinct of many military men. Hall was not one of them. He believed in God and gunnery, not necessarily in that order, and had been preparing for war most of his life. Born in the citadel of Anglicanism and Englishness known as Salisbury, he came from a family of naval men stretching back to his great-grandfather. At the age of 10, Hall accompanied his father on a warship's cruise, imbibed the aura of order and command, and that was that: young Rex resolved to join this nautical protector of Britain and empire.

He served on vessels and bases in North America and China, earning commendations as 'zealous, promising, smart and intelligent', and by 1905, at the precocious age of 35, was made captain. The fastest way to promotion during this era of relative serenity was to run a ship that excelled at seamanship drills and speedy coaling, but Hall, with his odd manner and odd ideas, found another, harder way. He specialised in gunnery – in making his ships effective killing machines. That required mathematical calculation, technical knowledge and psychological acuity so that loaders, gunlayers and officers worked in harmony. His teams broke gunnery records for speed and accuracy. No matter a target's size or speed or distance, Hall could destroy it.

At home he breakfasted on cold rice pudding and cold roast partridge and doted on his wife and daughter, who could do no wrong. Everyone else had to meet exacting standards. Hall inspired fear and respect. His physical presence, a historian would note, frequently nerved in men an impulse to do something heroic.

Hall's reputation as a disciplinarian resulted in the navy sending him troublesome characters to reform or break. Woe betide a sailor who was insubordinate or shirked a task because the captain's penetrating gaze would fix upon him during interrogation and judgement. During outbursts of anger – rare, shocking, memorable occasions – he resembled a crazed Mr Punch. Faithful and diligent sailors, in contrast, reaped his trust and a twinkly 'that's it, my boy'.

Hall's moral code had an Old Testament tinge, but he was an innovator. He abolished the *Queen Mary*'s naval police, improved living quarters and installed a chapel, bookshop and cinema, experiments that appalled some admirals as indulgent pampering, only to be later copied by the rest of the navy.

The Tsar and the princesses might have wondered about this twitching, unusual-looking officer, but Hall kept his guests' focus on his magnificent ship. It gleamed from bow to stern and threw the squadron's best party, leaving the Russians twirled, swirled and toasting England. The visit to St Petersburg was to underpin the Triple Entente, an understanding between Britain, Russia and France. Britain had not committed to a formal defence alliance but wanted a counterweight to the Triple Alliance of Germany, Austria-Hungary and Italy.

Hall had long anticipated a clash with Germany and authored essays on fighting tactics and combat-readiness. Years earlier the Kaiser, with his knack for tactlessness, had compared his armed forces to those of Attila the Hun that ravaged Europe in the fifth century. Hall, like others, embraced it as a derogatory term: the Germans were Huns.

On 3 July, while Berlin quietly encouraged Austria-Hungary to punish Serbia, in the Gulf of Finland the mighty British warships gave the Tsar, bobbing in his yacht, a final treat: a high-speed tactical exercise that involved criss-crossing each other at close range, a pirouette of giants at 27 knots. Their Russian ally duly awed, the visitors turned west for home. Hall stood at the bridge of his battlecruiser, the whole vessel throbbing with 75,000 horsepower, and studied the sky. There wasn't a cloud.

. . .

The next day, as Hall's squadron sliced through the Baltic, a whistle blew in Glasgow docks and the single-funnel passenger liner SS *Cassandra* eased through the River Clyde, bound for the Atlantic. The mostly Scottish passengers did not realise the tall, thin man who had embarked as a second-class emigrant under the name R. D. Casement was a famous knight. Six days since the parade at Antrim, Sir Roger was not quite incognito but keeping a low profile to avoid his journey drawing attention from the press or government snoops.

A ship named after a doomed prophetess did not feel propitious. 'Name of ill-omen!' he wrote. On the other hand it was 4 July, America's independence day. The gun-running plan hatched in London had raised £1,500 and was slowly unfolding – two yachts were to rendezvous in the North Sea and, all going well, return to Ireland laden with rifles.

But even if successfully landed, the cargo would not be enough. To be taken seriously and to pressure the government on Home Rule, the Irish Volunteers would need more guns. Which meant money. So Casement was now aiming for the hearts and wallets of Irish America.

The journey, via Canada, afforded time to reflect. While skirting Ireland's northern tip, Casement glimpsed the jagged precipices of Tory Island and recalled the night two years earlier when he organised a ceilidh for the islanders, and they had danced till dawn. It was one of his happiest memories.

It was also site of the 1798 rebellion's last stand. From Ireland's nationalist pantheon Casement most identified with Wolfe Tone, a

Protestant who attempted to unite Protestants and Catholics in resistance to English rule. Tone lobbied France's revolutionary leaders, and then Napoleon, to help liberate Ireland, and after several foiled expeditions was captured near Tory Island. He died in captivity. In this melancholic tale Casement found inspiration: with help from a major European power, and better luck, Ireland might win her freedom.

The *Cassandra* chugged for over a week through calm, grey seas. Near Newfoundland glittering icebergs appeared, filling Casement with a strange sense of poignance at such beauty, drifting to oblivion. 'Great Arctic palaces ... with a crystal sheen,' he wrote, 'they sailed past us bound to their doom in the Gulf Stream.'

Casement needed a different current. He was in many ways a solo act without a staff or budget or organisational support. He was on the Irish Volunteers committee and its arms sub-committee but lacked executive authority, and undertook the gun-running as a freelance effort. To navigate the US he would need a network, a sponsor. It was obvious who; the art would be in the persuasion.

Casement arrived at Quebec on 14 July and a few days later took a train to New York. Passing Lake Champlain, he rued the fate of the Mohicans, a tribe deemed savage that was wiped out, like the Gaels. 'Poor Indians! You had life – your white destroyers only possess things,' he wrote. 'The one lives and moves to be; the other toils and dies to have.'

A heatwave broiled Manhattan but otherwise it was the same city he had visited before: a handful of skyscrapers, yellow taxi-cabs, horse-drawn fire engines, wondrous ice box devices. Newspapers fretted not about diplomatic tension in Europe but a threatened baseball strike. Casement checked into the Belmont and made a phone call to request an audience with the old man. Then, killing time, he took a stroll down Broadway.

They met at Mouquin's, a Sixth Street cafe popular with writers and politicians, on 20 July. John Devoy was 72, short, stout, with a white beard and black hollows under the eyes, the result of insomnia that rendered him a 'sleepless demon'. He was gruff and crotchety, and this encounter was not likely to help his mood. This lanky visitor with a fancy title might be a spy, or just an idiot, and there was every chance Devoy would lie awake that night trying to figure out which. It was going to be a long lunch.

Devoy resembled Sigmund Freud but probably defied psychoanalysis. Stern and implacable, he was the leader of Clan na Gael, Irish America's leading nationalist organisation, and editor of the *Gaelic American*, a small, fierce weekly that hurled invective at England and anyone else who crossed him. After 43 years' exile he was still keeper of the flame of resistance and bore traces of a Kildare accent.

As a boy Devoy's family lost its farm in the famine so at school he refused to sing 'God Save the Queen', which earned a beating. Devoy spent the rest of his life hitting back. After gaining military experience in the French Foreign Legion he joined the Fenians, the underground revolutionary group, and secretly recruited Irish soldiers in the British army. A rebellion in 1867 unravelled in debacle – it was short on rifles and coordination – and landed Devoy in prison before banishment to the US.

Amid New York's immigrant slums he spent decades building America's first exile political movement dedicated to freeing his homeland 3,000 miles away. Even when Ireland's revolutionary spirit hibernated, Devoy used rally platforms and the *Gaelic American* to raise funds and spread the faith, fusing historic memories of English devilry in Ireland and America into a shared resentment. Forsaking marriage, Devoy lived for the cause. Home was a spartan hotel room, $1.50 a night, on 42nd Street, and indulgence was a cup of warm milk.

By July 1914 Devoy's network included judges, mayors, congressmen and former presidential candidates. He scorned Home Rule as an insipid sop to nationalist sentiment but welcomed the Irish Volunteers as evidence Ireland was stirring.

The old man had several reasons to cast a cold, rheumy gaze over Casement. He had heard of the investigator of Congo and Putumayo and assumed he was English. He certainly sounded it. And after decades serving the Crown, perhaps Casement's retirement was a ruse. Spies had infiltrated Devoy's organisation before, and contacts in Dublin counselled wariness about this knight who was so keen to offer his services. Plus Devoy faulted Casement for allowing moderate nationalists to join the Volunteer Committee. So Devoy had no intention of letting Casement anywhere near Clan na Gael.

Casement listened quietly to the charge sheet. When the old boy was talked out he politely and sweetly rebutted everything, point by point, and made his pitch. He spoke of his Antrim roots, his experiences in Africa, his dream of an independent Ireland and his work for the Irish Volunteers. He defended the committee decision as a tactical necessity to maintain nationalist unity. Perhaps conscious Devoy was half-deaf, Casement followed up the lunch with a letter reiterating his case.

It was like trying to charm a bullfrog, but Casement was able to share a secret sure to thrill Devoy: two yachts laden with guns were at that moment bound for Ireland. Guns. The magic word.

There was one catch. Casement did not know whether his friends had made it through the English Channel.

. . .

It had all been going according to plan. A tug with an arsenal bought from a Hamburg arms dealer rendezvoused with the yachts off Belgium's coast on 12 July. The *Kelpie* took 600 rifles and 20,000 rounds of ammunition, the *Asgard* took 900 rifles and 29,000 rounds, then they turned around, split up and headed for home.

Four days later a brisk breeze propelled the *Asgard* down the Devonshire coast. It was dusk, the sun sliding down the horizon. Soon the English Channel would give way to the Irish Sea and the final leg. The crew was covered in grease and perched atop mounds of rifles and ammunition boxes that covered the cabin, passageway and deck.

They resembled desperados, but with the exception of two Donegal fishermen they were members of Anglo-Irish society, all drawn into this adventure by the meeting at Grosvenor Road two months earlier. One was the cousin of Britain's ambassador to Washington, another the author of *The Riddle of the Sands*, a bestselling novel about a German invasion of England.

Night fell, revealing a half-moon. The *Asgard* ploughed through the gloom, waves slapping the hull. Then beams of light punctured the darkness, followed by the massive silhouette of a warship. Another silhouette loomed from the murk, then another, and another, until came the horrifying realisation that floating steel castles filled the entire sea.

The *Asgard* had sailed into an armada of destroyers, battle-cruisers, minelayers, submarines, auxiliaries and hundreds of other craft. Bow to stern, they would stretch 18 miles. 'Incomparably the greatest assemblage of naval power ever witnessed in the history of the world,' Winston Churchill, the First Lord of the Admiralty, would later declare, immodestly but probably accurately. It was to test the navy's mobilisation and intimidate potential enemies. By fluke, it now had the opportunity to intercept a yacht laden with illicit weapons.

The *Asgard*'s little crew gazed in disbelief at the naval swarm. Discovery seemed certain. A destroyer bore down then at the last moment swerved away, as if toying with them. Yet somehow they edged through the shifting maze. By 1 a.m. they were through, and the Irish Sea beckoned.

In the maritime host behind them floated Reginald Hall. He could hardly be faulted for missing the *Asgard*. He had not been tasked with scrutinising random yachts. But the gunrunner's moonlit escape was in a way a prelude to a forthcoming contest between the captain and Roger Casement. In this first skirmish, by proxy, the Irishman prevailed.

On Sunday 26 July, Casement was in Philadelphia agonising about the *Asgard*. It was several days ahead of the other yacht and he had received word it was due to land in Dublin at any moment, midday Irish time. A hundred things could still go wrong. With Joseph McGarrity, one of Devoy's Clan na Gael lieutenants, he walked to some fields and sat down to wait, willing the minutes and hours to pass. Eventually, the news came.

The *Asgard* had approached Howth, a fishing village near Dublin city, at the appointed time, with a female crew member on deck wearing a red skirt, a signal to those on shore. As it moored, hundreds of Irish Volunteers thronged the pier and unloaded the guns, not a policeman in sight. The Volunteers had spent the previous weeks marching up, down and around the city in apparently futile tramping until the police got bored and stopped following them.

Docking in broad daylight near the capital was a calculated risk and a public relations masterstroke. The rifles were, in truth, old and a small fraction of the arsenals landed in Ulster. So the Irish Volunteers magnified the impact by turning the unloading into a public spectacle. Toy soldiers no more, they were gripping Mausers. Hours later a crowd taunted British troops, who opened fire and killed four unarmed people, further boosting support for the Volunteers.

For Casement it was as if the Liberty Bell clanged over Philadelphia. Against the odds, the plan had worked. The bloodshed was tragic but made the cause only more just. Devoy proclaimed the gun-running the greatest deed in Ireland in a hundred years.

Casement's profile rocketed and newspapers clamoured for interviews. 'Utter kindliness ... radiates from him like an aura,' gushed one. Donations flowed. 'The Irish here would make me into a demigod if I let them,' Casement wrote to a friend on 29 July. 'May this bring a new day to Ireland. I see it coming – new hope, new courage.' Not even the 'stupendous war cloud' he noted over Europe could dent his exuberance. He signed himself, half in jest, as The Fugitive Knight.

· · ·

As Casement wrote these lines, Reginald Hall was in a convoy steaming east up the English Channel. The First Fleet had left Portland at 7 a.m. and upon reaching the Straits of Dover that night was to extinguish its lights, turn north and keep heading north. Winston Churchill was preparing his navy for war.

The assassination in Sarajevo four weeks earlier had not immediately derailed Europe's long peace. But Austria-Hungary's escalating moves against Serbia started a chain reaction so that when it declared war on 28 July it enlisted Germany, while Russia prepared to wade in on behalf of Serbia, which in turn would draw in France and possibly Britain, which had an understanding, the Entente, with France and Russia.

In his lyrical prose, Churchill recalled the moment an urgent update from the Balkans eclipsed a cabinet discussion on Home Rule. 'The parishes of Fermanagh and Tyrone faded back into the mists and squalls of Ireland, and a strange light began immediately, but by perceptible gradations, to fall and grow upon the map of Europe.'

Churchill ordered the fleet to a remote, impregnable sanctuary. Reginald Hall's new home was to be Scapa Flow, a base in Scotland's Orkney Islands. The *Queen Mary* arrived at 6.45 a.m. on 30 July.

. . .

Winston Churchill, as First Lord of the Admiralty.

The war swept away Casement's hopes and plans for America.

Vast armies of men, horses and artillery were moving across Europe to meet in titanic, slaughter-filled battles. America, secure on the other side of the Atlantic, gaped at the unfathomable spectacle and forgot all about Ireland. Momentum and money for the Irish Volunteers evaporated and Casement's US mission withered.

He despaired about the war; he had seen conflict and feared this would be suffering on an unprecedented scale, with England using Irish lives as cannon fodder. But the calamity also opened an opportunity – one that Ireland last had during the Napoleonic wars. An act of audacity could change everything.

Casement said nothing to his Clan na Gael hosts but at a rally in Philadelphia he did something curious. When a newspaper photographer raised a camera to take his picture, he turned and tried to shield his face.

Casement and John Devoy in the US in 1914.

CHAPTER FOUR

England's Difficulty

Reginald Hall stood on the bridge of the *Queen Mary* gazing over the waters of Heligoland Bight, a bay off Germany's North Sea coast. The sea glittered, serene. Beyond the haze was the mouth of the Elbe river. Action bells had rung and crews were at their assigned posts, nerves taut. Shells scrawled with messages such as 'love from England' and 'one for the Kaiser' filled the turrets. It was 28 August 1914, three weeks into the war, and shaping up to be an excellent day for an ambush.

The Royal Navy flotilla had crept overnight, undetected, into enemy waters. An advance guard of destroyers then approached the coast and revealed itself, prompting the Germans to scramble light cruisers and torpedo boats to confront the interlopers, unaware the *Queen Mary* and her fellow battlecruisers *Lion* and *Princess Royal* lurked beyond the horizon. The Germans would be outnumbered and outgunned. It was a trap.

This would be Hall's first experience of combat and his first chance to strike a blow against an enemy that was winning huge battles on land. German armies were routing the Russians in the east and sweeping aside the British and French in the west. A swift victory beckoned for the Kaiser, who had promised his troops they would be 'home before the leaves have fallen from the trees'. Bronze medals inscribed 'Entry of German Troops into Paris', showing the Eiffel Tower and Arc de Triomphe, had already been minted. This Royal Navy foray to the enemy's fortified coast was a relative pinprick in response. Until now the British and German navies had avoided contact, daring the other to make the first move.

The battlecruisers remained out of sight while the Germans took the bait and left the safety of their ports to engage the British destroyers. At 12.04 p.m. the leviathans steamed towards the kill zone. The smaller German and British ships were exchanging fire in a confused melee when the battlecruisers joined the fray. 'Like elephants walking through a pack of dogs, great and grim and uncouth as some antediluvian monsters,' one sailor recalled.

Hall passed a burning German ship, the *Mainz*, its decks covered in blood, and targeted the *Cöln*, a light cruiser about 5,000 yards away. His bridge shuddered with the first thundering salvo from 13.5 inch guns. The shells sailed high and landed near the coast but helped the gunners find range. The ship's pistons hammering, Hall pursued his quarry while turret crews reloaded.

Instead of fleeing, the *Cöln* headed *for* its executioner, blazing away with much smaller guns, some shots sailing high, others rifling into the sea. Hall's gunners unleashed fresh salvos that penetrated the enemy's hull with deep thuds before exploding. Another barrage obliterated her bridge and conning tower, creating an inferno. Still the *Cöln*'s remaining guns kept firing in suicidal defiance. The *Lion* joined the bombardment and the *Cöln* shattered. Her stern rose, the ensign with the German empire's black eagle still fluttering, the propellers still turning, and she slid into the depths. Of 367 men aboard, all but one perished. Bubbles and debris marked the spot. Some of Hall's men cheered, others looked away.

Dodging mines and suspected submarines, the flotilla steamed home. They had sunk four German vessels and killed 712 enemy sailors for some light damage and the loss of 35 British lives. They sailed into Scapa Flow to jubilation on the docks and congratulations from the Admiralty.

The Battle of Heligoland Bight was hardly Trafalgar but had an outsized impact. The Kaiser mourned his lost ships, his 'darlings', and dreaded losing more, so he chained his admirals. Instead of challenging the Royal Navy's growing blockade of European waters, the Hochseeflotte would huddle close to its North Sea and Baltic bases, sheltered and largely impotent. Britannia would rule the waves.

It was at this moment of personal apogee that Hall, so unassailable in command, so invincible on the bridge, encountered a foe that could not be smashed or sunk. It fluttered into his chest and seemed to deposit a patch of North Sea fog into his lungs. He began to wheeze.

. . .

Seven mornings a week, as Dublin woke, a slender man with a walrus moustache and hollow cheeks awaited a van's delivery of newspapers to his little shop at 75a Parnell Street, just off the northern end of Sackville Street in the heart of the city. He unpacked the bundles, arranged the titles on a rack and placed a billboard with the main headlines. Then, if his displays of tobacco, cigars, pipes, cigarettes and stationery were in order, and the floor was swept and there were no customers to serve, he would rest his elbows on the counter, adjust his glasses and read the news.

On Wednesday 9 September, a dull and damp morning, the papers reported a shift in fortunes on the Western Front. 'Allies' victorious advance', blared the *Daily Express*. 'Germans driven back . . . allies advance all along the line.' Page after page carried dramatic reports of a retreat by exhausted, over-extended German forces.

Tom Clarke was not a demonstrative man but this was reason to smile. For five weeks he had fretted over the Germans' seemingly unstoppable sweep through Belgium and northern France. The watch on his waistcoat chain had seemed to tick louder, as if time were running out. The worry was not that England would lose, the worry was the war would end too soon. These latest reports dissolved such anxiety. Germany's setback meant the conflict would drag on. Which gifted Tom Clarke more time to sharpen a dagger for England's heart.

The shop's facade bore his name in English and its Irish form, T. S. Ó Cléirigh, and advertised tobacco brands. The interior was narrow, spotless and brightly lit. Its owner was thin, grey and crumpled. Clarke was 56 but looked in his 70s, frail and weary.

Tom Clarke outside his shop at 75a Parnell Street.

Customers would sometimes find him sitting on a stool, trunk erect, hands on knees, gazing at a wall as if it stretched to the horizon. It was a posture from his years in prison when he would enter an almost trance-like state contemplating, among other things, his hatred for England and what to do with that hatred. It was not a hot hate that hissed and boiled; it was ice, the cold fury of a patient man.

Since his youth Clarke had waited for the enemy to become weak or distracted. 'England's difficulty is Ireland's opportunity,' went the venerable Fenian exhortation, and finally here it was, a war to drain England's life force and siphon her troops from Ireland. Clarke's duty was to strike while the opportunity lasted. This Wednesday night, in fact, he was to meet fellow conspirators to confirm a decision.

It did not matter to Clarke that most Irish people supported England in this crisis. Union jacks flapped across the city and Dubliners sang 'God Save the King'. The foaming over Home Rule had subsided. The government had promised to pass the legislation within weeks but delay its implementation until after the war, with a question mark over Ulster's inclusion. This postdated cheque was good enough for the Irish Parliamentary Party, which earned cheers at Westminster by asserting Ireland's fealty to the Crown.

Irish people lacked the intensity of English fervour to smite the Hun but viewed Germany as the aggressor. Clarke sold newspapers brimming with articles about German atrocities against Catholic Belgium and gallant France, prompting fulminations from Irish priests and bishops. Recruitment posters urged Irishmen to enlist and they did in their thousands, bands leading them in renditions of 'Let Erin Remember' as they tramped to ships that took them to British army training camps.

None of it mattered to Clarke because his Ireland knew who the real enemy was and demanded vengeance for centuries of grievous wrongs. Growing up in the famine's aftermath, he believed that England had starved not only the people but even the *idea* of Ireland. It was a reading of history that rinsed contradictions and left cold clarity. Clarke would break English rule, or die trying.

Caught and jailed for the Fenian dynamite campaign in 1880s England, for 15 years he was prisoner J464, selected for special punishment in what were dubbed Arctic cells. To allay hunger he chewed rags. A 'silent system' that forbade speaking drove inmates insane, but Clarke, sustained by some unconquerable will, recognised silence as an ally of secrecy and a weapon that in the future he too could deploy.

After release he moved to New York and worked for Clan na Gael under John Devoy, a mentor in the art of sustaining a revolutionary flame, then in 1907, bearing a faint American accent, returned to Ireland to seek opportunity to strike the enemy.

The Irish Republican Brotherhood, also known as the Brotherhood or the Organisation, was an oath-bound, clandestine successor to the Fenians, and the Clan's sister organisation in Ireland. Both sought an independent Irish republic through revolution. The IRB and Clan na Gael liaised via messengers who criss-crossed the Atlantic but were separate organisations, one completely subterranean and operating under the noses of British authorities while the other worked mainly in the open among Irish-Americans.

To his disgust, Clarke discovered the IRB had abandoned military training and study of revolutionary methods and atrophied into an old boys' club for drinking and reminiscing about rebellions of yore. Painstakingly he purged the useless, recruited young talent and sent reports to Devoy, who funnelled money, and bit by bit the IRB revived.

Clarke was treasurer on the supreme council but his real influence flowed through disciples who gravitated to his shop for instruction and inspiration. The taciturn man they called 'the old chap' had an aura. 'Almost all his loyalties to the colours and enjoyments of life had been burned away, leaving but a slender, intense flame of hatred to what he knew to be England,' recalled Sean O'Casey, a writer who knew him.

Irish people who had heard of the IRB assumed it was extinct or a cobwebby irrelevance, but by 1914 it had approximately 1,600 committed members. Like sleeper agents, they infiltrated mainstream, respectable organisations like the Gaelic League, Gaelic Athletic Association and the Irish Volunteers, and quietly dripped seditious sentiment. To strike the English, Clarke first needed to manipulate the Irish.

Roger Casement was not an IRB member and unaware of its reach. Before sailing to Canada he had offered his Irish Volunteer committee position to Clarke, who affected to be a simple political activist. Clarke declined, preferring the shadows. Plus, he suspected the former consul was a British spy.

The outbreak of war electrified Clarke – the whole British empire would be on the rack. But he needed time to plan, and the first weeks brought the alarming prospect of a lightning Teutonic victory. But Paris did not fall. And now, studying the news on this grey morning of 9 September, the shopkeeper found further reassurance. 'The Allies are gaining ground on their left along the line of the Ourcq and the Petit Marin ... the enemy has been pressed back in the direction of Rheims.' The Kaiser's troops would not be home before the leaves fell.

When closing his shop Clarke would slip the key into his pocket and put on a wide-brimmed hat and tweed overcoat, then head out with short, rapid steps, usually to a meeting. This particular night, mild and moonlit, he did not have far to go, just across the street to 25 Rutland Square.

IRB men and representatives of other groups – potential allies – sat around a table, some probably guessing why they had been summoned. Clarke was not one for fancy speeches; his presence alone commanded attention. Eyeing the men around him, he made a pledge, a declaration of intent: before the war ended the IRB would mount a rebellion against British rule in Ireland.

. . .

A momentous choice lay before Roger Casement. For all his recruiting and fulminating on behalf of the Irish Volunteers as a public figure, he was still, just, a respected and respectable former British government official. His role in the gun-running, if it became known, would not change that; Conservative MPs, after all, had openly cheered Ulster's illicit arms cargoes. Casement could stick to campaigning for the Volunteers in pursuit of Home Rule and wait to see what the war would bring. Or he could swerve into a plot to foment a rebellion in Ireland with German help.

For John Devoy, Clan na Gael's duty was to support its IRB confederates in Ireland with money, weapons and contacts. In New York it had access to German diplomats and could petition for help, just as earlier generations of Irish rebels had appealed to Scotland, Spain, France, the Pope and other foes of England. Now it was time to try the Kaiser.

For Casement, the implication was stark. He was a British subject, a knight no less. To consort with Germany would, in English eyes, be treason.

Without a cause, Casement was lost to melancholy, agitation and doubts about his purpose. With a cause, he felt alive and vital. Inhumanity in Congo and the Amazon had steered him towards noble goals and famous deeds. Now his third great vocation, Ireland, beckoned him across the Rubicon.

For Casement, the British empire was a malignant thread linking centuries and continents: it had strangled Ireland, carved up Africa and encircled Germany. Fearful of losing economic pre-eminence, the British sought to stifle her Teutonic rival by using France and Russia to box her in. This, Casement believed, was the war's root cause. In time some historians – not many – would share this view.

Casement went further. He did not speak German and had visited just once, a motoring holiday in 1912, but viewed the land of Goethe as a bastion of civilisation, an unblemished newcomer in Europe's grubby colonialism. He projected nobility, even benevolence, onto this young nation that dared to build a navy and overtake British commerce. This idealised image ignored Germany's massacres of the Herero and Nama in South West Africa, which a later generation would call genocide, and the Kaiser's inveterate provocations in foreign affairs.

In 1908 Casement outlined an idea for a novel, which he never wrote, about German forces landing in Ireland as liberators, culminating in an Irish flag flying over Dublin Castle. In 1913, under a pseudonym, he pondered Ireland's role in the event of a continental war in a series of articles titled *Ireland, Germany and the Freedom of the Seas*. In Casement's view, Britain had impoverished Ireland while using its waters to control the Atlantic. Now that war had broken out, Britain was using that power to blockade Germany and throwing Irishmen into the fight. 'I cannot bear to think of Ireland in this cauldron of hatred and murder,' he wrote to a friend.

So Casement did not hesitate. His worldview, a mix of insider knowledge, shrewd analysis, blinkered naivete and foaming anglophobia, and his need for a cause, impelled him across. And being Casement, he sought to go further. To consort with German diplomats in New York was not enough. He wanted Clan na Gael to dispatch him as an envoy. He wanted to *be* in Germany.

To reach Germany amid war-time restrictions was challenge enough without having his picture splashed in newspapers. That was why, anticipating such a voyage, he had tried – unsuccessfully – to dodge the press photographer in Philadelphia. The fewer images the British had of his face, the better.

Before attempting to evade the Royal Navy, however, Casement had to circumvent another formidable force, John Devoy.

They made an odd couple. One shaped like a barrel, the other a lamppost. Devoy had the sentiment of a Bronx precinct sergeant, Casement wrote poetry. Devoy growled orders and expected compliance, Casement smiled and did his own thing. The Clan na Gael leader trusted only Clan na Gael and IRB members, Casement was neither.

Casement's gun-running credentials had sufficiently impressed the old man to let Casement join fundraising efforts, but sending him to Berlin was a huge gamble and Devoy already had enough trouble sleeping at night. Casement was a conspicuous figure with no experience of disguise – an easy mark for the Royal Navy to intercept. If he did slip through, who knew what he would do in Berlin? The mercurial knight had a habit of ignoring instructions and blabbing confidences. Devoy worried Casement was too emotional and idealistic. 'As trustful as a child', he later noted. There was, at least, no longer suspicion he was a spy.

A group of Irish-Americans, probably with Devoy's knowledge, hired a private detective to watch Casement. One day, chatting to a friend in his hotel room, he broke into Irish. 'Oscail an doras,' he told her. Open the door. They found a waiter in the corridor apparently eavesdropping. A few days later Casement spotted him hovering in a drug store. 'Ah, George!' he beamed. Snoop or not, George fled. And competent or not, the detective reported nothing suspicious about Casement. Casement had assumed the British were watching.

Anticipating Tom Clarke's resolve in Dublin, Clan na Gael members met the German ambassador, Johann Heinrich von Bernstorff, at the German Club on East 59th Street on 24 August. Devoy's deafness hindered him in group settings so he let others make the pitch: if Germany supplied weapons and officers, the Irish would mount a rebellion that would siphon British troops from the Western Front. The ambassador listened intently and said he would consult Berlin.

Devoy had no particular love for Germany and viewed the proposal as transactional. Casement envisaged something grander, an alliance to break British mastery of the seas, and drafted a Clan na Gael letter to the Kaiser requesting help to liberate Ireland. In meetings with Bernstorff and the military attaché, Franz von Papen, Casement crystallised three objectives: obtain weapons, secure German recognition of Irish nationhood and raise an Irish brigade from British army POWs in Germany.

Devoy began to see advantages in sending Casement. The fellow had been thinking and writing about Ireland's relationship with Germany before anyone else and had an international profile and prestige. He kept meticulous accounts of expenditure, down to the last cent, and was frugal. Devoy had been astonished and impressed to discover Casement washed his own underwear. Whatever the role of laundry, the scales tipped. Devoy agreed to send Casement.

On the evening of Tuesday 13 October, as New Yorkers wrapped up against autumn's chill, Devoy and Joseph McGarrity and their designated ambassador took different routes to a rendezvous in mid-Manhattan. British spies had been hovering – targeting Clan leaders, not Casement, who was assumed to remain loyal to the Crown – so the conspirators took counter-surveillance precautions before gathering at East 94th Street, the palatial home of Daniel Cohalan, a New York supreme court judge and Clan member who balanced establishment respectability with revolutionary politics. Preparations for Casement's departure were almost complete. A false identity and berth on a Norway-bound passenger ship were arranged. This gathering was to fine-tune details and bid farewell.

Casement had recently sprung a surprise: he wished to bring someone on the voyage, a Norwegian sailor named Eivind Adler Christensen. It was a puzzling request so close to departure, especially since no one had heard of this fellow. Adler, as Casement called him, was an acquaintance who could act as interpreter, fixer and servant.

Casement had to get the tone just right. The Clan na Gael veterans were practised in the arts of deflection and subterfuge, and his proposal concealed two secrets. Casement was homosexual. And Adler was his lover.

He had shrouded the first secret for decades. In the Victorian and Edwardian eras it was taboo, a perversion, a crime, a sin, the love that dare not speak its name. And Casement did love. He loved the male gaze and male body, and loved sex. Prohibited from any open relationship, as a roving Foreign Office official he had furtive encounters in ports and cities around the world. Sailors, soldiers, students, clerks, whoever caught his eye, and returned his coded signals, would do. They were all races, white, brown, black, usually young, teenagers or in their 20s. Often he gave cash or little gifts which he viewed as tokens of appreciation, not prostitution.

While Oscar Wilde made the mistake of initiating a court case that exposed him, Casement cruised confidently through the shadows and found partners in London, Belfast, Dublin, Rio de Janeiro, Boma,

Madeira, Iquitos, Para, all without his closest friends or colleagues – or female admirers like Ada McNeill – guessing the truth.

For all his conquests, it was a solitary, conflicted existence. 'The Nameless One', a poem he dated 1900, expressed loneliness and wonder at why God made him this way:

> *No human hand to steal to mine,*
> *No loving eye to answering shine,*
> *Earth's cruel heart of dust alone*
> *To give me breath and strength to groan.*
> *. . . I sought by love alone to go*
> *Where God had writ an awful no.*
> *Pride gave a guilty God to Hell –*
> *I have no pride – by love I fell.*
> *Love took me by the heart at birth*
> *And wrought out from its common earth,*
> *With soul at his own skill aghast*
> *A furnace my mine own breath should blast.*
> *Why this was done I cannot tell.*
> *The mystery lives, inscrutable –*
> *I only know I pay the cost –*
> *With heart and soul and honour lost.*
> *I only know 'tis death to give*
> *My love – yet loveless can I live? –*
> *I only know I cannot die*
> *And leave this love God made, not I . . .*

Casement had compartmentalised his life. The British consul, the Irish nationalist and the sexual adventurer each had their place, sealed from the other. But now, unknown to the Clan na Gael leaders gathered in Manhattan, that discipline was breaking down.

Casement had encountered Adler on his stroll down Broadway in July while awaiting his first audience with Devoy. The former ship's stoker was 24, with fair hair, a powerful, compact physique and a gap between his front teeth. He spoke English with an American accent and was broke, marooned between jobs.

They stayed in touch and now, three months later, Casement proposed bringing Adler, breaching the barrier between his political and sexual life. He had recently turned 50 and perhaps felt his age and loneliness more than before. On a mission fraught with risk it was human to want company. Casement masked the nature of their relationship but did envisage Adler as a fixer and translator, and after a discussion Devoy and the others accepted the logic.

To deflect British attentions from his departure Clan na Gael publicised speaking engagements for Casement in Chicago and booked a hotel room there under his name. The next day would be Casement's last day as himself before adopting a new identity. He was going to need a razor and buttermilk.

. . .

As Casement prepared his disguise on Wednesday 14 October, Reginald Hall was 3,200 miles away assembling his crew on the deck of the *Queen Mary* for the bitterest moment of his life. On yet another frigid, grey afternoon at Scapa Flow, the captain was about to relinquish command of his battlecruiser.

The fleet's Orkney redoubt, a vast expanse of water dotted by treeless islands and jagged peaks, felt more Scandinavian than Scottish. When storms rolled in, everything disappeared in spray and cloud. Barrage balloons hovered in vigil over ships huddled side by side, as if for warmth. Some navy wit had penned an acidic ditty about the outpost:

> *They sprinkled it with raindrops, with sleet and hail and snow,*
> *And when they had it finished, sure, they called it Scapa Flow.*
> *... For years and years to come, whenever sailors congregate*
> *You may bet your life you may hear them sing that Scapa hymn*
>   *of hate.*

Hall had special reason for loathing. Since the Battle of Heligoland two months earlier the sub-Arctic conditions had gripped his chest, which was prone to infection, and nearly killed him. 'He could not last if he continued as he gets no better, in fact worse and looks an awful colour ... he has reached the limit of human endurance,' his commander, Admiral David Beatty, wrote in alarm.

The little captain had prepared for war his entire career and commanded one of the navy's finest ships and now, as Britain fought for her life, he had to give up his command.

The scarred, desolate landscape was an apt setting when Hall broke the news to his crew that afternoon. He lauded their dedication and courage and said if any man ever needed help they should write to him. 'Goodbye,' he said.

The cheers were deafening. 'They had begun by fearing him: now they loved him,' one officer recalled. Shortly after 5 p.m. Hall left the *Queen Mary* for the last time, boarded a harbour craft and headed for shore. Never again would he stand on the bridge of a capital ship and pound the enemy. But he was not leaving the navy and his war was not over. Like Roger Casement, Reginald Hall was heading for a new role. The Admiralty had offered him a job in London: chief of naval intelligence.

CHAPTER FIVE

Shark's Jaws

Reginald Hall encountered a capital utterly transformed from the peacetime metropolis Casement had visited in May. It was the wettest week of the year, but from dawn's first light it seemed every green space from Hyde Park to Hampstead Heath resounded to the barks of drill sergeants instructing recruits in khaki how to charge and make frontal assaults through shrubs and bushes, a spectacle that enthralled pensioners and terrorised squirrels.

Military bagpipers and drummers played rousing tunes as men still in civvies signed up at enlistment stations and tramped off through puddles to training camps. Herbert Kitchener, the war minister and legendary conqueror of Khartoum, gazed with blazing eyes and a magnificent moustache from posters that jabbed a finger, and an exhortation, at the soul of every Englishman: 'Your country needs YOU.' By mid-October almost a million had enlisted. A recruit named James Hodson caught the mood in an ode:

*'Give us men! cried England, cried Europe.
We have answered, we Kitchener's men,
and Kitchener is making us into men . . .'*

Each day brought evidence of the war's savage cost. Trainloads of wounded soldiers returned from France while women donned black armbands in mourning for sons, brothers, fathers and husbands who would never return. Refugees from Belgium, their number swollen by the fall of Antwerp, brought stories of burning villages and mass executions.

Government restrictions multiplied, with little dissent. Food was rationed, beer watered down, news censored, pubs and theatres shut early. Big Ben was muffled lest the sonorous bongs guide enemy airmen. And there was the blackout. Headlights, lanterns and street lamps were dimmed or extinguished and the windows of offices, businesses and homes, even Buckingham Palace, were boarded up so not a chink of light escaped. Night brought a smothering blackness.

'So impenetrable was the darkness that I did not know when we were crossing Waterloo Bridge . . . [with] the curious sensation that there were thousands of people near you, but invisible,' one visitor noted. With night came a hush as the streets emptied and searchlights stabbed the heavens, probing for Zeppelins that had yet to materialise.

With patriotism came fear and loathing. On the eve of Hall's arrival mobs of several thousand people attacked shops with German-sounding names in a fury of smashing, looting and bawling 'We want no Germans here!' Baron Northcliffe, a press magnate, believed Britons liked a 'good hate' and the *Daily Mail* obliged with reports of Teutonic outrages on the continent. At the war's outset *Punch* magazine caricatures had depicted the Kaiser as a sausage-eating buffoon, but now he was a blood-drenched ogre.

Spy mania gripped the public and Scotland Yard faced clamours for action based on wild rumours. German agents were under beds, behind bushes, up trees, they were impersonating British officers, sabotaging bridges, poisoning reservoirs. They were transmitting to U-boats, flickering lights to Zeppelins, dispatching carrier pigeons, coding messages via crossword clues and agony aunt columns. Tennis courts were gun emplacements for invading troops. Aristocrats and politicians with German ancestry, or German friends, were in league with the enemy. No one, however, suspected Sir Roger Casement.

Belgium's plight crystallised a belief that Britain was fighting for justice and decency. The Hun had invaded a small, neutral country, not part of any alliance or Entente, as a route to France. To punish Belgian temerity in resisting, German troops had massacred civilians and torched cultural gems like the university town of Louvain, part of an official policy of reprisals. The more Britain expended her own blood and treasure in fighting such a foe, the greater her determination to win, and vindicate the sacrifice, no matter the escalating cost.

War measures turned the mass of people for the first time into active citizens, the historian A. J. P. Taylor later wrote. 'Their lives were shaped by orders from above; they were required to serve the state instead of pursuing exclusively their own affairs ... the state established a hold over its citizens which, though relaxed in peacetime, was never to be removed and which the second World war was again to increase. The history of the English state and of the English people merged for the first time.'

As Director of Naval Intelligence, DNI, Hall would be at the heart of this new world. He could hear it being forged around him in the incessant hammering and banging of workmen erecting tin and iron structures for growing staff at the Admiralty. It was not the bridge of a warship, but immense power resided here.

First built in 1723, the Admiralty complex drew other offices of state that turned Whitehall into a hub of ministries with soaring porticos, polished granite columns and miles of corridors. One end of the thoroughfare led to Trafalgar Square, named after the battle that doomed Napoleon's naval dreams, the other led past the prime minister's residence at Downing Street to the Palace of Westminster.

When Hall entered the Admiralty he entered a shrine to the naval might that had turned this island on Europe's fringe into master of a global empire with 400 million subjects. An archway with mounted sentries led to a Palladian edifice topped by a glazed oval dome. The entrance hall displayed prows of sailing ships to honour victories in the manner that Rome commemorated vanquishing Carthage. In the boardroom a circular map of the world showed the position of British and enemy fleets while above it an antique wind dial, connected to a weather vane on the roof, showed the wind's direction. The roof also boasted a more modern technology: radio masts that allowed near instant communication with ships within a 1,600-mile radius.

Hall's office overlooked Horse Guards Parade, a ceremonial parade ground that hosted the Trooping of the Colour on the monarch's birthday. Such pomp had been suspended until the war ended, but the new DNI could still gaze on little rituals of power. Lord Kitchener would crunch over the immaculate gravel to his club at lunchtime, while Winston Churchill would trot in the other direction to Downing Street to confer with Herbert Asquith. Some evenings the prime minister would stroll past Hall's window to his own club, the Athenaeum.

For a sailor accustomed to brine, coal and gunpowder this was a rarefied environment where authority came not in barked orders but memos and murmurs. Hall's continuous blinking and odd, staccato way of speaking mattered little on ships where a captain's word was law, but here he would be scrutinised by admirals and ministers. 'I knew little enough about politicians, and had not a notion how to deal with them,' he later admitted.

Yet even in his first week in mid-October, Hall was not intimidated. On land or sea, he trusted his instincts and abilities. In Whitehall, battle meant fighting for budgets, turf and promotion, but Hall itched to get at the Hun, even if from a desk. A different type of gunnery, yes, but with multiple targets.

He started with office décor. Behind his desk hung a large steel engraving of the Battle of Waterloo, a reminder of British triumph, with Prussian help, no less, that Hall sensed would irk the French naval attaché, or any Frenchman, who visited his office. 'Take the damned thing away at once!' he told an assistant. The roving eye spotted a wallchart of the 'German Ocean', a common name for the sea between Britain, Norway and Germany. Hall ordered a brush and ink and within five minutes it became the North Sea.

From his window the DNI could see in a corner of Horse Guards Parade a recruiting tent where from dawn to dusk young men, rain bouncing off them, queued to join the fight. Shopkeepers, teachers, dockers, accountants, butlers, students, all classes, regions and religions, volunteering for the trenches. Some would not come back, but Hall would do his damnedest to make sure they were on the winning side.

Naval intelligence was a small department with 29 staff, mostly Royal Marine officers and clerks, tucked into the wider Admiralty bureaucracy. Its main function was to collect, analyse and relay information to aid strategy. Hall knew its history because his father, William Hall, had been appointed to set up the unit in 1882 amid a possible war with Russia. The war never happened, but when Hall senior returned to his ship six years later the unit continued whirring as a cog in Admiralty decision-making.

Blinker had got his first taste of intelligence work in 1909 when he was asked to quietly surveil German harbour fortifications during a courtesy visit by his ship, HMS *Cornwall*, to Kiel. No duck ever took to water with the alacrity of Hall's first dip into intrigue. The Germans were gracious hosts but kept the visitors away from key installations, so Hall devised a ruse: his men would hide a camera on a motorboat and feign engine trouble just as they passed the sensitive area, allowing discreet photography. The boat's owner, the Duke of

Westminster, endorsed the plan with a cry of 'Rule Britannia!' Hall's men got the pictures.

Taking his father's former post was a fluke. Soon after war broke out the head of naval intelligence, Rear-Admiral Henry Oliver – a control freak so taciturn he was nicknamed 'Dummy' – was promoted to another department, so the Admiralty needed a new DNI at the same time it sought to rescue Hall from Scapa Flow.

Even for this most undaunted of men it must have been difficult to know where to begin. Hall inherited an overworked department facing multiple, unfolding challenges. The navy was fetching troops from India and Africa, shuttling reinforcements to France and hunting enemy submarines – all of which cried out for good intelligence. Hall would need sources, agents, contacts. And more codebreakers. A handful had already been recruited and were in a room down the corridor studying a growing pile of intercepted, coded German messages.

Hall's department also had responsibility for collating and sifting information about the blockade of Germany, a linchpin of Britain's war strategy. Rather than a close-up blockade of German ports it was a 'distant' blockade that controlled entry to the North Sea. Vessels bound for Germany and neutral countries were to be intercepted and escorted to British ports, where cargo would be checked and passengers vetted. Many were trying to slip through with false identities.

. . .

On Thursday 22 October, as Hall neared the end of his first week as DNI, the Scandinavian American passenger liner *Oscar II* was seven days into its voyage from New York and the first-class passengers were growing increasingly fretful about the tall man with the long chin and strange accent. Most passengers were German or Austrian, or had sympathy with the Central Powers, and the closer they got to

Norway the more they feared being intercepted by the British and betrayed by this odd fellow. He said he was American but sounded English, and they suspected he was a spy.

Some turned mute within his earshot, which made for oppressive silences at mealtimes, while others squirmed and professed to want Britain to win the war. 'Well, I guess I don't,' said the purported American. 'You see my papa fought in the civil war and so did his too, and we ain't got no love for the British in my family.' He said this as if to lighten the atmosphere and reassure them, but perhaps it was a ruse to extract more information.

Casement was posing as a New York businessman, but nasal American vowels eluded him and he had little feel for US idioms. Instead of keeping a low profile and his mouth shut, he talked and talked. 'As a good American, I let myself loose some,' he later admitted. It caused ever more alarm to fellow passengers and undermined his alias, but Casement couldn't help it. He was a social creature. And ocean crossings were tedious.

On the evening of 22 October the Danish captain announced they would veer north and steam hard towards the Faroe Islands in a detour to try to evade British cruisers said to be patrolling north of Scotland's Shetland Islands and around the Orkneys. The British had many ships but it was a big ocean.

. . .

Casement's departure from New York had gone according to plan. A Clan na Gael member named James Landy, an estate agent, lent his identity, shared documents and business cards and tutored Casement in his background. The Austro-Hungarian consulate booked a first-class berth in Landy's name and a second-class ticket for Adler Christensen on the *Oscar II*.

To throw off any British surveillance Casement changed hotel and registered as 'Mr R. Smythe'. Before checking out on 15 October he wrote an emotional farewell letter to John Devoy – 'without you there would be nothing'. Then he shaved off his beard, which accentuated his chin, washed his face with buttermilk, which was said to lighten the complexion, and left by a rear exit.

At the port Casement changed places with the real Landy, who had briefly boarded the *Oscar II*. Emerging from New York harbour, it passed the scene of a collision – a vessel laden with coffee and bananas had been accidentally rammed and was slowly sinking, which fortuitously for the fake Landy distracted a British cruiser, the *Lancaster*, from its usual patrol, and vetting of passengers, outside the bay.

The single-funnel *Oscar II* was much smaller than the famous *Lusitania* and bound for Christiania, the Norwegian capital later renamed Oslo. The German and Austrian diplomats on board had immunity, but if the British boarded, the young men with fake passports who were trying to get home and report for duty risked arrest. So did Casement.

The ship ploughed through calm, grey seas. A newsletter compiled from telegrams provided updates on the war, which appeared to be settling into a bloody stalemate. Casement seethed at claims of German troops hacking off people's hands in Belgium, which he suspected was English propaganda repurposing parts of his report into atrocities by Leopold's regime in Congo. It used to be the Gaels that were demonised as savages; now it was the Germans. German atrocities were no myth, but Casement might have been right about the hand-cutting – the claims were never corroborated. Exasperated by having to conceal his true identity from fellow passengers, he had Adler distribute his booklet, *Ireland, Germany and the Freedom of the Seas*, though without claiming authorship.

Casement was delighted with his young companion. Adler did errands, kept his eyes and ears open and provided intimacy. There was a paternal element to the relationship. Adler said he had run away from home when he was 12 to escape a brutal father, a void Casement appeared to partially fill. Unlike the quasi-farce over Mr Landy, Casement's sexual relationship with Adler remained cloaked.

In his cabin Casement indulged his other passion, writing, filling page after page of letters, journals, jottings, ideas for articles; he usually averaged about 3,000 words a day. It was a way to impose order on churning thoughts. Weeks earlier he had joked about being a fugitive, and now he was plying the Atlantic just as Wolfe Tone and Benjamin Franklin had done centuries earlier to seek aid from England's enemies.

Casement's most precious document was an enciphered letter from Germany's ambassador, Count von Bernstorff. Addressed to the imperial chancellor, Theobald von Bethmann Hollweg, it endorsed Casement's credentials and urged the German government to consider his proposals to liberate Ireland.

. . .

In New York, Casement had impressed German diplomats. In fact, in a memo to Berlin the military attaché, Franz von Papen, called him 'the leader of all Irish associations in America', which confused Casement's prestige with authority. Von Papen also claimed most Irish people were 'ready to free themselves', a deluded reading of sentiment in Ireland. Before the war the Kaiser's government had shown little enthusiasm for Irish nationalism, lest it embolden restive groups within Germany's empire, such as the Poles. It had however hoped that Ireland's convulsions over Home Rule would deter British action on the continent, which had proved another delusion.

Bernstorff, the ambassador, was more cautious than his military attaché, but he sensed an opportunity for Germany if Casement could deliver on his plan to recruit, with the help of Catholic priests, an Irish brigade from Germany's growing number of captured British army soldiers. 'An Irish priest . . . and Sir Roger Casement are going to Germany in order to visit the Irish prisoners,' the ambassador said in a coded message to Berlin. It was marked telegram 172 and sent on 1 October.

German communications had a problem. On the first day of war a British ship lifted Germany's trans-Atlantic cables from the seabed and sliced them, instantly ending Germany's ability to send and receive cabled telegrams to and from much of the world. So it now relied almost exclusively on wireless – transmitting Morse code through the air. It had the world's most powerful transmitter at Nauen, a wireless station outside Berlin with a range exceeding 3,300 miles. It sent and received signals to and from German-operated radio towers around the world, including a 500-foot tower at Sayville in Long Island, New York.

Knowing the enemy could pluck messages from the ether, the Germans devised sophisticated codes and ciphers to render the messages as gibberish to anyone but intended recipients who had the correct codes and ciphers to unscramble the messages. There was supreme confidence in these safeguards. They were, after all, designed by the best scientific and mathematical minds, German minds. They were uncrackable: *idotensicher*, foolproof. So Nauen hummed and throbbed.

When British radio installations started intercepting some of these messages, Hall's predecessor Rear-Admiral 'Dummy' Oliver tasked a Scottish engineer named Alfred Ewing to try to make sense of them. Ewing enlisted a handful of academics and mathematicians as cryptographers. They had no expertise, but then came a wondrous gift: a copy of the German navy's cypher and signal book. It was the key to unlock intercepted messages sent in a code known as SKM. 'More precious than a dozen Fabergé eggs,' one historian wrote.

Retrieved by the Russians from a sinking German cruiser, a courier brought the intelligence treasure to London and solemnly handed it over to Winston Churchill. The First Sea Lord passed it to his naval intelligence department on the eve of Hall's arrival at the Admiralty. Eleven days later, as Casement's ship made its loop around the North Atlantic, the codebreakers were still working through the backlog of intercepted messages. Among them sat telegram 172.

. . .

On the afternoon of Saturday 24 October the captain of the *Oscar II* told passengers they would soon sight the Faroes, but at around 2 p.m., as they scanned the horizon to the north, the skyline to the south sprouted a pair of funnels. A British ship. It briefly headed west then swung around, closed in and fired a warning shot. The *Oscar II* cut its engines and wallowed in the swell. The interceptor was a battleship. 'Like a great granite battery, the seas washing over her,' Casement would recall. 'Her bows were covered with men, hundreds of them drawn up in three great rows right across the decks standing like statues.'

He hastened to his cabin to shave – his beard had partially grown back – and scour his papers. The innocuous could be left visible. Adler, travelling under his own name and less liable to scrutiny, would conceal incriminating but vital documents. A third category – papers not for British eyes, but dispensable – required a different fate. They included Casement's diary of his time in the US and this voyage. He opened a porthole and the bundle splashed overboard, ink and paper dissolving into the Atlantic.

Marines with rifles stomped aboard, took command of the bridge and aimed the *Oscar II* south, towards Scotland. Casement noted the name embroidered on their uniforms: HMS *Hibernia*, the Roman name for Ireland. He took heart; maybe it was a sign. They sailed through the night and at sunrise reached the Isle of Lewis, part of the Outer Hebrides. The rocks and cliffs resembled jagged teeth. 'It felt just like as if we were really going into a shark's jaws,' Casement recalled.

The ship anchored off Stornoway, an old Viking settlement. Four smaller captured steamers sat in the harbour, which was lined with brightly coloured houses and smelt of fish. British naval personnel questioned the *Oscar II* passengers and crew, relayed the information to the Admiralty in London, then awaited instructions.

Confined to the ship, some passengers wept. Time seemed to slow. Onshore, bells tolled for Sunday prayers. A castle looked down from a rise called Gallows Hill. The officer who shuttled on a tug between the *Oscar II* and the harbour was polite, even apologetic. A clocktower in the centre of town ticked the minutes.

There was no reason for the new director of naval intelligence to be alerted about the *Oscar II*. The interception was a routine affair that warranted the usual checks, nothing more. But Roger Casement's mission hung by a thread. The codebreakers worked seven days a week, a night shift and day shift, and at some point would reach telegram 172. British agents in the US had monitored Casement and his strident speeches for Clan na Gael. He was supposed to speak in Chicago but never showed up, then vanished. Where was he? They were checking his trail.

Casement's own actions increased the risk of exposure. In addition to subverting his Landy alias with fellow passengers, he had in effect put himself on a watchlist by penning a provocative 'Open Letter to Irishmen', signed under his own name, which the *Irish Independent*, a Dublin daily, had published on 5 October. It said Ireland had no quarrel with Germany and urged Irishmen to shun the British army – a public appeal that had jolted his former employers at the Foreign Office.

An intercepted telegram, seditious sentiments, a sudden disappearance, a passenger matching Casement's description, minus beard, turning up on a Norway-bound ship – a bright spark at Hall's department might have connected the dots. And right there the fugitive knight's gallop would have ended before it properly began.

But Sunday passed to Monday 26 October and the fake Mr Landy slipped through Britain's intelligence cracks. The codebreakers could not unscramble telegram 172, which was a diplomatic message that used different codes and ciphers from naval messages. British agents in New York visited Casement's last known hotel in New York but the trail went cold. And the authorities at Stornoway failed to detect anything unusual about the tall American passenger.

Instead, guards hauled away six Germans, including the ship's bandmaster and an assistant cook, and then released the *Oscar II*.

Shortly after 3 p.m. its propellers began to turn and the ship headed for Norway, taking with it any chance of a trophy catch by the Admiralty.

Having passed the British menace, tension on board dissolved. There was laughter, champagne and a transformed view of Mr Landy. He was no longer feared but toasted for having organised a collection that raised £65 for the six unfortunates who were interned. Casement discussed Ireland with an Austrian consul, one of several passengers who learned his real identity.

Just before midnight on Wednesday 28 October the *Oscar II* moored in thick fog at Christiana. Casement and Christensen passed customs and immigration control and took a taxi to the Grand Hotel, where they took adjoining rooms.

The next morning at 10 a.m. they stepped out to a bustle of shoppers and trams in the heart of Norway's capital. At the nearby German legation – a diplomatic office below the rank of embassy – they presented letters of introduction and requested visas to enter Germany. The ambassador said it would take at least a day. Returning to the Grand, Casement settled down to write letters and dispatched his companion to do some shopping. He had come to regard Adler as a 'treasure'.

Eivind Adler Christensen did not go shopping. In the waning afternoon light he headed up Karl Johans gate, the city's main thoroughfare, passed the national theatre and Palace Park, and made his way to a tree-lined residential neighbourhood with large, handsome houses. At 79 Drammensveien Street he turned into a driveway. It sloped upwards, leading to an imposing white mansion. He climbed sixteen steps and rang the bell.

CHAPTER SIX

Open Treason

Francis Oswald Lindley, first secretary of the British legation in Norway, blinked at the man seated before him and tried to process what he was hearing. The story was implausible, and certainly vile. It would have taken immense effort to not gape. The diplomatic mission's portraits of King George, at least, remained unperturbed.

The visitor had told the liveried doorman he wished to see the ambassador but the ambassador was out so it fell to Lindley, short, balding, son of a baron, to host this unexpected audience in an upstairs study. The young man refused to give his name, spoke English with a Norwegian and American inflection, and trembled, apparently with nerves.

He had, he said, arrived from the United States with an English nobleman – he withheld the name – who was in league with the Germans and wished to cause trouble in Ireland. This was astounding, if true, and it was not all. The fellow added that he had unnatural relations with the nobleman. Lindley would have heard outré stories during his postings, but treason *and* perversion; it was a lot to take in on a Thursday afternoon.

The first secretary admired Norwegian men as hearty, wholesome types who enjoyed salmon fishing as much as he did, but this specimen evidently belonged to another category. The meeting ended with agreement to reconvene the next morning when the ambassador would be present.

The visitor returned on Friday at 11 a.m. and it was the turn of Mansfeldt de Cardonnel Findlay to gaze down on the creature. Findlay was the tallest Englishman in diplomacy, 6 ft 9 in. of Victorian conviction, and gazed down on everyone, but he noted with particular disdain this caller's close-set eyes, the gap between his teeth and overall 'fleshy, dissipated appearance'.

Even so, the ambassador paid close attention. Elaborating on what he had told Lindley, the fellow said the nobleman had influential friends in New York who wanted German help for a revolt in Ireland. On the *Oscar II*, he had steamed open and copied letters – one was from the German ambassador in Washington to the German chancellor – which he now showed to Findlay. He repeated the avowal about a sexual relationship, which he said gave him power over the nobleman.

If even half-true these were sensational disclosures. Assuring the visitor that the British indeed paid for important information, and that he wished to see him again, Findlay extracted further details: the nobleman was travelling under an American alias, James Landy, and the German legation was preparing visas for the pair to enter Germany. Findlay pressed the mysterious informant for the nobleman's real name. A hesitation, then it came. Sir Roger Casement.

. . .

The unfathomable soul of Eivind Adler Christensen was forged in Moss, an industrial city 40 miles south of Christiania that clanked and clanged with shipyards, workshops and glassworks. Born in 1890, he was the eldest of five children of middle-class parents who believed in God, hard work and self-improvement. The greatest indulgence of his father, a machinist, was an occasional glass of port. The children did well at school and headed for respectable careers, all except Adler, who clashed with teachers, played truant and dropped out. He did odd jobs, hung out with petty criminals and stole cash, beer, boots, food, horseshoes. What he couldn't use, he sold. He lied, drank and gambled. It was as if the smell of sulphur that hung over Moss – a wood pulp factory used sulphate – seeped into him. Convicted of theft at the age of 16, he went to sea and didn't come back.

Adler Christensen, aged 25, in a studio portrait in Berlin in 1915.

For eight years Adler worked on ships and lived on his wits, drifting between jobs and ports, often destitute. In the US he acquired a wife and an infant son. And then in July he had encountered Casement. It may have been a reunion – there is evidence they met several years earlier in South America, and had a relationship, before crossing paths in Manhattan.

Adler's rough-hewn looks and manner bewitched Casement. The Norwegian cast himself as a tragic figure buffeted by life, and was sexually versatile – he liked women but could also have sex with men. Adler cursed like the sailor he was and would tell people to go fuck themselves. Casement, a linguistic prude, forgave such profanities; there was a hint of *Pygmalion* in his efforts to smooth out the younger man's coarseness, with Adler in the role of willing pupil. He possessed a blankness, accentuated by an immobile face, that let people project what they wanted to see. It never occurred to Casement that he had fallen for a sociopath.

Christensen's betrayal was merciless. He plundered Casement's innermost secrets, political and sexual, and laid them out like trophies to his enemies. But with Christensen nothing was straightforward. The boy from Moss sought to betray not only Casement but the British. Sulphur is a volatile gas.

After the first meeting at the legation Christensen returned to the Grand and burst into Casement's room with a breathless story: a stranger had accosted him and brought him in a chauffeur-driven limousine to 79 Drammensveien, where he was quizzed about his master's identity and intentions. Identifying the address as the British legation, Casement's heart hammered: the British were onto him. He had already been twitchy about possible surveillance, now there was no doubt. He had to reach Germany as soon as possible.

So began a surreal game of double and triple bluff in which only Christensen, the ringmaster, fully knew what was happening. Returning from his second visit to the legation – with Findlay on the morning of Friday 30 October – he told Casement the ambassador knew Casement's name and had said whoever 'knocked him on the head' need never work again; offered a reward, in other words, to kidnap or murder him.

More than frightened, Casement was affronted. This scoundrel of an ambassador was offering 'monstrous bribes' to commit a 'dastardly crime'. For all his anglophobia the former consul still believed in a code of conduct for English gentlemen. Well, he too could take the gloves off. Casement instructed Christensen to return to the legation at 3 p.m., as the ambassador had requested, and to feign cooperation. 'I advised him ... for the sake of appearances to "sell me dear" and to secure the promise of a very respectable sum for so very disreputable an act,' he later wrote.

Christensen played his assigned role at the legation but strayed beyond his instructions by letting the ambassador copy his copies of Casement's letters and also providing a sample of Casement's handwriting.

Findlay lacked authorisation to detain Casement in Norway so did the next best thing: he commissioned the informant to spy on him in Germany and supplied a line of communication: Christensen was to send coded letters to Herr Sigvald Wiig, a legation clerk, at 78 Thorvald Meyers gate in Christiania. Findlay paid the visitor an advance of 100 kroner, equivalent today to about £500, said more would follow based on results, and bade him farewell. What a coup! He had recruited a double-agent at the heart of an Irish-German plot. With cool understatement, the ambassador sat down to explain everything in a letter to the foreign secretary. 'My dear Sir Edward Grey ... I have the honour to submit the following account of two conversations ...'

Back at the hotel, Christensen showed Casement Findlay's cash and written instructions about clandestine contact. He added that Findlay had priced Casement's head at £5,000, equivalent today to about £500,000. Casement was perturbed at the bounty and exultant at subverting the ambassador's dirty tricks. What a coup! The English would stop at nothing but thanks to Adler he was onto them. 'That this man was faithful to me and the law of his country was a triumph of Norwegian integrity,' he later wrote.

A century later historians and psychologists still debate Christensen's machinations. A British reward was his most lucrative prospect, yet having created the opportunity he alerted his master. He fed truth and lies to each side, apparently improvising with no masterplan to see what might bring him most advantage. Sustaining the deceits could generate two incomes while figuring out the main payoff, but it was not just about money. Christensen appeared at times to genuinely care for Casement while inducing paranoia as if it were a game. It must have been thrilling to play important men against each other and watch them bumble in the dark.

After the second meeting with Findlay, Christensen returned to the Grand to find Casement packed and waiting. After 36 hours in Christiania the fugitive knight was seeing British shadows everywhere and itching to leave. The German legation had provided passes and a diplomat, Richard Meyer, to escort them to Berlin.

The three men caught the 5.38 p.m. train for Copenhagen. At Findlay's behest a British naval attaché, Captain Consett, lurked at the station and discreetly watched them board – he described Casement as 'distinguished looking' but with a flat-footed gait. Consett made no effort to stop them; a member of the trio, after all, was now a British agent.

The three passengers trundled south through the night. At Ängelholm junction they switched to a part of the train that broke off and headed for the Swedish port of Trelleborg. There they boarded a ferry, the *Queen Victoria*, and churned through a stormy Baltic to the island of Rügen on the Pomeranian coast. It was Saturday 31 October and Sir Roger Casement had made it to Germany.

By 7.45 p.m. he was in Berlin.

. . .

Meyer escorted the visitors to the Continental, an immensity of marble, pillars and chandeliers near the Brandenburg Gate in the heart of the city. Casement checked in under a new alias, Mr Hammond of New York, and took room 219, with Christensen in a cheaper room two doors up. Most of the 200-plus rooms were unoccupied, draping a hush over the hotel. Meyer told them to stay put until he had arranged documents for Casement. As an English speaker and British subject he was not safe on the streets.

There was a deceptive normality to Germany's imperial capital. Trams and taxis zipped down Unter den Linden, diners filled restaurants and shop shelves remained stocked. Berlin's football club had been back in action, playing Leipzig, and horse riders trotted through the Tiergarten. After dusk the city lit up – it was beyond the reach of enemy aircraft – as brilliantly as ever. Audiences packed theatres for plays and concerts.

But the war was everywhere. Trains and ambulances delivered wounded soldiers to hospitals and improvised medical centres in homes and museums. Families clustered in cafes to say farewell to sons, brothers and lovers heading to the front. Women worked as tram conductors and scouts delivered post. Music hall comedians made bleak jokes about being encircled by foes. 'Why does Germany understand war so well?' went one. 'Because it has been declared upon her eight times' – a pun on the word 'erklaren' which meant 'to declare' and also 'to explain'. Jubilation at battlefield victories came tinged with grief, with audiences falling silent during renditions of 'Nicht zu Laut':

> *Not too loud! Not too loud!*
> *Think just now while you laugh and cheer;*
> *Not too loud! Not too loud!*
> *Perchance a warrior fallen in the battle*
> *Lies beside his shot down steed*
> *And bids farewell to mother and bride;*
> *Not too loud! Not too loud!*

The failure to take Paris and the French Channel ports had not dimmed the German people's enthusiasm for the Kaiser and the armed forces nor dented confidence in eventual victory. Prussia had been 'hatched in a cannonball', said Napoleon, and a century of Hegel,

Nietzsche and other German philosophers underpinned belief in Teutonic moral and military superiority.

The goal had been to swiftly knock out France, then hammer Russia and end the war in about 10 weeks, before autumn turned to winter. Instead, after three months, there was stalemate in the west and mixed fortunes in the east, where Germany was routing Russian armies but other Russian armies were routing the Austro-Hungarians, leaving Germany, in an expression to become famous, 'shackled to a corpse'.

There was a hierarchy of enmity. War with Russia was providential, a clash of civilisations. War with France was natural, to resolve unfinished business from 1870. But for England to wade in was abominable, an act of jealousy and treachery by supposed cousins. Germans believed England cried crocodile tears for Belgium while coveting German colonies, patents and export markets. 'If my grandmother had been alive she would never have allowed it,' wailed the Kaiser, Queen Victoria's eldest grandson.

The notion that England was too mired in Ireland's Home Rule strife to join a European conflict had proved wishful thinking. On top of all this, the Royal Navy swept German ships from the oceans and imposed a blockade. Germany was building a Zeppelin fleet to cross the Channel and exact revenge from the air but it also enjoined divine retribution. *Gott Strafe England*, went the slogan. May God Punish England.

The hatred extended to the English language, which made it problematic for Casement to open his mouth in public. Without an official document to wave as a shield, he risked lynching or arrest. So he spent his first full day in Berlin, Sunday 1 November, cloistered in his mausoleum of a hotel writing letters and brooding. 'A state guest and almost a state prisoner,' he wrote.

On Monday came his mission's first test. Collected by Meyer, he walked to Wilhelmstrasse, Germany's equivalent of Whitehall, passed the shuttered Russian and British embassies and the Rococo palace that housed the Reich chancellery before turning into the wooden gateway of a plain white house: the Foreign Office. Compared with the sumptuous scale and opulence of England's equivalent, this was a shed, albeit with expensive upholstery and Hohenzollern portraits.

The chancellor and secretary of state were at the French front with the Kaiser so Casement was to see the under-secretary of state, Arthur Zimmermann. The building was underwhelming and Zimmermann was second-tier, but here pulsed German power, an awesome force that if persuaded, if harnessed, might succeed where imperial Spain and revolutionary France had failed, and help expel the English from Ireland.

Presenting himself as the envoy not just of Clan na Gael but Ireland, Casement pitched Ireland's cause as Germany's cause. The goal was not just material help for a rebellion but recognition of nationhood – a statement to the world that Germany endorsed Irish independence. Words alone had power; America's revolution began not with muskets but a declaration.

'If I win all it is national resurrection – a free Ireland, a world nation after centuries of slavery,' Casement later wrote. The grandiose framing elided the fact most Irish people wanted not independence but autonomy within the United Kingdom, and that Irish unionists did not want even that. But Casement was lucid about the symbolism of his mission, and where it might lead. Coming to Germany was a proclamation of intent, of defiance. The British would call it treason. So be it. Let it be, Casement wrote, 'one bold deed of open treason'.

Zimmermann greeted him warmly. A big, ruddy man, like Casement he had been an outsider who climbed the diplomatic ranks through the consular service. He listened sympathetically to the tale of Findlay's machinations – 'dastardly', he murmured – and then to Casement's proposal for a German statement. Such a gesture, said Casement, would curb Irish enlistment in the British army. He presented a draft outline he had written, which Zimmermann accepted with a smile. 'I accept it entirely.'

Casement knew that Zimmermann's boss, Foreign Secretary Gottlieb von Jagow, and Chancellor Theobold von Bethmann Hollweg would need to sign off on the draft, and that some in the government might oppose it, but this was an excellent start. The part of the enterprise that most enthused his hosts, he learned, was forming an Irish brigade from British prisoners.

That evening Casement received a card from the chief of the political police vouching for Mr Hammond of New York. For added protection he pinned a little American flag in his buttonhole. After dinner he took a stroll with Adler, relieved to escape the confines of the hotel, but found the shops and famous lime trees of Unter den Linden less impressive than expected, and the river Spree lacking in grandeur.

In the days that followed, the tension of the voyage should have begun to unclench, but instead Casement felt a fresh twinge of unease. He had eluded the British at Stornoway and Christiania and was beyond their reach, for now, but the hunt was just beginning. They would surely cast a wide net.

. . .

As the first rays of Friday 6 November glinted on the Thames an armed escort marched a prisoner in solemn procession towards the eastern wall of the Tower of London. A chaplain led the way, reading from a Bible. The procession entered a long shed at the end of which was a wooden chair tied to stakes. Carl Hans Lody turned to the officer in charge. 'I suppose that you will not care to shake hands with a German spy?' 'No,' the officer replied, 'but I will shake hands with a brave man.' Lody walked steadily and stiffly to the chair, sat down and braced for oblivion.

At the outbreak of war German spy chiefs had sent the naval reserve lieutenant, who spoke fluent English, to spy on British naval bases. Lody used an American passport in the name of Charles A. Inglis to pose as a US tourist while monitoring fleet movements in

Scotland. He was detected after sending telegrams to a cover address monitored by Britain's intelligence agency MO5(g), later renamed MI5, and eventually arrested in County Kerry, where he had tried to lay low.

Of his London interrogators, one stood out. 'Not only did he look at me, but he looked right through me,' he recalled. It was Reginald Hall's peregrine falcon gaze, and it stayed locked on Lody during his court martial at Westminster, which Hall attended, doing all in his power to ensure a death sentence.

Now, as an unusually warm November sun rose over the city, Lody crossed his legs and leaned back in the chair. 'Present!' cried the sergeant. Eight guardsmen charged and cocked their rifles and aimed. Beyond the Tower walls, vehicles rumbled across the bridge. 'Fire!' Eight shots rang out with one report, and the spy slumped.

Hall at that moment was probably at home at 53 Cadogan Gardens, a handsome four-storey redbrick in west London, and with luck was going to breakfast on cold rice pudding and cold roast partridge. He had no pity for enemies in wartime, his personal secretary, Hugh Cleland Hoy, recorded. 'If the power had lain in his hands [he would have passed] sentence of death on all the hireling spies who came before him. And they would probably have left this world of sorrows without so much as time to say their prayers.'

Less than a month into the job, the director of naval intelligence blew a 'crackling breeze' through Admiralty corridors, a historian noted. Lody's demise augured a busy Friday for Hall. In a few hours Britain was going to follow Russia and France in declaring war on Turkey, creating new opportunities and perils in the Mediterranean and Middle East. Hall was also eyeing a foray into postal censorship.

And this was the day his cryptographers would move to a new home. They had outgrown their cramped office overlooking Horse Guards Parade and needed more space, privacy and quiet. In addition to the codebook gifted by the Russians two other precious enemy codebooks had arrived, one seized from a German ship in Australia, the other dredged from a wreck in the North Sea, a bounty that became known as the 'miraculous draught of the fishes'. With additional signalling stations intercepting ever more messages, cryptography's potential was becoming boundless.

Hall went on a talent hunt for more codebreakers and found new digs – a hub of rooms on the first floor of a secluded Admiralty edifice known as the Old Building that offered silence and anonymity. By the end of Friday the unit was to be ensconced and out of sight. 'No admittance. Ring bell,' said a sign by the entrance. There was no bell.

Hall would have been aware of Findlay's dispatches from Christiania which revealed Casement's shocking treachery. The foreign secretary, Sir Edward Grey, had forwarded copies to Hall's boss, Churchill, as well as Asquith, Kitchener and Birrell, the Ireland secretary. The ambassador's telegrams laid out the purported plot by Irish-Americans and malcontents in Ireland to seek German help for an invasion, as well as Casement's 'unnatural relations' with the unnamed Norwegian informant. 'Story is extraordinary but I feel pretty sure it is true,' Findlay wrote. 'I am arranging to obtain news of what this man does after arrival in Germany.'

Extraordinary or not, Casement's skullduggery paled amid the titanic challenges facing the government. Hall's colleagues at MO5(g) had a card index of suspicious persons classified on a scale from AA to BB that used 'Boche', a pejorative French term for Germans. AA was 'Absolutely Allied', undoubtedly friendly, AB was 'Anglo-Boche', doubtful but probably friendly, BA was 'Boche-Anglo', doubtful but probably hostile. Casement appeared to be BB, Bad Boche, undoubtedly hostile, at least in spirit. But how much damage could he do? Ireland was calm and Britain controlled the seas, impeding any invasion. Whatever Casement was up to seemed embryonic. And he was being watched. As for unnatural vice, that might merit a sneer but not action. There was no category of Homosexual Boche.

. . .

After meeting Zimmermann, Casement was left to wait, worry and hope. His plea for recognition of Ireland's cause had to work its way through layers of government decision-making. He brooded. He needed to develop a plan to raise an Irish legion from prisoners-of-war and also itched to strike back at his would-be kidnapper, Findlay.

And there was something else. When the *Oscar II* was intercepted he had thrown his diary overboard. But there were other diaries stretching back to his time in South America and Africa. They were written long before his campaign for Irish independence and contained nothing seditious; they documented another type of transgression. They were not lyrical or subtle. They were explicit and forensic. Names of partners, dates, locations, payments, penis size, descriptions of mutual masturbation, oral sex, penetration, ejaculation – he had recorded it all, filling entire journals, year after year.

Why? That question can never be fully answered. But the tone of the diaries was not one of shame but exuberance, even joy. Underlinings, exclamation marks and comments added after the original entries show that Casement liked to re-read them. He could never discuss this part of his life, his identity, with even close friends. The trysts were clandestine and often fleeting, but this lonely man could return to these journals to recall a lover's touch and experience anew the frisson, the afterglow.

And here was the problem. The perpetual nomad, lacking his own home, had carted around his possessions, a biographer noted, 'like the shell on a snail's back'. Casement ended up storing trunks in several locations in London and Ireland. Some contained sex journals.

Now, amid the oppressive hush of his Berlin hotel, crept a cold, clammy realisation. His enemies could follow a trail that led to this hidden self. The implications were barely conceivable.

Casement did not know that Christensen had served the truth of their relationship on a platter to the English. But he knew he was a fugitive who had left loose ends. There was no easy remedy. Any letter to a friend in England or Ireland requesting concealment or destruction of the trunks risked backfiring if intercepted. The safer channel seemed to be via German diplomats in the US who liaised with Clan na Gael.

On 6 November, while gravediggers at the Tower dug a plot for Lody, and Reginald Hall rehoused his codebreakers, the Nauen transmitter pinged a message across the Atlantic. Casement wanted a Clan na Gael messenger to go to Ireland to dispatch a priest to Germany – and to tell Francis Joseph Bigger, a friend in Antrim, 'to conceal everything belonging to me'.

Five days later Casement wrote another note for Clan na Gael lamenting he had left 'papers' with Bigger and at a storage depot in London. 'How foolish of me not to have got them over to the USA. Now the enemy will get them I fear. They are in a state of mind that sticks at nothing.'

Casement appeared to have lost track of what was where. His storage depot trunks contained nothing compromising. It was his trunks at 50 Ebury Street, the boarding house with the sour milk aroma, that contained journals.

A week later Casement visited the German army's Western Front headquarters in Charleville, where he re-stated Ireland's cause, and then on 20 November it came, the official German government statement. It was splashed across newspapers. *'Deutsche Sympathie-Erklärung für Irland. Sir Roger Casement in Berlin.'*

The declaration trumpeted Casement's arrival in the imperial capital and said Germany had no quarrel with Ireland. 'Should the fortune of this great war, that was not of Germany's seeking, ever bring in its course German troops to the shores of Ireland, they would land there, not as an army of invaders to pillage and destroy, but as the forces of a government that it inspired by goodwill towards a country and a people for whom Germany desires only national prosperity and national freedom.'

It was not a full-throated cry for Irish independence but still a triumph for Casement that made headlines across Europe. In Britain there was shock. Some refused to believe it and assumed a German fabrication. Could Sir Roger even really be in Berlin? Others thought the hero of Congo must have gone mad, perhaps stricken with a tropical malady.

For Reginald Hall the explanation was simple. Roger Casement was a Very Bad Boche. And now he was a target.

PART II

Shadowplay

CHAPTER SEVEN

Sayonara

A heavy silence greeted Reginald Hall as he entered the room of the secretary of state for home affairs. The minister, Reginald McKenna, stood by the fireplace, clutching the lapels of his frock coat. He eyed the director of naval intelligence and said nothing. Hall took a seat beside Colonel George Cockerill, the deputy director of military intelligence at MO5(g), who had also been summoned to this conclave.

It was 11 a.m. At Horse Guards Parade troopers with gleaming breastplates and plumed helmets were marching out for the changing of the guard, a reassuring ritual, but McKenna's wordless glower had the opposite effect. Hall wondered if he should say something to break the silence. He gave a little bow and kept his mouth shut. It was the captain's first and possibly last time in the Home Office. He wondered if he was about to be fired.

The minister gave his lapels a little tug and marshalled his platform voice. 'Commander Hall,' he began, using a rank junior to captain. 'I have sent for you because it has been brought to my notice that without my express authority you have dared to tamper with His Majesty's mails. Is this true?'

Blinker blinked. 'Quite true, Mr Home Secretary.'

Another silence as McKenna digested the admission. He was one of the most powerful men in government, responsible for the UK's internal security, and had declared that Britain's civilian institutions and values should be 'business as usual' while it fought the war. The point, after all, was to remain British. Yet the director of naval intelligence had made it his business to steam open and read the country's mail. It was illegal, because civilian post could be opened only on the home secretary's warrant, and vexing, because an MP was kicking up hell about it, and apparently counterproductive, because the Foreign Office said interfering with the post would alienate neutral countries.

The minister's eyes locked onto Hall. Did he realise the heinousness of what he had done? Did he grasp that the home secretary had a duty to remove him from his post and take steps to have him brought to trial, and that if found guilty he would be jailed for two years?

It was late November, barely six weeks since Hall's appointment, and instead of scourging Huns he was facing disgrace and downfall. Instead of quailing, Hall had to suppress an urge to laugh. He visualised a judge's wig descending on the minister's bald head. The situation was absurd. Hall didn't fear prison, he feared civilians would shut his postal censorship experiment just when it was yielding dividends.

At the war's outset MO5(g) believed spies in Britain would post coded reports to Germany via neutral countries, so it dispatched a handful of men to the postal service's central sorting office at Mount Pleasant in Clerkenwell. They sought to monitor just a small fraction of mail – even this limited goal angered cabinet ministers – but the volume overwhelmed them. Hall heard about it and offered not just to help but to expand the monitoring to *all* foreign mail, a logistically daunting and politically explosive proposal.

'I must repeatedly have exceeded my authority,' he later wrote. 'I had come to the decision that if we were to get on with our job, there must be no slavish regard for peacetime precedents. There were certain things which in my view badly wanted doing, and I proposed to do them.' Wrangling £1,600 of funding from Churchill, Hall enlisted 200 volunteers from a conservative advocacy group, the National Service League, and set up a censorship unit to steam open, scan and reseal letters. Instead of missives from German spies, who had been rounded up and could no longer post anything, it stumbled across commercial correspondence that showed how Germany was sourcing supplies and contraband from overseas. It was an unexpected and momentous discovery that could help patch gaps in Britain's blockade and make it a stranglehold.

News of the censorship had leaked, prompting this summons by McKenna. But when Hall, backed by Cockerill, argued his case, the mood in the room, bit by bit, transformed. The 'eyes of hypnotic force' noted by a newspaper interviewer years earlier seemed to drill into the minister until his commitment to business-as-usual crumbled. By the end of it, McKenna agreed to consolidate and elevate Hall's censorship unit into a new War Trade Intelligence Department.

The next day Hall was invited to Downing Street to brief the prime minister on the proposed new department, and soon after that invited to a cabinet meeting. Standing by a doorway, he watched as Asquith smiled at the ministers seated around the oval table. 'Well, gentlemen, we have Captain Hall here, and I can see that you are all in agreement with his views. Good. Then we can take steps at once to form the new department.'

No debate, a fait accompli. Hall had steeled the government to usher in a surveillance state that by the end of the war employed thousands of postal censors. He walked back to the Admiralty almost in a daze, mulling the implications. 'I knew as clearly as if I had been told by Mr Asquith himself that in a little while the ID [intelligence department] would be doing work far wider in scope than any Admiralty official that day would have dared to prophesy,' he later wrote.

Some historians date the birth of Britain's modern secret service from this time. It also marked Hall's emergence as a Whitehall player. Through force of personality and willingness to take risks his Admiralty cog was becoming an intelligence hub that radiated far beyond naval matters, giving Hall access to the nation's power-brokers. 'Cabinet ministers were at first not sure what to make of this man of unusual appearance and abrupt manner, but his obvious sincerity of purpose, his mastery of his subject, and his eagerness to help them with their problems soon won their complete confidence,' a biographer noted.

Hall widened his reach yet further by hiring Lord Richard Herschell, a confidant of British and Spanish royalty, and Claude Pearce-Serocold, a stockbroker with connections to the City, as personal assistants and fixers. He cultivated relationships with police detectives, administrators, academics and bankers in methodical acquisition of information, assets and influence.

Roger Casement's name had proliferated in Whitehall in-trays since the German declaration about Ireland on 20 November. The former Foreign Office hero had metamorphosed from Irish nationalist gadfly to apparent traitor. Having won Berlin's qualified support, the British expected him to return to the US to mobilise Irish-American sentiment. On 25 November the Foreign Office cabled diplomatic missions around Europe to keep a lookout. 'He may be travelling under his own name or that of James Landy.'

The following night ambassador Findlay in Christiania cabled London with a dramatic update. The Norwegian informer – his still-unnamed double-agent – had visited the legation that day and disclosed that Casement was still in Berlin, had met the Kaiser and by late December intended to sail from the Schleswig coast to rendezvous with another ship that would land weapons and men in Ireland. 'Vessel is to put Casement on board rich American yacht coming from America with body of conspirators at a fixed rendezvous off

Irish coast ... he will be accompanied to Ireland with a picked band of German officers.'

The informer corroborated his assertions by showing Findlay letters that Casement had entrusted him to send to Clan na Gael citing German support and pending action in Ireland. Findlay urged his masters to take 'prompt and drastic measures' and vouched for the informer. 'I believe information he has given to be genuine. He is not clever enough to invent it.'

The ambassador's information trove included a particular sting for Hall. One letter recounted the *Oscar II*'s internment at Stornoway and mocked the Admiralty as 'London weekenders' who were too focused on Sunday dinner to properly vet the passenger list, resulting in his escape and the arrest of harmless men. 'What fools the English can be!' Casement wrote. 'Fancy bothering about the 2nd cook, two poor stowaways, the bandmaster and a couple of sailor boys.' Casement did not know who occupied the post but was taunting the head of naval intelligence. Hall must have seethed. The Bad Boche with a taste for vice with his servant was now also an impudent Boche.

And possibly an expensive one. The Foreign Office authorised its ambassador in Norway to pay the informer up to £5,000 – about £500,000 in today's money – for information leading to Casement's capture.

The informer's evidence pointed to Casement plotting a landing on the west coast of Ireland, but jittery diplomats reported sightings across Europe. The ambassador in Brussels suggested Casement had boarded a New York-bound ship in the Netherlands. The ambassador in Madrid reported he was on the *Manuel Calvo* that left Cadiz on 1 December before conceding two days later the report was wrong.

All this piled aggravation on Hall. Sir Roger was turning into some sort of Celtic Pimpernel, everywhere and nowhere, betrayed by a mystery informant, yet still out of reach. And so arrogant. *What fools the English can be!* Hall's patience with the dull grind of intelligence work, the gathering and sifting of information, the penning of reports and memos and bureaucratic minutiae, had a limit. What set his pulse racing was action, a show, and there were few more tempting targets than this blighter in Berlin.

The DNI was pondering options when a visitor from Scotland Yard called into his office. Cropped hair, elegant suit, silken voice – the unmistakeable figure of Basil Thomson, assistant commissioner of the Metropolitan Police. Spycatcher extraordinaire, if you believed the papers. And friend of cannibals and nemesis of pirates, if you believed Thomson's memoirs. 'With his moustache, wing collar and white handkerchief nattily tucked in his breast pocket, he [looked] more a dapper boulevardier than a detective,' one historian observed.

Some in Whitehall bristled at the police chief's self-promotion, but Hall appreciated good yarns and Thomson had plenty. As a colonial administrator in the South Pacific he had saved a man from drowning, dynamited a murderous alligator, hanged pirates and befriended reformed cannibals, including an old chief who recommended as particularly tasty the upper arms of people aged between 15 and 20. As the prime minister of Tonga, Thomson modernised the tax system, arbitrated tribal disputes and was designated *Koe tangata Fakahinohino*, Expounder of the Dark Ways of Civilised Man.

Basil Thomson, assistant commissioner of the Metropolitan Police.

Returning to England, he acted as guardian for Siamese princes, wrote books and articles, befriended Baron Northcliffe, owner of *The Times* and *Daily Mail*, and was appointed a prison governor, which required him to supervise more hangings. Thomson despised those who sought clemency for condemned men without considering the victims. 'An approaching execution never failed to produce droves of them, for the most part women and long-haired sexless men,' he wrote. Executions were swift affairs. 'In thirty seconds from the forming of the procession, the man was dead; the fall of the drop could be heard outside the walls, and there was a confused roar of voices like the moaning of the wind.'

In 1913 Thomson became assistant commissioner at the Met and head of its Criminal Investigation Department, CID, overseeing 700 detectives. When interrogating suspects he favoured guile over intimidation and placed them in a low armchair so they had to look up. After war broke out Thomson also took charge of the Special Branch, a unit originally set up to hunt Fenian dynamiters, and CID became the executive arm of War Office and naval intelligence, which lacked the manpower and legal right to arrest suspects. When detectives scooped up Lody and other hapless German agents, the press, briefed by Thomson, anointed him the nation's spycatcher.

He visited Hall on this winter morning to discuss Ireland. His colleagues at the Royal Irish Constabulary had been tasked with investigating rumours of German submarines refuelling at remote coves on the west coast, but found nothing. Thomson wanted additional scrutiny and he had an idea: why not send an American yacht, with a few English agents aboard, to scout the inlets in the guise of a pleasure cruise?

Hall blinked at his visitor. Wheels in his mind turned. The Americans would make trouble if they heard of the misuse of their flag, but the idea was good. And perhaps it could be tweaked to combine another, bolder objective: perhaps the expedition could pose as an emissary of Casement, win the confidence of Irish radicals, uncover their plans and intercept the knight upon his return to Ireland.

Thomson agreed. It was the birth of a partnership between two kindred spirits, and of a game of shadows with their quarry.

To allay Irish suspicions the yacht's captain and crew would impersonate Americans and the owner pretend to be German-American. Hall was delighted. A masquerade! They would need to work quickly; Casement was expected within weeks.

On the morning of Tuesday 15 December the *Sayonara*, a 760-ton steam yacht, prepared to sail from Southampton. Anthony Drexel, an American banker based in London, had agreed to charter his beloved craft, which now had a concealed wireless radio for contact with the Admiralty.

The gum-chewing skipper affecting an American drawl was Lieutenant Simon, a Royal Navy officer who had served on US ships and had a talent for mimicry. He told his crew of 50 naval ratings to replace their British uniforms with American kit and to copy his accent, which they attempted with gusto. Wilfred Russell Howell, a former British army major, strutted on deck sporting an upturned Kaiser-style moustache, a Homburg hat, a thick German accent and what passed for a Teutonic pout. With the Stars and Stripes fluttering, the *Sayonara* slipped its moorings and headed for the Irish Sea.

. . .

Anthony Drexel's steam yacht Sayonara, *1912.*

That evening, as Hall's decoy steamed west, the target of its mission was at the Continental Hotel in Berlin when in walked Adler Christensen, freshly returned from Norway, where he had spent three weeks lying to the English ambassador. It was a joyful reunion. Casement listened with delight to Adler's account of feeding Findlay a farrago of nonsense that doubtless had been passed to London. 'It is quite delicious,' Casement wrote in his diary.

He had devised the ruse to chasten the scoundrel ambassador and bamboozle the British with fake letters that outlined a fictional plan to rendezvous with a tycoon's yacht and sail to Ireland. Casement's goal was to elicit proof about the purported effort to kidnap or murder him and to confuse London about his intentions. From Adler's account, the ambassador swallowed every word.

Casement's beard had grown back and he looked like his old self, and the return of his lover to Berlin was cheering, but he was anxious. Everywhere he turned he faced doubts and dilemmas. It was as if the cold and dark of winter was seeping into his mission.

His hosts wondered if the attempt to entrap Britain's ambassador in Norway was worth the trouble. And they didn't like Adler, who was accused of 'disquieting' misbehaviour in Berlin, possibly financial rather than sexual. Even so, Casement planned to send Adler back to Christiania with more misinformation.

Since the German statement about Ireland three weeks earlier, Casement had obtained an imperial passport, number 2192, in his own name, letting him travel around Germany, but his momentum had stalled and anxieties pecked at him.

He bristled at some of the responses in Britain to his presence in Germany. The *Manchester Guardian* condemned 'an act of monstrous baseness at first thought incredible'. Some former friends suggested a mental imbalance, that he was not bad but mad. Questions in the House of Lords about what punishment awaited the renegade consul prompted bravado. 'They have to catch me first,' he wrote.

Casement thirsted for news from Ireland and the US but was shorn of contact with friends. Had British censorship stifled news of the German declaration? Did people know about it, did they care? Were Irish boys still enlisting for the British army? He could only guess. Isolation fuelled delusion – he attributed Britain's restoration of diplomatic relations with the Vatican to fright over his mission. He risked sending a letter, via neutral Holland, to a friend in London, with an enclosed note for another friend in Dublin.

In December he met some Irish prisoners-of-war on a preliminary visit to their camp and encountered indifference, auguring poorly for the proposed Irish Brigade. Colds and insomnia did not help his spirits.

Casement also discovered some German officials disliked the Irish enterprise. Some hoped to negotiate peace with England, others prickled at the idea of meddling with soldiers' loyalties. 'In my heart I am very sorry I came!' he confided in his diary on 12 December. 'I do not think the German government has any soul for great enterprise.'

Casement's faith in ordinary Germans remained undimmed, as did his appreciation of the male form, though without sexual references. His diary noted 'handsome' soldiers in Berlin's Tiergarten and 'fine, strong, well-shaped bodies' marching through Frankfurt. He also observed a French prisoner-of-war with 'splendid calves and the figure of a young Hercules'.

On 18 December, three days into the *Sayonara*'s cruise, church bells rang in jubilation across Berlin and Casement's hopes revived. The pealing was for another apparent victory over the Russians, and it was the day Casement finally met the chancellor, Theobold von Bethmann Hollweg. In a palace by the Reichstag the two men smoked and talked, in French, about the war, British skullduggery and the potential of an Irish brigade. The chancellor made no promises but made encouraging noises and wished Casement 'all success in your aims and projects'.

On Christmas day Casement bade farewell to Adler, who left for fresh intrigue in Norway. Casement was going to miss his lover but had begun to worry about his volatility. 'Adler's deepest affection is won by extreme rascaldom,' he wrote in his diary. 'Utter unscrupulousness of action, so long as it succeeds, is his ideal he confesses.'

Snow coated Berlin and the city was sombre. Food prices deterred feasting and black mourning ribbons hung from Christmas trees.

Casement spent much of the day in his hotel room, melancholic. It would have cheered him to know a British ship was chasing his shadow off the coast of Ireland, but all he knew was that he was again alone in a cold city.

. . .

Six days later, on the last day of 1914, Reginald Hall's Admiralty office overlooked a wintry scene: heavy snow had collapsed a recruiting tent at Horse Guards Parade and made the other sag. Despite coal rationing the DNI kept a blazing fire. When it dwindled, his private secretary Cleland Hoy recalled, Hall would summon the office gopher and point at the hearth, then at a coal cart outside the window. 'Maskell, that's wanted here.'

'Yes, sir,' replied Maskell, who would disappear and return with contraband replenishment to restore a full, illicit blaze.

'You see, Maskell,' Hall said, 'Hoy is used to South Africa and cannot stand this climate. If we lose him we lose the war.'

Maskell nodded. 'Yes, sir.'

On a bad day Hall's temper was legendary, but he was ending the year on a high. His codebreakers – informally designated Room 40, or 40 OB, after one of their offices in the Old Building – had refined their art and were now giving the Admiralty advance warning of German naval operations.

However they still could not crack intercepted German diplomatic messages that piled up, their contents a mystery.

Despite a life at sea, the DNI had an instinct for the psychology of Whitehall. One night he was locked in a marathon argument with Churchill, who deployed all his oratorical brilliance and stamina to clinch his point. Hall found himself sagging into an almost hypnotic state, a common condition for anyone who dared to challenge the First Lord, but refused to submit. Recalling a fragment from Kipling's *Kim*, in which the protagonist strives to retain his identity, he began to chant: 'My name is Hall, my name is Hall . . .'

Churchill frowned. 'What's that you're muttering?'

'I'm saying that my name is Hall because if I listen to you much longer I shall be convinced that it's Brown.' Churchill burst out laughing and dropped the argument.

In addition to squeezing Germany with the blockade, Hall was juggling bribery in Turkey, propaganda in the US, surveillance in Spain. Postal censorship continued yielding results, including the letter Casement sent via Rotterdam to London.

And tantalisingly there was the *Sayonara*. Hall tracked its progress up and down Ireland's Atlantic coast with childlike glee. Unaware of its real identity, Royal Navy patrols repeatedly boarded it and notified the Admiralty about the owner being an 'obvious Hun'. The Royal Irish Constabulary also raised the alarm, as did the Marquess of Sligo, who came to London to denounce the crew as spies. Hall was delighted. Everyone was fooled, leaving the *Sayonara* a free hand to dupe the Irish radicals said to be awaiting Casement.

'He was fascinated by the Great Game, the world of spies and agents, deception, bribery, disinformation, destabilisation, all that side of intelligence now stigmatised as the "dirty tricks" department,' a British former intelligence officer later noted. Another observer put it more simply: Hall was 'half Machiavelli and half schoolboy'.

The floating pantomime – which incurred the very real risk of German mines – reached farcical depths in early January when its skipper and owner trekked through a howling storm on Achill, an island off the coast of Mayo, to the cottage of Darrell Figgis, a writer and nationalist suspected of being in league with Casement.

Figgis invited the visitors in for a drink by the fire and was mystified by the one who resembled a Teutonic caricature. 'He lifted from my mantelpiece a bust of Beethoven and gently extolled the greatness of German gifts to the world,' Figgis recalled. The Hunnish visitor claimed he had the 'high honour' of Sir Roger Casement's friendship and hinted the knight may be concealed on his yacht offshore.

The scene turned slapstick when a neighbour arrived and told Figgis the police, suspicious of the visitors, had surrounded the cottage, but not to worry because the young men of the village had surrounded the police.

The *Sayonara* resumed its prowling and was poised, Hall thought, to spring the trap. Based on reports from Findlay, he expected Casement to depart Germany on 8 January on a Danish steamer, the *Mjölnir*, and reach Ireland a week later. 'It is possible Casement will be accompanied by six to eight German officers,' Hall wired his decoy. It was all too delicious.

But then the ambassador in Norway said Casement was not in fact aboard the *Mjölnir* and that his informant had vanished. Findlay confessed that Casement's servant, who was supposedly too dim for duplicity, had outplayed him. 'I deeply regret failure . . . it is impossible to follow the workings of a mind absolutely unregulated by any rules of intelligence or morality.'

Reginald Hall's fantasy of catching the fugitive knight dissolved in the Atlantic spray and the *Sayonara* was recalled. This was probably a cue for the legendary temper. Hall family lore does not record the date, only the event: one day the captain returned home early from the Admiralty, stomped through the living room, where his wife was hosting ladies to tea, glowered at everyone, kicked over a table and stomped out, banging a door behind him.

CHAPTER EIGHT

Brotherhood

The car splattered up the hill through rain, mud and fading light. On a good day you could look down the valley and see vineyards, picturesque houses and the medieval cathedral of Limburg, but the afternoon was wretched and Roger Casement was headed up, towards the camp.

It was 5 January 1915; the war was a stasis of mud, blood, frost and barbed wire. The military sweeps across Europe of the previous summer and autumn had ended in a 350-mile scar of trenches stretching from the Channel to the Alps that left both sides glaring across no-man's land. Unable to flank the enemy, generals threw infantry into frontal attacks against machine guns and artillery, exchanging stupendous quantities of lives for a few yards of terrain that changed nothing.

Casement, however, now had an opportunity for breakthrough. His attempt to dupe the British was almost played out – they would soon realise he had not left Germany – but that was a sideshow to his main mission, which entailed raising an Irish brigade, a legion of men drawn from British army prisoners who would fight for Ireland if given the chance. This was the day to start making it happen. The car splattered on up the slope, engine whining.

A few thousand or even a few hundred well-equipped volunteers, if landed in Ireland, could kickstart a rebellion. Set against the wider war it would be a modest military force but a symbol that Ireland's fight was not with Germany but England, a symbol that might halt Irish enlistment in the British army and sway US public opinion. The propaganda value would be worth 10 army corps to Germany, an official told Casement.

The Germans had siphoned about 2,200 Catholic Irishmen from other POW camps to this purpose-built camp outside Limburg, a Catholic town 340 miles south-west of Berlin. It had sturdy wooden huts, warm blankets, better food, pictures of the Pope and anti-English literature, including articles by Casement. Now it was up to him to convert these soldiers, who had sworn an oath to the Crown, to a new allegiance.

History, Casement told himself, was on his side. For centuries Irishmen had fought in foreign armies in hope of returning home to win Ireland's freedom. John Devoy had evangelised the Fenian faith among the British army's Irish regiments in the 1860s, only to see the work unravel in a botched rebellion. In South Africa scores defected from the British army to fight for the Boers.

Casement had addressed a first batch of prisoners during a preliminary visit in early December, when the camp was being built. They were grubby, scruffy and had 'horrid beards', and most proved apathetic or hostile. A discouraging start, but since then he had negotiated an agreement with the Germans, which he called a 'treaty', establishing that while Germany would train and equip the brigade it would fight 'solely in the cause of Ireland'. Casement assured his hosts Clan na Gael would pay the brigade's expenses, which jolted John Devoy, who found himself scraping the clan's coffers to honour the promise. Casement had also commissioned distinctive uniforms with a harp emblem and obtained the services of two Catholic priests, Fr John Crotty and Fr Canice O'Gorman, to act as chaplains.

So there was reason, as the car swung through the gates into the camp, for hope. It was five months since he had won cheers from Irishmen at the burial mound of Shane O'Neill in Antrim, and these prisoners, though in British uniform, were also Irishmen.

The plan was to start with a group of about 70 inmates. Clutching an umbrella, Casement mounted a table. The faces that gazed back were curious, some unsure who he was. A Fenian? A Boer?

Casement identified himself and declared his purpose. Home Rule was a 'pretence' to keep Ireland indentured, he said. If they joined him, Germany would strive to land the brigade in Ireland to fight English rule. If Germany could not deliver them to Irish shores, each man would be offered passage to America and £10 to £20 to start a new life.

After about 15 minutes, with Casement's voice ringing out in the dusk, the listeners grew restless. There was hissing, boos. Then insults. A sergeant-major of the Dragoon Guards called him a traitor. And right there, Casement's mission imploded. The word gleamed with a malignant power from which there was no escape.

The audience began to push, jostle and heckle. 'How much are they paying you?' someone shouted. Casement stepped off the table and tried to answer back amid the scrum. He swung his umbrella, but nothing could ward off the humiliation. His own compatriots were jeering him and the fantasy of leading a force of liberation. Casement retreated and was driven away in darkness.

He did not understand these men. He did not understand where they had come from or what they had endured or what he was asking. Many were from slums and relied on army wages to feed wives and children. They had pride in their regiments, the Dragoons, the Royal Munster Fusiliers, the Connaught Rangers. 'In addition to being Irish Catholics, we have the honour to be British soldiers,' a group of

NCOs had told camp officials. They had witnessed devastation in France, heard of atrocities in Belgium and lost friends to German bullets, bombs and bayonets. In captivity they were often cold and hungry and bullied. Now this visitor with his suit and posh voice was asking them to commit treason.

Casement seethed. For him, these men cared only for England's king and his shilling, and nothing for Ireland. He had hoped for lions and found hyenas. 'More English than the English themselves,' he wrote. For two weeks he hunkered at Limburg's Nassauer Hof hotel, sending emissaries to the camp, poking at the cinders of the brigade dream. Endless rain bounced off the town's cobbles and his teeth ached, requiring dental work. Dreams of Congo and Putumayo haunted his nights.

Eventually a handful of prisoners volunteered for the brigade, embers amid the ash, but he told German officials there was little hope and returned to Berlin on 23 January.

Despair hovered. The mission was slipping away and with it his purpose. What was the point of being in Germany? Even if he could leave, where would he go? The US, perhaps, but he sensed Clan na Gael's confidence in him was withering.

And then Adler Christensen, back from Norway, presented a gift. Before his final double-cross of Findlay he had wrangled from the ambassador a note on British legation notepaper offering Adler immunity from prosecution and £5,000 for information leading to Casement's capture.

Casement rejoiced. 'The letter is the most damning piece of evidence, I suppose, ever voluntarily given by a government against itself,' he exulted. It proved a 'dastardly criminal conspiracy' that he would publicise.

In a 3,000-word open letter to his former boss, Foreign Secretary Sir Edward Grey, he accused England of trying to kidnap and murder him and to corrupt his 'faithful follower'. His German hosts dutifully sent copies to the international press and embassies around Europe.

Casement hoped for a sensation – English perfidy unmasked before the world – but the world didn't care. Some Norwegian newspapers ran the story, then lost interest, and elsewhere the tale was ignored or scorned. Casement's letter denouncing the hapless British effort to catch him was a rant built on a molehill: the British offered a reward for his capture, so what? He was a fugitive.

The debacle crushed Casement. Cut off from friends and grieved by a sense of failure and abandonment, he checked into a clinic outside Berlin. 'I am in my room at the sanatorium writing up my diary and eating my heart out,' he wrote on 11 February. He managed a few more lines then put down his pen, unable to continue. He was done with diary writing.

. . .

In Dublin, Tom Clarke's morning ritual remained unchanged. As the city woke, he emerged from his newsagent's shop at the top of Sackville Street and placed on the footpath a billboard with the day's headlines. It was a duty he took seriously – his livelihood was selling papers – but as February 1915 wore on, no amount of creative phrasing could disguise the fact the war had become a grim monotone.

For Clarke, the stalemate made for a repetitive billboard but bought more precious time for the Irish Republican Brotherhood to plan a rebellion while England's difficulty lasted. The old chap, as younger IRB men called him, had seldom felt so alive yet weary. The conspiracy needed a military strategy, money, men and weapons, all of which required endless messages, any one of which could be intercepted, or leaked, and lead to arrest. Some days stressed Clarke to the point of exhaustion, leaving him feeling, as he put it with an accent from his New York days, 'moidered'.

Gardening brought him solace, and it was almost spring, planting season, but a fresh worry had sprouted: Roger Casement. Reports from Berlin left a question mark over whether Clarke could rely on German help – and on Casement. Clarke was working on a solution.

He was a deceptive figure, this prematurely aged ex-convict with sunken cheeks who spent his days sweeping the floor, arranging shelves and serving customers before closing his shop and heading into the night to organise insurrection. Clarke had prospered enough to move his wife and two sons a few months earlier to a fancier house. After decades of suffering and deprivation he had built a comfortable life. It changed nothing; he was willing to lose it all.

For Clarke it was simple: Ireland was subjugated and its spirit smothered; only a rising – the connotation of awakening made it the rebels' preferred term for insurrection – could rouse the nation and oust the occupier. The mandate came not from the people, who slumbered, but history. It was the clarity of a fanatic and also of a man who looked in the mirror and sensed he had not much time left. The conspiracy required no pretence of democracy or much consideration about who would govern an independent Ireland. The goal was ending English rule. Nothing else mattered. When fellow radicals baulked at the implications, or favoured alternative strategies, he dropped them until his loyalists became a clique within a clique, hermetic.

The rebellion had to be kept secret until the last possible moment to offset the enemy's overwhelming presence. The war gave authorities new powers to intern suspects and confiscate property, and Clarke, as a parolee, was vulnerable. One wrong move and he could be jailed. Detectives from the Dublin Metropolitan Police's G Division, for political crime, followed him and staked out a building overlooking his shop to monitor who came and went.

He was careful. He stashed gold sent by John Devoy in a cellar; if he couldn't shake off surveillance he skipped or cancelled IRB meetings; he limited the conspiracy to a tight group, leaving the G-Men, and their colleagues in the Royal Irish Constabulary, who covered political crime outside the capital, struggling to penetrate the plot's inner sanctum.

It was a sign of Clarke's success that Dublin Castle, lacking good intelligence, muddled the IRB with Sinn Féin, a fringe political party whose name meant 'We Ourselves' in Irish. Its leader, Arthur Griffith, advocated non-violent means to achieve independence yet 'Sinn Féiner' became a British catch-all term for dangerous separatists.

For Clarke, the biggest impediment to fighting the English was the Irish. Each step of the conspiracy had to navigate compatriots' hostility, indifference and suspicion.

Despite lengthening casualty lists, Irish people still supported the war effort. John Redmond, the influential leader of the Irish Parliamentary Party, urged enlistment to demonstrate Ireland's worthiness for Home Rule, which was being kept on ice until the war ended. Food and recruits flowed to England while troops from across the empire used their leave to visit Dublin and enjoy the sights, bars and brothels of a city that faced no air raids and had no blackout. Khaki-clad groups would amble past Clarke's shop en route to their next adventure, oblivious to the gaze of the little man at the counter with the pince-nez.

Clarke had to gain control of two organisations. The first was the IRB itself. He was part of an 11-man supreme council that presided over 2,000 members organised through regional 'circles' and 'centres'. Some opposed a rebellion unless it had popular support, which evidently did not exist, or met other conditions. For Clarke this was a recipe for procrastination. He wanted a stand-up fight, the sooner the better, and proceeded to outmanoeuvre dissenters so that in January 1915 the supreme council, with some misgivings, endorsed his hawkish policy.

The other organisation was the Irish Volunteers. Since the outbreak of war the original 130,000-strong force had split into those who believed Ireland had a duty to support England and a minority of about 10,000 who said they would stay in Ireland and hold onto their weapons to make sure England delivered Home Rule.

Clarke welcomed the emergence of this smaller, flintier Irish Volunteer force. It remained legal and could operate openly, albeit with police monitoring. Clarke's challenge was to infiltrate and mould the Volunteers into a revolutionary instrument without the police, or the organisation's putative leaders, noticing until it was too late. The IRB secretly recruited Volunteer commanders, who then dripped IRB radicalism into the bigger organisation. Like an apothecary, or poisoner, Clarke had to gradually increase the dose.

With surveillance, secrets, lies and intrigues on multiple fronts, no wonder Clarke felt 'moidered'. On top of all this there was the Roger Casement dilemma. His messages from Berlin suggested the Irish Brigade was floundering and that the Germans would not send a sizeable force, or any force. But what about weapons? And what about Casement? There were growing doubts about the envoy.

Clarke wanted his own man in Berlin to assess the mission and talk directly to the German government. It would be a perilous journey through frontiers filled with spies and secret police. Clarke had just the fellow. Young and committed, knew Casement, knew the continent, spoke several languages. Plus he was dying. And who would suspect a dying man?

. . .

Joseph Plunkett was thin and pale with huge brown eyes that gave the impression of an owl. As the day of departure approached he tried to disguise himself by growing a beard, but it came out thin and scraggly and he still resembled an owl. He also destroyed photos of himself and spread a story that he was moving to Jersey in the Channel Islands, for his health.

It was a plausible fiction for Dublin Castle's G-men. Since Plunkett was two years old, bovine tuberculosis had been attacking his glands and lungs in escalating efforts to kill him. Now, as long as he didn't expire before reaching Berlin, the disease was going to prove useful.

Plunkett was 27 and not afraid to die but hoping for deferment. He had devoted his life to pondering the mysteries of divinity, love and, most recently, revolution, and sensed that with enough time he might do something important. He was the privileged yet unfortunate son of wealthy parents who owned dozens of properties around Dublin. His father, George, was a scholar of medieval and renaissance art who preferred Botticelli to parenting, and who had been made a papal count, a Vatican title of nobility, for donations to charity. Plunkett's mother, Josephine Mary, was a former society beauty who was capricious and dictatorial with her seven children. She gave most of them versions of her name – Joe's middle name was Mary – and dressed them in strange clothes, disrupted their schooling and presided over a domestic chaos of unpaid bills and aggrieved servants. She loathed most of the guests her husband brought home for dinner, including Casement, during his visits to Dublin.

Plunkett spent much of his youth convalescing in bed, where he would play the fiddle, devour books and write poems. Illness whetted rather than suppressed his zest for life. When well enough he joined family tours of galleries and museums across Europe and dabbled in languages, gadgets and philosophy. In Algiers – dry heat was good for him – he raced camels and roller-skated.

That sojourn ended, like so much else, with a summons back to Dublin from 'Ma', who controlled her children's lives with fickle financing. Patchy education and social awkwardness left Plunkett virtually unemployable and dependent on her whims. Instead of a coat she got him a blue cloak with a velvet collar, which he combined with bangles and large rings. If a project caught Ma's imagination or snobbery she could be generous. She published a book of Joe's mystic-infused poetry, which critics lauded, funded his small theatre company and paid £200 for the *Irish Review*, an arts magazine he edited from 1913.

Shy yet playful – his party-piece was dancing while sitting on a chair – Plunkett joined Dublin's swirling zeitgeist of arts and activism. 'The youth of that period were like the 1960s, full of utopianism, a lack of realism, but well intentioned,' a historian noted. 'In some ways the enemy was their parents' generation as much as the British state.'

The English had executed a famous ancestor and archbishop, Oliver Plunkett, in 1681, but it was the Home Rule convulsions of 1913–14 that radicalised Joe. He steered the *Irish Review* towards political commentary and commissioned articles from Casement, who excoriated English villainy under a pseudonym because he was still with the Foreign Office.

The aftermath of a lung haemorrhage did not stop Plunkett joining the Irish Volunteers' committee in 1913, a swerve into a world of marching, drilling and adventure. And then came a tap on the shoulder and a murmured invitation to join 'the organisation'.

Tom Clarke cared little for intellectuals or prophets, but he saw value for the IRB in young poets like Plunkett who were willing to pursue something others thought unobtainable. The revolution, if it happened, would need public faces other than Clarke's grizzled countenance. It would need men who could orate, write and inspire.

Plunkett's visits to Clarke's shop, and the militant tone of *Irish Review*, put him on a watchlist. A frequent visitor to his home who professed to be a poet, and produced feeble verse, turned out to be a police spy. Anticipating the magazine's suppression, Plunkett committed editorial suicide with a provocative edition that disputed Ireland's allegiance to England. Copies were duly seized, ending the *Irish Review*.

It left more time for IRB business, which uncorked Plunkett's enthusiasm for subterfuge and intrigue. '*They say I sing in secrets*,' one of his poems began. A favourite novel was G. K. Chesterton's *The Man Who Was Thursday*, a thriller about an anarchist group infiltrated by police. Some thought Plunkett too keen on cloak and dagger. 'He revelled in passwords, ciphers and the mummeries of dusty conspiracies,' said one historian.

After induction into the IRB, Plunkett vindicated Clarke's faith by revealing he had a military plan for a rising – a pet project he had been working on for years. He had no military training but read Clausewitz and played *Little Wars*, a game of toy soldiers and strategy based on a wargaming manual by H. G. Wells. These were dubious credentials, but his core idea had audacity: instead of guerrilla action in the countryside the rebels should seize Dublin and make the capital the battlefield.

By February 1915 Clarke accepted this as the keystone of a more detailed plan that Plunkett and others would flesh out. The strategy could incorporate but did not necessitate German troops. The IRB had no desire to replace the British occupier with another foreign force, no matter how benign. It wanted Irishmen to do the fighting, and hopefully the Irish Volunteers would oblige, but the IRB did want Germany to supply officers and, above all, weapons.

Among Clarke's tight circle of conspirators the obvious candidate for Berlin was the experienced traveller with a plausible cover story. Through February and early March Plunkett stopped shaving, taught his sister Geraldine a cipher to decode his letters and spread the cover story about a health-boosting holiday in Jersey. Openness about his departure followed a dictum from Chesterton's novel: 'If you don't appear to be hiding, nobody seeks you out.'

It was around this time he composed a poem that suggested readiness to die – but not quite yet:

> *My hour is not yet come*
> *And shall I do this thing*
> *For them that need a sign?*
> *Not you, nor I, but some*
> *That thirst shall hear me sing . . .*
> *When my life-blood runs bright*
> *To grace the gods' repast.*

Plunkett sailed from Dublin's North Wall port on the SS *Carlow* on 17 March. A G-man observed his departure but his chiefs in Dublin Castle were not concerned. They ranked the poet low in the hierarchy of radicals and apparently believed his cover story. No one checked whether he turned up in Jersey.

Joseph Plunkett in a studio portrait taken for his German visa in 1915.

On Tuesday 20 April, 34 days later, the 8.30 a.m. train from Basle chugged into Berlin's railway terminus, Anhalter Bahnhof, and Plunkett stepped onto the platform, half-dead. He had zig-zagged through England, France, Spain, Italy and Switzerland in an odyssey of detours, delays and interrogations, ingested vast quantities of quinine, creosote, chlorodyne and cognac for bronchitis and fever, toured churches and galleries and written poems, shed the name Plunkett and adopted the alias James Malcolm, and after nearly two days without sleep all but collapsed on the train ride from Basle.

But he had made it to Berlin.

CHAPTER NINE

Love Your Enemies

Shortly after lunch on Wednesday 21 April 1915 – a day after Joe Plunkett's arrival in Berlin – Reginald Hall's assistant, Claude Pearce-Serocold, made two phone calls from the Admiralty. He instructed the customs authorities in London, and the senior naval officer at the port of Harwich, to halt all traffic with the Netherlands. There were to be no crossings to or from Amsterdam, Rotterdam or the Hook of Holland until 3 May. He gave no explanation and hung up.

It was a cue for Hall to emit one of his cackles. The Germans would note the halt in sailings and, with luck, leap to an incorrect conclusion. At such times the schoolboy in him bubbled out, his secretary, Ruth Skrine, recalled. 'The fun and hazard of it all would fill him with infectious delight. "Adventures are for the adventurous!" he would chant, rubbing his hands and grinning like a crafty French abbé.' Her chief was a gambler, she said. 'One of his favourite sayings was: "Mistakes may be forgiven, but even God himself cannot forgive the hanger-back." We all followed with a blind devotion the risks he took, because we were sure he would win.'

The stakes this time were particularly high. The Allies were about to strike against Turkey in the Gallipoli peninsula so Hall was disrupting traffic in the English Channel to trick the Germans into expecting an Allied operation on the Belgian coast. He had no way of knowing that the gambit would not only work but set in motion a chain-reaction that would lead, in 16 days, to one of the war's greatest acts of infamy, and an eerie, recurring motif in his hunt for Roger Casement.

For Hall the ruse was one of multiple operations he was running and another topic to advertise – or conceal – at his weekly press briefing. Other military men shunned journalists as pests, but the director of naval intelligence, ever the innovator, hosted British and American correspondents at his office on Wednesday afternoons and plied them with tea, cigarettes and stories.

Hall could give a positive framing to the war. Having survived the previous year's enemy onslaught, and retained control of the seas, initiative now rested with the Allies. The French were preparing big offensives, Russia was still standing and Britain was marshalling the resources of a global empire. The Germans were making sporadic Zeppelin bombing raids over England and U-boats had started sinking merchant vessels, but time surely was against the Hun. A ditty in that day's *Westminster Gazette* depicted an isolated, desperate foe:

> *They cry and rave, and stamp their feet,*
> *Because they've got a bottled fleet;*
> *They kill the babies in their beds*
> *By dropping bombs upon their heads;*
> *They sink the peaceful trading ships;*
> *Watch women drown with smiling lips,*
> *And then wonder, when it strikes 'em,*
> *Why it is that no one likes 'em.*

Hall wanted more of that sentiment in the press. British enlistment rates were falling – unless more men volunteered there would have to be conscription – and US public opinion still favoured neutrality, keeping President Wilson on the sidelines. It was vital to project confidence in victory and stoke loathing of Germany. So as the correspondents puffed on their cigarettes, Hall provided material.

There were, of course, unmentionable topics. Room 40 – technically a separate department to Hall's intelligence division – remained secret, a holy of holies veiled even from admirals and ministers. The *Sayonara* expedition, which had ended three months earlier, was classified. Nor could Hall disclose his attempt to bribe Turkey into breaking its alliance with Germany.

But there were things he could share – insights into the blockade of Germany and the hunt for U-boats, analysis of the enemy's strategy and dilemmas, anecdotes from field agents, hints of pending operations, Admiralty gossip. His audience listened, rapt. To cover the war from London was to grope through mists of rumour, obfuscation and censorship. It might be months before the Admiralty admitted losing a dreadnought or the War Office disclosed a German offensive. In Hall's office some of the mist lifted.

The intelligence chief told stories that could be published without attribution and others that were never to emerge in print. To be fed scoops and be trusted with secrets thrilled the journalists, who adored Blinker. 'His charm would carry everything before it,' Skrine recalled. 'Representatives from every newspaper would throng into his inner room, thirsty for sensational news, and they never went away disappointed.'

The awe Hall inspired emerged in tributes after the war: 'We thought him the real Sherlock Holmes' (*Guardian*), 'The world's super spy' (*Derby Evening Telegraph*), 'The wizard of Whitehall' (*Belfast News Letter*). American correspondents felt privileged to enter 'the sacred precincts of his office which always had an air of mystery or suppressed excitement', the *Daily Arkansas Gazette* wrote.

To have the press feasting on his every utterance must have been gratifying, but this was a means to an end. Hall no longer unleashed fusilades at enemy ships, but articles that boosted morale or demonised the enemy were ammunition for other targets. So too were fake stories planted to confuse or bait the Germans. One entailed a fictitious gold shipment by which Hall hoped – in vain – to lure a German ship into a trap. Editors who knowingly ran such stories did so from patriotism. Hall freely used the mass circulation penny press such as the *Mail* but rationed fakery in *The Times* to not undermine its authority. 'Whatever you ask them to publish must be within the bounds of reason,' he later wrote.

He deployed a socialite and dilettante called Ralph Neville to amplify rumours – for instance fleet movements, or a planned offensive – around London clubs frequented by diplomats of neutral countries. 'A good lunch with the selected victim, a game of *écarté* afterwards and the tongue strings were loosed,' Hall wrote. The misdirection would end up cabled to the diplomat's capital, where it would be shared with German diplomats and forwarded to Berlin.

Some journalists were not willing accomplices but dupes. During one briefing Hall, feigning distraction, left on his desk a fake Admiralty telegram about the sinking of three German submarines. Other deceptions seemed pure mischief – later in the war he told the US naval under-secretary about agents infiltrating Germany through Denmark, a fiction Franklin Roosevelt still believed and repeated decades later when he was president.

In this murky arena of feints and traps a bullseye gleamed on the aggravating, tantalising figure of Roger Casement. An amateur intriguer, yet three times – the gun-running, Stornoway and the Findlay farrago – he had bested Hall. Hardly a fair scoreline since on the first two occasions Hall was not properly in the game, but those indirect brushes with the fugitive knight would have irked. In Berlin Casement was safe from retribution, not so his reputation.

Newspapers regularly published titbits on his doings, or alleged doings, and denounced him as an odious traitor. The *New York World* said Casement had accepted German gold to foment rebellion and attributed the report to a Berlin correspondent, which it did not have. Historians think the likeliest source was British intelligence.

Hall had a sign on his wall with a striking message: 'Love your enemies.' It was a joke.

This was a merciless conflict, the dawn of 'total war' that exposed entire populations to aerial bombing and hunger and invented new horrors. On 22 April, German troops opened the valves on 6,000 tanks filled with 160 tons of chlorine gas and released a grey-green cloud towards Allied lines near Ypres – the first use of lethal gas on a battlefield. Some 2,000 Canadians suffocated as fluid filled their lungs, a gruesome death.

Even with all this, Hall could respect some enemies, such as the spy Carl Lody, who did his duty as a German officer and went to his death without flinching. But a traitor who broke his oath to the King and sought to induce British army soldiers to do the same was a different category. Unlike Lody, Casement chose to become a Boche, betraying not just his country but relatives serving with British forces. On 23 April, another Casement – Roger's army medic cousin, Frank – tried in vain to save the poet Rupert Brooke, who died en route to Gallipoli.

English cinemas at this time were showing a French-made film of Victor Hugo's novel *Les Misérables*, which depicts a police inspector, Javert, making an obsessive hunt for the fugitive Jean Valjean. Hall did not have Javert's joylessness or blind respect for authority, but there was a Javert tinge to his Manichean morality and shadowing of Casement. Basil Thomson joined him in the hunt. The *Sayonara* expedition had been a debacle but sealed a partnership with Scotland Yard's assistant commissioner.

They tracked their quarry with singular zeal and ferocity, an English journalist who knew Thomson later wrote. 'These two staunch servants of the British empire seem to have conceived a hatred much more persistent and merciless for the renegade British consul than for the Kaiser and his armies.'

In January, Thomson's detectives had trawled Casement's bank accounts, which led them to Ebury Street. A cheque to a Mr Doubleday piqued interest until it was established he was the fishmonger at number 63. There were also payments to a Mr Peacock at number 55, a tailor and landlord, and one to W. P. Germain, Casement's landlord at number 50. For a brief moment Casement's lodgings interested the hunters, then like a roving searchlight their gaze moved on. His treason, after all, began only after he left England and there were other, more promising leads.

In February, Dublin Castle sent London a 13-page statement about the fugitive from Bryan Kelly, a young Dubliner recently returned from Germany. Kelly had been learning German when war broke out and was interned with other British subjects in Berlin. Casement had obtained his release to help with the Irish Brigade so Kelly had travelled with Casement and witnessed his humiliation at Limburg. Dispatched to Ireland to deliver messages, the student instead reported everything to the authorities, providing Hall and Thomson with a detailed insight into Casement's activities and agitated state of mind.

Hall's secretary, Cleland Hoy, stumbled across another source: his own nephew, Gerald Hoy. Like Kelly, the teacher from County Tyrone had been extracted from internment by Casement on the promise of delivering messages back in Ireland. Like Kelly, young Hoy betrayed his benefactor and ended up giving a statement to Hall in London that further thickened the bulging Casement dossier.

Casement's trail gifted the captain another line of attack. Findlay had told London of Adler's 'unnatural relations' with Casement and in February the ambassador returned to the topic to ask if sodomy was the reason Casement had left the consular service, and to pose a related question: 'Is he generally known to have been addicted to sodomy?' Here was ammunition for Hall's press briefings: the renegade knight was not just a traitor but a degenerate.

But Hall held fire. Conceivably he considered the allegation irrelevant or unproven or, more likely, premature. Hall liked to conserve ammunition to maximise impact. 'Very often valuable information will come in which of itself would be of little use at the time,' he later wrote, 'but which if kept till the proper moment will have due effect'.

. . .

On 30 April, nine days after Hall ordered a halt to sea traffic with the Netherlands, Room 40 learned that four U-boats had sailed from Heligoland and another two from Emden. Usually the Germans had an average of just two submarines in the Atlantic or North Sea at any one time. Now they had six. Hall's ruse had worked – the Germans were scrambling to attack troop transports of a fictitious English invasion fleet.

The enemy was exposing its precious subs to needless risk on a wild goose chase. But the deployment also multiplied the risk to Allied and neutral ships. In February Germany, in retaliation at Britain's blockade, had declared the waters around the British Isles a 'zone of war' and begun sinking vessels without warning.

On 1 May the *Lusitania*, a British-owned Cunard passenger liner, sailed from New York, bound for Liverpool. The Admiralty knew from intercepts that the Germans were broadcasting the *Lusitania*'s schedule, and by 6 May it knew that at least one submarine, *U-20*, lurked along the liner's route, but relayed no warning nor offered an escort.

There are innocent explanations. Room 40 could not always pinpoint and track every enemy submarine and the need to shield the codebreakers' existence limited use of their information. But it was also true that Winston Churchill wanted neutral shipping in the danger zone. 'We want the traffic, the more the better; and if some of it gets into trouble, better still,' he privately wrote. Dead Americans, after all, would inflame US public opinion.

On the afternoon of 7 May, *U-20* was cruising off Ireland's southeast coast when a lookout spotted a large vessel with four funnels. Captain Walther Schwieger submerged and ordered Lieutenant

Raimund Weisbach to prepare a G6 torpedo. It streaked through the water, arcing froth over the surface, and hit the *Lusitania*'s starboard side.

The liner sank within 18 minutes, tumbling screaming crew and passengers into the sea. A total of 1,198 people died, including 127 Americans and 27 infants. *U-20* returned home to congratulations – it had destroyed a symbol of British maritime prowess – but the glee curdled when German authorities grasped the scale of a public relations catastrophe that made them a symbol of barbarity around the world. 'The poor babies who perished in the ocean struck a blow at German power more deadly than could have been achieved by sacrifice of 100,000 men,' Churchill noted.

Suspicion lingers to this day that the Admiralty deliberately left the *Lusitania* unprotected in hope that the Germans would sink her. But not even the far-seeing Hall could anticipate that his ruse about a fake British flotilla would multiply German submarine patrols and lead to an atrocity with such a propaganda windfall. Or that it would add another thread to the dark braid connecting him with Roger Casement.

On Tuesday 18 May, a crisis unrelated to the sinking engulfed Hall. Jackie Fisher, the First Sea Lord, had abruptly quit in exasperation with Churchill, his micromanaging civilian boss. In a tribute to Hall's reputation for guile, senior admirals asked their junior colleague to liaise with Downing Street to help fix the mess. When the dust settled, Churchill and Fisher were both ousted and Hall, amid his intrigues, had won the confidence of the Lord Chief Justice, Rufus Isaacs – a potentially useful ally in any courtroom battle.

There were more political convulsions. The Liberal administration, weakened by the Admiralty row and a controversy over army munitions, fell and formed a government of national unity with the Conservative and Unionist party. Edward Carson and his 'galloper' F. E. Smith, who just a year earlier had led the Ulster Volunteer Force in a seditious revolt against Home Rule, became respectively attorney general and solicitor general. Their elevation humiliated the Irish Parliamentary Party and cast fresh doubt over Ireland obtaining self-government after the war. It also meant some of Roger Casement's bitterest political foes were now in government.

. . .

By May 1915 the cluster of offices known as Room 40 did not just hum, it whumped and clattered. The expanding network of signal stations around Britain's coast was now sending hundreds of intercepted messages daily so a new system funnelled them into a basement in the Admiralty's Old Building where they were sorted, inserted in dumbbell-shaped canisters and placed into vacuum tubes that sucked them up with a *fwump* and deposited them, with tremendous clanging, into baskets.

Hall had continued recruiting more codebreakers and administrative staff, including a troupe of female typists nicknamed 'Blinker's beauty chorus'. They were overseen by the formidable, cigar-chewing Lady Hambro, who was assigned her own nickname, Big Ben, because she was so striking.

In addition to Oxford and Cambridge dons the codebreakers included an actor, an art expert, a dress designer, a Catholic priest and a music critic, all products of Hall's endless, eclectic quest for talent. It resulted, said William James, a colleague and biographer of Hall, in 'an atmosphere vibrating with excitement, expectation, urgency, friendship and high spirits'.

At some point that spring Hall met a naval officer invalided home from the Persian Gulf. He recounted a wistful tale about how the British and their tribal allies had raided a German consulate and pursued a diplomat, Wilhelm Wassmuss, who had been fomenting revolt against British rule. Like Lawrence over in Arabia, he wore flowing robes. Wassmuss escaped on horseback, leaving behind his luggage and a cloud of dust.

Hall's antenna quivered. The material seized from the consulate and Wassmuss's luggage – where was it? A search located the stash in the cellar of the India Office, a three-minute walk from the Admiralty, where it had lain undisturbed since being hauled from Persia. Among it was a German diplomatic codebook, Code No. 13040.

Since the previous autumn, signal stations had intercepted non-naval messages that defeated the codebreakers. The communications had piled up, gathering dust, their meaning locked. Here was a key. It was found to be one of two codes used for communication between Germany's embassy in Washington and Berlin. Room 40 now had another reason to vibrate.

As spring edged into summer the codebreakers worked through the backlog, and bit by bit Hall was able to catch up on months-old messages between Ambassador Bernstorff and his masters at Wilhelmstrasse. They included some messages from Casement to Clan na Gael. 'The enemy are greatly alarmed,' said one dated 6 November. 'They are ignorant of the true purpose of my coming to Germany but seek evidence at all costs.' That made Hall smile. All costs? A touch of vanity, Sir Roger.

These were old messages. The reason for Hall to rub his hands and grin like a crafty French abbé was the ability to eavesdrop on messages to come.

CHAPTER TEN

The Fools, the Fools, the Fools

The train jolted into motion and pulled out of the station, spiriting Joseph Plunkett and Roger Casement away from Limburg. A baking sun threatened to turn the carriage into a sauna but that was a small price to pay to escape the valley and get some distance, however temporary, from the hilltop camp and the Irish Brigade.

Three weeks of renewed recruitment efforts among the 2,500 prisoners had yielded a grand total of 53 men, a feeble result, but no one had the heart to rename the force the Irish Platoon, or completely abandon it. Like some creature conjured by Mary Shelley, the brigade idea was dead yet not dead, revived yet pitiful, and could not be disowned.

It was 1 June, six weeks since Plunkett's arrival in Germany, and he was returning to Berlin to resume petitioning the government for military aid, which was the main reason Tom Clarke had sent him. Casement was accompanying Plunkett just to Frankfurt for a few hours' respite and sightseeing before returning to Limburg.

They had lunch and visited the former home of Charlemagne. History remembered the Holy Roman Emperor as a great diplomat for wrangling the Franks, Lombards and Merovingians, but Plunkett was earning a little niche for contending with Roger Casement, Adler Christensen and their German liaison, Captain Hans Boehm. Managing this trio while seeking access to the Kaiser's most senior officials was a fraught balancing act and Plunkett was only halfway across the tightrope. He still did not know if the Germans were going to aid a rebellion in Ireland.

After bidding goodbye to Casement, who returned to Limburg, Plunkett took the overnight train to Berlin to resume his mission's core objective – obtain weapons.

Their reunion in April had been warm, an opportunity to reminisce about Casement's suppers with the Plunkett family, amid Ma's glowers, and his contributions to the *Irish Review*. Casement had installed Plunkett in his hotel, the Eden, and introduced him to friends and contacts.

But the younger man was wary. Casement had intellect and courage but was depressed, and his relations with German officials had soured. And he was stubborn. When Plunkett revealed plans for a rising that would use the Irish Volunteers as a rebel force, Casement stuck to his view about the need for German manpower and said to go ahead without it would be 'folly' and 'criminal stupidity'.

Still, the pair had agreed on the need for weapons and collaborated on what became known as the *Ireland Report*, a 32-page analysis of the strategic possibilities of a German force invading the west coast to link up with Irish Volunteers, who would seize towns and disrupt British logistics. Threading solid intelligence with creative licence, it dangled the prize of Germany ending up with precious naval bases.

Insisting on German troops reflected Casement's view, but the report's core message was that Ireland could create big problems for England. It was a sales pitch to persuade German diplomats and generals that the potential reward justified the risk of sending weapons and men through 2,000 miles of hostile waters. Plunkett and Casement had submitted the report in early May.

Through all this Plunkett, weakened by fever, navigated Adler Christensen. He found the Norwegian had a 'curiously immobile face, not easy to decipher', and did not trust him. Plunkett withheld his real identity and told Adler only his alias, Joe Peters. But Casement's affection for his servant, a near constant presence in Berlin, had required Plunkett to establish a rapport and play along with Casement's efforts to find an honest career for Adler – there was talk him selling vacuum cleaners, building boats or learning photography and making a film of the Findlay affair, all of which came to nothing.

While awaiting a response to their report, Plunkett and Casement had decamped to Limburg to try to salvage the Irish Brigade. The scaled-down goal was 200 men. 'We'll get them if we have to kidnap them,' Plunkett declared. Casement was appalled and ruled out subterfuge. By the end of May they still had fewer than 60 volunteers. The midget force was to move to a training camp near Berlin.

Limburg's beer and Bulgarian sour milk had seemed to help Plunkett's health and sustained him through long talks with Captain Boehm, who was seconded from military intelligence to work with Irish rebels. Unlike other liaisons who were sceptical or uncomprehending, the ebullient Boehm fizzed with enthusiasm, which was refreshing, but also a challenge because his ideas were half-mad.

As a brewery manager in Milwaukee, Boehm had imbibed can-do American optimism that he channelled into schemes to set Ireland aflame. One involved decorating Zeppelins with Irish tricolours and dispatching them to drop seditious newspapers over Irish cities. 'Sensational and perhaps theatrical, but certainly effective!' he declared.

When Plunkett parted from Casement at Frankfurt, and arrived in Berlin on 2 June, his mission hung in the balance. The Irish Brigade was a sideshow; what really mattered was German aid for a rebellion. For the next four days he held talks with officials. There are no records of the discussions, but for Plunkett something crystallised. Early on 7 June, as church bells tolled over a sleeping city, he was wide awake in his rented apartment and writing a poem called 'The Spark':

> Because I used to shun
> Death and the mouth of hell
> And count my battle won
> When I should see the sun . . .
> Now I have seen my shame
> That I should thus deny
> My soul's divinest flame
> Now shall I shout my name,
> Now shall I seek to die
> No more shall I share ease
> No more shall I spare blood . . .
> Now Death and I embark
> And sail into the dark
> With laughter on our lips.

It was as if the prospect of German aid had gifted the 27-year-old a sense of agency over his own fate. After so many years staving off tuberculosis, he now glimpsed a chance to end the struggle on his own terms. 'After many years of fighting to live, he had decided to fight to die,' said a biographer.

Casement returned to Berlin and for a week the two Irish envoys held talks with officials over the terms of any German support. Exactly what was agreed remains unclear but it sufficed for Plunkett to deem his mission complete.

He could not depart immediately. Irish newspapers had reported that an unidentified bearded man other than Casement had addressed prisoners at Limburg, so Plunkett awaited an all-clear from Tom Clarke before risking a return. He accompanied Casement to a spa in Bavaria, where a final dilemma awaited.

Casement said he wanted to go home too. It was a cry from the heart; he was worn out. The IRB approved Plunkett's return, but he received no reply to his request about Casement, leaving him to make the decision alone. The poet appraised his old friend. The hero of Congo had become gaunt and jittery and was desperate to escape Germany. But he was a liability. His high profile made it harder to evade the English. And if he did make it to Ireland he might meddle in the rising plan. It was a choice between compassion and the revolution.

Stay, Plunkett told him. So Casement stayed.

Plunkett made it back to Dublin, alone, and undetected by British intelligence, in mid-July. A friend recognised him on a tram and as a joke said in a loud voice: 'I don't believe you were in Jersey at all, Plunkett, I think you were in Germany.'

. . .

The Alps soared in the distance and Lake Ammer glittered on another humid, sultry Sunday, but the last thing Casement wanted was to join the smiling faces aboard the yacht. He liked Charles Curry, the wealthy Irish-American expat who owned the boat, but had no desire to spend more time with his party of German officers and Bavarian aristocrats. They were going to sail just five miles from Riederau to Diessen, where a military band was going to oompah, but Casement had had enough of the company. To escape he proposed a bet – he would try to beat them on foot. The yacht slid from the jetty, Casement headed for the woodland path and the race began.

His Africa treks had been legendary. Joseph Conrad witnessed Casement disappear into a wilderness and emerge months later browner, leaner, serene. Once, discovering a rubber worker flogged to pieces, Casement put the man in his hammock and escorted him 50 miles for medical treatment. That was the man dubbed *Monafuma*, Son of a King, in his prime, fit, fearless, impelled by a humanitarian impulse that made him synonymous with nobility.

A different figure strode along the shore. Sunken cheeks, grooves in the forehead, silver peppering the black hair – he looked older than 50. What Casement termed a 'campaign of infamy' by a 'reptile press' and 'hired pens' in the British and US press had depicted him as a German stooge who cut prisoners' rations if they shunned his traitors' brigade. As in Congo, Casement had acquired a dog – a terrier he named Rebel – but in Riederau there was no great injustice requiring his intervention. His chivalry was limited to liberating cows from a paddock, which he considered cruelly confining, and leading them to a field.

It had all seemed so clear a year earlier. Germany, unjustly assailed, could perform a service to the world by supporting a rebellion that ended England's stranglehold over not just Ireland but the Atlantic. Casement could complete the mission Wolfe Tone had begun 120 years earlier. But everything had gone wrong. The Kaiser's officials had no interest in liberation; Ireland was at most a means to distract the English, and even this shrivelled vision was dogged by Prussian obduracy and barks of 'ausgeschlossen' – out of the question. The Germans had lost faith in Casement and he in them.

Clan na Gael also seemed to have turned against him. German diplomats had shown him letters saying the organisation regretted sending Casement. They were not written by John Devoy but were wounding nevertheless.

Young Plunkett's visit had been cheering but also concerning. To launch an insurrection without German troops was madness, a futile spilling of blood, and the war had enough ghastly slaughter. 'The whole world has become a terrible place,' Casement lamented to a friend. Sinking the *Lusitania* was further folly – he warned his hosts the English would use all their cunning to bring America into the war.

Casement's despair was not visible to the revellers skimming the lake on Curry's yacht. What they saw was a tall figure striding along the shore path with an astonishing pace. The scenic haze and crunch of his boot could lift Casement's spirits only so far. He was relieved to be out of Berlin, but loneliness had followed. Plunkett had gone and soon so too would Adler, who was preparing to return to the US. He sought fresh opportunities, and Casement, seeing the Norwegian's restlessness, wasn't going to stop him. Plus Adler had acquired a German girlfriend who planned to go with him.

Casement's attempt to find other companionship, or just company, in Berlin had backfired. One night in the Tiergarten he had been on a bench with a young soldier when a guard appeared with a lantern, questioned them and took Casement's name. The pair had just been talking, but the park was a cruising ground for homosexuals, prostitutes and their clients. Casement was so distraught – a perception of sexual impropriety would be his mission's final humiliation – he sought advice from Magnus Hirschfeld, a prominent author, sexologist and homosexual. Hirschfeld's memoir did not elaborate on their discussion, but one can surmise that the Casement who relocated to Bavaria in June 1915 was chastened, and more careful.

Munich's American colony of pro-German expats welcomed Ireland's rebel envoy as an exotic addition. The consul-general, Thomas St John Gaffney, a jovial man with Limerick roots, hosted Casement to dinners that clinked glasses to British defeat. Casement stayed at the Basler Hof and worked from the cavernous Luitpold cafe. He chain-smoked, drank up to eight cups of coffee daily and worked through meals, almost oblivious to whatever was on his plate.

He moved to the picturesque village of Riederau, where Curry, another leading member of the American colony, was president of the yacht club and had a large summer house. When other guests got on his nerves, Casement moved to the Black Eagle inn right by the lakeside, where he would take cooling swims and trek up to a monastery.

This was the landscape of King Ludwig II, whose building of fairytale castles ended in madness, a cautionary tale for a man in Casement's position, but as June slid into July he found solace in the tranquillity of the lake and mountains. He played chess, hiked with students and struck up a friendship and correspondence with a teenager, Max Zehndler. Casement's postcards, written in passable German, betray no sexual intrigue but confirm enduring need for male companionship.

The following year a German biographer interviewed locals, who depicted Casement as a secular St Francis of Assisi who spent his melancholy, sunlit sojourn by Lake Ammer communing with nature, befriending the humble and doing good deeds. Encountering two peasant women with heavy baskets, Casement allegedly took one basket, ordered a companion to take the other and hauled the load up a mountain. However romanticised, the portrait suggested that even this hollowed man had a hidden store of resilience.

On that sultry Sunday he strode into Diessen behind the yacht, losing the race, but his speed left the passengers 'astounded'.

A sense of premonition seemed to shadow Casement. A few weeks later he visited the historic city of Augsburg during a solemn festival that raised funds for wounded soldiers. The renegade knight left an inscription in a visitor's book. 'Roger Casement – Sacrifice Day, 1 August 1915'.

. . .

That same afternoon hundreds of people watched in silence as Tom Clarke clicked across a tiled floor to a coffin in the domed rotunda of Dublin City Hall. He closed the lid over a glass cover, beneath which lay a wizened corpse, and draped a tricolour over the casket. Irish Volunteers in green uniforms carried the coffin through the portico out to a wreath-covered hearse and a city bathing in brilliant sunshine.

An honour guard of armed Volunteers and a cavalry unit waited at the head of 20,000 mourners that included representatives of churches, political groups, labour unions and sports and cultural organisations. Thousands more lined the route to the cemetery. Marching bands played not laments but patriotic tunes to create an air of celebration and defiance.

Tom Clarke was attempting to alchemise the bones of a forgotten, musty Fenian named Jeremiah O'Donovan Rossa, who had expired weeks earlier aged 83 in New York, into a challenge to British rule. He wanted a pageant to stir dormant rebel spirit – and to test the authorities in Dublin Castle, who had to decide whether to intervene and risk bloodshed, or to let Clarke take over the city for a day.

Rossa had masterminded a dynamite campaign in England in the 1860s before spending decades feuding with other Irish exiles, but in such unpromising material the shopkeeper at the end of Sackville Street sensed an opportunity to showcase separatist ideals. 'If Rossa had planned to die at the most opportune time for serving the country, he could not have done better,' Clarke told his wife.

During Joe Plunkett's four-month absence, Clarke, like a patient chess player, had moved his pieces on the board. While some lieutenants worked on details of the rising, others steered the Gaelic League, which promoted the Irish language, towards politics. Other IRB men burrowed deeper into the Irish Volunteers, though the organisation remained under the nominal control of a university professor called Eoin MacNeill.

Plunkett's news, when he returned in mid-July, was encouraging: the Germans seemed prepared to send weapons, perhaps even officers. It was not a cast-iron guarantee but enough for the IRB to start scouting locations to land arms. And to tap young Joe for another overseas mission.

The political climate had also evolved. Casualty lists chronicled the growing number of Irishmen killed in France and the Dardanelles. Tales of battlefield heroics would have brought consolation and pride, but the war minister, Lord Kitchener, refused to create new Irish divisions – he didn't trust the Irish – and instead scattered Irish recruits across the armed forces. With their valour not even celebrated, what were Irish boys dying for?

Some Irish bishops echoed the Pope in calling the war futile. Enlistment rates slumped, prompting rumours of conscription. On top of all this was the spectacle of Home Rule's bitterest enemies – Edward Carson and F. E. Smith – entering government, as if their reckless rabble-rousing in Ulster had never happened.

Apathy about the war came tinged with something else. 'At the back of it was a vague feeling that to fight for the British empire was a form of disloyalty to Ireland,' a chronicler wrote. The Royal Irish Constabulary reported that 'a spirit of disloyalty and pro-Germanism, which hitherto had been confined to a small number, was spreading'. A satirical song captured the leaking credibility of John Redmond's Irish Parliamentary Party, which still urged enlistment on the promise of Home Rule:

Full steam ahead John Redmond said
That everything was well, chum,
Home Rule will come when we are dead
And buried out in Belgium.

So Tom Clarke did not need to sabotage faith in Home Rule – the British government was doing that for him. But the IRB remained a tiny, secret group and complete separation from Britain remained a fringe idea. To legitimise revolt Clarke wanted to stir old passions and show the possibility of an Ireland that did not yet exist. Then Rossa helpfully died. Mainstream, respectable Irish people sniffed at contemporary radicals but were suckers for old, dead rebels.

While John Devoy shipped the body from New York, Clarke chaired a funeral committee with 11 sub-committees to arrange hotels, trains, publicity, badges, banners, flags, booklets, speeches, security. He had seen New York parades and wanted that same flair – Dublin was to have its first Tom Clarke production.

When the coffin arrived on 27 July it was taken to a catafalque at St Mary's Pro-Cathedral, where the next day Rossa's widow and daughter joined a packed Solemn Requiem high mass. A Volunteer guard of honour escorted the coffin to City Hall, where for four days mourners, some ferried to Dublin on 17 special trains, paid homage. And then on 1 August, with all the trappings of a state funeral, Clarke closed the casket and a procession that included phalanxes of Volunteers – illegally displaying rifles – prepared to move.

If the Castle was going to intervene, now was the moment. The provocation was literally on the doorstep of British rule – City Hall was wedged between two main entrances to the Castle. But there was no shrill pierce of whistles, no clatter of army boots and shouted commands to lay down weapons. There was not a British soldier to be seen the length of the procession, just a handful of policemen who kept a discreet distance. The chief secretary, Augustine Birrell, had weighed options and decided to do nothing.

The war had put Home Rule on ice and averted the prospect of civil war in Ireland but created delicate dilemmas. Birrell's task was to keep Ireland quiet, encourage enlistment and once the war was over deliver some version of Home Rule that probably excluded most of Ulster. The vast majority of the Irish were loyal, but what was he to do with the vexatious radicals who paraded and sought to contaminate others with their ideas? Arrests and weapon seizures risked bloodshed and uproar. Better, therefore, to do pinpricks: close their little newspapers, deport some loudmouths and monitor the rest. Rossa's send-off would give the radicals a platform, but better that than intervening and causing a riot. So Birrell let Tom Clarke put on his show. It was, after all, just a funeral.

The cortege, stretching two miles, wound its way through the city, marshalled by pickets of Volunteers, among them Joe Plunkett. With no khaki in sight, the armed men in green resembled the nucleus of an Irish army. 'The tide is turning – the tide is turning at last,' an elderly Mayo man whispered to a companion. 'The people are answering the old call.'

Bands played 'The Dead March' as the hearse entered Glasnevin cemetery, home of fallen nationalist heroes. A priest said prayers in Irish while the coffin was lowered. Then a Volunteer officer stepped forward. Tall, heavyset, handsome: Patrick Pearse. The Volunteers' director of military organisation by day, leading IRB conspirator by night. When Clarke chose him for the oration, Pearse asked how far could he go. 'Make it hot as hell,' Clarke replied. 'Throw caution to the winds.'

Among the eclectic group that formed Clarke's inner group, Pearse stood out. Physically imposing, he had an intensity that stopped people in their tracks. There was a story, widely believed, that as an infant he knelt by his bedside and took an oath to live and die for Ireland. Pearse believed the Irish had lost not only their language but their soul and had set up a school, St Enda's, to turn pupils into warrior scholars.

Personally ascetic yet financially reckless, reverential to his mother yet scared of women, a dour loner yet with magnetic presence, obsessed by Napoleon yet averse to conflict, Pearse, a biographer said, embodied 'enough material to occupy a symposium of psychiatrists for a week'.

Where some saw messianic absurdity, Clarke saw potential. For national rebirth Pearse believed the Irish needed to be goaded into rebellion, even hopeless rebellion, and he sought to be the instrument. He had a droopy eye and slight stutter, but on a platform his slow, grave cadences, controlled passion and crafted phrases could mesmerise. So Clarke had fast-tracked Pearse through the IRB, just as he had with Plunkett, and now tasked him with the graveside oration.

It was five minutes of propagandistic brilliance. A new generation had been re-baptised in the Fenian faith, Pearse told the crowd, packed amid the tombstones. 'Life springs from death, and from the graves of patriot men and women spring living nations.' They were gathered in a place of peace, but they pledged war, unceasing war, until English rule was ended. Seeds sown by previous rebellions were coming to a 'miraculous ripening' that would soon change everything.

'They think they have pacified Ireland,' the voice cried out in the evening sun. 'They think that they have purchased half of us and intimidated the other half. They think that they have foreseen everything, think that they have provided against everything; but the fools, the fools, the fools! – they have left us our Fenian dead, and while Ireland holds these graves, Ireland unfree shall never be at peace.'

The voice faded away but the words crackled in the air, electric, a call for resistance that would be quoted that night in trains and bars and homes, and the day after that at football and hurling matches, and all the days beyond.

CHAPTER ELEVEN

Blinker's Web

On the evening of Wednesday 3 August 1915 a tall, well-tailored passenger named Emile Gaché steamed out of New York aboard the Holland-America liner *Noordam* and wondered if the anxiety he felt was paranoia or foreboding. The ship was bound for Rotterdam, in neutral Holland, but would, of course, dock in England for inspection.

Gaché had a Swiss passport, a photograph of his parent's holiday cottage in the Alps and encyclopaedic knowledge about nephews, nieces, aunts, uncles and other relations. His initials were sewn into his linen and he had documents detailing a business trip to France to buy wines. Even so, as the Atlantic stretched before him, his nerves required steadying. He headed to the dining salon and ordered a drink.

The 38-year-old was in fact Captain Franz von Rintelen, Germany's most audacious and successful spy. He had created the alias with help from a real Gaché – the Swiss wife of a German naval officer – who coached him on her family tree and the Swiss civil code. The alias had worked before, and Rintelen never lacked self-confidence, but doubt had nagged at him since the wireless message from Berlin recalling him from the US. It obliged him to run the gauntlet of the British blockade just when his mission was ripening into a harvest of sabotage, strikes and potential revolt.

Well born and with excellent English, before the war Rintelen had served in the navy and represented German banks in Latin America and New York. When war broke out he rejoined the navy as a financial adviser in Berlin and was selected for a delicate operation. All the combatants were struggling to produce enough artillery shells, but Germany's enemies filled their gap by buying vast quantities of American munitions that rained down on German trenches, while Britain's blockade prevented Germany importing a single American shell. The German high command tasked Rintelen with disrupting the flow. 'I'll buy up what I can, and blow up what I can't,' he vowed.

Arriving in April, he kept his word. Unable to buy controlling stakes in arms companies, Rintelen turned to sabotage. He recruited a chemist to make time-bombs and via Clan na Gael enlisted Irish stevedores to plant them on munition ships bound for Britain, France and Russia. The explosions caused fires, diversions and sinkings. Rintelen also fomented strikes among dock workers and fanned strife in Mexico to deflect US attention from Europe. He nicknamed himself the Dark Invader.

Then came the disquieting order to return home. Rintelen did not trust the security of Germany's enciphered wireless communications but had to obey. So he revived Emile Gaché, boarded *Noordam* and had a fortifying drink. On 12 August, England's chalk cliffs hoved into view and the ship slowed to a crawl, sending Rintelen back to the bar. Early the next morning a steward knocked on his cabin door. 'Some British officers wish to have a word with you.'

The indignant Monsieur Gaché was escorted ashore and then to Scotland Yard, protesting all the way at the outrageous violation of Swiss neutrality and demanding to see the Swiss ambassador. He was ushered up a winding staircase into a room where a small man in naval uniform awaited. He had blue, blinking eyes. Reginald Hall already knew the answer so there was no need to bark the question. It could float out, almost gentle. 'Do you know a Captain Rintelen?'

. . .

A giant, invisible web was catching German signals across the Atlantic and depositing them into Room 40, where codebreakers transformed ciphered secrets into daily reports for Reginald Hall. The web didn't catch everything – some telegram routes remained, for now, undetected – but according to one estimate during the war, Room 40 handled 37,000 intercepted naval messages, and thousands more non-naval ones.

Combined with the War Office's codebreaking department, it was an unparalleled intelligence feat, wrote one historian. 'The geographical spread and range of topics covered in those messages is astounding. They ... gave British military and government leaders an extraordinary oversight of their enemies' activities on every continent and on every ocean of the land war, the sea and air war, the espionage and sabotage war, and the propaganda and diplomatic war.'

Another chronicler put it this way: 'Wherever Germans were plotting, Hall was listening and, like dogs who can hear high-pitched sounds that never reach the human ear, Hall could hear intrigues hatching anywhere in the war. The more Room 40 decoded, the more came into his net.'

Even so, Rintelen was such a polished performer he all but convinced other British interrogators he was Emile Gaché, but Hall – on this occasion operating without Basil Thomson, who was away – could not be deceived. His alias crumbling, the Dark Invader faced a grim choice: extradition to the US to face criminal charges, or internment in England as a prisoner-of-war. He confessed his identity and was sent to Donington Hall internment camp.

The director of naval intelligence faced a problem with this bounty. Technically, it wasn't his. Room 40 was a separate section of naval intelligence headed by Alfred Ewing, the Scot who had recruited the first codebreakers on behalf of Hall's predecessor, Rear-Admiral Henry Oliver. Ewing still answered directly to Oliver, who was now chief of the Admiralty war staff, which also made him Hall's boss. Neither man liked Hall, whom they considered pushy, but as DNI Hall was entitled to access Room 40's intelligence and recruit staff. The chain of command was a bureaucratic mess.

Ewing was no pushover, but Hall gradually sidelined him. He inserted loyalists into Room 40 and encouraged the cryptographers to bypass Ewing. 'If ever we dug out anything of importance we were to take it direct to him [Hall] without showing it to Ewing,' one recalled.

Hall also kept Ewing away from the diplomatic annexe, based in Room 45, which he set up after obtaining the codebook seized in Persia. This let him eavesdrop on the enemy's political analysis, intrigues and gossip. Of 30,000 diplomatic messages intercepted during the war, 90 per cent were decoded.

The correct procedure was to pass this trove without comment to his political masters, especially the foreign secretary. From his office, Hall could pick out Sir Edward Grey's second-storey window on the other side of Horse Guards Parade. But the more people who knew about the intercepts, the greater the chance a leak would alert the enemy to their compromised communications. Room 40's existence needed to remain cloaked.

Plus Hall did not trust the judgement of many of his superiors, military and civilian, who in his view were more concerned with bureaucratic 'punctilio' than winning the war, a nervous condition that seemed to especially afflict the Foreign Office. So of the great coup in cracking the enemy's diplomatic code the Admiralty's intelligence chief breathed not a word. He abrogated to himself the task of reading the daily trove and deciding which messages, if any, to pass up the chain.

'He had unbounded confidence in his ability to decide how much of the information in the messages should be passed on to other government departments,' wrote a colleague and biographer. It was his nature, another chronicler observed. 'Years on the bridge had not only disciplined him to lonely decisions but given him a positive taste for them. He relished the responsibility of sole command.'

Many deciphered messages ended up in Hall's personal archive – by the end of the war he had stashed 10,000 diplomatic decrypts in his basement at 53 Cadogan Gardens. It was a high-stakes act. When Hall made the right call, Britain benefited. If he made a mistake, there was no one to challenge him.

Hall's antenna did not rest. When he heard that a Munich artist had made a commemorative medallion about the *Lusitania* he enlisted the department store Selfridges to make 300,000 copies. The medallions were intended to be satirical and had no official backing, but Hall fostered a perception the German government was celebrating the atrocity. It was inspired propaganda.

Adventures were for the adventurous, and rules were pliable. Once a friend, Lady Dorothie Feilding, arrived at the Admiralty just as her car ran out of petrol, which was strictly rationed. Hall pressed the buzzer under his desk to summon Maskell, the office gopher whose duties included circumventing coal rationing.

'Maskell, steal petrol.'

'Yes, sir.' Ten minutes later Lady Dorothie was back tootling down Whitehall.

The mischief had a darker side. Hall allegedly punished a lenient judge by orchestrating a Zeppelin raid over his country estate. Whatever the truth of the story, which sounds improbable, the significance is that Hall himself recounted it with relish. There is also unverified evidence that in August 1915 Hall, or others in British naval intelligence, ordered the killing of a spy who supplied German codes to London but became a security risk.

Convinced he was on the right side, Hall made no secret of his ruthlessness. 'I'd serve under the devil if he was proficient,' he said. News of enemy losses, such as a sunk U-boat, would prompt a cheerful instruction to a lieutenant: 'Willoughby, fetch the rum.' Ed Bell, a US diplomat in London who worked closely with him, made a pointed tribute: 'A perfectly marvellous person but the coldest blood proposition there ever was – he'd cut out a man's heart and hand it back to him.'

Some compatriots inside and outside the Admiralty began to view Hall as a menace. 'They were a little frightened of him; they never knew what he was going to do next,' wrote his biographer. 'Men who had all their lives been accustomed to work to certain rules and conventions became apprehensive when they heard that the director of intelligence was on the war-path.'

Some compared the DNI to Sir Francis Walsingham, a Tudor spy chief and consummate plotter who ran a team of codebreakers and used torture, bribery and blackmail against Queen Elizabeth I's enemies, including Mary Queen of Scots, who was tricked into disclosing evidence that sent her to the block.

By September 1915, the war left little room for pity. Bulgaria joined the conflict on Germany's side, auguring fresh carnage in the Balkans. The British and French launched an offensive at Loos and Champagne that after a week cost 300,000 casualties for no strategic gain. All the suffering hardened the public mood and deterred the combatants suing for peace and declaring the war a mistake. That month, Hall's 17-year-old son John started his last phase of naval training before entering the cauldron.

Informants and spies in New York added more strands to Hall's network. Britain's naval attaché, Guy Gaunt, teamed up with a Bohemian émigré who infiltrated enemy diplomatic missions with Czechs and Slovaks who worked as maids, chauffeurs, clerks and cleaners. Gaunt also hired private detectives to monitor the docks and liaised with the US secret service, which was now paying closer attention to Irish radicals. Combined with the intercepted wireless messages, New York had become the stickiest part of Hall's web.

In the first week of September, Joseph Plunkett sailed straight for it.

. . .

There was a drawback to sending a dying man on an overseas mission. His condition might allay suspicion of conspiratorial intent but raise alarm about infection. Immigration officials took one look at Joe Plunkett's swollen glands and barred entry. America didn't need another tragic poet.

Tom Clarke had dispatched Plunkett to update John Devoy on preparations for the rising, but US rules on tuberculosis left his envoy marooned on Ellis Island. If US or British intelligence learned of the presence of a leading Irish Volunteer and suspected IRB member, the entire conspiracy was at risk. Plunkett might withstand interrogation, but his hollowed walking stick contained documents detailing the rising plans.

Devoy swiftly worked his political contacts. Messages pinged between the Democrats' New York fiefdom, Tammany Hall, and the Senate, and on 11 September the labour secretary granted permission for Plunkett to enter the US, under a thousand dollar cash bond, for three months of 'literary work'.

Days later Plunkett was in Manhattan. Through luck and guile he had slipped through Hall's web. Oblivious to the poet's significance, Dublin Castle had not flagged his journey to the Admiralty or anyone else.

Sensitive Irish communications between the IRB and Clan na Gael were done the old-fashioned way: courier. Sometimes the plotters entrusted cyphered documents to a sympathiser who worked on a liner, other times they used a passenger with a plausible cover story. Short of betrayal it was a relatively secure system, though slow. Messages for the Kaiser's government, or Roger Casement, were then passed to German diplomats in New York to be transmitted to Berlin.

No one realised the weakest link was the Germans with their modern technology and supposedly uncrackable codes.

For Plunkett the mission was a welcome distraction from a broken heart – a young woman, the object of his unrequited ardour, had convinced him to drop the pursuit. Bereft, he sought refuge in the conspiracy, and poetry. Shortly before sailing he wrote 'Big Talk':

I have found a thing to do in the world,
It is to break chains.

He updated Clan na Gael leaders on the rising plans and possibility of German help. What remained undecided was the date. In his free time Plunkett met other writers, and appeared to steer clear of his mother, the mercurial Ma, who was visiting New York for a campaign to canonise the martyred Archbishop Plunkett.

John Devoy was on his own path to some sort of Irish revolutionary sainthood. Each day brought fresh trespasses that the 73-year-old had to try to fix or forgive – his hand was so stiff from writing he now dictated letters to an assistant – before spending another sleepless night in his cheap hotel room battling powerful anxieties and a weak bladder.

In July the *Gaelic American*, his fiery weekly, had almost gone bankrupt, with just $22 and a few cents left in its bank account. Clan na Gael was also broke, its coffers drained by funnelling $7,740 to Casement and thousands more to the IRB. Devoy averted financial collapse partly by using a late brother's bequest and was able to dispatch Rossa's body to Ireland.

In return Tom Clarke had sent him a tubercular courier, but he had resolved that. Roger Casement, in contrast, seemed to defy any fix. When they had lunched at Mouquin's 14 months earlier, Devoy had intended to rebuff the exotic knight, only to relent, a decision that now haunted him.

He credited Casement with reaching Berlin, no mean feat, and persuading the Germans to issue a declaration stating they had no quarrel with Ireland. But it was downhill since then. The futile pursuit of Findlay, the bungled brigade recruitment, the soured relations with the hosts. Casement's tradecraft was also wanting. Instead of concise notes that Berlin's couriers could easily conceal on Atlantic crossings – a slow, low-tech alternative to the mighty Nauen transmitter – Casement sent Devoy bulky packages of newspaper cuttings and longwinded letters.

Devoy dreaded the letters: page after page of Casement explaining why he had ignored instructions and done things his way. The agreement with the Germans over the Irish Brigade, which Casement grandly termed a 'treaty', included a provision that if a landing in Ireland was not possible the unit might fight the British in Egypt, which Devoy considered lunacy. And there were the endless requests for money. Casement was personally frugal but wanted Clan na Gael, not the Germans, to fund the brigade.

Still, the old Fenian thought the brigade concept might yet be salvageable, and chafed at untrue press reports that German guards beat and starved recalcitrant recruits. A small, well-organised unit could refute such calumnies and prompt Irish soldiers in the British army to ponder their allegiance.

So Devoy and the IRB agreed to send an officer to lead the brigade: an Irish Volunteer captain named Robert Monteith, recently arrived in New York from Ireland. The question was how to spirit him to Germany.

Devoy had just the man: Adler Christensen.

Since returning to the US in July, Casement's ever-persuasive former servant had convinced Devoy he could be an asset and was now entrusted with escorting Monteith to Norway – an operation, Adler explained, that required significant money.

Devoy's other task was to update German diplomats on preparations for the rising. All going well it would fall to him, at some point, to notify the Germans that the insurrection was going ahead. He had been waiting for such a message from Dublin most of his life, and it would be an honour to pass it on for transmission to Berlin.

On 6 October, Robert Monteith stowed on the SS *United States* under the direction of Adler, who travelled as a regular passenger. Three days later, Plunkett followed them across the Atlantic in the SS *New York*. The three men did not know the extent of Reginald Hall's surveillance network but through luck and guile slipped through undetected, Monteith and Adler to Christiania, and Plunkett to Liverpool.

Plunkett had the chutzpah to bring two swords dating from the US civil war, which required an import licence under the Defence of the Realm Act. They resembled stage props, and Plunkett ran a theatre company, but the swords were for the rising. When the time came to rebel, he wanted to do it in style.

. . .

On the morning of Wednesday 27 October, while Plunkett recuperated in Dublin and Monteith teamed up with Roger Casement, the high windows in Reginald Hall's Admiralty room looked out on a ritual as old as warfare.

Amid a thin, autumnal mist, teams of men wheeled and dragged 24 captured German field guns and howitzers into a wire-fenced enclosure on Horse Guards Parade and lined them up. A distance of 10 feet separated the muzzles, which were trained on St James's Park. Captured trench mortars and machine-guns completed the array.

The Romans called ceremonial displays of a conquered enemy's weapons *tropaeum*. A century earlier prizes taken from Napoleon's army had been displayed at Horse Guards Parade and now it was the turn of wrecked but still impressive German hardware. Crowds streamed into the parade ground for the spectacle.

The guns were hauled from the cauldron of mud known as Loos, but even with these souvenirs hulking outside his window Hall had reason to ponder another type of battlefield and a very different trophy. Ireland remained calm but it was a troubling arena in the intelligence war. Dublin Castle reported growing support for Sinn

Féiners but declined to crack down, saying it could backfire and was not necessary.

Hall was less sanguine. The backlog of intercepted German messages dating from the previous summer – which he had not shared with the Castle – detailed Irish intrigues with the Kaiser's US diplomats. Fresh intelligence from New York, in fact, had prompted him to visit the Donington Hall prisoner-of-war camp and confront the Dark Invader.

'What did you discuss with the Irish leaders in America?' Hall demanded. 'What have you been planning?' Rintelen had left behind a group of saboteurs, who remained at large, but whatever he knew about plans for an Irish rising was months old, and in any case he played dumb. 'What Irish leaders?' he replied.

When not haunting John Devoy's sleepless nights, Roger Casement was swimming through Reginald Hall's imagination as the malign linchpin between the Boche and the bad Irish, the pivot on which everything turned. It made sense. The rogue knight had the greatest prestige and profile of any Irish radical and everything seemed to hinge on him returning to lead a revolt. To catch him – now there was a trophy. But when would he leave Germany? And how? These were questions to occupy Hall as he gazed over the captured guns.

It was exactly a year since Casement had sailed out of Stornoway on *Oscar II*, free to taunt the hunters. *Fancy bothering about the 2nd cook*. And to do so again after bamboozling Ambassador Findlay and provoking the *Sayonara* farce. Well, Casement was not crowing anymore. Hall was tracking his mission's disintegration.

In the public mind the humanitarian hero was now a spiteful, hapless Hun stooge. In early October former Limburg inmates, repatriated to Britain in a swap of wounded prisoners, had spoken scornfully of the traitor's 'temptations'. Casement had become a liability to his friends. The US consul-general in Munich, Thomas St John Gaffney, was fired after American and British newspapers howled that he had honoured the rascal at a dinner. War Office sources said Casement had lost the confidence of the Germans.

So much was going wrong for Sir Roger, and if he did attempt a homecoming he faced being snagged. Signalling stations continued to multiply around Britain's coast. With luck one would pluck from the ether a message about what was afoot, and with a *fwump* and clatter it would land in Room 40.

As an extra precaution there were Irishmen, loyal to the Crown, manning a secret coast-watching network around Ireland.

All that was left for Hall was to wait. And enjoy the view of the captured Germans guns, which had the decency to point at the Foreign Office.

CHAPTER TWELVE

We Have Decided to Attack

Captain Robert Monteith marched the column out of the gates in good formation, eyes straight, rifles at the shoulder, boots striking the asphalt in unison. The cold turned their breaths into plumes and a bright sun hung overhead. It was 14 December 1915, a crisp, beautiful day. The Irish Brigade remained tiny, just 56 men, but after a month under Monteith's command the former prisoners-of-war once again looked and acted like soldiers, though instead of khaki they wore green, and home was no longer Limburg but Zossen, a training camp 30 miles south of Berlin.

The tall, lean figure of the chief was waiting, as usual, at the crossroads. 'Eyes right!' Heads swivelled as they drew level, and Roger Casement acknowledged the

Captain Robert Monteith.

salute. He fell into step and joined Monteith at the front. Trees with gaunt, naked branches lined the road to Mittenwalde and decaying leaves scented the air, but a route march made them feel alive.

The chief couldn't restrain himself to military pace for long and he soon loped ahead of the column. Monteith, almost as tall, and burly, matched his stride, and thus they would walk and talk about the men, the war, Ireland and Africa, always Africa, where both had served, and as they reminisced it was as if the years slipped away and the north German lowland became velds. Eventually Monteith would halt them to let the column catch up, led Sergeant-Major Michael Keogh, puffing. 'Aw, Sir Roger, you're killing us!' Casement would laugh and, funds-permitting, treat the men to lunch at a roadside tavern.

Members of the Irish Brigade in Germany.

By the time they marched back to Zossen it would be dark, stars glittering overhead, and they would sing 'Clare's Dragoons', about Irish exiles who centuries earlier fought against England in continental wars.

When on Ramillies' bloody field
The baffled French were forced to yield,
The victor Saxon backward reeled
Before the charge of Clare's Dragoons . . .
Viva la, the new brigade!
Viva la, the old one too!
Viva la, the rose shall fade
And the shamrock shine forever new!

Weary but ebullient, the men would return to their barracks, Casement would retire to his room at the Golden Lion inn and Monteith would give a silent thanks that his chief, for at least that night, had solace and rest. 'I knew that after the road work he could always sleep,' he recalled.

Monteith had reason to scorn Casement. They were both Irish Protestants who had served the empire – Monteith as a soldier in India and South Africa, where he won medals and decorations – before embracing Irish independence. But Monteith, 36, was a generation younger, a family man, and a professional soldier who favoured practice over theory and had no time for histrionics.

His success in drilling Irish Volunteers in Dublin had alarmed the authorities, who fired him from his Ordnance Survey job and kept him under surveillance. When the IRB asked Monteith to go to Germany to try to salvage the Irish Brigade he hesitated – it would mean leaving his adored wife, Mollie, and their two young daughters. Mollie, a Fenian's daughter, urged him to accept, so he did. To allay suspicion the IRB first relocated the family to New York – even there British agents monitored Monteith – before dispatching him as a stowaway with the unpredictable Adler Christensen.

Adler overcharged for the service and exposed Monteith to extra peril in Norway by making a detour to visit his family in Moss, but the worst surprise came in Germany: arriving in late October, Monteith found Casement in Munich not only 'very ill, despondent and nervous, and in a state of fretfulness', but no longer seeking recruits for the brigade, deeming it pointless because there was no way to land them in Ireland. Having left his family and risked his life in response to Casement's request for an officer, Monteith might have erupted. Or elbowed Casement aside and taken over the mission, which would have delighted Tom Clarke and John Devoy.

Instead, this tough, no-nonsense soldier all but fell to his knees in reverence. In Casement he saw greatness, and goodness. 'Here was a man who had made, and was still making history; the man who had walked through savage Africa armed only with a walking stick, whose written word had shaken the throne of King Leopold II of Belgium, a man who had saved millions of lives in the Congo and Putumayo,' he later wrote. For Monteith, Casement's mission was no different from Benjamin Franklin seeking French help for America's revolution, or the English enlisting Prussian help against Napoleon.

Monteith was also enchanted by Casement's 'sinuous and panther-like' movements and blue eyes. 'I have known no eyes more beautiful . . . blazing when he spoke of man's inhumanity to man, soft and wistful when pleading the cause so dear to his heart.' It was Monteith's honour to serve such a chief.

Monteith spent most of November at Limburg trying to recruit more men but found them hostile to the brigade, and to guards. 'The German soldier is not tactful,' Monteith observed. He then moved to the training camp at Zossen to take command of the original 56-strong group recruited by Casement and Joe Plunkett. They were sullen – they lacked boots, blankets and weapons and were ambivalent about the idea, if landing in Ireland was not possible, of fighting the English in Egypt.

Monteith also worried about his family in New York – 'sweetheart mine . . . kiss the little ones for me', he wrote to Mollie – and above all he worried about Casement, who was back in Berlin, unwell and quivering like a leaf. 'I am seriously concerned he contemplates self-destruction,' he wrote in his diary. Monteith improved conditions for the men, got them guns and began training. He also persuaded his chief to move to the Golden Lion, about two miles from the camp, and to join marches.

Casement's vigour was a revelation but his morale could crack like the frost. He clucked over the men like an anxious hen and gifted them his own meagre belongings. At his behest they had switched allegiance, earning the contempt of former comrades and exposing them to an English noose, and they were still guarded by Germans, stuck in a camp they called the Birdcage.

Monteith imposed order and channelled the men's boundless energy into football and boxing bouts, but rowdiness still erupted. While Casement spent Christmas with friends at Dresden, the brigade's festive shenanigans with local women resulted in five marriage requests and a new year's day brawl with German soldiers that smashed up a canteen. In a world gone mad, there were worse ways to usher in 1916.

In mid-January, Monteith received an urgent summons to the Golden Lion. A midday winter sun gleamed outside but the room was dark and stuffy. Opening the curtains, he saw the chief prostrate in bed, ashen. His hands were burning, his forehead icy. On the table lay letters from Clan na Gael critical of his work, the final straw. Casement turned to the wall and wept, convulsed with grief over his failures. 'That day I believe his heart broke,' Monteith recalled.

Casement struggled into a dressing gown and fell. Monteith caught him and carried him to a couch, where the chief gazed up, like a child. 'Captain Monteith, you know what I have sought to accomplish, and that even one person should know is sufficient for me.'

Casement refused to see a doctor, citing expense, but Monteith insisted. Advised to take a 'nerve rest', on 19 January Casement moved to a sanatorium outside Munich.

. . .

The same morning, Joe Plunkett surveyed the bare walls and spartan furniture of the safe house, and waited. From the window he could see a quiet street, a damp, grey Dublin afternoon, and still no sign of them. Usually he could use lulls to work on a poem, or read, but tension was not conducive to concentration. Plus a gland on his right cheek throbbed.

It was 19 January 1916. Since returning three months earlier from New York, with his two swords, life had astonished Plunkett by producing one marvel after another. He suspected he was never meant to be so happy. He was in love – this time with a woman who loved him back – and the plot to end British rule was on track.

Except for one glitch. A trade union leader called James Connolly, who had his own tiny labour militia, was threatening to launch his own insurrection – a solo run that would goad the British into arresting everyone and neutralise the IRB before its own plans were ready.

Tom Clarke had tried talking sense into the man without disclosing the IRB's plan for its own rising, but Connolly still seemed bent on launching his own small, hopeless revolt. So he was to be brought to this semi-abandoned house where Plunkett and other IRB leaders would try to convince him to join them. It wouldn't be easy. Connolly thought they were all just talk.

Plunkett's unfamiliar sense of happiness gave him more to lose. He had stumbled into a headlong ardour for Grace Gifford. She was 28, smart, slender, elegant, with a biting, mordant wit, and now *his*, gloriously his. She shared his unconventional spirit and penchant for large rings and flamboyant style. How had he not noticed her before? Even her name evoked something divine.

An artist, Grace had contributed satirical caricatures when he edited the *Irish Review*. She favoured Home Rule but came from a Protestant, unionist family. In defiance of a domineering mother – Joe could empathise – Grace had developed an interest in Catholicism and sought his counsel. Conversations on theology nurtured friendship, then romance.

A recent poem suggested physical consummation:

The day I knew you loved me we had lain
Deep in Coill Doraca down by Gleann na Scath [. . .]

Till wild between us drove the wind and rain.
Breathless we reached the brugh before the west
Burst in full fury – then with lightning stroke
The tempest in my heart roared up and broke . . .

They became engaged in early December, though Joe warned her about complications. 'I am actually a beggar. I have no income and am earning nothing,' he wrote in a letter. 'Moreover there are other things more desperate, practically speaking, to prevent anyone marrying me.' That was an elliptical way of saying he was terminally ill and plotting a revolution but Grace seemed to think her fiancé merely had bronchitis and a sideline in political activism. For Plunkett, marriage and insurrection were not rival commitments but, as one biographer put it, the 'repeated overlapping of two strands like the twisting of a rope'.

During the courtship the Plunkett family estate, Larkfield, in the suburb of Kimmage, turned into an armed camp. It had a large house, two cottages, sheds and a mill spread over eight acres, affording space and privacy for military drills, a shooting range and making grenades filled with shotgun pellets. An attempt to make a field gun using rainwater piping packed with gunpowder blew up. Joe also had a team working on a radio. The advent of conscription in Britain – but not Ireland – produced a trickle of returned emigrants to the estate, which became known as the Kimmage Garrison.

Ma Plunkett's absence – she extended her trip to the US – facilitated the estate's transformation, but she had bequeathed financial chaos. To sort out the books Plunkett hired one of the returned emigrants, a 25-year-old from Cork who had clerked at a post office in London. Quick, able and confident, and with a bone-crushing handshake, he was soon assigned additional tasks. His name was Michael Collins.

When Joe's illness flared up he would retreat to bed and study maps acquired by Robert Monteith before he was fired from his Ordnance Survey job. Other IRB leaders, save Clarke, who was too closely watched, visited Larkfield to discuss the rising. Instructions were not written down but memorised. Soon after Christmas Plunkett, still digesting his engagement, got his other marvel. Enough of the planning had fallen into place to fix a date for the rising.

23 April 1916. Easter Sunday.

It was the culmination of slow, zig-zag plotting since August 1914, but formidable obstacles remained: taking full control of the Irish Volunteers, landing weapons from Germany, seizing the capital, all with secrecy and surprise and a tight timeline. None of it would happen, however, if James Connolly first provoked a British crackdown. The trade union leader's impetuosity had deterred the IRB from including him in its plans, and now it was obliged to stop his own planned rising.

So Plunkett found himself on this drizzly Wednesday at an empty house not far from Larkfield waiting for his comrades and Connolly. He had rebuffed IRB entreaties to meet so he was to be waylaid in the city centre and brought here for a parley.

Finally the car arrived. Out stepped Connolly, his bow-legged gait unmistakeable. Short, stocky, balding, with a thick moustache, he looked older than 47 and had a tendency to scowl, and this summons – only half in jest he called it a kidnapping – was not likely to improve his mood. He had better things to do than listen to bourgeois blabbers. Connolly was born in Scotland to Irish parents and after 20 years in Ireland still chafed at the Irish habit of procrastinating, mixing the serious with the trivial and bringing God into everything. He didn't smoke or drink or chit-chat and wished people would get to the point.

Connolly's experiences in the British army and the slums and factories of Edinburgh and New York, and voluminous study, had convinced him Karl Marx was right: workers needed to unite to resist oppression. In Dublin he helped found the Irish Socialist Republican Party and the Irish Transport and General Workers' Union (ITGWU). A speech impediment tripped up certain words, including socialist, which he rendered 'solist', but he projected seriousness and on a platform would 'throw off gloom like a cloak and pour out eloquence like molten metal that scorched and burned all before it'.

The war shattered Connolly's dream of an international labour uprising. Instead of uniting against capitalist overlords, workers flocked to national banners and slaughtered each other. For Connolly, Germany's rulers were as noxious as Britain's. 'We serve neither King nor Kaiser, but Ireland!' proclaimed a banner over his headquarters at Liberty Hall.

Connolly synthesised Irish nationalism and socialism into a resolve to create a workers' republic. The instrument would be the Irish Citizen Army (ICA), a 300-strong militia originally formed to protect striking workers from marauding police. It was small but cohesive and could, he hoped, strike a first blow to inspire wider revolt.

Unaware of the IRB plan for a rising, Connolly had lost patience with Irish Volunteer leaders and their endless speeches, especially Patrick Pearse, who droned on about blood sacrifice and Ireland's soul. Connolly didn't care about religion or graves or dead Fenians, he wanted economic redistribution and, above all, *action*. While middle-class Volunteers talked and talked, he had drilled the ICA in urban warfare – even staging a mock attack on Dublin Castle – and his newspaper, *Workers' Republic*, blasted defiance. 'The time for Ireland's battle is NOW, the place for Ireland's battle is here,' the forthcoming issue declared. Connolly was goading not just the British but the Irish Volunteers, daring them to act.

He tramped into the house and was ushered into an upstairs room with a table and chairs and not much else. Whatever they had to say, he would hear them out. But really he was done with talk. It was time for grit and gunpowder. The sight of Joe Plunkett would not have reassured him. A workers' revolt didn't need a posh poet with a cloak.

Plunkett was not the only IRB leader present but did most of the talking – his mission to Germany, the prospect of weapons, the strategy to seize Dublin, out it poured, targets, dates, logistics, tactics.

Hours passed, the capital slunk into thick winter darkness, and still Plunkett talked. Connolly paced and fired questions. Both accomplished debaters, it became a duel, the mystic versus the Marxist.

Wednesday turned to Thursday and on it went, Connolly digesting, disputing, probing, Plunkett and his comrades rebutting, reassuring, elaborating, including a promise that the new Irish state would have social equality and religious freedom. Plunkett took breaks lying on a bare iron bedstead. Friday dawned and still Connolly paced and interrogated until it was Saturday, 22 January, and the marathon ended. Connolly agreed to halt his solo run and join forces with the IRB.

Plunkett later said he had never talked so much, never been so tired and never enjoyed anything so much. The alliance suited both sides: the IRB averted a premature insurrection and could add the Irish Citizen Army to rebel ranks; Connolly joined the inner sanctum of IRB planners. It cleared the way for a rising at Easter. A propitious date: the previous Easter the Volunteers had mobilised for harmless manoeuvres, so the British might not suspect any menace from bank holiday mobilisation. Plus Easter symbolised resurrection.

It also promised a more visible role for women. They played key roles in the nationalist and labour movements, took the same risks and made the same sacrifices as the men and did so while defying societal pressure to stay in the kitchen. The ICA admitted women and had a prominent female leader, Constance Gore-Booth, better known as Countess Markievicz. The Volunteers had a female equivalent, Cumann na mBan, or League of Women, that had its own uniform and trained in first aid and weapons. Overlooked by police, they acted as couriers and gathered intelligence. The IRB excluded women but Tom Clarke entrusted his wife, and Joe Plunkett his sisters, with vital duties. With the ICA on board, the rising, if it happened, would promise equal rights, unlike Britain, where women were denied the vote.

Plunkett was considering including Grace in the rising plans, but in a letter on 27 January he stuck to romance. 'I know that there is great happiness in store for you if you love – the greater your love the greater the joy,' he wrote. In a tinge of foreboding, however, he said he would 'go into darkness, danger and death' for love. As Grace read these lines an IRB courier sailed for New York with the message John Devoy had been awaiting for half a century.

. . .

Three days after Plunkett's letter to Grace, in London, Reginald Hall sat down to pen a very different type of letter to the mother of Harold Tennyson. Harold, a grandson of the poet laureate, Alfred, Lord Tennyson, had served on the *Queen Mary.* He had escorted the Tsar's family during the St Petersburg visit and proved to be a fine violinist as well as sailor. Now at the age of 20 he was dead, killed by a mine while serving on another ship.

'He never failed me, and his fine character had such an influence with the men,' Hall wrote. 'I love to think of his fine, good face with the straight eyes. Indeed is it not so wonderful that God took him for Himself.' The captain's tribute, Lady Tennyson later said, 'brought unspeakable comfort to our stricken hearts'.

So much grief, so much waste, and Hall knew he would continue writing such letters – and might receive one from his son's commander – until the war was won. The intelligence chief had notched up more successes. Intercepted documents had exposed enemy intrigues in the US, which Hall passed to US officials and leaked to the press, resulting in expulsions of Austrian and German diplomats, including Franz von Papen, the German military attaché and liaison with Clan na Gael. A search of von Papen's luggage on his way back to Berlin revealed cheque stubs detailing payments to saboteurs, a fact that was duly shared with US officials and leaked to the press, creating another howl. Still President Wilson kept the US out of the war, but Hall would keep chipping.

Room 40 hummed on, a hive-like organism still a secret even to most admirals and ministers.

The night shift was tasked with discovering the cypher key, which the Germans changed at midnight. Others, armed with codebooks, processed the daily deluge of intercepts. As the calendar flipped to February, Hall could be confident that whatever the year would bring, he would be forewarned. The naval messenger who delivered Room 40's output in a locked box each day to Hall's office confided that those fellows in the Old Building had the war's cushiest job. All they did was crossword puzzles.

. . .

On the morning of Saturday 5 February, the twin afflictions of a New York winter and Adler Christensen made John Devoy feel every one of his 73 years. Freezing temperatures gripped Manhattan and the Clan na Gael leader was still recovering from flu. He was not sure if there was any remedy for Casement's former servant.

Devoy had contracted the Norwegian to smuggle men to Germany, as he had smuggled Monteith, only for the plan to end in expensive fiasco, with none of the men leaving New York. It exposed Christensen as a double-dealing charlatan and definitively ended his involvement with Irish rebels, but he still had one card to play in Roger Casement's story.

Devoy had spent the morning stewing on Christensen when he received a message from Tommy O'Connor, a young IRB member and purser with the White Star Line. Tommy was in town and wished to see him. He had a message from Dublin. The old man crunched over snow past City Hall to Haan's on Park Row, where the East Side streetcar clanged to a halt. The restaurant was an oasis of wood-panelled walls, oil paintings and leather booths – good for discreet talks.

During lunch Tommy passed a sealed envelope. Devoy opened it and deciphered the code with Tommy's help until the second sentence, which said the message was only for Clan na Gael leaders. Devoy hustled back to his office on William Street and completed the deciphering. It was from the IRB supreme council. They were going ahead with the rising, had a date, Easter, and wanted weapons delivered on the eve of fighting.

Devoy stared at the words, shocked. He had not expected an insurrection until the war turned in Germany's favour. And so soon! Less than three months to prepare. Despite his autocratic temperament the old Fenian accepted the home organisation's right to make the supreme decision. His duty was to help. He could only hope his friend Tom Clarke, pulling the strings in Dublin, knew what he was doing.

Devoy shared the news with other Clan na Gael leaders and two days later met a German contact. Whatever his anxieties about the rising's timing, this was a moment to savour. He had kept the flame of resistance alive and believed, against overwhelming evidence, that his people would rise up. Here, in this message from Dublin, was the proof, and he had been entrusted to pass it to the Germans.

From Germany's New York diplomatic mission it was relayed to the embassy in Washington, where it was reviewed by the ambassador, Count von Bernstorff, and encrypted. On Thursday 10 February a communication numbered 79 and marked 'very secret' was sent to the German-owned Sayville radio station on Long Island.

Addressed to the imperial chancellor, Theobald von Bethmann Hollweg, it requested a shipment of weapons and ammunition to arrive in Limerick at Easter. 'Unanimous view that action cannot be postponed much longer. Delay means disadvantage for us ... therefore we have decided to attack.'

These few lines unfurled the most audacious challenge to British rule in centuries, and now the wonder of German technology was casting them across the Atlantic.

CHAPTER THIRTEEN

Conjurer's Box

Whatever way they looked at it, the officers of *Abteilung IIIb* came to the same conclusion: they would support the Irish, but not too much. As the military intelligence department of the German General Staff it was their job to weigh risk and reward, and the calculus decreed modest investment in the Irish venture.

Since the initial message from John Devoy on 10 February, the embassy in Washington had forwarded to Berlin more communications that expanded the rebel wishlist to German officers and artillery teams. To which the answer was *ausgeschlossen*, out of the question. Not one German would land in Ireland. But by the end of February, the intelligence chiefs concluded weapons could be dispatched.

Partly it was a question of resources. The previous week the German army had begun a titanic assault on Verdun to shatter French resistance and morale. Significant forces were also needed in the Balkans and on the Eastern Front, where Russia was preparing a fresh offensive. The Reich was overstretched. Partly it was the risk that any vessel dispatched to Ireland would be sunk or captured; evading the

British blockade would depend on the skill of the captain and the fortunes of war. And partly it was doubts about the rebels. Did they have support in Ireland, and did they know what they were doing? The Irish Brigade fiasco did not inspire confidence.

On the other hand a rebellion could yield effective propaganda and tie down British troops. Conceivably, though it strained reason, the rebels might actually win.

Whatever the fate of the enterprise, it would at least find a use for Sir Roger Casement and his little brigade, and that promised respite to Captain Rudolf Nadolny, head of the political section, who had wearied of Sir Roger's visits to his office on Moltkestrasse for petitions on behalf of the brigade. A fervent Prussian with a thin moustache, Nadolny's agents had infected Allied shipments of horses, mules and sheep with anthrax, and he might have been tempted to add some to Sir Roger's coffee during his visitor's longwinded effusions. It would be a relief to pack him off to Ireland.

In a message to John Devoy on 1 March, sent via the German embassy in Washington, Nadolny said the navy could land 20,000 rifles, 10 machine-guns and explosives at Fenit pier, in County Kerry, between 20 and 23 April. He then sketched the plan to Robert Monteith, who had been training the Irish Brigade at Zossen.

Monteith went to Munich to brief the chief, who had been largely confined to a sanatorium bed since his breakdown in January. Casement jolted as if dunked in cold water. At first he welcomed the news. After so much stasis, action! Two years earlier he had helped run guns for the Irish Volunteers and now he could do so again, and in the process escape Germany. But he worried over what exactly was planned in Ireland. A rising, presumably, but when exactly, and with what support?

. . .

Casement arrived in Berlin on the 8.40 a.m. train on Thursday 16 March, the mild spring day some compensation for returning to an imperial capital he now loathed for its heel-clicking officials. Monteith accompanied him to the *Abteilung IIIb* headquarters, where Nadolny and two other officers greeted them with smiles. So began the pantomime, one side lying, the other feigning credulity while introducing its own lie.

After showing a message from Devoy detailing the rising plan and request for support, Nadolny said an arms shipment would leave around 8 April, in three weeks, and take about 10 days to reach Ireland on the eve of the rising. Once Casement and his brigade landed with the arsenal the rebels would surely prevail and compel England 'to surrender' control in Ireland, Nadolny declared, keeping a straight face as he predicted a feat worthy of Baron Munchausen.

Casement listened in silence, his thoughts swimming. He considered a rising without German troops to be 'stupendous idiocy' and 'foredoomed failure', and viewed the weapon shipment as an attempt to provoke a bloody diversion, using cheap Irish lives, for minimal German effort. He said none of this. He nodded and smiled, as if accepting the fiction, because he did want the arms shipment to go ahead. Casement was not going to go down in Irish history as the man who stopped his comrades getting weapons – weapons that could be stored for a future, properly planned rising.

And he had a plan – he had been anticipating this moment since Munich – that required Nadolny's cooperation. Casement wanted the Germans to provide a submarine so he could reach Ireland *before* the arms ship. Whatever facility for lying he had acquired in the Foreign Service – reasonable tone, eye contact, open gestures – he now used.

Arriving early, he told Nadolny, would permit him to ensure a smooth landing of the weapons and help launch the rising. The request hung in the air. Nadolny eyed him. The real reason was the opposite. Casement wanted to stop the rising.

A lifetime ago he had penned 'The Dream of the Celt', excoriating English domination, and then devoted his existence, risked everything, to ending that domination. But he believed this envisaged rebellion was warped, that the Germans had made hollow promises to gull his comrades into a futile bloodbath, and he wanted to warn his comrades before it was too late.

So Casement projected enthusiasm for the whole enterprise as he made his pitch for a submarine. Nadolny, possibly sensing a hidden agenda, smiled back – sustaining the fiction of two allies, working in concert – but lamented that for technical reasons the Admiralty had already ruled out sending a submarine. Casement said the matter was of supreme importance and that he would speak to the Admiralty.

There was one area of sincere agreement between Nadolny and Casement. Devoy's message had included an order that his envoy 'remain in Germany as Ireland's accredited representative until such time as the provisional government may decide otherwise'. The old Fenian wanted to keep Sir Roger and his meddling ways parked in Germany and well away from the rebellion.

His envoy, as ever, felt free to disregard instructions. It was his duty to accompany the brigade, Casement said. Nadolny, just as keen for Casement to leave Germany, nodded. 'Of course it is impossible for you to remain behind. You must be there with them. Everything forces you to go.'

That, at least, was decided. What remained unresolved was when Casement would leave, and how.

. . .

Five days later, on Tuesday 21 March, as Casement continued to lobby Berlin's decision-makers for a submarine, black clouds sent a squall howling through Wilhelmshaven, the naval port on Germany's North Sea coast. Lieutenant Karl Spindler tramped into his quarters, freezing and wet from a stint of outpost duty. Rain hammered so hard the windowpanes threatened to shatter.

Instead of the Royal Navy, Spindler was spending the war battling the weather. It was a sour joke that the Kaiser had built up a fleet to make Germany a world power with a 'place in the sun' only for the fleet, once war came, to huddle in its ports, keeping the monarch's 'darling' dreadnoughts safe and impotent.

Spindler, 28, had his own frustrations. As a boy in Königswinter, a small town by the Rhine, he had built rafts and spent his days on the river seeking adventure like some Westphalian Huckleberry Finn. He became an ocean liner officer and when war broke out joined the navy, hankering for action and command, but he lacked the connections and aristocratic pedigree for quick promotion. After two foggy, uneventful winters at Wilhelmshaven, Spindler had clawed his way to command a small flotilla of patrol boats but yearned for excitement and glory. He consoled himself by painting dramatic seascapes.

Spindler was trying to get warm and dry when there was a knock on the door. The chief wanted to see him. Tramping through the downpour to headquarters, he listened in growing wonder as the commander outlined a special expedition – its nature could not yet be disclosed – that required an officer, five petty officers and 16 men, all volunteers and unmarried. 'I have proposed you for the command of this expedition. How does that suit you?'

Spindler grinned. In his sodden uniform, with the wind shrieking, he felt the luckiest man on Earth.

. . .

That same Tuesday evening, Reginald Hall could study sheets of rain billowing across Horse Guards Parade. It was supposed to be the start of spring but monsoon-like torrents had flooded rivers and left London saturated and bedraggled. It was a day for Maskell to warm the room with a good blaze because Hall had information to digest and decisions to make.

Room 40 had intercepted and deciphered the German embassy's communication of 10 February disclosing John Devoy's message about the planned rebellion. Several more messages since, flowing both ways across the Atlantic, had elaborated on the planned rendezvous off the Kerry coast between 20 and 23 April. 'Irish pilot boat to await . . . at dusk, north of the island of Inishtooskert, at the entrance of Tralee Bay, and show two green lights close to each other at short intervals,' said a telegram from Berlin.

And this very day had brought another gift from the ether – codewords. 'As a sign that something untoward has occurred, BRAN. FINN means that the cargo has left at the right time,' said telegram number 686 from Washington, in the name of Devoy and Ambassador Bernstorff.

Hall surely smiled. So thorough, these conspirators, and with a nice Celtic touch; in Irish mythology Finn McCool was a hero whose hound, Bran, alerted him to danger. If this information harvest continued, Hall was going to have to erect a shrine to the Nauen transmitter, that embodiment of German technological prowess, for services to British intelligence.

The message from Devoy instructing Casement to remain in Berlin appeared to have eluded interception, so Hall could assume the renegade consul would come to Ireland.

The question for Hall was what to do about this forewarning. He could not sound a klaxon about a German-Irish rebellion without imperilling Room 40's secrecy, which remained paramount. One of his cardinal points of intelligence work was 'covering up all tracks so that the enemy may remain in ignorance of the fact than any of his secrets have been discovered'.

Plus he did not trust all his superiors to make sensible decisions. He had withheld sensitive political information about the US from Arthur Balfour – Churchill's successor as the navy's First Lord – and was even less inclined to trust his civilian colleagues with secrets about Ireland.

Knowledge about the planned rising had to be used selectively and its provenance concealed. So for over a month Hall had sat on the intercepts, but with April approaching it was time to issue discreet warnings. Vice-Admiral Lewis Bayly, the Admiralty's senior commander in Ireland, was told to increase patrols on western approaches. Hall's army intelligence counterpart was due the next day, 22 March, to notify Major-General Lovick Friend, the army's commander in Ireland, that an 'absolutely reliable source' said Irish radicals hoped to land German aid on the west coast for a possible rising at Easter.

Without knowing the actual source, neither Bayly nor Friend could judge the quality of the information – in Whitehall random rumours were also attributed to 'reliable sources' – so the admiral and general could be expected to take some preventive action but not scramble to battle stations. This suited Hall. Precipitous action now could unnerve the rebels and forestall Sir Roger's departure, scotching any chance of catching him.

Hall did not pass the intelligence to Downing Street or Dublin Castle. Inside the Castle walls the chief secretary, Augustine Birrell, and his under-secretary, Sir Matthew Nathan, weighed the familiar dilemma: let the Irish Volunteers and Irish Citizen Army continue to march and shout, or swoop and risk provoking a backlash? Lacking Room 40's information, Birrell and Nathan relied on old-fashioned spies. The Dublin Metropolitan Police's G Division had two informants, code-named Granite and Chalk, who had infiltrated the Irish Volunteers. Around the third week of March, Granite said there was no fear of a rebellion while Chalk said something was stirring. Whom to believe?

. . .

The police and soldiers waited for sunset before staking out positions and surrounding the estate. It was late March and after months of surveillance, and alarming reports, the order had come to lay siege to Larkfield, the Plunkett family estate in south Dublin.

Inside the grounds Joe prepared a defence – men were posted at hedges and laneways while in the main house windows were shuttered and furniture heaped against doors. In the stairwell, maids screamed. Dublin seemed poised to have its own Alamo.

Since January the estate had become increasingly militarised and now hosted about 90 Volunteers, nicknamed 'the Liverpool lambs', who had fled conscription in England and turned the mill into a barracks. In anticipation of a rebellion – there were no details, just rumours – they had multiplied the stock of home-made bombs.

Now the police and soldiers outside the gates seemed poised for a pre-emptive strike. Gripping rifles, shotguns and revolvers, the defenders braced for a shout to surrender, or a volley of gunfire. Minutes passed. Nothing happened. Joe's younger brother, George, investigated and returned to announce that the police and soldiers had gone, melted into the night.

Intimidation? A scouting exercise? Joe could only guess what it meant. The truth was that despite this brief show of force, Dublin Castle had favoured Granite's reassuring report and decided against a crackdown, at least for now.

The conspirators did not know this and worried a swoop might come at any moment, before they were ready. For Plunkett, every day mattered. For over a year he had been walking a tightrope, eyes fixed on revolt, and now it was just three weeks away, but the closer he got to the end point the more he had to juggle.

In February his sister Philomena, known as Mimi, had couriered a message to John Devoy. Upon her return – a chamois bag strapped to her thigh had $2,000 in Clan funds – Joe was dismayed to learn that Devoy's messages to Germany had given a four-day window, 20–23 April, to land the arms.

The rebels already had enough guns to start the revolt so Joe wanted the arms ship to come no earlier than 23 April, Easter Sunday, the day of the rising, lest an earlier landing expose the conspiracy and lose the element of surprise. So he had sent Mimi back to New York to specify a narrower timeframe for delivery. 'Arms must not be landed before midnight of Sunday 23rd. This is vital.' There was, Joe assumed, time for this tweaked timetable to reach the arms ship before it sailed.

Making the revolution an all-family affair, Joe also had a mission for his father, the papal count. The 65-year-old was to travel to Rome to inform Pope Benedict XV about the plot, and hopefully obtain his blessing, to avert condemnation by Irish bishops once the shooting started.

Since their talking marathon in January, Plunkett and James Connolly, the Irish Citizen Army leader, had developed a rapport and refined tactics for the coming battle. Patrick Pearse, meanwhile, used his oratorical gifts to condition Volunteers for insurrection without alarming the British. Pearse announced there would be manoeuvres over Easter – as the previous Easter – to test mobilisation and equipment, implying a routine affair.

It was equally important to keep the ostensible leader of the Volunteers, Eoin MacNeill, in the dark. The IRB had quietly extended its sway over the Volunteers but the history professor still believed he was in charge, still commanded some loyalty in the ranks and opposed any rebellion. He had to remain ignorant about the rising until the last possible moment.

The need for secrecy complicated planning but preparations to receive the shipment were underway in Kerry, where local IRB men would stake out the beach near the landing point and organise manpower and transport. So many balls in the air, and as March drew to a close Joe Plunkett had one other thing to juggle – his wedding. Grace had proposed they marry at Easter. Plunkett gazed at his fiancée. 'We may be running a revolution then.'

. . .

Karl Spindler stood on the ship's bridge, feeling the throb of the unfamiliar engines, and steered a course out of Wilhelmshaven. The crew bustled around him, still learning the vessel's idiosyncrasies. It was shortly after 2 p.m. on Friday 31 March, for once a fine spring day in the North Sea, and they were bound for Lübeck, on the Baltic coast, for final preparations.

It had been a hectic 10 days since Spindler swapped his regular duties to plan the expedition. He had selected 21 men, all volunteers and unmarried, like himself. Summoned to Hamburg docks, he had expected a sleek patrol vessel with modern devices but found himself gazing on a far bigger, bulkier ship – the SS *Castro*, a 1,200-tonne Wilson Line cargo freighter that had been seized in the Kiel canal along with other British ships when war broke out.

It was to become the SS *Aud* – in fact a doppelgänger of the *Aud*. The real version was a Norwegian steamer that was at that moment hauling cargo off the coast of Spain. Royal Navy reference books listed the names and descriptions of virtually every vessel afloat, and the *Aud* was marked as Norwegian, and thus neutral. German naval intelligence chose the *Castro*, languishing in Hamburg, as the imposter because it was of similar dimension and shape, with a single funnel. With adjustments it would appear all but identical to the actual *Aud*.

One important change had already been made. Beneath a sofa bunk there was a hidden entrance that led to a series of manholes, ladders and a clandestine hold roomy enough for 50 men. An iron bulkhead – a partition wall – at one end was matched at the other by a dummy bulkhead, giving the impression of a watertight compartment with no opening. Beneath wooden planks there was another secret hold. The plan was for Spindler to dodge or bluff through the British blockade with the weapons and Casement's Irish Brigade concealed in the belly of his ship. The secret compartments were nicknamed the conjurer's box.

From Hamburg Spindler had sailed the vessel, temporarily renamed the *Libau*, down the Elbe to Wilhemshaven, where carpenters and welders, working behind screens for secrecy, began transforming her into the *Aud*. Now on the last afternoon of March he was sailing for Lübeck for final adjustments and the loading of the weapons and the brigade.

Spindler assembled the crew on deck and ordered them to strip. If the ship was to be Norwegian, so too its crew. In place of imperial German navy uniforms they donned sweaters, caps, trousers and oilskins used by Scandinavian merchant sailors. German naval intelligence, ever thorough, had stamped buttons with the name of a Norwegian firm.

Spindler also told the men to grow beards, drop the heel clicking, speak a Low German dialect that might pass for a Scandinavian tongue and adopt a rolling gait with hands in pockets. He was no longer Herr Lieutenant but Cap'n. The crew exchanged looks. Was he serious? With some pride Spindler noted how his sailors struggled to shed military polish and turn slovenly, but they persisted. Success or failure hinged on the credibility of their pretence, just like the *Sayonara* voyage that Reginald Hall had dispatched.

After mooring at Lübeck on 1 April they loaded coal, provisions and water. Then 4,000 wooden boxes, each with five rifles, plus crates with machine-guns and ammunition, disappeared into the conjurer's box. On top went a camouflage cargo of pit-props, tin baths and door and window frames, all stamped for transport to Genoa and Naples. With the transformation nearly complete, Spindler took a train to Berlin for a final round of briefings at the Admiralty.

. . .

By Friday 7 April, Roger Casement had met and taken a liking to the genial lieutenant who was going to risk his life to bring weapons to Ireland. But he was damned if the Irish Brigade was going to set foot on the *Aud*. It was due to sail in just over 48 hours and would do so with barely an Irishman aboard. Casement had changed the plan.

After two weeks of fruitless lobbying Casement had all but abandoned hope of racing in a submarine ahead of the arms ship to call off the rising. But he had resolved to save his little brigade from what he considered criminal folly. Even if the *Aud* evaded the Royal Navy, which seemed unlikely, the boys faced death in a futile rebellion or execution as traitors. He would not permit it.

Captain Rudolf Nadolny, the intelligence chief, had glared like an enraged bullfrog. Dropping any pretence of fraternity, he roared that the men would sail or rot in jail, or worse. He threatened to halt the arms shipment altogether and to blame Casement, making him a traitor to Ireland. When threats did not work, a Nadolny aide tried and failed to bribe Robert Monteith to take the brigade.

And so with the expression of a man who has swallowed his own anthrax, Nadolny agreed that almost all the men would stay in Germany. After all the effort to recruit them, they were to remain at their training camp and sit out the rebellion. Only Casement, Monteith and a brigade volunteer called Daniel Bailey would sail on the *Aud* to link up with their comrades in Kerry. If the British showed up, Monteith and Bailey were to hold them off with a machine-gun.

Although he considered Lieutenant Spindler a fine fellow, Casement was sure the *Aud*, even if it avoided interception, would deliver him to a hopeless enterprise. Sparing the brigade from that fate was his only consolation. 'Only God can save the situation,' he wrote in his diary. 'I go with a brain appalled and a heart sick to death and longing for death.'

On the evening of 7 April, the eve of departure, came a minor miracle: Casement got his submarine. A last-ditch appeal to a government intermediary did the trick. The U-boat would leave a few days after the rifle-laden steamer but, taking a more direct route, arrive first. Casement's hope of averting the rising trembled back to life.

At 6 p.m. on 9 April, as a church tower clanged over Lübeck harbour, the imitation *Aud* slipped its moorings and chugged out to sea. Tramp steamers usually had dogs so a last-minute addition to the crew, an ancient bear of a mongrel called Hector, prowled the deck. It was Sunday, according to sailor lore a good day to start a journey. Karl Spindler stood on the bridge, eyes fixed on the approaching dusk.

CHAPTER FOURTEEN

Calm Lies the Sea

In the anonymity of the Baltic sea, beyond prying eyes from the shore, Karl Spindler's crew spent their first night completing the ship's metamorphosis. Men with paint and brushes were lowered on planks over each side to write *Aud-Norge* in six-foot white lettering. A Norwegian flag was planted on the stern and red lead paint was applied to the funnel to simulate rust. By the morning of Monday 10 April the disguise was complete.

On the bridge and in the cabins anything German-made or German-looking was collected and stashed in the conjurer's box and replaced with Norwegian sardine tins, torches, linen, surgical dressings, maps, charts, flags and Christiania newspapers. Freshly forged cargo manifests, bills of lading, certificates and other documents were creased and aged with soot, oil and grease.

Sailors who struggled to grow Viking-worthy beards got similar treatment, with oil and coal dust applied to chins and cheeks. Each crew member received photographs and letters of fake Norwegian families and practised pronouncing their Norwegian aliases. On deck, in addition to the rolling gait, they now clamped pipes in their mouths and made a great show of spitting. A stoker was supplied with bacon to keep Hector visible and vocal while passing other vessels.

Only now did Spindler disclose to the crew that their mission was to run guns through the British blockade for a revolution in Ireland. 'They were almost wild with delight,' he later wrote. 'No one thought about the dangers that lay before us. A single desire animated us all. On, on, into the enemy's territory; and then home again, covered with glory. With such a splendid crew one could cheerfully face the devil himself!'

Before them was a perilous 2,000-mile route through Scandinavian waters with a wide loop around Scotland before sweeping down Ireland's Atlantic coast. One danger came from German submarines that did not know the *Aud*'s real identity – seven months later, in fact, a U-boat would sink the genuine *Aud*, which was carrying British coal. Other risks were the weather, reefs, mines and Royal Navy patrols. Spindler estimated the voyage would take about 10 days and aimed to arrive on Thursday 20 April, the start of the four-day window.

Unarmed and alone – there were no deck guns or radio, lest the aerial thwart its disguise – the *Aud*'s only chance, if intercepted, was to deceive the enemy, like a floating Trojan horse. Plan A was to play the innocent Norwegian and ply any boarding party with brandy and whisky. If rumbled they would try to overpower the boarding party with revolvers, knives and crowbars secreted around the ship. The last resort was self-destruction; a codeword shouted three times was the signal to detonate explosives placed below deck.

Late on the Monday, entering the strait between Denmark and Sweden, Spindler shook off a Danish pilot boat seeking business and passed a Danish torpedo-boat with a blinding searchlight before entering the Skagerrak strait, gateway to the North Sea. To fob off a curious Swedish cruiser he faked a diphtheria outbreak by raising a quarantine flag and splashing the deck with carbolic acid.

By Wednesday 12 April, the *Aud* was a lone speck in a world of sullen sea and sky. Spindler, resting in his cabin, woke to a shout. 'Smoke cloud on the port beam!' A lookout clambered to the foretop and scanned the horizon through binoculars. The source of the distant wisp of smoke had a high mast with spotting-top. A British warship. It seemed to be heading straight towards them.

Spindler ordered emergency stations and told the engine room to reduce smoke while the *Aud* tacked east. Maybe they had not been spotted. Minutes passed, then a joyous shout from the lookout. The warship was veering west. They were 75 miles east of the Shetland Islands and had escaped their first brush with the British blockade – the easternmost tip of a flotilla that formed a cordon around the Shetlands. Studying his charts and pondering options, Spindler set a course towards the Arctic Circle.

. . .

As the *Aud* wheeled north, Roger Casement was a thousand miles south, in Wilhelmshaven, having breakfast on *U-20* while the crew loaded provisions and readied for departure, a process that usually entailed jamming every available space with supplies, butter under the bunks, sausages next to grenades, hammocks suspended beside torpedoes.

Casement had spent a fraught final few days in Berlin settling his affairs and writing letters and diary entries that justified his actions in the tone of a man eyeing posthumous publication and posterity. After bidding goodbye to the brigade boys, he wept.

The Germans issued him, along with Monteith and Daniel Bailey, commando kits comprising revolvers, daggers, maps, binoculars and curare, a poison, should they prefer suicide to capture. From Zoo station at Kurfürstendam they took an overnight train, travelling in separate compartments as a precaution against spies, and arrived at the port on Wednesday morning, a steam cutter delivering them to *U-20*, bobbing in the harbour, in time for breakfast.

Casement had shaved off his beard and was virtually unrecognisable, repeating his ritual from New York 18 months earlier. But then he had sailed with hope. Now his dreams were ash. John Devoy had lost faith in his envoy. And the Germans, despite granting the submarine, had no intention of landing him before the arms shipment. 'HQ attach importance to getting the Irish ashore at the last possible minute,' said a confidential German Admiralty order.

And even if Casement did reach Dublin before the rising, what could he do? He was so disconnected from the conspiracy he did not know who was orchestrating it. And he overestimated the significance of German troops. The plotters were prepared to proceed without any German soldiers. Isolated and discounted by his own side, Roger Casement was a rebel leader only in the imagination of the British.

Even so, Casement was able to muster a smile at Wilhelmshaven. He had escaped Berlin and its Prussian bullfrogs and if a rising were to go ahead, however doomed, his place was with his comrades. And his escort was an affable, experienced captain. Eleven months earlier, peering through *U-20*'s periscope, Walther Schwieger had given the order to fire the torpedo that sank the *Lusitania*. Yet he had charm and Casement couldn't help liking him.

The humanitarian and the revolutionary battled inside Casement. He could support violence in the abstract for a cause while recoiling from actual bloodshed. He disapproved of the *Aud* cargo including bombs, which seemed unchivalrous, and hoped the Volunteers would ditch them. He conceived the rifles as instruments to resist conscription and thus save Irishmen from the trenches. Yet in a choice between peaceful, limited autonomy for Ireland – Home Rule – or a German invasion to support insurrection, Casement chose the latter.

This was the bundle of paradoxes that clambered down the conning tower and took his place, with Monteith and Bailey, in the captain's quarters. The Irish guests could not resist bragging to their hosts that an Irishman, John Philip Holland, had pioneered submarine design six decades earlier with a prototype called the *Fenian Ram*, intended to attack the English navy.

Submarines could travel faster and further on the surface and typically submerged only to attack ships or dodge destroyers. With twin diesel engines that could generate up to 15 knots, and a shorter route, *U-20* was expected to reach Kerry first despite the *Aud*'s head-start. But a day and a half into the journey the crank actuating the diving fins broke and *U-20*, amid crackling radio messages for a replacement submarine, limped to a naval base at Heligoland.

The Irish passengers transferred to *U-19*, which was commanded by Raimund Weisbach, who had served on *U-20* and helped turn Irish waters into a graveyard. It was another swirl to the *Lusitania* leitmotif linking Casement with the British intelligence chief who hunted him.

U-19 left Heligoland at 1.26 p.m. on Saturday 15 April, tasked with making up for lost time to rendezvous with the *Aud* and the Irish pilot boat on the evening of 20 April. It ploughed north through a choppy sea and at 9 p.m. made its first dive, a daily drill known as 'shaking the bubble' that brought awe and terror. At the sound of a bell, men scrambled into positions and sealed hatches while Weisbach switched from diesel to electric engines and opened valves to fill tanks with seawater. With descent came a thick, heavy silence as the crew listened for leaks. Fully submerged, *U-19* glided like a bird. Casement sat, wordless, with an expression of childlike wonder.

The terror came in many forms. In this era before sonar, submerged submarines were blind and relied entirely on sea charts to avoid hazards. A mine or an uncharted wreck or reef could shatter the hull. If spotted before diving it could be rammed or shelled as it descended, never to rise. Doomed men were known to rip off fingernails scrabbling at hatches. Ascent brought its own fear because before the periscope broke the surface there was no way to know what lay above. Crews called it 'the blind moment'.

Casement, without beard, and German crew members aboard U-19.

That at least was a shared dread. Additionally, Casement had a private fear about what awaited when he surfaced from the fathomless murk of his mission to Germany to face the enemy. He had mocked and challenged the English and had a presentiment about the price he would pay, a dark vision that saw beyond a defeated rebellion to something far more personal.

'The English government will try now most to humiliate and degrade me. They will not honour me with a high treason trial … they will rob Ireland of that and they will charge me with something else – something baser than "high treason" – God knows what … they will seek through some dastardly means to assail me otherwise and break their vengeance on me and Ireland by a coward's blow. I go to far worse than death – death with the cause of Ireland to sustain me would be a joyful ending – but I go to a show trial, to be wounded in my honour; to be defamed and degraded with no chance of defence.' Casement wrote these lines in a letter to Charles Curry, his friend in Munich, weeks earlier, on 26 March. He repeated the prediction in another letter, on 6 April: 'By assailing me and my character they will hope to blacken my cause too.'

It was a pre-emptive effort to defend his reputation. Casement had seen Oscar Wilde's fate, jailed, humiliated, destroyed, and he feared his own sexuality could be weaponised. He did not know Adler Christensen had revealed their relationship to the British but decades of homosexual cruising had left a trail, and since his arrival in Germany he had fretted about the enemy obtaining trunks with his 'papers'.

On that first dive Weisbach kept the boat submerged for more than two hours. Underwater, the interior temperature rose and so did the reek of sweat and diesel and the claustrophobia of knowing a mistake, or bad luck, could condemn them all to suffocation in a darkened steel tube. At 11.20 p.m. *U-19* climbed and broke to the surface. Water sluiced over the deck and the crew opened the hatches. There were no British destroyers, only a black sea and a three-quarter moon.

. . .

As the men aboard *U-19* gulped cold North Sea air, in London it was 10.20 p.m. and Reginald Hall had reason to be pleased with his day's work. It had been a raw day, wind slicing and slashing as if spring had never arrived, but the ether had proved kinder.

The Nauen transmitter, normally so garrulous on Irish matters, had been quiet of late, leaving the director of naval intelligence to speculate whether the Boche really were going to help Casement's little revolution. Then a signalling station on England's east coast picked up message fragments that suggested two submarines had departed, or were about to depart, for Ireland's west coast. Another fragment enquired 'whether German auxiliary cruiser vessel which is to bring weapons to Ireland has actually . . .' The rest of the message was corrupted and indecipherable, but Hall could surmise a surface vessel was also en route.

Another Room 40 coup, and the usual dilemma: to share or not to share? Political intelligence, especially of this sensitivity, was supposed to be passed to civilian superiors, no matter what Hall thought of their judgement. But Saturday passed and no report went to Downing Street or the Foreign Office. Herbert Asquith and his cabinet remained unaware that a German arms cargo was en route to Ireland for an insurrection scheduled to begin in eight days.

However, Hall did – now for the second time – notify Vice-Admiral Bayly, the Admiralty's senior commander in Ireland, who operated from Queenstown, a port outside Cork on the southern coast. Hall's first alert to Bayly the previous month had prompted extra patrols on the Atlantic coast. This new message indicated the weapons shipment and rising were imminent, demanding maximum vigilance. Before turning off his light and going to sleep, Hall could be confident of two things. Bayly would take necessary measures. And the next week was going to be interesting.

The next day, Sunday 16 April, Vice-Admiral Bayly sent his commanders a confidential report about a German shipment. 'This landing is expected to be connected with a rising which some say may be expected around Easter. Whether the arms and ammunition will be in the submarines, or whether they will escort the steamer carrying them cannot be stated; both contingencies have to be allowed for. Armed trawlers have been established along the coast from Galway to Dursey.' The report did not specify Tralee Bay, which lay between Galway and Dursey.

Bayly also verbally tipped off Brigadier-General William Stafford, the army garrison commander at Queenstown, about a possible landing of arms and rebellion over Easter. Stafford put this in a letter to his superior in Dublin, Major-General Lovick Friend, who on Monday 17 April showed the letter to Matthew Nathan, the under-secretary, who showed it to the heads of the Royal Irish Constabulary and Dublin Metropolitan Police.

A warning about a conspiracy to stage a Hun-supplied revolt in the heart of the British empire, it landed with all the force of a small plop. With the source unclear and the transmission haphazard it disappeared into Dublin Castle's puddle of rumours – the same murk that swallowed conflicting reports from the police agents Chalk and Granite. The officials tasked with ruling Ireland concluded that the Sinn Féiners might be up to something, but probably weren't.

. . .

Joe Plunkett mingled with the other conspirators amid the crowd lined up outside the Coliseum theatre on Henry Street. He looked awful, as if he had been shot. Tubercular abscesses on his cheek and neck had been operated on, leaving a swath of bandages, but he was not going to miss this meeting.

The theatre doors would soon open to a show by a music hall troupe from England. It promised a night of entertainment for Dubliners who had abstained for Lent and were looking forward to tea with milk, or maybe a Guinness, on Easter Sunday. It was Tuesday 18 April, so five more days to go.

The Irish Republican Brotherhood's military council had come not for the show but to review a draft proclamation of independence and finalise plans for their own spectacle. To avoid surveillance Jennie Wyse-Power, a sympathiser who owned a shop and restaurant beside the theatre, suggested they meet at her premises under cover of the audience arriving and leaving.

The counter-surveillance ruse seemed to work – there was no obvious posse of G-men stalking the council members. Trams and shoppers still bustled on Sackville Street but the General Post Office, hulking over the corner of the thoroughfare and Henry Street, had shut for the day. Passing the mass of Georgian granite and fluted Ionic columns, all topped with a statue of Hibernia resting on her spear and holding a harp, Plunkett could only hope the landmark was as solid as it looked. It was to be the revolutionary government's headquarters.

Word of what was to come had filtered down to some Volunteers, prompting a scramble for bandoliers, belts, haversacks and other equipment at Lawlor's on Fownes Street. Chemists found themselves selling out of first aid kits while Fred Hanna, a bookseller on Nassau Street, wondered at all the requests for tomes on military strategy. Liberty Hall, the dingy home of James Connolly's Irish Citizen Army, swarmed with men and women stocking food, melting lead into bullets and delivering messages. It became so crowded someone pasted a notice on the stairs: 'Please keep to the right.'

As the audience filed into the Coliseum, and the orchestra awaited the conductor's signal, the military council trooped into one of Wyse-Power's private rooms next door, all gathered together perhaps for the last time.

The draft proclamation was a single page printed on a rickety press in the basement of Liberty Hall. With a mix of typefaces, it declared an Irish republic in the name of a provisional government; the culmination of so much work and hope, it felt precious, even sacred. Each of the seven – Plunkett, Tom Clarke, James Connolly, Sean McDermott, Eamonn Ceannt, Patrick Pearse, Thomas MacDonagh – read and approved it in turn. The occasion's solemnity was not aided by next door's booming ditties and English accents:

> '*Chorus, gentlemen, chorus, please!*
> *All together with a fallallay!*
> *Tol-lol! Lal-de-riddle! That's the way!*
> *Roar it louder than you've ever done a'fore!*'

If all went well – if the arms ship arrived and the Volunteers turned out in force – it was the proclamation that would roar and shake the whole British empire. The plotters could only hope Irish people would approve because no one was consulting them in advance. Even most of the Volunteers, in fact, were to remain in the dark until the last moment.

As the Coliseum continued to throb – at the interval a piccolo player led the orchestra in a chirpy rendition of 'The Deep Blue Sea' – Plunkett updated his comrades. His father, the papal count, had returned from Rome saying the Pope had given his blessing to the Volunteers, though not the rising, and was meeting bishops to pre-empt pulpit denunciations once the shooting started.

Joe had also printed and distributed copies of what would become known as the 'Castle document', which purported to reveal a sweeping, imminent British plan to disarm the Volunteers and arrest potential troublemakers, including moderate nationalists and even the Archbishop of Dublin. It was either a fabrication or an exaggeration of a British contingency measure, and it served a crucial purpose: Eoin MacNeill, the Volunteers' chief-of-staff, believed it.

The history professor could obstruct mobilisation because he did not want the militia – unaware of the extent of IRB infiltration, he still considered it *his* militia – thrown into a needless conflict. But the Castle document convinced him the English were about to swoop and that the Volunteers must prepare to resist. Plunkett's creative handiwork would electrify all of the city the next day when an alderman bypassed censorship by reading it out at a Dublin corporation meeting.

Plunkett, looking round the table at his comrades, could also confirm that by now his sister Mimi had reached New York and given John Devoy the message, to relay to Berlin, specifying the arms should not arrive before Easter Sunday, 23 April. If the ship had already sailed, the Germans could surely radio the tweaked date to the skipper.

The ship's arrival was to act like a spring that activated an intricate clockwork of plans in County Kerry. To avoid leaks, information was being rationed to a handful of people and shared as late as possible. A local boat pilot who could guide the German ship to shore would be briefed on the eve of her arrival.

A plan for a Volunteer training camp on the beach – a pretext to monitor the bay for the ship – had to be scrapped when the organiser ran into problems with police. But a team dispatched by Plunkett would seize a radio transmitter to communicate with the ship. Volunteers would also seize Tralee post office to control telephone and telegraphy lines and contain police in their barracks. Members of James Connolly's transport union would help run a train to Fenit's pier to load the weapons, which would be distributed to units across the west and south of Ireland. The stage had been set. All that was needed was the ship.

For those of his comrades yet to hear the news, Plunkett had a final flourish. He was going to marry Grace Gifford on the morning of Easter Sunday. The rising, after all, was not due until evening. There would be time.

A full moon glimmered as the theatregoers streamed out of the Coliseum. The conspirators slipped in among them and headed their separate ways, satisfied with their plans, untroubled by the fact that the arms ship had sailed before Devoy's message, it had no radio, and a submarine bearing Roger Casement was also coming.

. . .

While the conspirators dispersed into the Dublin night, from the conning tower of *U-19* Captain Raimund Weisbach could see no moon, only a ceiling of black clouds that blended into a dark sea that chopped and churned and hurled spray across the deck. His charts told him the loop around Scotland was complete and they were between the Shetlands and the Faroes and heading south, towards Irish waters.

After midnight it would be Wednesday 19 April, four days since departing Heligoland. Skimming low and fast on the surface, they had avoided British patrols, but rough seas and a brutal storm had hindered the effort to catch up with the *Aud*, assuming she was still free and on course for the 20 April rendezvous. If they missed her, so be it. Weisbach would transfer his passengers to the Irish pilot boat, and start hunting ships to sink.

Weisbach was 29, blond, and a model of clean-cut Prussian manhood who played Schubert and Mozart on his violin. A navy lieutenant when war broke out, how proud he had been when transferred to the submarine corps, the best chance of breaking the English stranglehold, and prouder still to win the Iron Cross for torpedoing the *Lusitania*. He had been given command of *U-19*, the navy's first diesel submarine, just four weeks earlier, and already the crew had nicknamed him *Kleinerlöwe*, Little Lion.

U-boat success was measured in tonnage sunk and Weisbach itched to prove himself, but first he had to complete this *sonderkommission*, a special mission. Only after delivering his three passengers could he begin hunting prey.

Sir Roger was a curious passenger. Seasick, barely able to eat, morose, yet his powerful baritone had enthralled the crew with Irish ballads. And he was a great talker, especially about the history of his homeland. They would be sailing over the graveyards of Spanish and French ships that paid the price of challenging England. Weisbach had no intention of joining them. He planned to slip in and out of Tralee Bay before the enemy realised he was there.

U-19 throbbed south through a paling sky.

Approximately three hundred miles south, Karl Spindler watched the sun rise on Wednesday 19 April and wondered when his luck would run out. Two British auxiliary cruisers had passed close during the night and ignored the *Aud* – no interception, no boarding party – just like other patrols in previous days. It was uncanny. He flew a neutral flag but why no checks?

Against the odds, Spindler had pierced the blockade and now, after 10 days and more than 2,000 miles, reached the west coast of Ireland. In fact, at their current rate they would reach Tralee that evening, a day early for the rendezvous. Spindler told the engine room to cut speed to five knots. They would waddle awhile to time arrival for the following afternoon.

At times during the voyage it was as if Njord, the Viking sea god, was toying with these fake Norsemen. To avoid the Royal Navy cordon around the Shetlands they had veered up to the Arctic Circle. Amid frigid emptiness they paused to retouch the *Aud-Norge* paintwork and tempted fate by playing 'Calm Lies the Sea' on the gramophone. Turning southwest they ran the gauntlet of the British 10th Cruiser Squadron, which had about a dozen large auxiliary liners to patrol a 200-mile expanse between Iceland and the Faroe Islands. Three times ships emerged from fog and approached the *Aud*, only to veer away. Then a storm with waves the size of houses nearly ran Spindler's crew onto the treacherous Rockall reef.

Battered and dazed, they entered Irish waters on 18 April, safely past the 10th Cruiser Squadron but now subject to scrutiny from coastal patrols. The two cruisers that had approached that night, then vanished, fuelled Spindler's unease. 'The business began to look queer,' he recalled. 'Did they want to lull us into a false security?'

As the sun rose higher on 19 April the *Aud* dawdled south, the Irish coast still invisible, and another cruiser appeared. Her deck guns were manned and blue-jacketed British marines crowded the rail, watching them. Spindler's crew slouched on deck, feigning nonchalance, and Hector played his part, barking furiously. After what seemed an age the enemy again just drifted away.

There was no trick, no trap. Vice-Admiral Bayly had instructed his Atlantic flotilla to be on the lookout for submarines and a disguised steamer but the patrols did not suspect the *Aud*. Lots of neutral steamers plied these waters and patrols had multiple tasks. The 10th Cruiser Squadron had been testing a new tracking system and rough seas made a boarding risky. By 19 April conditions were calm, but Bayly's coastal patrols had no description of the mystery ship and may have envisaged a small trawler, not a sizeable cargo ship.

That night, chugging south, Spindler ordered the crew to open the hatches and dump the fake cargo. Door frames, zinc buckets and tin baths splashed overboard, clearing the holds for quick unloading of the weapons.

Thursday 20 April unfurled a fresh, glorious morning. The air was still, a gentle northwesterly swell on the water. By noon they were 52º N and 11º W, about 45 miles from Tralee. Spindler ordered full-steam ahead. An intoxicating thought infused the crew. They were going to make it – make a revolution, maybe history.

As stokers fed the boilers other crew members prepared steam-winches and unloading tackle, uncovered hatches and placed the top boxes in slings for immediate landing. Spindler estimated it would take seven to eight hours to unload the weapons. As agreed with Sir Roger, the machine-guns would emerge first so the Irish on the quay-side could fend off any English intervention. Spindler ordered the crew to wear uniforms, pistols and daggers beneath their Norwegian kit. And he primed more explosives in the bow, to scuttle if necessary.

Shortly after 1 p.m. what appeared to be bluish cloud banks on the horizon solidified into land – the first glimpse of Ireland. Spindler assembled the men for final instructions. Their uniforms might not save them from execution if caught, he said. Nobody demurred; they had not come this far to turn back. He told the engineers to prepare to pump out water tanks to lighten the ship for the shallow channel leading to Fenit. Surgical dressings were doled out and the medicine chest was placed in the mess room. Then: 'Every man to his post.'

The coast was sublime. Jagged cliffs soared over a shore which splintered into little islands, inlets and coves. Navigating from three peaks known as the Three Sisters, Spindler approached Tralee Bay, uncomfortably aware that a signal station at Loop Head was probably observing them. The chronometer said 3.30 p.m. Hector prowled while the men on deck sucked on pipes and spat. A green flag flew from the masthead and a man with a green jersey stood at the bow – the agreed signals.

The bay was deserted. A handful of cottages on the southern and eastern banks indicated Fenit must be close. Wary of reefs, Spindler nudged the *Aud* a mile northwest of Inishtooskert, a tiny, uninhabited island carpeted in daisies, and reached the rendezvous point at 4.15 p.m.

He cut the engine. Water slapped against the hull, the ship barely moving. In the stillness, Spindler could feel his heart. At any moment the Irish pilot boat should appear. Perhaps Casement's submarine as well.

His binoculars swept the bay. Nothing. Minutes passed. Gulls circled, sunlight glinted. Spindler's chest tightened. Where was the pilot? Or the submarine? By 4.45 p.m., still nothing. His orders were to wait 30 minutes and if nobody appeared to use his judgement whether to turn back.

Spindler blazed with questions. Had the submarine sunk, or come and gone? Had rebellion broken out early and diverted the Irish? Was it an English trap? Perhaps the Irish would come after nightfall. On that hope, he decided to linger.

At half-speed, he edged around Inishtooskert and through his binoculars studied Fenit, which was just a pier and a collection of buildings. Barely a soul stirred. Dusk came as a welcome shield from any British observation, though at intervals Spindler flashed a green light to shore from a paraffin lamp, the glass coated in soot to dim the beam. Dropping anchor between two rocky scimitars, the *Aud* hunkered in darkness, a black silhouette.

. . .

As the tranquil Thursday night deepened Mortimer O'Leary continued gazing at the ship from the window of his cottage on the island of Illauntannig. He had noticed her in the bay before dusk, upon returning home, and could still see her outline. A ship of her size, around 1,500 tonnes, just sitting there, it was odd, and the day's second mystery.

Mort was 19, and yet to obtain his pilot's licence, but plied these waters every day in his currach. He was a Volunteer and that afternoon, in a quiet corner in the town of Castlegregory, the captain of his Volunteer company had made a startling request. A steamer with arms was due to arrive. Would he keep lookout and guide it ashore? Mort said yes.

It would arrive in three nights, on Sunday, and was a small steamer, he was told. To Mort that sounded like a trawler, perhaps 150 tonnes. He was to go to Tralee town on Saturday for a full briefing and to collect signal lamps. Until then he was not to know more. 'All right,' Mort replied, though he had a hundred questions.

Then he returned home to the puzzle of this freighter poking around the bay. Whoever it was, they had picked a balmy night for a visit. Around midnight Mort cast a final glance at the shadowy hulk, then went to bed.

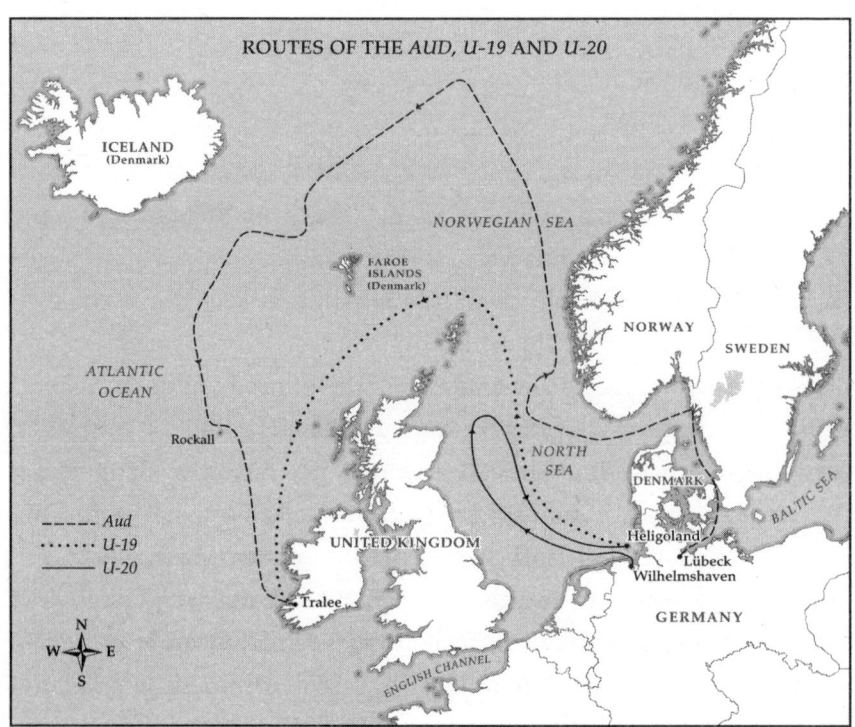

CHAPTER FIFTEEN

Good Friday: In the Name of King George

U-19 slid into Tralee Bay 10 minutes after midnight, its electric motors softly *phut-phutting* through water flat as glass. A moon that had glowed golden and low on the horizon vanished behind Mount Brandon, casting the inlet into Stygian darkness. In the conning tower the German officers and their three passengers vied with suppressed excitement to be the first to spot the green signal light.

The boat slowed to a crawl and in the stillness it seemed to Robert Monteith the water was whispering, and that he could hear the thumping hearts of his companions. A gold-rimmed watch the IRB gave him before he left Ireland a year before ticked in his pocket. Monteith had lived his share of adventures, fighting for the British in India and Africa, and then drilling Irishmen to fight the British, but nothing compared to this moment.

Like Sir Roger he believed a rising now was premature but the guns were precious, and there was something symbolic about landing them here, an extremity of Ireland associated with saints and scholars and a folklore prophecy about a mystical liberator.

Monteith's binoculars were useless against the blackness. All those moonlit marches with the chief and the brigade at Zossen, and now not a glimmer from the heavens. He rubbed his eyes and peered into the murk. There! A twinkle! It disappeared. The others didn't see it, and in any case it wasn't green. Monteith wondered if it had been real.

The submarine crept east, then west, adjusting position, scouring the void for a hint of emerald. The blackness, unbroken. Minutes passed, then an hour, and exhilaration gave way to a numbing realisation. They had travelled 1,300 miles and arrived, just a few hours late, to a silent, empty rendezvous. The crew was at diving stations lest a patrol appear but even the British seemed to have forsaken this eerie Atlantic terminus. As far as they could tell, *U-19* was alone.

The *Aud* might have been intercepted, or sunk, or come and gone, but where was the pilot boat? What sort of rebellion was this? Monteith spoke little German, but he understood the officers quietly cursing the Irish. Shame engulfed him. 'Our boys have failed us!' he thought. Monteith had left his Mollie and two girls in New York, and risked his life to help Sir Roger, the greatest man he had ever met, and here they were back in Ireland abandoned by their compatriots. He wanted to tear something, to fight someone.

It was the slow unfolding of one of the great what-ifs of Irish history. IRB leaders in Dublin and their comrades in Kerry were in their beds, oblivious that the precious cargo on which so much depended had arrived, and that Casement too had come. Slow and cumbersome communications between Dublin, New York and Berlin, unclear wording, heedless assumptions, bad luck, all played a role in leaving two German vessels marooned in Tralee Bay, blind to each other.

U-19 passed probably within a mile of the *Aud*, but from the submarine's perspective Spindler's ship was swallowed in blackness, its lamp signals too faint for detection. *U-19*, emitting no signals, was a grey ghost. After an hour of prowling, Weisbach had enough. Lingering was dangerous and futile. The passengers would be put ashore in a dinghy.

Gathering their packs below deck, Monteith watched the chief scribble a few final lines in his diary. The man had barely eaten or slept in days. His hands were almost devoid of flesh, like a skeleton, and quivered. When Monteith tried to show him how to load a Mauser pistol, Casement demurred. 'I have never loaded one. I have never killed anything in my life.' If they encountered hostile people on shore, they must be tied up, he said.

The chief was calm, fatalistic. 'It does not matter so much about us but the English patrols will catch the arms ship. The pity of it!' Monteith disagreed. It did matter what happened to Casement. If the world lost him, it would not be the same.

Shivering in the cool air, they stowed their kit in the dinghy, a semi-collapsible tub of wood and canvas. An outboard engine would be too loud so they would row ashore, said Weisbach. Monteith protested but Casement smiled. 'Hush, it will be greater adventure going ashore in this cockle shell.'

Donning life-vests, the Irishmen murmured farewells to their escorts and clambered into the craft. It was 2.15 a.m. *U-19*'s propellers whirred and it dissolved into the gloom, bound for the open ocean for *Kleinerlöwe*, to hunt prey – hours later he would sink a British cargo ship.

The three men in a tub, Montieth, Casement and Bailey, bobbed in its wake. Monteith surveyed his crew mates. The smallest invading party known to history, he thought. Two miles away, barely visible, lay Kerry, where in a few hours church bells would announce Good Friday, the day Jesus was crucified. It occurred to Monteith, with horror, that he had been tasked with personally ferrying the chief to his death.

Casement sat at the stern, steering with an oar, and Monteith and Bailey rowed. For an hour they fought a southward drift, the only sound the slap of wood in water, then came a faint thunder of breaking waves, and a line of white foam. The boat began to rock. 'Only two hundred yards more,' said Casement.

A wave roared over them, then another, tumbling them overboard. Gasping, they heaved back into the boat and veered onto a sandbank. Struggling free, they aimed for shore. Finally, a beach loomed out of the darkness. The boat shuddered to a stop, its bow wedged in sand.

Bailey helped Casement ashore while Monteith tried to puncture and sink the boat. It refused to be scuttled and the effort wrenched Monteith's ankle. He hobbled to the others and collapsed alongside them, drenched and exhausted. They were at Banna Strand, seven miles north of Fenit.

When Monteith opened his eyes it was still dark, but skylarks were launching from the dunes, warbling. Surf lapped at the chief, who drifted in and out of consciousness. In the gloom he resembled a sleeping child. Later, Monteith would wonder if he should have let him die there, but he roused him.

A shadow on a ridge caught Monteith's eye, then vanished. His nerves prickled. They needed to move. Kerry farmers were not revolutionaries or likely to take kindly to bedraggled strangers. They needed to get to Tralee to find Volunteers, find out about the arms ship and get a message to Dublin. Perhaps there was still time to call off the rising, and failing that, join it.

Teeth chattering like castanets, and too weakened to carry much, they buried pistols and ammunition in the sand, then trekked inland over swampy terrain. At 5.20 a.m. they passed a low wall and a farmhouse where a servant girl with tousled hair, leaning over a half-door, spotted them. She stiffened. Monteith did not like her stare and muttered a curse, earning a rebuke from the chief.

They pushed on. After hiding from two men pushing a cart with seaweed they came to a rath, an ancient earthen fort ringed with furze bushes and blackthorn, and paused to rest. A mile to the east was the village of Ardfert, and six more miles to Tralee, but the chief was spent. They made a plan: Casement would hide here while Monteith and Bailey, leaving their waterlogged overcoats, continued to Tralee to find Volunteers and return with a car. It was 6 a.m. With luck they would be back by 10 a.m.

. . .

As Casement's comrades bade goodbye and disappeared through the foliage, Karl Spindler was six miles south, still in Tralee Bay, sucking hard on his pipe while giving some Royal Navy visitors a tour of the *Aud*.

The patrol boat had appeared an hour earlier, briefly inspiring hope it was the Irish pilot until Spindler saw the mounted deck gun and British naval ensign. Sybil Head signal station, perched high above the bay, had been monitoring the *Aud* and dispatched the *Setter II* to investigate.

When a boarding party with rifles clambered aboard and demanded to see the captain, Spindler took his time opening his cabin door and did so in the guise of Niels Larsen, a gruff Norwegian who was sleepy, tousle-haired and indignant at the intrusion. 'What's the meaning of this?' he barked in English. 'If you wish to speak to me, be good enough to wait until I have dressed.' He slammed the door in their faces.

So began a pantomime that mirrored the *Sayonara* cruise of 16 months earlier, though this version risked exploding into violence. Spindler, concealing his nerves, played the role of a brusque but cooperative neutral. A storm had battered the *Aud*'s engines so they were in the bay effecting repairs, what was the fuss? A racket below deck – an exuberant bashing of spanners on pipes – suggested the engineers were hard at work.

When the British demanded to see the holds, Spindler led them on a tour and opened the hatches. Not all the fake cargo had been dumped and what was left just about covered the top of ammunition boxes. Spindler invited the visitors to climb down the ladder for a closer look. 'Not that you will see very much.' The storm, he explained, had jumbled things and made quite a mess.

The visitors declined but requested the *Aud*'s papers. Spindler produced creased, cocoa-tinged manifests and bills of lading, all in Norwegian, and steered the British skipper to the sofa in his cabin. Might he fancy a coffee, or something stronger?

John Donaldson had the uniform but was not a full Royal Navy officer. He was a Scottish fisherman from Aberdeen who had been drafted, along with his boat and crew, into the Royal Naval Reserve Trawler Section for mine clearing and patrols. The *Setter II* and other auxiliary craft had been sent to Ireland weeks earlier to keep watch for a disguised German ship, and the signal station suspected something off about this vessel, but Donaldson saw no Hunnishness.

The two skippers clinked glasses, felt the bite and then glow of White Horse whisky, and discussed the war, the sea and women. The strains of 'It's a Long Way to Tipperary' wafted from the gramophone in the saloon, where Donaldson's men enjoyed their own tipples. On his second scoop, Donaldson confided they were on the lookout for a German steamer come to help an Irish revolt.

Spindler burst out laughing. It was the least funny thing he had ever heard but his nerves were shot. 'Yes,' Donaldson continued, 'they are terribly stupid, in spite of all their cunning.' Twenty minutes later the visitors were clambering back down the ladder to their own boat and bidding goodbye to the friendly Norwegians.

Spindler sat down to think. The British had been expecting him. All hope of delivering arms to the Irish was gone. The only thing left was escape, perhaps to Spain. They were under observation from signal stations and to flee immediately would expose the lie about engine repairs. They would sit tight for a few hours, then leave. A long day beckoned, and not yet 8 a.m.

. . .

The clock tower pealed eight times and Robert Monteith's anxiety probably worsened with each one. He and Bailey were seated on a wall by a bridge, trying to look inconspicuous as the river Lee gurgled beneath them and families passed on the way to church. Tralee was a handsome market town, but on this day of penance and prayer, shops and pubs were shut and the interlopers didn't have names or addresses of local Volunteers. The shadow on the beach, the servant girl and then passing a quizzical policeman on the walk to Tralee made it urgent to get off the street and retrieve the chief, but a false move could lead to arrest.

They made another pass through town and found a newsagent open on Dominick Street. It sold copies of the *The Irish Volunteer* and other nationalist titles. 'You sell the right sort of papers,' Monteith told the newsagent.

The man stiffened. 'Yes, sir, I sell all sorts.'

Monteith took a gamble and asked to be put in touch with the local Volunteers. The shopkeeper, his name was George Spicer, eyed the strangers coolly and asked why they wanted such information. Monteith went all in: they were not police spies, they were Volunteers and needed help. Spicer told them to wait and dispatched his son.

The boy returned and said the Volunteer commander told him he would come after finishing breakfast. Monteith and Bailey waited. Then waited some more. Some men arrived and scrutinised them, apparently at the behest of the commander. A clock over the street's jewellery shop ticked past nine.

Eventually, he came. Austin Stack, a 36-year-old sporting hero with thin lips and weighty responsibility. He had captained Kerry to the 1904 All-Ireland Gaelic football championship and now was leader of the local Volunteers as well as the IRB. He was tasked with landing and distributing the weapons cargo, mobilising hundreds of men, seizing communications installations, paralysing the security forces and – the IRB leaders in Dublin had stressed this – keeping all the preparations secret until the last moment on Sunday. The plans were not written down, nor shared with lieutenants, but stored in Stack's head.

After confirming Monteith's identity, and hearing his tale, Stack may have felt like throwing up his leisurely breakfast. The arms ship might have come and gone, or arrive any minute, and Sir Roger Casement was out in some field hiding under a bush with an urgent message for Dublin. Yet Stack was not supposed to do anything that might alarm the authorities before Sunday, and he didn't have a car. He considered his options.

At approximately 11 a.m. a sympathiser named Maurice Moriarty, driving his employer's car, collected Stack, another IRB man named Con Collins and Bailey, who was to act as guide, outside the Mercy Convent on Pembroke Street. Monteith, his foot swollen, remained behind. Taking back roads to avoid Ardfert, which had an RIC barracks, it was about seven miles, or 20 minutes, to Casement's refuge. The car sped out of Tralee, dodging potholes.

. . .

Constable Bernard Reilly was not used to seeing the sergeant so animated, or being told to grab his rifle and go on a manhunt, but he was having to get used to a lot of things this morning and it was barely 11 o'clock. A mystery boat, buried weapons, three strange men, what next? Ardfert had never seen the like. Shouldering his carbine, Reilly wheeled his bicycle onto the road to join Sergeant Thomas Hearn. They would first try Brandonwell bog, where men had been sighted hours earlier.

Reilly had the standard Royal Irish Constabulary look: bushy moustache, tall, sturdy, cutting a fine figure in the dark green, almost black, uniform. Men of good character with sober, honest habits, the cream of Irish manhood: that's how the RIC billed itself, a semi-military force of 10,000 men scattered across Ireland in small stations called barracks. With the Dublin Metropolitan Police taking care of the capital, the RIC was Dublin Castle's eyes and ears in hamlets, villages and towns. 'If a cow farted, the RIC knew,' one historian noted.

The force suppressed the Young Ireland rebellion of 1848, then the Fenians in 1867, for which a grateful Queen Victoria bestowed the royal prefix. Things settled down and by the time Reilly became RIC constable 60449 many Irish mothers were proud to have a son wear the uniform. Its badge had a crown, and senior officers were mostly Protestant, but the badge also had a harp and in the south of Ireland the lower ranks were mostly Catholics – moderate nationalists who supported Home Rule while remaining loyal to Britain.

Many enlisted to fight in France and those who stayed kept a beady watch for signs of sedition and pro-Germanism. The RIC in this part of Kerry had seen the Kaiser's work firsthand when some *Lusitania* victims washed ashore months after the sinking. Bodies without heads, without limbs, monstrous, pitiful things, and it had been their job to collect and bag them. Now the sea had delivered another test.

For Reilly the drama began at 8 a.m. when Pat O'Driscoll rode into Ardfert on his horse, which he usually used to deliver milk, to announce that his uncle, John McCarthy, had found a boat with a dagger in the Banna surf, and then spotted footprints that led to buried pistols and boxes of bullets. McCarthy had fetched Pat to help drag the boat ashore, then dispatched him to notify the RIC.

To this day it remains unclear why McCarthy, a farmer, was on the beach before dawn. He claimed he was on his way to pray at a holy well but there is speculation that authorities paid him to keep an eye on the sea, and that he may have been the shadow Monteith reported seeing. Unlike the Admiralty, however, the RIC had no warning that a German arms ship or submarine were expected.

Sergeant Hearn had cycled off with Constable William Larke to Banna Strand to investigate, leaving Reilly at the station. He was a lowly barrack orderly but took it on himself to phone Ballyheigue barracks, five miles away, to request support. When the sergeant returned – Larke remained at the strand to guard the boat and guns –

he said a servant girl had seen three suspicious men coming from the direction of the sea. He alerted headquarters at Tralee and told Reilly to grab his rifle.

It was after 11 a.m. when Reilly and his sergeant pedalled down the road to Brandonwell bog. It proved a false lead – the men spotted earlier were labourers cutting peat.

The two policemen caught their breath. Maybe the mystery trio had cleared off. But if they were still in the area, where would they hide? The constable and his sergeant surveyed a landscape of stubbly fields.

. . .

Four miles to the north, Austin Stack had multiplying reasons to swear as he stood on the roadside beside Moriarty's immobilised car. It was 11.30 a.m. and they had not found Casement. First, Bailey wasn't sure of the exact location. Then they got a puncture near Banna Strand, where RIC men from Ballyheigue were buzzing like sand flies. And now a busybody sergeant named Daniel Crowley was quizzing Stack and his companions and looking unconvinced by their claim to be out motoring for pleasure.

When they finally fobbed off Crowley and replaced the wheel it was midday. They headed north to confer with a contact of Stack's before looping back towards Casement. Except at a crossroads Crowley turned up again – he had followed on his bicycle – for another round of questions. By the time they were back on the road they were still headed north, away from Casement, and it was 12.45.

. . .

The *Aud*'s bell had just chimed 1 p.m. when the lookout spotted a finger of smoke approaching from the north. Karl Spindler focused his binoculars and studied the steamer's outline. He froze. She had a long gun on the forecastle and her top mast indicated a wireless installation. Another Royal Navy vessel. Abandoning the plan to sit tight to feign engine trouble, Spindler's command crackled through the voice pipes. 'All hands on deck! Stand by to weigh anchor!'

He could guess what had happened. *Setter II*'s cheery endorsement of the *Aud*'s innocence had not convinced the watching signal stations so this bigger, faster patrol vessel was coming to investigate. It was time to run. Spindler took the wheel and aimed for the open sea. The pursuer was doing 12 knots. The *Aud* had never exceeded 11. He ordered all available hands to the stokeholds.

. . .

As the *Aud* fled, Constable Reilly and Sergeant Hearn tramped towards the next potential hide, McKenna's Fort, a rather grand title for a mound of earth and brambles. The mist had cleared, unveiling a warm afternoon sun. In the distance, cows grazed. Bees hummed. There was little else to break the silence.

Weary of investigating shrubs, Hearn dawdled on the perimeter, puffing a cigarette, and let his underling battle the blackthorn. It was 1.20 p.m. Clambering through, Reilly spotted the head and shoulders of a man hunkered about 50 yards away. Reilly paused. The fellow was possibly armed, and where were the other two?

He dashed forward, rifle aimed. 'If you move hand or foot, I'll shoot.'

The man stood up. He was tall and thin, maybe foreign. 'That's a nice way to treat an English traveller.' The accent, posh.

Reilly kept the rifle aimed. 'Have a care now.' He blew his whistle.

The man smiled. 'I'm not armed, you know.'

Hearn blundered through the shrubs and gaped at the stranger. 'What are you doing here?' he demanded.

The man was calm, equable. 'By what authority do you ask this question? Am I bound to answer you?'

'I can ask you any question I like,' said Hearn. 'What's your name?'

'Richard Morten.'

'Where do you live?'

'The Savoy, Denham, Buckinghamshire.'

'Your occupation?'

'I am an author.'

'Give me the name of some book you have written.'

'The Life of St Brendan.'

Casement hadn't missed a beat, naming an English friend and authentic address, and citing the patron saint of Kerry as a plausible book subject. But the policemen's eyes travelled down to his wet trousers and boots, coated with sand, and they kept their rifles pointed. 'I must ask you to come along to the barracks with me,' said Hearn. 'There are some other questions I must put to you.'

No heroics, no fight or flight, just an attempt to bluff his way out, then submission. The renegade knight came quietly.

Casement had waited at the fort exhausted, famished, anxious, yet with a tinge of rapture. He was back in Ireland. The skylarks brought him back to his boyhood, where their song signified spring, and the landscape of peaks and valleys was sublime. Violets and primroses carpeted the earth. For fleeting moments, he had been happy. Then he saw the policemen approach. He tried to burn documents but the matches were wet and just had time to stuff some papers in rabbit holes before the constable's challenge.

Checking the overcoats, Reilly discovered a train ticket for Berlin to Wilhelmshaven. He wasn't sure what it was but knew it wasn't Irish. The stranger denied having seen it before. They took him to the Allman family farm to ask the servant girl to identify him. Yes, she said, he was one of the men she saw that morning.

A 12-year-old boy who was passing with a pony and trap agreed to take them to Ardfert, and on the way observed the suspect rip pieces of paper and drop them behind his back. The boy retrieved them – they were parts of a code to communicate with Germany – and handed them to the police.

The folklore prophecy of a liberator mocked the dishevelled figure who rattled into Ardfert. Casement had been snared not by the Saxon foe but his own compatriots, inhabitants of the land he had idealised in 'The Dream of the Celt'. He was put on a horse-drawn sidecar and brought to the RIC barracks in the centre of Tralee, arriving just before 3 p.m.

Sergeant Hearn formally charged the suspect in connection with the cache found on Banna Strand. 'In the name of His Majesty King George the Fifth I arrest you on a charge of illegally bringing arms into the country, contrary to the Defence of the Realm Act.' The police did not know the same sovereign had made this man a knight. The gaunt, beardless suspect was an enigma.

He was so unwell the district inspector, John Kearney, put him not in a cell but the billiards room, which had a crackling fire. When the prisoner requested a doctor two hours later, Kearney assented. As a Catholic the DI had won promotion the hard way, with ferocious diligence, and he had been scrutinising this fellow until his brain hurt. There was something familiar about him.

. . .

Karl Spindler was 90 miles out in the Atlantic, steaming south, doing a mental countdown to sunset. It was 5.45 p.m., another 95 minutes before darkness cloaked the ocean.

Half-naked and coated in sweat and coal-dust, the men had shovelled until the furnaces vibrated and the chief engineer wailed that the boilers would burst, but the *Aud* reached 13 knots and outran the pursuer, the *Lord Heneage*, which dwindled to a speck. But a speck with a radio, and sunshine still lit up the ocean.

If they made it to Spain, Spindler planned to sell the weapons and convert the *Aud* into a raider to hunt Allied ships. The stuffed shirts in Berlin would see the mettle of a boy from Königswinter.

Just before 6 p.m. a lookout spotted smoke clouds to the southwest: a two-funnel steamer doing 20 knots. By 6.15 p.m. she was upon them: HMS *Bluebell*, a Royal Navy sloop bristling with deck guns and machine-guns. The previous year she had fished for corpses after Raimund Weisbach's torpedo hit the *Lusitania*. Now she raised a signal flag of command to the ship laden with a rebellion's hopes. 'Stop.'

. . .

Doctor Michael Shanahan arrived at the barracks shortly after church bells tolled the 6 p.m. Angelus. He shooed the RIC men out of the billiards room and turned to the patient. The man was jittery but coherent and had a question for the GP. Was he in sympathy with the Irish cause? Yes, said Shanahan. The patient whispered he was Sir Roger Casement and wished to send word to the Volunteers.

On his way out of the barracks, the doctor was stopped by Kearney. The district inspector read several newspapers a day and had been rummaging through an old pile, seeking a photograph, which he found, of a handsome, famous, bearded man. He showed it to the doctor, then used a piece of paper to cover the beard, and asked if it resembled the prisoner. Shanahan shook his head. But he could see the policeman knew.

Shanahan hastened through quiet streets and found some Volunteers. Sir Roger Casement was at the barracks and only lightly guarded, he said. A few determined men with pistols could spring him. The Volunteers behaved oddly and fobbed him off. He was mistaken, it was not Sir Roger, they said. Shanahan insisted, in vain, and left in fury and disbelief.

The Volunteers knew the prisoner's identity but Austin Stack, upon returning to Tralee from his thwarted mission to McKenna's Fort, had vetoed a breakout attempt. His instructions from Dublin were clear, do nothing to provoke the authorities before Sunday, and Stack was not going to imperil the rising, not even for Sir Roger. Then Stack himself and his IRB comrade Con Collins were detained – on the orders of DI Kearney, who had grown alarmed by Friday's events – and put in cells down the corridor from Casement.

At a stroke the Volunteers of Tralee, who for two years had proudly drilled and marched for Ireland's honour, were paralysed. Dr Shanahan had appealed for bold action from confused, frightened, leaderless men. Robert Monteith was isolated in a safe-house – Daniel Bailey in another – unable to help. As daylight drained from the sky, so did the opportunity to rescue Casement.

The prisoner asked for a priest, and at around 9 p.m. it was the turn of Fr Frank Ryan to lean into a fireside whisper and learn that this was Casement and that he wanted to send word to the Volunteers to call off a rising. 'Do what I ask and you will bring God's blessing on the country.' Fr Ryan opted for balance by relaying the message to the Volunteers *and* the RIC, who thanked him.

It was the day everything went wrong for the rebels, and Good Friday was not finished.

At 9.30 p.m. a car with four men – part of the team sent from Dublin to seize radio transmission equipment to communicate with the *Aud* – got lost in the dark and drove off a pier at Ballykissane, south of Tralee. Three drowned. The arms ship, in any case, had no radio, and was beyond saving. As midnight approached two destroyers joined the escort bringing the *Aud* to port, blocking any escape for Karl Spindler.

Roger Casement remained under guard, his identity still unknown to the authorities in Dublin, but his shadow play as a fugitive at an end, when the chimes of Tralee's churches ushered in Saturday 22 April.

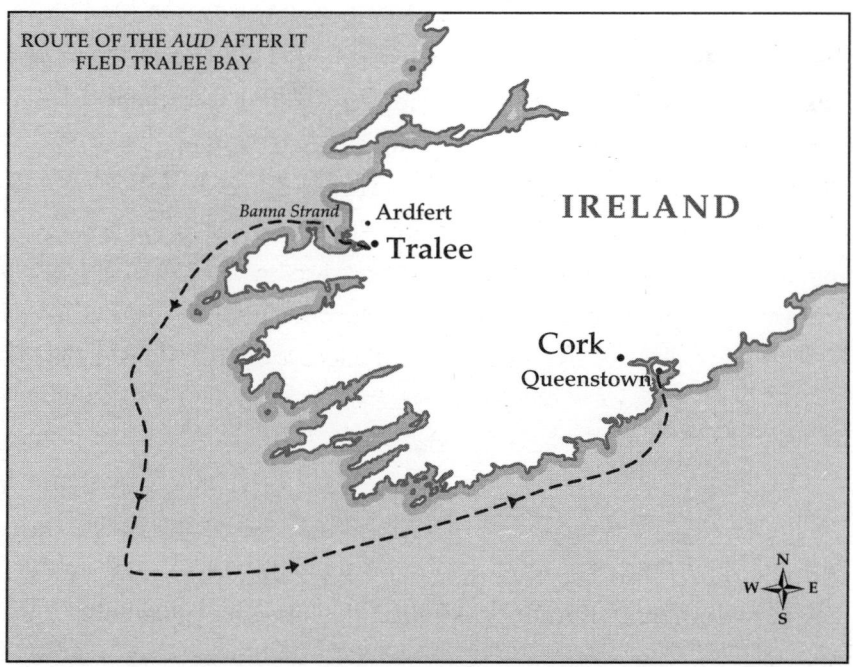

PART III

Terrible Beauty

CHAPTER SIXTEEN

Holy Saturday: The Professor

Joe Plunkett was supposed to be in bed to let the neck wound heal, but as Dublin woke to a cool, gloomy morning on Saturday 22 April he was in a car feeling every jolt and shudder from the rutted driveway of Woodtown Park.

If he had slept at all it was a miracle. News of Casement's capture had reached IRB leaders the previous evening, giving Plunkett the night to brood on his comrade's unexpected arrival and possible fate. Then he learned about the drowned radio team. Of the arms shipment there was no news, leaving hope it might somehow arrive despite Friday's disasters. But cargo or no cargo, the rising was to go ahead on Sunday afternoon – in about 32 hours.

Events in Kerry did not break the capital's bank holiday weekend torpor. Newspapers were reporting the discovery of a small boat with guns and ammunition at Banna Strand, and the arrest of a stranger of unknown nationality, nothing more. The upcoming Irish Grand National, a horse race that united all classes, occasioned more excitement.

Plunkett had left his nursing home to come to a semi-rural estate in the Dublin mountain foothills, because in the final countdown to revolt the rebels' biggest worry was not the British but the man who lived at the end of the driveway: sober, cerebral, dithering Eoin MacNeill. In the elaborate machinery of the plot, the Volunteers' chief-of-staff was a pivot around which other parts turned. It was paramount the pivot itself remain fixed, unmoving.

For the conspirators, the history professor had served his purpose by giving a sheen of respectability to the militia that marched and drilled to ensure the slippery English delivered Home Rule. As a distinguished Irish language scholar and former civil servant with a pince-nez, MacNeill was a reassuring figurehead who did not alienate moderate nationalists or panic the British. He was a radical who believed in Irish independence, yes, but reasonable. Everyone knew he preferred books to barricades.

Except now the time had come for barricades and the conspirators needed MacNeill to stay on the sidelines. The IRB plotters had thoroughly infiltrated the Volunteers but MacNeill's remaining authority could make problems unless contained.

Plunkett brought Thomas MacDonagh, a fellow conspirator and academic colleague of MacNeill, to help wrangle the professor. The car halted in front of an imposing Victorian villa that was home to MacNeill and his wife and eight children. MacNeill was 49, with a trimmed blond beard and figure kept lean from cycle commutes to and from the city. He invariably puffed on a pipe as he treated visitors to tea with a view of the city below.

MacNeill was no pacifist. He envisaged the Volunteers as leverage over the British government and the nucleus of a future Irish army. If the English tried to disarm and disband the 12,000-strong force, MacNeill was prepared to fight a guerrilla campaign of resistance. But he considered an unprovoked rebellion as a folly that would devour his precious force in futile sacrifice.

The professor knew some Volunteers were IRB members but he had not grasped the extent of infiltration. His home was remote and lacked a telephone and he preferred to dwell on Celtic antiquity rather than the possibility he was being manipulated. To avoid arguments or splitting the Volunteers, he overlooked warning signs. Earlier that week the 'Castle document' had convinced him the British were planning to round up nationalists.

But then on Thursday 20 April his deputy, Bulmer Hobson, had discovered evidence that a rising was planned. Hobson had long suspected it and kept sniffing till he found proof. A furious MacNeill confronted the conspirators and threatened to upset their plans.

So on Friday the IRB did two things. It kidnapped Hobson, depriving MacNeill of his shrewdest consigliere. And it told MacNeill a German arms shipment was imminent and would trigger a real British crackdown. MacNeill, cornered, accepted the logic: to survive, the Volunteers would need to resist.

But the conspirators worried the professor might yet meddle. What mattered was that he should not interfere with the Volunteer manoeuvres on Sunday, which were the cover for mobilisation. So Plunkett and MacDonagh had trekked to his estate to make sure the chief-of-staff was safely contained.

Sipping tea as rain clouds menaced the city below, Plunkett had a sweetener for the conversation: according to his father, the Pope had sent blessings to the Irish Volunteers and in particular to their chief-of-staff. The precise hotchpotch of lies and half-truths that followed remains unclear, but by the time the visitors drained their tea and trundled back to the waking city they were confident the professor would remain quiescent. All the rebels had to do was keep him that way until the next day when the Volunteers deployed, and then it no longer mattered what Eoin MacNeill said or did.

. . .

'All hands to quarters. Ready with the fuses and incendiary bombs. Stand by to run up ensign.'

It was 9.25 a.m. and Karl Spindler was preparing the *Aud*'s final act as it approached Queenstown harbour.

The crew had spent the night burning documents and disabling equipment as they were escorted to this British naval hub on Ireland's southern coast. The British could not be sure the *Aud* was the arms ship until she berthed and was searched, but Spindler was not going to gift his ship and her cargo to the enemy.

He slowed to a crawl as they entered a harbour brimming with Royal Navy vessels. 'All ready?' 'All ready,' came the reply from the engine room. 'Hard a-starboard!' The engine-room telegraph clanged three times.

The German naval ensign was hoisted and the crew flung their Norwegian jackets overboard, revealing German uniforms. A muffled explosion deep within the *Aud*'s belly showered deck planking and splinters into the air. Flames erupted from the holds and water roared into a 15-foot gash in the stern. The ship began to list.

'All hands to the boats!' cried Spindler.

The men clambered into two lifeboats and the skipper counted: 21 men. One missing. A shout from the burning deck. 'Captain, I have just saved the gramophone!' A stoker, sprinting through the smoke with a big box under his arm.

The precise fate of the mongrel Hector is unclear, but he did not survive. The lifeboats pulled away as more explosions shuddered through the ship. It sank stern first. Her crew watched in silence as the bow rose and pointed at the sky before sliding beneath the water with a loud hiss.

A flotilla of British marines closed in to take the crew prisoner while beneath them the thousands of boxes with rifles, machine-guns and bombs meant for Ireland's revolution swirled through 15 fathoms of clear blue water and silently came to rest on a seafloor of sand and shingle.

. . .

District Inspector John Kearney nodded it was time and the little procession filed out of the barracks into Tralee high street for the short walk to the station and the 10.30 a.m. train. Sergeant James Butler led two constables and the prisoner. He was not handcuffed but onlookers could see the tall, gaunt figure in a grubby suit was a captive. Several times he slipped in the mud.

The town swarmed with RIC men and soldiers – a hundred additional troops had arrived overnight – to hunt the two suspects from the dinghy that remained at large. Of the Volunteers there was no sign.

The previous night Kearney had guessed the prisoner's identity but took pity and invited him to supper in his family's private quarters in the barracks. The policeman's wife cooked a steak while Casement played with the children, then by a fire the men discussed Irish history and the war. The guest left his hosts a pocket watch as a memento. And to show no hard feelings, or perhaps it was the act of a lonely man desperate to connect, he also gifted his captors his oak walking stick.

The police were so confident, or complacent, only Sergeant Butler boarded the train with the prisoner. En route they heard that two men had driven into the sea and drowned. Casement assumed it was Monteith and Bailey. 'It was on my account they were there,' he sobbed. 'They were two good Irishmen.'

As the train chugged through Ireland's flat, rain-soaked midlands the prisoner's identity began to leak out. 'The authorities believe his capture is of great importance,' said an article poised to roll off the *Kerry Evening Post* presses. 'A rumour is around that he is no less a personage than Sir Roger Casement.'

The authorities in Dublin had known since morning and notified Whitehall. When the train pulled into Dublin's Kingsbridge station at 5.30 p.m., the air scented with hops and barley from the nearby

Guinness brewery, six constables were waiting. A fateful decision had been made. The renegade knight would not be tried in Dublin. He was being summoned across the Irish Sea, as if drawn by a gravitational pull, to face judgement in London.

. . .

From his window overlooking Dublin Castle's cobbled yard Sir Matthew Nathan could see the statue of Lady Justice with her scales – her back turned to the city, as nationalists loved to point out – while he weighed his options. The lunatic traitor Casement was to be packed off to England, well and good, but what about the other scoundrels?

It was supposed to be a sleepy Saturday yet startling reports kept landing on the desk of the under-secretary for Ireland. A suspect who turned out to be Casement, a car with drowned men, a disguised German ship scuttling itself, all apparently connected – and the Volunteers planning a march through Dublin the next day.

Sir Matthew possessed a luxuriant moustache and abundant self-belief, which he needed this afternoon because the chief secretary, Augustine Birrell, and Major-General Friend, the army chief, were in London, leaving him to mind the shop. The viceroy, Lord Wimborne, would need to be informed and then, as ever, ignored. Sir Matthew had little interest in the counsel of excitable aristocrats. He had served across the empire and won promotion on the basis of cool, sensible judgement.

In other eras the Castle had responded to trouble by planting ringleaders' heads on spikes, but Sir Matthew knew that just produced martyrs and rebel ballads for another generation of trouble. His duty was to keep Ireland calm, and Irish men enlisting, until the war ended. So he had tolerated the Sinn Féiners because arrests could trigger, as opposed to avert, an insurrection.

But the telegrams from Tralee and Queenstown added up to a crisis that evidently required some form of action. Sir Matthew's pen hovered over a blank page. His analysis and recommendations needed to be in the courier's bag and on the next mail boat to Holyhead.

Had the scales abruptly tilted towards sweeping up the extremists? Tom Clarke, Patrick Pearse and dozens more – the Castle had files on them all. Now with evidence that they were in cahoots with Germany, what better time to strike?

On the other hand, and Sir Matthew always evaluated the other hand, perhaps it was better to gather more intelligence so the police and army could prepare targeted raids that caused the least political damage. There was surely time. Whatever the rogues were planning had evidently fallen apart. They had lost not only the arms ship but Casement, who seemed key to the whole business.

In fading afternoon light the under-secretary's pen skimmed across the page, giving his verdict to London. The security forces should raid sites where the Sinn Féiners made and stored weapons – Joe Plunkett's Larkfield estate was one of them – but first obtain more information. There was no need for hasty scramble. 'I see no indication of a rising,' he wrote.

. . .

Lamps and headlights glowed from the bicycles and cars that worked their way through the deepening dusk to 53 Rathgar Road, summoned by the fury of a man betrayed. Eoin MacNeill had discovered everything – the arms ship sunk, his deputy kidnapped, the Castle document fake – and convoked this emergency gathering to process the fact that some of his supposed comrades had been lying, lying, lying.

After Plunkett and MacDonagh left that morning, the professor had spent a pleasant afternoon at home discussing the ancient high kings of Ireland with an archaeologist friend until 6.15 p.m., when three genuine comrades, Volunteers who had discovered the truth, arrived with disclosures about the scuttled cargo, Bulmer Hobson and the doctored Castle document.

Like a startled bat the Volunteer chief-of-staff swooped from his woodland estate to the home of a friend in Rathgar, which had a telephone and was close to the city, to consult supporters. Now cars filled the street, bicycles lay in the garden and the visitors huddled while MacNeill held court like King Lear, belatedly realising he had been played for a fool.

The plotters on the Volunteer committee had smiled and saluted him, nodded at his advice, relayed his orders, all but clicked their heels, and it was all a show, a puppet show, with him dangling on their strings. They had been undercutting his instructions, whispering their own commands, winking at confederates.

MacNeill felt that Plunkett in particular had been duplicitous. So did Bulmer Hobson, who later observed: 'Most of us were hoping to outwit the common enemy but Joe Plunkett devoted his talents to outwitting his friends.' For MacNeill, the subterfuge could lead only to catastrophe – a doomed rebellion that the British would probably *welcome* as an excuse to crush the Volunteers. Adding to the sting, he assumed Casement, his old friend, was part of the plot. Why else would he have come?

Plunkett and MacDonagh briefly joined the summit at Rathgar Road to plead their case – deceit had been unfortunate but necessary – and to find out what MacNeill intended to do. He told them: he was going to dispatch an order to Volunteer commanders cancelling the next day's manoeuvres, which he now fully understood were cover for a rising. 'I have been grossly deceived all along,' he said.

Plunkett left, his mind reeling. Losing the arms ship meant insufficient rifles, losing MacNeill could mean insufficient men. The rising risked unravelling without a shot fired. Should it go ahead, be postponed, cancelled? Returning to the city, the trams, theatres and tourists of Sackville Street carried on, just another Saturday evening, oblivious to the rebel countdown.

The normality was encouraging. Perhaps the thing was salvageable. Perhaps surprise was still on their side. Despite discovering the arms ship, the British were not rounding up suspects, at least not yet.

MacNeill could send his order but he did not know which Volunteer commanders were part of the conspiracy. Might the professor, after all, be contained? For Plunkett and the other conspirators it would be a night of frantic messages and meetings. All was flux, their plans oozing out as if from a shattered egg.

There was no time to think of Roger Casement, who passed within a mile of them, a prisoner of the Crown.

. . .

The waiting constables had escorted Casement from the train station to Arbour Hill, a military barracks, where he was roughly handled, then he was driven through the city centre eight miles south to Kingstown.

It was the harbour town of his birth, 51 years earlier, a child of wandering parents who himself became a wanderer, an imperial consul with no home or settled identity until Congo's tragedy put him on a winding path through empires and dreams of liberation, only to find himself back in the salt air of Kingstown.

At 8.55 p.m. the whistle blew and RMS *Ulster* pulled away from the pier, bearing 223 mail bags and 120 passengers. They were unaware of Casement's identity but a steward, noting the military escort, gifted the prisoner cigarettes and whispers of encouragement. The mail boat throbbed past the Howth peninsula, where two years earlier the *Asgard* had landed rifles for the Volunteers, and by 9.24 p.m. was past the shallow sandbanks. The boat picked up speed, twin propellers trailing foam in a dark, smooth sea. Lights twinkling along the arc of Dublin Bay grew fainter and vanished into blackness.

Approximately an hour later the phone on Basil Thomson's desk rang. The assistant commissioner of the Metropolitan Police was doing a night shift at Scotland Yard in case of a Zeppelin raid, but the skies were empty and London, draped in blackout, was silent and still. Faint glimmers hinted at the Thames flowing beneath his window. Thomson picked up the phone.

'Is that you, BT?' The clipped staccato of a familiar voice.

'Do you know,' Captain Reginald Hall continued, 'who it was that landed in that canvas boat?'

Thomson had seen the reports of an unnamed suspect. 'No, do you?'

'I do. It was that blighter Casement.' Currently en route, express delivery. The interrogation would be at Scotland Yard at 10 a.m.

Thomson replaced the receiver and surely smiled. They had him.

. . .

The clocks had struck midnight, ushering in Easter Sunday, when Eoin MacNeill left the gathering at Rathgar Road, wheeled a bicycle out of the gate and swung onto the saddle. He turned left and pedalled towards the city.

For the professor it was a simple equation: to save the Volunteers, cancel the mobilisation. Messengers were bearing his handwritten order to commanders across the country. Some would obey, but those stricken with rebellion fever, he knew, would go ahead and draw British wrath on the entire organisation.

But a message to *all* the Volunteers, an edict promulgated to the rank-and-file and impossible to miss, could reassert his authority and abort the madness. The fizzing fuse had almost reached the barrel – mobilisation would begin later that morning. His deceivers believed, hoped, they had run down the clock, that he was too late, a historian out of time.

MacNeill pedalled on, over the canal and through Portobello, skirted Iveagh Gardens and Trinity College, pushed into the city centre, past pubs with the night's rearguard of drinkers, over the tide-swollen Liffey, then turned onto Middle Abbey street, and stopped. To save money the city had dimmed street lamps, but it was impossible to miss the bustle of men and vans outside Independent House, home to one of Ireland's bestselling newspapers, the *Sunday Independent*. Within hours it would be on sale in every village and town.

MacNeill presented a note to the young duty editor, Fred Cogley, and requested immediate publication, stressing it was a matter of the gravest necessity. Cogley hesitated. The note would make for dramatic news but it was a decision for his boss, who was absent, and the printing presses were already thundering with early editions. So, no.

The professor gazed at the newsman. For too long he had failed to impose his will on younger men. In this most pivotal moment of his life, he was not going to back down.

As the sun rose on Easter Sunday, 23 April, newsagents across Ireland snipped twined bundles and placed the *Sunday Independent* on racks. The headline of the lead news item came, unusually, with an exclamation mark. 'NO PARADES!' it declared. 'IRISH VOLUNTEER MARCHES CANCELLED. A SUDDEN ORDER.'

The professor's message ran below the article. 'Owing to the very critical position, all orders given to Irish Volunteers ... are hereby rescinded, and no parades, marches, or other movements of Irish Volunteers will take place. Each individual Volunteer will obey this order strictly in every particular.' It was signed Eoin MacNeill, chief of staff, Irish Volunteers.

Casement, inset, and members of the doomed radio team, depicted in a contemporary mural in Belfast.

CHAPTER SEVENTEEN

Easter Sunday: This Festering Sore

Six hours after starting its run through Welsh and English countryside the Irish mail train slowed and shuddered to a halt under the cavernous iron roof of Euston station at 6.10 a.m. Carriage doors swung open and the platform filled with voices, bags and trollies. Even at this early hour other platforms swarmed with families coming to London for parks, museums and shows, or escaping it for the seaside.

Stalls sold chocolate eggs, hot cross buns scented the air, and red and white roses sprouted from caps and lapels because this Easter Sunday, 23 April, coincided with St George's Day, when England celebrated the slaying of a dragon. The bagging of its most notorious traitor elicited no cheers because Roger Casement's arrest and arrival in London remained secret.

He passed from the custody of an army major to a burly Scotland Yard inspector, Joseph Sandercock, who escorted him through the throngs, an anonymous figure in a suit sticky with two-day-old Atlantic brine.

Two years earlier, on 8 May 1914, Casement had stridden through the same concourse. It was the day he had testified at Royal Commission House about Foreign Office reforms, then met friends, including Eoin MacNeill, to discuss buying rifles for the Volunteers. Now the 'dark beauty' that had so enchanted men and women was hollowed and haggard. Without the beard Casement looked gawky, a crumpled Samson.

Sandercock led the prisoner through the Great Hall out into a cool, sunny morning and a waiting car. Zipping through streets emptied of traffic by the holiday weekend, Casement glimpsed the city he once knew so well. Some changes – khaki uniforms, recruiting posters, dirigibles – would have been apparent; others, like women doing men's jobs, wearing trousers, smoking, he could only imagine. The parks, and their riots of daffodils and swallows back from Africa, he could not see.

Big Ben still towered over Whitehall but instead of his old stomping ground at the Foreign Office he was delivered to the red-brick fortress on the other side of the road, Scotland Yard. They gave him breakfast, which afforded a chance to compose his thoughts. Six frenetic weeks had vaulted him from a Munich sanatorium to the enemy citadel while God-knew-what was unfolding in Ireland. Was an insurrection underway, imminent, postponed? He was agitated and dazed but clung to one resolve: call off the rising. Shortly before 10 o'clock he was summoned.

It was an agreeable walk from the Admiralty to Basil Thomson's office and Reginald Hall had done it many times, but seldom with such relish. The fugitive knight, snared at last. A day, surely, for Willoughby to fetch the rum.

Legally the Admiralty could not arrest or charge suspects so the director of naval intelligence had formed a partnership with Thomson, who headed Scotland Yard's Criminal Investigation Department, CID, which encompassed the Special Branch. Hall would supply suspects' names and the assistant commissioner supply detectives to scoop them up, then together they would interrogate them.

Hall did not begrudge BT's flamboyance. The former colonial administrator, with his tales of cannibals and pirates in the South Seas, and disregard for Whitehall punctilio, was a kindred spirit. The natives in Tonga, after all, had called him *Koe tangata Fakahinohino*, Expounder of the Dark Ways of Civilised Man.

For 18 months they had hunted Casement. The *Sayonara* expedition did not flush him out but they had tracked his efforts to recruit civilian internees and prisoners-of-war in Germany, intercepted his letters to England and Ireland and eavesdropped on communications between New York and Berlin. They had also reports from Christiania about his unnatural proclivities.

Some enemies Hall could respect, such as the audacious Captain Rintelen. Casement was another category. A Boche by choice, a traitor and a pervert who tried to induce – perhaps the better word was 'seduce' – others into stabbing Britain in the back while loyal Irishmen and Englishmen were serving and dying. The task now was to extract as much information as possible before consigning him to the scaffold.

There was a deceptive congeniality to Thomson's office, a big, carpeted room with a fireplace, armchair and large windows overlooking Victoria Embankment. An oak-framed roll of honour listed convicts who had swapped prison for the trenches and died with honour, and included a quote from Pericles. 'Even those who come short in other ways may redeem themselves by fighting bravely for their country; they may blot out the evil with the good.'

Soft furnishings, a view of the Thames, a hint of absolution – it was a stage for confession, but few who sat in the armchair were given the option of washing away sins.

Hall and Thomson were joined by Major Frank Hall, an officer with the army intelligence agency MI5, and a clerk to take notes. Casement entered, and they surveyed their catch. 'Tall and thin, and rather cadaverous, with thick black hair turning grey and a long pointed chin,' Thomson later wrote. 'He had thin nervous hands, mahogany coloured from long tropical service; his forehead was much wrinkled, his complexion deeply sunburnt.'

Casement sat in the armchair and they began. The tone was courteous, gentlemanly.

'We were waiting for you, Sir Roger,' said Blinker.

Thomson, who took the lead in interrogations, sought to establish the basics for the record. 'What is your name?'

'You know it already,' the prisoner replied.

The assistant commissioner persisted. 'Who are you?'

'Officially, I am Sir Roger Casement.'

'There may be people impersonating Sir Roger Casement.'

'I don't think there are many people who would care to impersonate me,' came the wry reply.

Anything Casement said could be used in evidence, Thomson warned. 'You are not charged at present but it is certain that you will be.' He displayed the train ticket from Berlin to Wilhelmshaven found in the overcoat at McKenna's Fort. 'Is that your property?'

'No, it is not my property.'

Thomson showed the code – retrieved by the young boy near the fort – for communicating with Germany. 'Have you seen that?'

'Yes, I have seen it.' Casement could see, in fact, that they could link him to the boat and pistols at Banna Strand, and link those to Germany. Not that he had any intention of denying his mission to Germany.

'Do you realise, sir,' Blinker interjected, 'that you have committed treason of the most heinous kind?'

'Yes, I do. I have committed what you call treason over and over again,' said Casement. 'I am not endeavouring to shield myself at all. I face all the consequences. All I ask you is to believe I have done nothing dishonourable. To you all I am of course is a desperate villain. I never want to hurt your country as England, but to help Ireland. I am a rebel.' He meant every word, but to the inquisitors it came across as histrionic, theatrical.

The questioning continued, still polite, cordial, but the unspoken purpose was clear: they meant to kill him.

Thomson asked about the Irish Brigade, funding sources, German attitudes to Ireland, the submarine journey. Taking care to not name or incriminate anyone else, Casement answered some questions and defended his actions as those of an Irish patriot. Growing more animated, he rose from the armchair and perched on the edge of Thomson's desk.

To encourage the prisoner's flow the clerk was for a time dismissed, leaving sections of the interrogation unrecorded in the notes, but recollections later by Thomson and Casement filled some gaps.

Casement said he had done nothing treacherous to his homeland, which was not England. 'I have committed perhaps many follies in endeavouring to help my country according to what I thought was best, and in this last act of mine in going back to Ireland I came with my eyes wide open, knowing exactly what was I was going to do, knowing that you were bound to catch me. Knowing all the circumstances, I came from a sense of duty.'

And there Casement sprang his surprise: he had come not to lead but to *stop* the rising, he said. Meagre German aid condemned it to futile bloodshed and failure so he had come to tell his comrades to call it off. And he still wished to do so. Let me send a message, said Casement. Let me make a public appeal to the plotters: stand down.

It was a dumbfounding assertion. Casement had loomed as the nefarious force binding Irish radicals to German conniving. Now he was telling his inquisitors it was the reverse. And offering to douse whatever flames might be kindling in Ireland.

The security chiefs digested this bewildering twist. Casement repeated the offer, imploring.

Eventually, Reginald Hall gave the answer. No. No message, no public appeal. Then he delivered his own surprise. He did not want Casement, or anyone else, to avert the rebellion.

'No, better let this festering sore come to a head.'

Ten words – not recorded by the clerk, but recalled by Casement, for whom the meaning was limpid. Rather than avert rebellion, allow it. Allow Ireland's extremists to expose themselves like a noxious ulcer that could then be cut out. An insurrection would end the tip-toeing around Irish sensibilities and justify clear, firm action.

There is no document proving Hall wanted the rising to go ahead to justify the repression he thought necessary, but the evidence points that way. In addition to Casement's recollection, there is context. The intelligence chief routinely withheld information from political masters and in the case of Ireland left the authorities unclear about the rebel threat. 'Hall . . . was determined to act as he saw fit, even to the extent of apparent distortion of evidence to force Dublin Castle into repressive action against the separatist movement,' one scholar concluded.

There was an *Alice in Wonderland* quality to the scene in Scotland Yard: an Irish rebel who did not want rebellion was being interrogated by British officials who did want rebellion, and both sides mistakenly believing the rebel had sway over his comrades.

After Casement declined to identify ringleaders – 'Under no circumstances am I going to hurt any Irishman, not a hair of his head' – questioning ended for the day, to resume the next. Before the prisoner was led out, Thomson told him the charge would probably be high treason.

Casement seemed relieved. 'I hope so.'

. . .

'What's that?' James Connolly roared, rising to his feet and grabbing the newspaper. His eyes locked on Eoin MacNeill's announcement in the *Sunday Independent*. He paled.

Moments earlier the trade union leader had been content, breakfasting with comrades in Liberty Hall, his Irish Citizen Army headquarters by the Liffey. Despite the calamities in Kerry and the loss of the arms ship the 300-strong workers' militia still planned in a few hours to march out and join the Volunteers in seizing Dublin. ICA men with bandoliers and rifles filled narrow, dimly lit passageways, the air thick with expectation. Gelignite stolen from a quarry supplemented their home-made bombs. Connolly had been quietly singing to himself:

*'We've another saviour now,
That saviour is the sword.'*

Then a female aide entered with a copy of the newspaper. 'Look, Mr Connolly, the *Independent* says "no manoeuvres today".'

Connolly stared at MacNeill's announcement. 'All orders given to Irish Volunteers are hereby rescinded . . .' It was inconceivable, yet the text was there in black and white, filling half a column, and being read across the country. A rebellion that hinged on secrecy, cancelled in the press. Was this some devil's comedy?

News of the countermand would swiftly spread among the 12,000 Volunteers. The British, surely, would grasp what had been afoot and come swooping. The word 'treachery' ricocheted around Liberty Hall. Some rebels vowed to shoot MacNeill. Others slumped, speechless.

As Casement's interrogation unfolded in London, the seven lead conspirators held an emergency conclave at Liberty Hall. With reports streaming in about Volunteer units dispersing in confusion, they faced an agonising debacle.

For all the curses directed at Eoin MacNeill, the plan for action outside Dublin had always been shaky. Orders for deployments overlooked the IRB's patchy influence and the meagre weapons. Many Volunteers by now had been told, or guessed, the real purpose of the manoeuvres but others remained oblivious and might have baulked at being thrown into a fight.

While Liberty Hall's sentries kept a lookout for a possible British raid, the rebel leaders debated. Rationally, all hope of military success had evaporated. They lacked men, weapons, public support and appeared to have lost the advantage of surprise. Joe Plunkett's finely tuned military plan lay broken and splintered. To proceed verged on suicide.

Yet they could not turn back. It was their purpose, an act of faith. Perhaps there would be miracles, perhaps despite all the confusion the men would mobilise, the people would rise and the Germans would come. And if not, if the rising was crushed, it would at least salvage Ireland's honour. Centuries of occupation, yet a nation still. It was the resolve of fanatics or, a kinder word, visionaries.

The only question was timing. Tom Clarke favoured striking that afternoon, per the original plan. The others outvoted him, citing too much disarray. They sent an immediate order to all commanders *confirming* MacNeill's countermand, to avert any half-cocked eruptions that day, and prepared a second order, to be dispatched that night, ordering units to mobilise at midday the next day, Easter Monday. In the basement of Liberty Hall rickety flatbed presses started to print copies of the proclamation of independence.

Shortly after 1 p.m. the conspirators dispersed across a city stubbornly heedless of their dramas. Sprays of Easter lilies adorned the white linen and gleaming candelabra of church altars. Men in bowler hats and women in long skirts strolled across Stephen's Green. Passengers in open-deck trams felt the sun's rays. The anti-climax and uncertainty brought Tom Clarke close to tears.

Joe Plunkett returned to his nursing home, a bachelor still. He was supposed to have married Grace Gifford that morning but cancelled it to attend to the conspiracy's multiple crises. Instead of placing a ring on her finger he sent an aide to give her a pistol and cash for emergencies. Grace had zingy one-liners for most occasions but probably not that one.

Joe had devoted his life to poetry and cheating a raspy, wheezing death, then discovered revolution, and love, but the conspiracy's unravelling had left no time for nuptials. Within hours – unless the British arrested him first – he would be gripping a rifle.

At 9 p.m. he wrote a letter to Grace urging her to trust in providence and the possibility they still might have a future. He also wrote a testament. It was concise, just a few lines. 'Will of Joseph Mary (Patrick) Plunkett made this day April 23rd 1916. I give and bequeath everything of which I am possessed or may become possessed to Grace Evelyn (Mary Vandeleur) Gifford.'

He signed it and slipped it into his pocket.

. . .

'I want between sixty and a hundred of the ringleaders arrested tonight,' Lord Wimborne declared to his visitors. He had long wanted the troublemakers rounded up and now there was eminent justification. No more dallying, tonight!

It was 10 p.m., which left enough time to organise raids before dawn, and Sir Ivor Churchill Guest, the 1st Viscount Wimborne and Lord Lieutenant of Ireland, believed it was also time to assert his authority.

Since Wimborne was posted to Ireland the chief secretary, Augustine Birrell, and under-secretary, Sir Matthew Nathan, had kept him on a tight leash while allowing the Sinn Féiners to roam free. Well, no more. The viceroy had summoned Nathan and security chiefs to the drawing room of the viceregal lodge, his residence in Phoenix Park, to demand action.

Previous viceroys had been content to host receptions and act as ceremonial adornments but Wimborne, with Churchillian energy and pugnacity, fancied some actual ruling and chafed at constraints on him imposed by Birrell and Nathan. Cousin Winston would never have stood for it.

The weekend's developments, however, had steeled Wimborne's impulse for swoops on Liberty Hall and other Sinn Féiner nests. They had been consorting with the enemy, what more was needed? The leaders could be jailed before sunrise.

Sir Matthew, as ever, poked a hole in viceregal reasoning. 'On what charge? To hold them on a charge of "hostile association" would need the agreement of the Home Secretary.'

'They could be kept on remand,' said Wimborne. 'Anyway, I'll sign the warrants and accept full responsibility.'

The under-secretary demurred. Earlier that day he had learned of the gelignite theft, and received from Tralee a report detailing the confession of the fugitive Daniel Bailey, who had been captured and disclosed details of Casement's submarine journey to Ireland, and plans for a rising. On the other hand Eoin MacNeill had cancelled the Volunteers' mobilisation, which seemed to confirm the rising was off, voiding need for any intemperate response.

Army commanders cited another reason for caution: to raid Liberty Hall it would be advisable to have artillery, and the nearest guns were 80 miles away. After Monday, it was also pointed out, there would be fewer holidaymakers in the city.

Punctured by Nathan's incisions, the viceroy's resolve began to deflate. They debated past midnight and in the end agreed to joint military-police pre-dawn round-ups – later in the week. Wimborne had to admit the logic. MacNeill's announcement showed the Volunteers' tails were between their legs. And their leader Casement was safely locked up in London. The raids could wait a few days.

. . .

While Dublin slept through the first hours of Easter Monday, 24 April, serene, the inmate registered as Mr C.R. spent his first night behind the brick walls of Brixton Prison in south London. The identity of Reginald Hall's trophy catch was to remain secret, for now, even to warders.

Casement had another secret – a concealed vial of curare, a poison, for escape to another realm. He did not take it. Before leaving Germany he had tortured himself with the idea that the English would charge him with 'something baser' than high treason. *'I go to a show trial, to be wounded in my honour; to be defamed and degraded.'*

Yet the interrogators had asked nothing about his private affairs and indicated he would be tried for treason. Amid the cinders of all his hopes and plans, he might at least march to the gallows with dignity, and there was solace.

CHAPTER EIGHTEEN
———

Easter Monday: Left Turn, Charge

Joe Plunkett sat on the edge of the bed while a nurse bandaged his throat. He closed his eyes. The pain came and went in waves, but the fatigue loitered. Finally the big day, and him in a nursing home in his pyjamas, not sure he could stand.

Michael Collins prowled the room. The former post office clerk from Cork with the bone-crushing handshake had become Joe's bodyguard and aide-de-camp, and on the basis of the chief's current state those duties included helping him to dress. Another Volunteer also hovered, barely able to disguise his shock at Plunkett's condition.

A matron entered and implored her patient to stay in bed, but Plunkett smiled and waved her aside. The world saw a frail poet with poor eyesight but somewhere within that carbuncled body resided an extraordinary will. The conspiracy was to blaze into open revolt at midday and Plunkett was not going to miss it.

Flamboyance had not deserted him. Plunkett covered the bandage with a silk scarf and with Collins's help donned a green tunic with gold braid and leather riding boots with spurs. He completed the outfit with bangles, large rings and a sabre. Whatever happened, he was going to look fabulous.

Plunkett hobbled down the stairs and propped himself between his two comrades in the back of a cab. They passed slum tenements, then the elegant shops and hotels of Sackville Street. It was a bank holiday; Dubliners were having a lie-in, soaking up the sunshine or heading for the Grand National at the Fairyhouse racecourse outside the city.

The Great War was raging through a third year – the Germans were encountering stubborn French resistance in the wastelands of Verdun and battling the Canadians and British for possession of craters at Ypres; the Russians were launching fresh offensives in the east while the Turks were grinding down a British-Indian garrison besieged at Kut-al-Amara; a litany of bloodbaths yet neither side able to break the wider deadlock. Irishmen in British uniforms were dying every day but for Ireland the carnage felt distant. It had no air raids or blackouts or conscription. The only soldiers on the capital's main thoroughfare this morning were off duty, sauntering amid the women promenading in their finery.

The cab turned onto Eden Quay and dropped Plunkett and his escorts at Liberty Hall. Inside, seated amid piles of freshly printed proclamations, the leaders were receiving grim tidings. Only a fraction of the Volunteers were turning up at designated muster points. Confusion over Eoin MacNeill's countermand had rolled a giant bowling ball through the ranks. Many units had not received the mobilisation order – a countermand of MacNeill's countermand – issued the previous night. The military plan that Plunkett had spent two years developing verged on collapse.

Well, they were still going ahead. The targets to be seized remained the same and commanders would have to make do with what they had. James Connolly, who had developed an affection for Plunkett since their wordy duel three months earlier, projected a cheerful fatalism. 'We are going out to be slaughtered,' he announced.

A comrade looked crestfallen. Was there no hope? 'None whatever.' For the socialist, any revolution was better than no revolution, and he had been given the honour of being the overall military commander in Dublin.

Connolly's authority was unquestioned, but with his pot-belly, bandy legs and disorderly moustache he did not look like a general, and the gathering outside Liberty Hall at 11.30 a.m. did not look like an army. About 250 mostly boys and men with a jumble of pistols, rifles, shotguns and pikes – six-foot poles with bayonets – that resembled Tudor halberds. Plunkett's cavalry-themed attire added its own effect. 'Ludendorff,' a voice whispered, making a mocking comparison to the Prussian general. 'Dressed to death,' came a murmured reply.

A sister of Patrick Pearse caused a scene with a last-minute appeal to her brother: 'Come home, Pat, and leave all this foolishness.' The other women present, mostly ICA members, had come to fight.

At 11.50 a.m. Connolly's voice rang out. 'Left turn! Quick march!' A first section of rebels marched down the quay, crossed the bridge and split into smaller groups bound for landmarks on the southern side of the river. Eight minutes later another command from Connolly propelled the remaining 150 rebels into motion. Four-abreast, they marched up Lower Abbey Street, tailed by two horse-drawn carts piled high with homemade bombs, food, axes, pick-axes and crowbars. A group of urchins jeered. Other onlookers shrugged, assuming the oddball caravan was another Volunteer route march.

They turned onto Sackville Street and headed up the broad boulevard, the spectacle drawing grins from British officers lounging outside the Metropole Hotel. The column halted when it drew abreast of the General Post Office, its Palladian bulk surmounted by the figures of Hibernia, Mercury and Fidelity.

There was a pause. Two Volunteers linked arms around Plunkett to keep him from being knocked over in what was about to happen. The roar from Connolly was as much a cry of desperation and defiance as a command. 'Left turn, charge!'

The rebels broke formation and swept towards the edifice with cheers and whoops, a human tide crashing through the main entrance and into the marbled hall. Staff and customers froze, bewildered. An English officer who had been writing a telegram was seized and trussed up.

'Everybody out!' shouted Connolly. A mass scramble for the exit left the rebels in command of the building. Connolly surveyed the new rebel headquarters. 'Smash the windows and barricade them.'

Joe Plunkett leaned on a counter and smiled. The rising had begun.

As other rebel units attempted to seize landmarks around the capital it fell to Patrick Pearse to proclaim the republic. Of the document's seven signatories, he was designated president of the provisional government and commander-in-chief of its army. Tall and grave, Pearse looked the part, and his oratory could enthral.

Emerging from the GPO portico and its fluted Ionic columns, he read the document to an audience of quizzical onlookers. 'Irishmen and Irish women, in the name of God and of the dead generations from which she receives her old tradition of nationhood, Ireland, through us, summons her children to her flag and strikes for her freedom,' he began.

Citing help from 'gallant allies in Europe', he proclaimed a republic that was a 'sovereign independent state' and guaranteed 'religious and civil liberty, equal rights and opportunities to all its citizens'. The provisional authorities would 'cherish all children of the nation equally' – a reference to unionists – and step aside once elections established a new government.

The proclamation was a distillation of nationalist doctrine, concise, potent, eloquent, and it flopped. Pearse was addressing not the converted, as at Jeremiah O'Donovan Rossa's funeral, but a random group of Dubliners. 'The response was chilling,' a witness later wrote. 'A few thin, perfunctory cheers, no direct hostility just then; but no enthusiasm whatever.' It was, another observer wrote, the antithesis of the storming of the Bastille. 'They were posing as the saviours of their country... and doomed by the verdict of their own countrymen.'

That was a sweeping extrapolation based on a few onlookers, but there was no denying the lack of mandate. The rising was a renunciation not only of British rule but the wishes of most Irish people. Ireland was no powder keg of resentment. Outside the tiny rebel ranks there was no chafing at oppression or desire to expel the occupier or even agreement there was an occupier. The Irish were different from the English, and the English had inflicted grievous wrongs over the centuries, but that was history.

Modern Ireland encompassed Sackville Street's bronze statue of Daniel O'Connell, who won Catholic emancipation, and the granite column honouring Horatio Nelson, Britain's naval hero. Many Irish nationalists took pride in the achievements of Irish soldiers and administrators who helped build the empire, and the tens of thousands now fighting to defend it.

Ulster's unionists were also Irish and they did not want Home Rule let alone independence, and were prepared to fight to avert it. The rebels elided this reality by insisting the unionists would see sense and that the real foe was England.

The rebels lacked even the support of fellow separatists such as Arthur Griffith, the leader of Sinn Féin, and many fellow members of the Irish Volunteers and Irish Republican Brotherhood, who favoured other means to obtain independence. They were a minority within a minority, a junta. In the absence of support from the living nation, they claimed to represent one that used to exist, and might again.

As poets and playwrights they lacked military expertise but understood the power of words and symbols. Pearse faced a tough crowd, but the proclamation was a lucid evocation of national struggle. Numerology imbued the number of signatories – seven – with mystical resonance. It was Easter, the Christian calendar's week of sacrifice, resurrection and renewal. And they had the General Post Office, a granite stage in the heart of the capital.

After the proclamation, people on Sackville Street spotted figures moving on the GPO's roof. A dark, nondescript blob rose jerkily to the top of a flagpole only to flap down listlessly in the warm midday air. 'A few half-hearted, half-mystified cheers greeted its appearance,' wrote one chronicler. 'It was not until a sudden breeze stirred it gently that anybody could make out what it was – a green flag on which was written in bold Gaelic lettering, half-gold, half-white, the quite incredible legend: IRISH REPUBLIC.'

Other rebel units had mixed success in seizing targets. To the west one group took the Four Courts and adjacent streets by the river while another occupied an industrial district around the Guinness brewery. In the south and east a group seized Boland's mill and bakery by the canal, another took Jacob's biscuit factory, another dug trenches in Stephen's Green and smaller units took over houses and pubs overlooking junctions.

Depleted manpower restricted operations and inexperience led to missed opportunities. There was no attempt to seize the Shelbourne Hotel, which overlooked Stephen's Green, or Trinity College, a strategic asset in the heart of the city.

The most glittering prize of all, Dublin Castle, was there for the taking. A detachment of about 30 rebels shot dead a policeman at the gate, captured six soldiers in a guardroom and swept into the yard. Sir Matthew Nathan was in his office, talking to an army intelligence officer, Major Ivon Price, about the planned arrests of Sinn Féiners, when they heard shots. 'They've commenced!' shouted Price. He scrambled down into the yard and blazed with his pistol. And then, inexplicably, the rebels withdrew.

The seat of British power was at their mercy – the garrison at that moment comprised fewer than 25 soldiers at an adjacent barracks. Perhaps it appeared too easy and the rebels feared a trap, or were intimidated by 700 years of Castle symbolism, or were diverted by an instruction to occupy the neighbouring City Hall. Whatever the reason, they retreated, and like the Cheshire cat the opportunity to capture the Castle vanished, leaving the rebels a mocking grin of what might have been.

The mobilisation chaos crippled action outside Dublin, leaving the capital the crucible. The conspirators had expected the British to hit back hard and fast, but Monday afternoon passed with a feeble response. A fusillade from the GPO repulsed a force of lancers, killing three, plus a horse.

Almost everything had gone wrong for the rebels yet they managed to seize strongholds because the British produced their own debacle. They had failed to arrest the conspirators before it was too late and left the city virtually undefended. Garrisons were below strength and some officers were literally at the races, leaving just 400 troops immediately available for action.

Since February naval intelligence had known the date of the rising yet the shambolic cavalcade from Liberty Hall struck the authorities in Dublin like a bolt from Mount Olympus. The result was that insurgents controlled much of the capital. It was going to take reinforcements, and a grim fight, to dig them out. Put another way, a festering sore had come to a head.

. . .

'I want to tell you something I was not in possession of yesterday,' Reginald Hall told the prisoner. 'We now find that Monteith was with you. The other man has been arrested and made a full confession.'

It was the second day of interrogation and the director of naval intelligence was making a point of telling Casement that his U-boat companion Daniel Bailey was singing like a canary about the Irish Brigade, the mission to Ireland, everything. News of the rising had not yet reached Scotland Yard but, curiously, all telegrams from Dublin had ceased at midday.

Bailey's confession further undermined Casement's position but there was comfort in the thought that Robert Monteith, his loyal lieutenant, may have escaped. 'He came only to help me,' he said.

Quizzed about places, names and dates, Casement turned vague, eliciting a jab from Basil Thomson. 'There is no secret about it. We have had it from another source.' The assistant commissioner did not specify intercepted messages but the meaning was clear: they had a bounty of evidence.

Shortly after 3 p.m. a report from Dublin claimed that rebels had seized the GPO and by 7 p.m. it was clear a rising was underway. The army mobilised forces in Ireland and selected two brigades from England to cross the Irish Sea. General Sir John Maxwell, a veteran of the Boer war and campaigns in Egypt, was tasked with taking overall command and crushing the rebellion.

Adventures are for the adventurous, went Reginald Hall's maxim, and Ireland was now well launched on hers. The vexing troublemakers had finally made their play, gifting the army an opportunity to snuff them out. There remained the matter of bringing Sir Roger's role in the affair to a satisfactory conclusion. There was enough evidence to try him for high treason, and doing so in England would avert any Irish jury waywardness.

First Hall needed to announce the arrest. For 18 months Casement had hovered in English consciousness as a spiteful gadfly buzzing in Germany. News of his capture would electrify the public. The traitor knight, back in London, not for honours but judgement. The Admiralty drafted a press release to be issued at 10.25 p.m., in time for the next morning's newspapers.

. . .

The proclamation had summoned Ireland's children to her flag but those swarming through the smashed shopfronts on Sackville Street were keener on loot. It started with Noblett's, an Aladdin's cave of confectionary. The plate-glass facade shattered, a hand grabbed a jar, then it was a mob ransacking and devouring Turkish delight, glacier mints, fruit bon-bons and sweetmeats. With the munching and crunching came a sweet, intoxicating realisation: no one was in charge.

The city that housed them in squalid, pestilential slums, and displayed fancy wares in shops they were not welcome to enter, with prices they could never afford, had slipped into a twilight without authority. No owners or guards or police, only opportunity.

The throng moved onto a hat shop and emerged with silk hats and bowlers, then moved to a department store. 'All who were underdressed before were overdressed now, and for the first time in their frosty lives the heat of good warm things encircled them,' the writer Sean O'Casey observed.

Crates of whiskey and champagne, cases of salmon and sardines, boxes of butter and jam, bags of onions, pianos, chairs, all spilled out onto a thoroughfare that turned into a bacchanalia. Drunks danced with mannequins and toasted and cursed the rebels. A woman wailed that someone had stolen her stolen tea while another knelt with hands outstretched, clasping a rosary, to implore the Virgin Mary for 'Ireland to be a nation once again'. An urchin brandished Thomas More's *Utopia*, others played cowboys and Indians with toys guns. An enterprising soul swiped a pile of proclamations hoping to 'sell them for a fiver after the beggars were hanged'.

A shoe shop hosted a fashion show. 'Bare-footed little devils with legs buried in Wellington top-boots, unable to bend their knees, and drunken women brandishing satin shoes and Russian boots till it seemed the whole revolution would collapse in ridicule or pandemonium,' one observer wrote.

The rebels brandished batons and fired into the air, to no avail. As the evening wore on, the mood darkened. Gunfire echoed from the river and Sackville Street was a debris of wrecked trams and barricades. Shouts of 'the British are coming' would briefly scatter people until it became clear the British were not coming, not yet, but somewhere in the darkness, they all knew, reinforcements were on their way. So-called 'shawlies' – wives of men serving in the British army – rained epithets on the rebels: 'Shitehawks! Lousers! Bowsies!'

It was all a jarring counterpoint to the proclamation's ideals, and the heavens did not help by unleashing cold rain on the first night of the provisional government, but the rebels remained in good spirits and continued to fortify their headquarters. Food and ammunition came in trucks while sealed orders came and went in motorcycle pouches, all passing through checkpoints with passwords. Some messages were dated '1st day of the republic'.

James Connolly hustled up and down the GPO's three storeys barking commands and radiating confidence. This was not the revolution his beloved Karl Marx had predicted but it would do. Men from units that had not mobilised trickled in, swelling the garrison to more than 200 defenders. They filled sandbags, punctured masonry for loopholes and tunnelled through neighbouring and adjacent buildings, including the waxworks museum, which yielded the triumphant capture of George V and Lord Kitchener, who were carried back as prisoners-of-war. The tunnels' purpose was to create a warren of defences against infantry attack. Connolly was sure the British, as rabid capitalists, would abjure artillery to minimise damage to property.

Patrick Pearse, the orator president, floated about, not interfering, almost detached, as if wafting on history. 'There was a mystic atmosphere about his personality which inspired confidence and an urge to achieve great things,' one comrade later wrote.

Tom Clarke watched it all with paternal pride. Without his implacable resolve and moulding of the IRB there would have been no rising. A last-ditch appeal from his wife to consider their family had splintered on his indomitable will. 'My children will have to accept it the same as you. We are going to make a bid for freedom no matter what happens.'

Clarke's was the first name on the proclamation, but he let the younger men take command. His work was done. The Irish Citizen Army and Irish Volunteers had fused this day into the army of the republic, which colloquial usage was already turning into the Irish Republican Army, or IRA.

As the night deepened, street arc lamps lit up the GPO in pale blues and greens. Inside the granite walls, Joe Plunkett made his way to the first floor and amid the dust and hustle of his comrades lay down on a pallet, enfeebled but serene. He spotted a fellow poet, Desmond FitzGerald. 'I must have a rest. Can't you sit down and let us talk?' FitzGerald obliged, and while rain bounced off the roof, and rifle-fire cracked in the distance, they talked of poems, books, monarchies and republics, and wondered what would become of theirs.

Earlier that afternoon Plunkett, as often happened, got a burst of energy. He joined the Volunteers erecting barricades outside and noticed that home-made bombs placed in an empty tram were not detonating. 'Joe put another bomb in the tram and shot at it with his Mauser from about 30 yards – he was a beautiful shot,' his sister Geraldine, watching from across the street, recalled. The bomb exploded and smashed the chassis, adding an immobilised tram to the barricade.

Back in the GPO, Plunkett confronted a man who accidentally discharged a shotgun, knocking plaster from a ceiling. He turned out to be a Finnish sailor who had embraced the rebel cause. 'Amazing, but obviously that man there is a danger,' said Plunkett, who transferred the Finn to making grenades.

Vigour spent, Plunkett passed the rest of the afternoon on a mattress. Of the four proclamation signatories in the GPO – the other three were at other posts – he was the least known, and his attire and supine position drew reproachful remarks. Who was this bejewelled, horizontal fellow? James Connolly growled a response. 'That's Joe Plunkett, and he has more courage in his little finger than all the other leaders combined.'

As Plunkett talked through the night with his fellow poet he seemed happy, though his thoughts kept veering to a counterfactual realm where Eoin MacNeill did not cancel the mobilisation, and the

German arms landed, and they had a chance in the fight. Such thoughts might have been depressing but for some reason were not, Desmond FitzGerald recalled. 'Plunkett found comfort in speaking of what might have been.'

Amid the first paling of the sky on Tuesday 25 April, two rebels on the roof of a building near the GPO heard unmistakeable rat-tat-tat bursts from across the river. 'The British?' asked one.

'Must be, I suppose,' his comrade replied. After a pause, he added: 'We have no machine-guns.'

CHAPTER NINETEEN

Easter Week: Don't Be Afraid

The press release from Reginald Hall's office had been terse and saved the most striking detail till last. 'The secretary of the Admiralty makes the following announcement: during the period between p.m., April 20, and p.m., April 21, an attempt to land arms and ammunition in Ireland was made by a vessel under the guise of a neutral merchant ship, but in reality a German auxiliary, in conjunction with a German submarine. The auxiliary sank, and a number of prisoners were made, amongst whom was Sir Roger Casement.'

There was no mention of the rebellion in Dublin, which initially was under a news blackout, but Casement's name was enough to have the newspapers of Tuesday 25 April crackling with shock and marvel. 'CAPTURE OF SIR ROGER CASEMENT', the *London Daily News* blared across its entire front page. 'One of the great sensations of the war was announced last night,' the article began. The trophy capture all but eclipsed other war news.

Other papers cleared space on their front pages for biographical details to remind readers about this former consul who had been honoured by the King and retired on a Foreign Office pension before surfacing in Germany where he acquired, as *The Times* said, 'remarkable notoriety'. The reports reprised his efforts to enlist prisoners-of-war into 'sedition' and 'treason', and quoted Casement's denunciations of England and praise of the Kaiser's Germany.

For Hall, doing his daily press review, this was a satisfying result that would set the tone for the forthcoming trial. But the coverage accomplished something else not even he, credited by admirers as the 'eyes of the navy', foresaw.

One and a half miles from Whitehall, at 50 Ebury Street, the boarding house perfumed by fish, cheese and sour milk, William Patrick Germain felt a pang of duty. He was 52, too old to fight, and managing a house full of lodgers did not contribute much to the war effort, but this morning brought an opportunity to do something. The bearded face that gazed from front pages, and the name shouted by newspaper sellers, were familiar. The knight-turned-villain had been a lodger.

During his stay in May 1914 – when he testified at the Royal Commission – Sir Roger had asked Germain to mind two locked wooden trunks, which he had loyally done. But now a greater loyalty called. Whatever they contained, the luggage might be useful to the authorities. Within hours the trunks were sitting at Scotland Yard.

Up the stone staircase leading to Basil Thomson's office, their owner was again seated in the assistant commissioner's low armchair.

. . .

As Casement faced his third day of interrogation, Dublin woke to the second day of the rebels' republic. A lull hung over Sackville Street. The rain had ceased and only a few souls were out stepping over the broken glass and debris. At 9.30 a.m. Patrick Pearse issued a communiqué from the GPO to the press and public. 'The republican forces hold all their positions . . . [and] everywhere are fighting with splendid gallantry. The populace of Dublin are clearly with the republic, and the officers and men are everywhere cheered as they march through the streets.'

The schoolmaster-turned generalissimo was peddling fables to rival his beloved Celtic myths. The rebels had lost the Castle, City Hall and Stephen's Green and they were not marching, or being cheered, but hunkering at a handful of fortified bastions, awaiting attack by the British. The most realistic goal was to hold out for as long as possible and perhaps the survivors could escape to the countryside.

Between swills of brandy at the viceregal lodge Lord Wimborne was finally getting a chance to show he was a Churchill and could handle a crisis. He issued edicts down the phone – 'It is His Excellency's command' – and declared martial law in Dublin for the first time since the 1798 rebellion, giving the military wide powers to punish rebels. Reinforcements from Belfast and the Curragh had brought the total troop level to 4,650 men, outnumbering the rebels almost five to one, a superiority that would further increase with two brigades from England and four eighteen-pounder field guns en route from Athlone. Once the army secured a line of communication through the city, the plan was to isolate and squeeze the main rebel positions.

Louis Redmond-Howard, a young writer, staked out a position near the GPO to observe what was to come. He disapproved of the insurgents but feared for them. 'We knew they were our own flesh and blood that had rebelled: it would be strangers who would conquer, and yet we knew that order was right.'

. . .

'Since I saw you yesterday what we thought would happen has happened,' Basil Thomson told the prisoner. 'There has been more or less a rising in Dublin, and a good many have been killed, and that is all the good that has proceeded from your expedition.'

Casement eyed the assistant commissioner and digested the information. All his efforts to avert the folly, in vain. From Berlin,

Kerry and this interrogation room he had tried to call the thing off. He could only imagine what was unfolding in Ireland. If he could not stop the rising, he had wanted to join it; too late now.

If the rebels had only the rifles he helped to send in July 1914, God help them. When the *Asgard* dodged the entire Royal Navy and landed the Mausers he had been so proud, but that seemed a lifetime ago.

His inquisitors, this duo of the policeman and the little navy captain who kept blinking, pressed on. They seemed convinced the Germans had sent a second arms ship, which had yet to be intercepted. 'There is another ship,' Reginald Hall insisted.

Unknown to Casement, one week earlier, on 18 April, the US secret service had raided a German government office in New York and discovered months-old messages between the IRB, John Devoy and Berlin, including one that suggested the Germans would send two ships to Ireland. Hall had received this information the previous day and now demanded to know if there was indeed a second ship. 'There is not, on my word of honour,' said Casement.

The interrogation continued, delving back into the Irish Brigade, Casement's negotiations in Berlin and his sea voyage. There was probably a break for lunch. Much of the questioning was ground already covered.

Casement talked, the clock ticked. Below the window, figures strolled on the Embankment. Barges glided on the river, a picturesque scene, though some were sludge vessels laden with human waste. On the opposite bank a new county hall was rising from scaffolds, a skeleton of pillars and beams. The metropolis thrummed with afternoon traffic, oblivious to the courteous, lethal game playing out in this corner of Scotland Yard.

It was Thomson who asked it. A query so out of context, so divorced from everything else, it seemed to come from another interrogation.

'Have you got some trunks at 50 Ebury Street?'

The question hissed towards Casement like a torpedo. Thomson added: 'I propose having them down and examined.'

It may have taken Casement some moments to register the significance. For two years he had fretted that his scattered possessions might reveal his secret life to the British. *Conceal everything belonging to me*, he had exhorted a friend in Antrim. *I go . . . to be defamed and degraded*, he had predicted on the eve of sailing.

In London most of his possessions were in a storage depot, and harmless, but one of the Ebury Street trunks contained, along with a canvas hold-all, a box of visiting cards, a trinket box with pills, a brass syringe, ointment, cotton, a picnic set, an address book, periodicals, tobacco tins and 23 books, four diaries.

Spanning 1903 to 1911, they comprised jottings, observations and financial accounts of the then-consul's travels through Africa and South America and visits home to Ireland and England. Much was mundane – ship sailings, hotel bills, office minutiae – but the distinctive spidery handwriting also recorded sexual encounters, hundreds of them, with dates, locations, names and details. Oh such details. The point of recording it all was to be able to revisit these moments, this private realm, and hold the memories.

The 1903 pocket diary, bound in blue-green leather, had brief references to partners, some of them named, *Arthur, Henry, Aghostino, Juan, Pepe, Yves*, and their penis sizes. *Enormous. Huge one.* He had written some phrases in the Congolese language of Kikongo. *Mu nua ami* [in my mouth].

The 1910 diary, with a dark blue cover, gave more elaboration. 13 January: *Gabriel Ramos – deep to hilt . . . in very deep thrusts.* 28 February: *Deep screw to hilt . . . lovely, young – 18 and glorious. Biggest since Lisbon.* 1 March: *Breathed and quick enormous push. Loved mightily.* 12 March: *Splendid erections. Ramon $7.* 28 May: *Rode gloriously – splendid steed.*

The 1911 cash ledger, a hardback notebook, had more names and descriptions. The 1911 diary, with a green leather jacket, had the most frequent, loquacious entries. 1 January: *Took in mouth with much groaning and struggle and moans of love.* 1 October: *He took off boots and trousers and gave a tremendous one.* 2 October: *Bathed and then he entered and did it hard and kissed and loved.*

Page after page of his innermost self, the one the world was never supposed to see – in the hands of a policeman and a Royal Navy captain. An abyss yawned before Casement. When British marines had stomped aboard the *Oscar II* he had thrown his New York diary out the porthole but here there was no ocean to swallow his secret, only the glinting gaze of mortal enemies asking about trunks.

Casement's diaries and ledgers, now held at the National Archives at Kew.

'There's nothing in them,' Casement replied, mustering bravado.

In later years Thomson gave conflicting accounts of the trunks' arrival at Scotland Yard, and how he introduced the topic into the interrogation. The likeliest version is that detectives cracked open the trunks, swiftly gleaned the gist of the diaries and briefed Thomson, who then asked the prisoner about the trunks to gauge his reaction – to toy with him.

Casement tried to brazen it out, and the moment passed. Questioning turned to German support for the rising and Casement's nationalism, but towards the end Thomson returned to the delivery from Ebury Street, masking the taunt as a prosaic observation. 'Sir Roger, your trunks are here but there are no keys.'

Casement: 'Break them open.'

So ended the third and final day of interrogation, and the prisoner was led away.

News of disturbances in Dublin reached the House of Commons that afternoon, prompting clamours for action. 'Is it a fact that Sir Roger Casement has been brought to London, and can the prime minister give the House and the nation an assurance that this traitor will be short forthwith?' asked one MP. Cheers and laughter almost drowned out Herbert Asquith's reply. 'I do not think that is a question that ought to be put to me at present.'

Brixton Prison no longer housed the traitor. He was transferred to military custody and by Tuesday night was in a cell at the Tower of London.

. . .

It was dark when Captain Fred Dietrichsen, an English officer with Danish ancestry, led his men onto the pier at Kingstown in the early hours of Wednesday 26 April. He didn't know what awaited but at least knew they were in Ireland, unlike some fellow Sherwood Foresters who were convinced they had just landed in France.

It had been a hectic scramble across England and then the sea, leaving many lads woozy, but it seemed the battalion from Nottingham and Derbyshire – nicknamed after Robin Hood's forest – was finally going to see action.

As a married man of 33, Dietrichsen could probably have sat out the war and continued practising law, but as a patriot he enlisted in 1914, only to be kept in England commanding recruits who knew as little about fighting as he did. His current lot were mostly teenagers – clerks, shop assistants and factory workers – who were just weeks in uniform and barely knew how to handle a rifle. Still, everyone was determined to do their best. The pity was they would be fighting not Germans but Irish brethren – Dietrichsen's wife was from Dublin.

At 10.35 a.m., amid warm sunshine, the battalion started the six-mile march to the city centre. The sight of young women along the route prompted cries of 'bonjour mademoiselle!' Residents of the plush southern suburbs turned out to cheer the troops and there among them, to his complete astonishment, Dietrichsen spotted his own Beatrice and their two young children – unknown to him they had come before the disturbances to visit her parents. The captain stepped out of the column and the family embraced in brief, joyful reunion.

By 12.30 p.m. Dietrichsen and other officers were leading the men in columns of four up Northumberland Road, still a mile from the centre, when shots rang out. Soldiers crumpled. Another volley, and more bodies fell. 'Drop!' an officer shouted. The soldiers dived but bullets seemed to whistle from every angle. 'There! That house there!' shouted a captain, pointing. 'Prepare to fire!' The soldiers fired. The captain rose to his feet, brandished a sword and yelled, 'Charge!'

It was not Dietrichsen. He was dead, caught in the first volley. So he did not see the massacre. Unable to locate the snipers, the English soldiers presented easy targets. 'It was not like killing men,' said one vivid description. 'It was more like trying to slaughter a great insect or animal . . . as one man was killed another crawled up and over him.'

The firing came from just a handful of well-placed rebel sharp-shooters, some using Mausers landed by Casement's gun-running scheme two years earlier. By dusk, when the snipers finally withdrew, they had inflicted more than 220 casualties. Dietrichsen died with a note from his five-year-old son in his breast pocket. *'Dear Dad, thank you for choc, love from Christian.'*

. . .

As the British treated their wounded and counted their dead that night, Casement was curled under a blanket and quietly using his spectacles to slice a cut in his finger. Tasting blood, he extracted his vial of curare.

It was his second night at the Tower. The rising had gone ahead, the enemy knew his secret and he was the Judas of England. He was in the same stinking clothes and besieged by lice. There was no word from any friends, who appeared to have repudiated him. He craved sleep but an overhead bulb glared without cease and two guards sat in the cell, staring at him, silent sentinels on suicide watch. Another kept vigil from the corridor through a small window on the door. 'Sleep became impossible and thoughts became a page of hell,' he later wrote.

With enough dosage the curare, made from a South American plant toxin that indigenous tribes put on arrow tips, paralysed and killed by asphyxiation. Having concealed the vial, possibly in his hair, Casement now rubbed some of the crystals in the wound. He prayed and waited.

Without a watch he could only guess the time. He would shut his eyes and open them to see the guards still there, staring. Wednesday passed to Thursday, and no spasm came. His veins still pulsed, and his thoughts still clawed and scratched. His finger swelled, and that was it. He would live to see the dawn. The German poison was useless.

. . .

One hundred and seventy miles to the east, in trenches close to the French village of Hulluch, the British army's 16th (Irish) Division greeted the paling sky of Thursday 27 April with foreboding. Aerial reconnaissance, and a German deserter, had suggested the Bavarian troops on the other side of no-man's land were preparing gas canisters.

The enemy was close enough to have held up placards that week: 'Irishmen! Heavy uproar in Ireland. English guns are firing at your wifes and children!' It was an exhortation to Irish regiments on this section of the front to mutiny, and hadn't worked. The Royal Dublin Fusiliers had heard of the rising and were disgusted. They were nationalists and wanted Home Rule but England was not the enemy. Plus their army wages fed families back in Dublin.

Just before dawn German artillery erupted, then a thick, dark cloud wafted towards the Irish lines. A massive chemical attack – 3,800 cylinders of chlorine and phosgene – and the British army gas masks did not work properly.

It was a hideous death. First a burning in the throat and eyes, then a sensation of asphyxiation, intense thirst, headache and a stabbing in the lungs. Eventually skin turned greenish black and yellow and eyes became glassy, unseeing stares. 'There they lay, scores of them in the bottom of the trench, in every conceivable posture of human agony; the clothes torn off their bodies in a vain effort to breathe,' a chaplain wrote. Some 538 Irishmen, plus hundreds more Allied soldiers, perished at Hulluch.

. . .

Dublin was 400 miles from the gas attack but parts of the city centre now resembled ruins on the Western Front. On Thursday afternoon the British shelling edged up Sackville Street, ever closer to the rebels' citadel, where their military commander lay stricken.

As an authority on human endurance Joe Plunkett could tell that even James Connolly, the GPO's irrepressible talisman, would soon reach his limit. 'Thursday, 4th day of the republic,' Plunkett wrote in his notebook. 'About one o'clock Commandant General Connolly was wounded in the left arm and ten minutes later in the left leg (by a sniper). The leg wound is serious as it caused a compound fracture of the shin bone.'

Through clenched teeth Connolly still issued orders from a mattress, but he could no longer patrol the GPO to encourage and reassure its anxious garrison. Plunkett was a dusty, coughing effigy in cavalry fancy dress and just as horizontal, but he could, with effort, get up and walk. With his dangling sword he started to shuffle between the sandbags, speaking quietly to defenders.

The garrison had grown to about 400, including dozens of girls and women who cooked, tended wounded, delivered messages and were prepared to fight. Throughout the city the rebel force now numbered 1,250, with British forces approximating 20,000.

Earlier in the week a sighting of smoke in Dublin Bay had prompted wild hopes of German submarines – perhaps the 'gallant allies' referenced in the proclamation had sent more weapons, or even officers. Instead the British closed in, and did not repeat the blunder at Northumberland Road. Instead of infantry charges, as the rebels had expected, the enemy methodically cut off each garrison.

Artillery bombardments began on Wednesday, exploding Connolly's assurance that capitalists would not destroy property. After pounding Liberty Hall to rubble the British gunners demolished other targets while snipers and machine-gun crews found vantage points from which to rain bullets. Improvised armoured trucks gave the attackers another edge.

Isolated rebel outposts ran low on food, ammunition and sleep and struggled to hit back at the darting khaki specks. Patrick Pearse, president of the shrivelling republic, gave stirring speeches in the GPO about the country rising up and Volunteers columns marching on Dublin to relieve the defenders. Privately, he recognised military reality. 'When we are all wiped out, people will blame us for everything, condemn us,' he confided to a comrade. 'In a few years they will see the meaning of what we tried to do.'

Resistance outside the capital remained paltry save for a unit in north county Dublin that improvised guerrilla tactics for highly successful, mobile attacks – a potential template for a different type of rebellion.

Pearse was right about people blaming the rebels. The middle class condemned the anarchy and looked forward to the authorities restoring order. The poor had even more reason to resent the insurgents given most of the fighting was happening in their areas, the crossfire scything down women and children, including two-year-old

Sean Francis Foster, killed in his pram, all consequence of the rebel decision to make the city a war zone. 'They ought all to be shot,' was a common refrain.

By Thursday there was hint of another sentiment. Previous uprisings had collapsed ignominiously, sometimes within hours, but these fellows were showing the English that Irishmen could fight. It did not signify approval or sympathy but, in some quarters, grudging respect.

By Thursday evening Sackville Street was in flames, sending black plumes over the city.

Inside the GPO Connolly lay on his mattress, grimacing. Words, for once, failed Pearse, who lapsed into silence. Tom Clarke clutched a pistol, vowing to fight to the last. Plunkett continued to reassure the defenders.

'Joe moved amongst us all the time, his eloquent comforting words at odds with his bizarre, eccentric appearance,' one rebel recalled. 'We all, somehow, and in many differing ways, responded to his gentle urgings and praise. He was greatly loved. Most of us by now knew that he'd risen from his deathbed to lead us.'

Fires torched and toppled buildings in what one witness called 'a gigantic waterfall of fire'. An oil works opposite the GPO exploded. 'A solid sheet of blinding white-death flame rushes hundreds of feet into the air,' said one account. The conflagration spread to the Imperial Hotel and Clery's department store, forcing the rebels in these outposts to flee – some wrapped in mattresses as improvised bulletproof vests.

Even from miles away the inferno mesmerised. 'The most awe-inspiring sight I have ever seen,' a witness recalled. 'It seemed as if the whole city was on fire, the glow extending right above the heavens . . . the whole air seemed to be vibrating.'

In the baking GPO defenders drenched sandbags with water to prevent them igniting. Fears of dying in a granite oven were briefly deflected by Plunkettian exuberance. 'It's the first time this has happened since Moscow,' Joe declared. 'The first time a capital city has burned since 1812!'

By dawn – Friday 28 April, day five of the republic – the firestorm opposite the GPO burnt itself out, leaving a grim spectacle. 'All the barbaric splendour that night had lent the scene has faded away, and the pitiless sun illuminates the squalidness and horror of the destruction,' one chronicler wrote.

The end was near. Pearse ordered the two-dozen girls and women to evacuate, prompting fierce protest. 'No! We'll stay with the men! You told us we were all equal! What about women's rights?' Eventually, most left. In a final communiqué, with his eye on posterity, the republic's president paid tribute to his rebels. 'If they do not win this fight, they will at least deserve to win it. But win it they will although they may win it in death ... they have redeemed Dublin from many shames, and made her name splendid among the names of cities.'

The men, plus Connolly's indefatigable secretary Winifred Carney and a handful of female nurses who were allowed to stay, braced for the final assault. Infantry or artillery? The answer came at noon when an incendiary shell hit the roof. More followed. Flames crackled down, devouring each floor, the smoke making Plunkett retch.

By evening, with gunfire peppering walls, Pearse gave the order to evacuate. They would try to reach a nearby factory to create a new redoubt. Units took positions by different exits and waited for dusk, a flimsy cloak against bullets but better than nothing. Among shards of falling timber someone launched into 'A Soldier's Song', a Volunteers' marching tune. Others joined in, their voices rising over the roar of flames and explosions:

Our camp fires now are burning low
See in the east a silvery glow
Out yonder waits the Saxon foe
So chant a soldier's song.

It would, in a future inconceivable in that moment, become Ireland's national anthem.

From a side courtyard, silhouetted against flames, they made a dash. A group of about 20 elected to not flee but charge the enemy, and was cut down. The rest made rushes across Henry Street amid sprays of bullets. Plunkett ordered a van to be pulled across a lane as a barrier and sent comrades across in batches, each time lowering his sword and shouting, 'On! On! Don't be afraid, don't be cowards any of you!'

Seventeen were injured but they all got across, only to come under fresh volleys from another angle. A rebel took a bullet to the chest and toppled over Connolly's stretcher. They took refuge in a terrace of small houses on Moore Street. Night brought a lull in gunfire. The rebel leaders shared a tiny room with, and cared for, a wounded British soldier. Grimy, parched, exhausted, they slept like the dead.

Saturday 29 April, day six of the republic. The GPO a scorched, abandoned shell, gunfire crackling around the city, Plunkett and the other proclamation signatories cloistered in a room overlooking a landscape of debris and corpses, including civilians. They considered a last stand, guns blazing. But what would it achieve? More civilians would die. And so too younger rebels, junior officers, who might otherwise live to lead a future rebellion. They decided to surrender.

At noon, while an emissary approached British commanders, Plunkett wrote a letter to Grace Gifford. 'This is just a little note to say I love you and to tell you that I did everything I could to arrange for us to meet and get married but it was impossible. Except for that I have no regrets . . . I wish we were together. Love me always as I love you.' His will, leaving his meagre possessions to Grace, remained in his breast pocket.

Orders to surrender went out to the remaining rebel outposts. Tom Clarke, the old Fenian who had orchestrated it all, wept tears of frustration, grief and pride. When all was ready, Plunkett emerged and stood alone in the middle of Moore Street with a white flag. A barricade of British soldiers watched in silence. About 120 rebels filed from their hideouts and assembled, rifles over shoulders. They marched in fours to Sackville Street, the crunch of their boots breaking the hush.

A bright sun shone on it all – dead horses, dead people, tangled machinery, charred ruins. An Irish tricolour still flew from the gutted GPO. The column halted a hundred yards from the British lines. At a command, the rebels advanced five paces and laid down their weapons. It was over.

Ruins in central Dublin in the aftermath of the Easter rising.

CHAPTER TWENTY

Into the Dark

Reginald Hall arrived at the Admiralty on Monday 1 May 1916 under a rapturous sun that heralded summer; the type of sun that bounced off the breastplates of the mounted troopers, threw a radiance over the sweep of Horse Guards Parade and seemed to follow him to his desk where reports from Dublin bathed the morning in the glow of the three most satisfying words in the English language: I was right.

Right that the rebellion would be a shambles, right that it would be crushed and right that the Sinn Féiner canker could now be extirpated once and for all. What a sight it must have been, two days earlier, when the scoundrels surrendered and were marched down Sackville Street past the jeers and insults of their countrymen. There were accounts of chamberpots being thrown and of exhortations to the British troops to 'bayonet the bastards'. Several thousand had been arrested and 400 were already en route to prison camps in England and Wales.

Ireland's vituperation was something to behold. The Irish Parliamentary Party and Catholic bishops – loyal nationalists – were condemning the rebels and demanding retribution. Hall's analogy of separatism as a festering sore found echo in an editorial in the unionist *Irish Times*. 'The state has struck but its work is not yet finished. The surgeon's knife has been put to the corruption in the body of Ireland and its course must not be stayed until the whole malignant growth has been removed.'

The fury was understandable. Bodies were still buried under rubble – the eventual confirmed death toll was 84 rebels, 144 soldiers and police and 276 civilians, plus thousands injured. More than 200 buildings were damaged, entire blocks pulverised and countless livelihoods destroyed.

In Hall's calculus this was unfortunate but did not alter the fact he had rolled the dice and won, netting not only the fugitive knight but the whole rotten gang of extremists. As *Punch* magazine drolly put it: 'Sir Roger Casement, it appears, landed in Ireland from a collapsible boat. And by a strange coincidence his arrival synchronised with the outbreak of a collapsible rebellion.'

As a result, pusillanimous government tolerance for Hun-inspired Irish intrigues had given way to political resolve, martial law and a military governor. Hall had little time for theatre but London was celebrating the tricentenary of Shakespeare, and the Bard supplied a pithy endorsement for those who seized opportunity. *'There is a tide in the affairs of men which, taken at the flood, leads on to fortune.'*

For the intelligence chief there remained two delicate matters.

He had a cardinal rule about 'covering up all tracks', but a pending official inquiry into how insurgents managed to seize the Irish capital in the middle of a war – to lesser minds, a calamitous intelligence failure – risked shining a light on his foreknowledge and Casement's offer to avert the outbreak. Hall had no desire to testify or appear in the final report; like H. G. Wells's *Invisible Man*, there were parts of a story that required one to vanish.

And there remained the Sir Roger business. Hall had favoured a swift court martial but the government decided on a civil trial held in public 'lest in after-years,' as the attorney general put it, 'we should be reproached with having killed him secretly'. So be it. The evidence of high treason was abundant.

Basil Thomson's detectives had found more of Sir Roger's trunks at another lodging house and a storage depot, yielding his consul's ceremonial sword and tricorn hat, among other possessions, but nothing comparable to the cache from 50 Ebury Street.

It was difficult to know which was more extraordinary – the degree of debauchery, or the blighter's practice of writing it all down. Once read, the diaries were not easily forgotten. Hall was a devout Christian but hardly naive about the existence of sodomy. Royal Navy tradition, went the joke, was 'rum, buggery and the lash'. At 46, he was old enough to remember Oscar Wilde's court case. And Sir Roger's inclinations had been known since Adler Christensen betrayed his master to British diplomats in Norway. But none of that had prepared Hall for the sheer volume and detail and *celebration* of unnatural acts.

A big mouth choked with love ... softly fingering and milking ... splendid erections. Dear God, there was no end to it. Rather than shame, the diaries were exulting.

A later era would question the youth of Casement's partners – many were teenagers – and the power imbalance of a privileged European having sex with poor, brown-skinned partners. They were not prostitutes, but Casement's habit of bestowing cash or gifts showed a transactional element and, in some cases, grooming of potential partners.

For Hall, a product of Victorian Britain, the issue was homosexuality – a crime as well as a sin. More charitable souls suggested it was a mental affliction, perhaps a disease. Whatever the cause, Hall had only to stroll over to Scotland Yard to view, in Casement's own hand, page after page proving he was 'addicted to sodomy'. In all the war there was not a trove like it.

Which begged the question: to use or not to use?

The diaries predated and were unrelated to Casement's treason. They were his private life and not needed to hang him. To exploit them would not be gentlemanly. But Hall was not in the business of being a gentleman – the British empire was fighting for its life and what counted was victory. In any case, for the intelligence chief it was clear that the rogue knight, for all his talk of honour, was no gentleman.

Something else had crystallised. The trial was going to be a public spectacle, giving Casement a platform to pose and preen and play the martyr – to turn his death, if executed, into a gift to Sinn Féiners, or what was left of them. The fellow was locked up in the Tower, but it turned out the hunt was not quite over. His persona, his reputation, could still stir trouble.

Unless, of course, the world learned the truth about the real Sir Roger. Shakespeare, as ever, put it well. *'Tremble, thou wretch. That hast within thee undivulgèd crimes. Unwhipped of justice.'* So, yes, the diaries would be used.

Gazing out the window on the brilliant blue sky, the director of naval intelligence might have had a twinge of sympathy for the Scotland Yard detectives who would be spending the coming weeks hunched over desks copying and photographing the smut.

. . .

General Sir John Maxwell wished he were back in Egypt, digging up mummies, but the army had sent him to Ireland to put bodies *in* the ground, so that was what he would do. The first three death sentences had been passed that morning.

It was Tuesday 2 May and a bitter vapour of charred wood still lingered over central Dublin. Residents wandered the ruins, agog at the devastation and gaping voids where landmarks once stood.

As military governor it was Maxwell's duty to punish the rebels and restore order. The chief secretary, Augustine Birrell, had resigned, the under-secretary, Matthew Nathan, would soon follow, and Maxwell was free to ignore the viceroy, Lord Wimborne. 'I am going to ensure that there will be no treason whispered – even whispered – for a hundred years,' he had declared.

Possessor of a sunny nature and a great slab of a nose – source of his nickname Conky – the general had made his reputation in colonial wars in Africa before heading the British army in Egypt, where he became enchanted with archaeology and pharaohs' tombs. A plainer affair awaited the rebel ringleaders – a freshly dug 28 ft × 9 ft pit at Arbour Hill barracks.

Things were going rather well, given the circumstances. Casement's arrest, Maxwell was sure, had helped to limit the revolt, and the army had acquitted itself honourably, notwithstanding some shootings of civilians, an unfortunate business to be resolved discreetly, without fuss. The police were making fresh arrests and cattle boats were deporting rank-and-file rebels to England and Wales – their dispirited letters were further evidence the flame was extinguished.

For Maxwell, justice and decency demanded executions. The insurrectionists had conspired with the enemy and betrayed not just Britain but their own brethren who were loyally fighting in the trenches.

The first courts martial had taken place that morning at Richmond barracks, some army officers acting as prosecutors, others as judges. There was no defence counsel and the hearings were in private. It turned out that some of the proclamation signatories were poets. A curiosity, but now was hardly the time for verse. The general favoured prose.

. . .

'My comrades and I believe we have struck the first successful blow for freedom.'

In the darkness of the tiny cell, Tom Clarke peered at Kathleen to make sure she got it – his wife had to memorise the whole message. He continued. 'It will not come today or tomorrow and between this and freedom Ireland will go through hell, but she will never lie down again until she has attained full freedom.' Clarke paused. A guard watched from the open doorway, impassive. 'With this belief, we die happy.'

Right to the end, the old Fenian was going to stick it to the English. In a few hours the sun would rise over Wednesday 3 May and he would be taken from this cell in Kilmainham gaol to be shot, but that still left time to entrust Kathleen, granted a final meeting with her husband, with his clarion call to the Irish people, plus his detailed instructions for rebuilding the Irish Republican Brotherhood after the executions.

It was Clarke's unappeasable will, some iron in the soul, that had sustained him through English prisons, American exile and the sharpening of the IRB into a revolutionary instrument. He was the true leader of the rising.

Through the gloom of the cell – the jail had lost its power supply during the fighting – Kathleen peered back at her husband. Of Fenian stock herself, she believed in the cause. But the price, the price. A happy marriage and three sons had not deflected Tom, and now at 38 she was to be a widow – a pregnant widow. 'I don't know how I am to live without you,' she said. 'I wish the British would put a bullet in me too.'

Clarke told her to be brave and to not let his death shadow the boys' lives, as if that were within her power. Then he returned to IRB business. The prematurely aged 58-year-old was rejuvenated – exalted that the rebels had held out for a week and full of hope for the future. He meant every word of the dictated message. Happy. He would die happy. A guard escorted Kathleen down the corridor and the cell door clanged shut. Decades later, when she was an old woman, she would still remember how the key sounded when it clicked in the lock.

. . .

Grace Gifford opened her eyes and sat up. She had barely slept yet felt she was being pulled from a torpor, as if summoned. She put on a dress of check fabric, a hat, coat and stepped into the dazzling sun of Wednesday 3 May. The late edition newspapers reported three executions that morning: Tom Clarke, Patrick Pearse and Thomas MacDonagh. There was no news of Joe.

Gifford went to see a priest and said she had to marry that day.

He eyed her. 'Must you?' Such requests usually signified an out-of-wedlock pregnancy.

'Yes.'

Clerical paperwork secured, Gifford headed to Grafton Street, its boutiques largely unscathed, and in a jewellery shop asked to view wedding rings. The owner noticed the stifled sob and red-rimmed eyes. Gently, he asked what was wrong. 'You should not cry when you are going to be married.'

She hesitated, then poured out her engagement to Joe and the probability of his imminent execution. The jeweller, thunderstruck, helped her select a ring, which she bought in cash. By 6 p.m. she was at the gates of Kilmainham gaol petitioning to see, and marry, her fiancé.

It was just four miles from Gifford's handsome family home in the posh suburb of Rathmines to the forbidding limestone walls, with an entrance framed by chained, writhing serpents, but the journey had started years earlier when Grace veered off her life's pre-ordained path of respectability. A talented artist, she plunged into Ireland's Celtic revival and a bohemia of writers, actors and activists.

Stylish and witty, Grace had no shortage of suitors but fell for Joe. He was misty, intense, playful, sometimes secretive, often sick, never boring. She had converted to Catholicism in advance of their planned wedding on Easter Sunday, then their world blew up. Now, four days after the surrender, she was in a disused prison bristling with soldiers, begging the governor to let them wed.

To plead pregnancy would have bolstered her case, plus it had the virtue of probably being true – there is evidence Grace was indeed pregnant. In a courtyard, she awaited the decision. Night fell, shrouding the decrepit bastille in darkness. At 11.30 p.m. guards escorted her through a labyrinth of stone and iron and halted at a small chapel. Inside, flickering candles illuminated dark shapes – soldiers with rifles and bayonets, a priest and a tiny altar. There were footsteps, then from the gloom emerged Joe, flanked by two sergeants. They removed his handcuffs.

Bride and groom beheld each other in silence. The chaplain performed a brief ceremony. Two soldiers signed the marriage certificate. Plunkett was again manacled and marched out. The only words the newlyweds had spoken to each other were 'I do'.

Joe returned to his cell to wait. He was serene. His poem 'The Spark', written a year earlier in Berlin, had expressed a wish to die on his own terms, and it was coming to pass. They would come for him at dawn:

Now death and I embark
And sail into the dark
With laughter on our lips.

The English had executed his ancestor, the archbishop Oliver Plunkett, three centuries earlier on a trumped-up charge of treason, but Joe *had* consorted with the enemy and conspired against the Crown, and was proud of it.

Illness and an erratic upbringing had left him a misfit full of knowledge and passions, a dilettante with a cloak, until the Irish Volunteers and then the IRB supplied a purpose and launched him on the great adventure. He had criss-crossed Europe and the Atlantic and threaded the plot until his deceptions unravelled, yet still the impossible happened, a rebellion. Earlier that day General Maxwell had paid a backhanded tribute to Plunkett's contribution in a memo to Downing Street. 'This man, being of good education, exercised great influence for evil over the other members.'

Unlike Patrick Pearse and his fixation on blood sacrifice, Joe did not *want* to die. Grace Gifford was a reason to live, as was the possibility of becoming a father. But he preferred to die for a cause rather than let tumours do the job.

Shortly after 2 a.m. the door opened – it was Grace, brought back for a final farewell. Soldiers clanked into the cell with her. She sat on a bench and Joe kneeled before her, talking quietly. She was tongue-tied, stricken with realisation that their entire marriage was this moment, this cell. She noticed how filthy his bandage was. A sergeant broke the spell. 'Your ten minutes are up.'

Grace was escorted out and Joe was moved to another cell with three other condemned prisoners.

By 3.40 a.m. streaks lightened the eastern sky. The door opened and guards marched Edward Daly down a corridor. Minutes later came a crash of gunfire. Then Willie Pearse, Patrick's brother, was taken, then Michael O'Hanrahan. Joe was last.

He gave a priest his spectacles, for his mother, and his ring, for Grace. 'Father, I am very happy,' he said. 'I am dying for the glory of God and the honour of Ireland.' He seemed utterly calm, the priest later recalled. 'As cool and self-possessed as if he looked on what was passing and found it good. No fine talk. No heroics. A distinguished tranquility.'

A guard tied the prisoner's hands behind his back, placed a blindfold over the eyes and pinned a white cloth over the heart. He was led out to the yard and placed against a wall. It was chilly, the dawn still murky, the city beyond the gaol silent and still.

Sherwood Foresters, survivors of the Northumberland Road massacre, formed the firing squad. Six knelt, six stood behind them. They charged and cocked their rifles, aimed. At an officer's signal, the rifles boomed, and Joseph Plunkett sailed into the dark.

CHAPTER TWENTY-ONE

The Other Thing

News of the executions reached Casement in whispers. The guards were not supposed to speak, but the silence in the cell was oppressive and some felt sorry for the prisoner who spent day and night curled on the bunk. They brought bleak tidings: the rebellion was crushed and the leaders were being shot in batches.

Casement could envy them. They had fought together and could die with dignity, unlike him, a wretch in the Tower awaiting display, like a specimen. Other parts of the old fortress were open to the public, who came to gawk at the ancient bolts and chains, the pitiful scratches left by captives, the stone paving where Guy Fawkes was fastened, the block on which Anne Boleyn was beheaded. Soon it would be his turn to be paraded and judged.

He had made another suicide attempt – swallowing crooked nails to rupture the intestines – and again survived. The only refuge from loneliness was rapport with a Welsh Guards corporal who flouted the injunction of silence and urged him, of all things, to 'cheer up'. The corporal knew nothing of the prisoner so Casement brought him up to speed: 'I'm supposed to be a traitor. I'm not a traitor. I'm an Irish rebel.'

On 9 May a trim, dapper man appeared in his cell like an angel in tweed: George Gavan Duffy, an Irish solicitor, hired by friends and relatives. They had not repudiated him, Duffy explained; the authorities had blocked all access, but he was fixing that. It paved an emotional visit from Elizabeth and Gertrude Bannister, cousins who were like sisters to Casement. Horrified by his filthy, spectral appearance they returned with fresh clothes and soap.

The Bannisters also brought gladdening news: Robert Monteith, his faithful lieutenant, had escaped the British dragnet in Kerry and was still on the run, still free. Casement would have been cheered and dismayed to learn two other facts that remained hidden to him. Back in Zossen, the military camp outside Berlin, the men of the Irish Brigade had come to understand that the chief had not abandoned but saved them from a doomed mission, and hoisted an Irish tricolour in his honour. They would stay in Germany and, after the war ended, make their way home.

In Philadelphia, a gap-toothed blond man presented himself to the British consulate and offered to testify against Casement: Adler Christensen, re-emerging from the shadows to work an angle, a final betrayal of his former master. Wary of a man who had double-crossed them before, the British eventually declined the offer.

In the Tower, Casement revived. He still had friends, he was not alone, not quite. His appetite returned, his mind cleared. And his old campaigning spirit stirred. The executions in Dublin – on 12 May it was the turn of James Connolly and Sean McDermott, bringing the total to 14 – brought him grief, but also responsibility. With the other leaders dead, Casement became custodian of the dream, the idea, of independence.

He dreaded his trial, but it would be another arena, another opportunity, in the struggle. Speeches from the dock by Wolfe Tone and Robert Emmet still resonated centuries later. Casement would have to make the most of his. 'He saw it as the case of Ireland, a trust in his keeping,' a biographer noted. 'He saw himself quite properly as a symbolic figure: he was Ireland, the point at which her melancholy history came to a focus in the eyes of the world.'

He immersed himself in legal documents and wrote copious notes for Duffy. Not that he expected to escape the gallows – no previous occupant of his cell had done so. 'I don't think I am likely to prove an exception to the rule,' he told a visitor with a smile. The goal was to turn the trial into a proclamation of nationhood.

A preliminary hearing at Bow Street police court on 15 May presented the first test. With a seething, angry mob gathered outside, Casement took long, slow strides to the dock and sat with Daniel Bailey, the Irish Brigade member caught in Kerry, who was also charged. As prosecutors outlined the case, all eyes were on Casement.

'A tall, slim figure, with nerves vibrant as violin strings and a classical head poised between slightly drooping shoulders,' *The Times* reported. 'The comments he passed to his counsel were written quickly and were in a bold and apparently firm hand.' An illicit courtroom photo of Casement was published around the world. When Casement spotted two female friends in the packed public gallery – almost certainly the Bannisters – he bowed and waved.

The three-day hearing was a legal skirmish, a warm-up. He was now back in civil rather than military custody so when the hearing concluded on Wednesday 17 May he was taken not to the Tower but Brixton Prison.

It was another fine afternoon in the capital. Crossing the bridge, Casement could glimpse the gothic towers of Whitehall, heart of the empire he had once served. He was up for the fight, whatever they threw at him.

. . .

As Casement passed on the other side of the Thames, Reginald Hall was hosting his weekly gathering of newspaper correspondents in his room at the Admiralty. The 4 p.m. Wednesday 'tea talk' drew a regular group of British and American reporters who sat, smoked and quizzed the little captain, their private oracle.

Unlike other military officials who regarded the press as pests, the naval intelligence director treated them more like pets and fed them stories that could be published, invariably without attribution, and other tales that might entertain or elucidate but were not to leave his sanctum.

This session perhaps touched on the continuing maelstrom at Verdun, a German attack in east Africa, Casement's hearing at Bow Street and the launch that day of the Royal Commission into the Irish rebellion. Doubtless to Hall's satisfaction, and perhaps due to discreet string-pulling, it had not asked him to testify.

Tea drunk, stubs extinguished, the correspondents were filing out when Hall asked Ben Allen to stay behind. The 33-year-old Californian worked for the Associated Press, an American agency that supplied copy to newspapers around the world. From a pigeon-hole in his desk Hall pulled out a rolled manuscript with a rubber band around it. Might the AP be interested in an exclusive?

Allen, a diligent, by-the-book reporter, beheld the captain and his offering. Was this how Adam felt when Eve presented the apple? It was not the first time Hall had dangled what he termed 'the Casement diary' to Allen. Unrolled, the manuscript comprised loose pages with ragged edges, as if torn from a notebook. To Allen the delicate handwriting suggested a person of culture, but the content reflected the 'ravings of the victim of perversions'.

Unlike Adam, Allen didn't bite on the offering. As on the previous occasion, the journalist told Hall his agency was not interested in scandal for its own sake but would consider using the material on condition that he could visit Casement in prison to verify its authenticity.

Hall blinked. Such a punctilious fellow, this Yank. He did not formally reject Allen's request, he simply rolled the pages back together and returned them to the pigeon-hole. He was not going to gift Sir Roger a platform to the American media to say God knows what. Perhaps young Mr Allen would prove more receptive the following Wednesday, and if not, there were plenty of other correspondents.

And there was plenty of time. For now, Hall was merely setting the stage. The trial was at least a month away and it was not necessary or advisable to splash things in the press before then. Newspapers were already skirting contempt of court by calling Casement a traitor. Branding him a degenerate too, at this point, could damage the trial, which had to be seen as impartial and scrupulously fair.

Meantime there were more discreet ways to spread the word. Hall's network included socialites who sowed misinformation over brandy and cigars in London clubs, usually to diplomats of neutral countries who were a conduit to Berlin. In the case of Sir Roger the target audience was British and American, and there was no need to invent anything. It was a matter of whispering the existence of the diaries, showing extracts to the right people and letting tongues wag.

The scheme reeked of vendetta. Casement was a prisoner, largely helpless and already vilified as a traitor. But there was a pragmatic reason to use the diaries. To sustain immense sacrifices the public needed regular reminding that the enemy was loathsome – 'a good hate', as the press baron Viscount Northcliffe put it. The message was also aimed at the US lest it pity this enemy of England.

To destroy a defenceless man's name was merciless but it was not in the strict sense slander – the information was true. At sea, Hall had specialised in gunnery, and in the era of total war, with aircraft bombing cities and submarines sinking passenger liners, he would use whatever ammunition was available. It took nerve. Hall had no clearance from superiors, at least not yet, to leak the diaries. As with a gas attack, a shift in the wind – in political calculation – could blow the poison back at him. 'A lesser man would never have done it,' an English author concluded in 1956. Perhaps. One can also say a kinder man would never have done it.

Two versions of Casement materialised in London that balmy May of 1916.

At Madame Tussauds, workers poured hot wax into a life-size clay mould figure that was shaped and painted and given a prominent spot at the wax museum. The notorious knight looked rather handsome. In rarefied clubs and salons, a steady drip of malice slowly gave form to the other version, the grotesque.

. . .

'The prime minister should know that the bodies of all the executed rebels are buried in quicklime, without coffins, in the Arbour Hill prison grounds.'

It was 26 May and General Sir John Maxwell, having put 15 men in the ground – 14 in Dublin, another in Cork – was damned if he was going to dig them up. He was rejecting a request from relatives to retrieve bodies for reburial, his letter told Downing Street. 'Irish sentimentality will turn these graves into martyrs' shrines.'

Excavating tombs in Egypt was scholarship, here it would be mischief, and there was enough of that already – the military governor was receiving disquieting reports about sympathy for the rebels. Three weeks earlier they were the destroyers of Dublin, now they were, in some quarters, heroes, with the British cast as villains. It made no sense.

Instead of executing hundreds, Hun-style, he had called a halt at 15 and commuted dozens of death sentences. At Downing Street's insistence, no woman had been shot, not even Countess Markievicz, whom the general felt sorely deserved it. Since a visit by the prime minister two weeks earlier the prisoners at Richmond barracks were receiving better food than the guards. Martial law had been declared but not enforced – the checkpoints, searches and other measures were conducted under the regular war-time regulations.

There had been regrettable incidents. James Connolly's wounds required him to be tied to a chair when shot. It emerged that soldiers killed 13 civilians during fighting on North King Street, and that at

Portobello barracks a captain, apparently insane, executed another three civilians, including a prominent pacifist called Francis Sheehy Skeffington, which was causing uproar. For Maxwell, such unfortunate events were 'happily few', given the cauldron of the rising.

Yet Maxwell was being assailed on all sides. As early as 8 May the viceroy, Lord Wimborne, warned of potentially 'disastrous consequences' if executions continued. The Bishop of Limerick called him a cruel dictator. Most damaging of all was a denunciation in the House of Commons by John Dillon, an Irish Parliamentary Party MP. 'You are washing out our whole life work in a sea of blood . . . this series of executions is doing more harm than any Englishman in this House can possibly fathom.'

Maxwell was baffled. Where was the sympathy for the soldiers and police who died? Or the civilian casualties who bore the brunt of the rebellion? Where was the outrage at the conniving with Germany?

He was no brute, nor stupid, but wobbling on a tightrope: on one side, a mandate to punish the insurrectionists; on the other, Irish history and psychology. Despite the curses and chamberpots hurled at the rebels immediately after the rising, public sentiment was more ambiguous and nuanced than first appeared. The general thought he had shown restraint, but for many in Ireland the private courts-martial and executions were like watching blood seep from a closed door. If there was equilibrium between coercion and conciliation, Maxwell could not find it. He wasn't Cromwell, but the situation required Solomon, and he was just Conky.

As May progressed, more vexing reports landed on his desk. People were wearing Sinn Féin badges more frequently and openly. The RIC detected 'sudden unfriendliness or even hostility' towards the police. There was 'sullenness' among the Dublin poor.

A month earlier most of the rebel leaders were unknown, but now their pictures gazed from newspapers along with articles about their families, writings and Catholic devotion. Connolly and Patrick Pearse, especially, were catching the public imagination.

So too was Joe Plunkett. Ever since a jeweller told the press about the veiled, weeping beauty who bought a wedding ring, the public could not get enough of the candle-lit ceremony and the bride who became a widow. They were already singing ballads. *'God bless thee, Grace Plunkett, thy faithful devotion, has won the great heart of a nation to thee . . .'*

So the general's letter to the prime minister was firm: no executed men would be dug up, they would remain in their pit, dissolving in quicklime. There would be no martyrs' shrines.

. . .

The bells tolled for Joe Plunkett two weeks later, on the morning of Thursday 8 June, at the Carmelite church on Whitefriar Street, near Dublin Castle.

More than a thousand worshippers watched in silence as the poet's parents, the papal count and countess, and his widow, Grace, took their pew. 'Your prayers are requested for the repose of the soul of Joseph Mary Plunkett,' intoned the deacon, and every head bowed. Requiem masses for other executed leaders were scheduled at other churches throughout the city.

When the service for Plunkett ended, the congregation erupted in cheers for his parents and his widow. The symbolism was perfect: the rising's tragic, romantic heroine mourning her love in the one church in Ireland that held the relics of St Valentine.

Ireland's most celebrated poet, William Butler Yeats, disapproved of the rising but sensed changing sentiment towards the dead rebel leaders, and began sketching notes for a poem. 'A terrible beauty,' he wrote, 'has been born.'

General Maxwell, pen in hand, was also trying to articulate the shift. 'The Irish,' he wrote in a fresh letter to Downing Street, 'are impossible people.'

. . .

'Oh, Roddie! To think I should see you here!'"

On the same day Dublin was praying for Plunkett, in Brixton Prison Richard Morten gripped Casement's hand and wept. It seemed inconceivable his best friend, the man he considered a brother, should go on trial for his life.

Confidants and confreres, they had known each other for decades. With his wife, Morten had often hosted 'Roddie' – a term used by Casement's closest friends and relatives – at their Buckinghamshire home. When arrested in Kerry, the fugitive had blurted out Morten's name and address as his own, an emergency measure forgiven by the actual Morten.

It was a poignant reunion. Morten was one of the few Englishman who wanted to save Casement. He did not endorse his actions in Germany but would not abandon his friend – no matter what was said. He wondered if, or how, to broach that.

Since the preliminary court hearing three weeks earlier, Casement's mood had slalomed between defiance and despondence. It helped that the prison medical officer had rid him of the lice and lifted a prohibition on cigarettes, and he had better food and access to books and newspapers. The trial for high treason had been fixed for 26 June, in just over two weeks.

Wreathed in smoke, the men talked and talked and the allotted time neared its end. Morten was on the point of leaving when the words bubbled out. 'What about the other thing, Roddie?'

The other thing. It needed no description, no elaboration.

Casement looked at his friend. He had heard rumours that the diaries were circulating but did not know how widely. Now the man probably most dear to him in the world was asking about them.

The cell went quiet. 'Dick, you've upset me.'

Before sailing from Germany Casement had predicted that through 'dastardly means' the English would charge him not with treason but 'something baser'. They had not charged him with homosexuality – at least not yet – but here, in Morten's stricken expression, he could see the outworking of the enemy's machinations.

Morten left, bereft, and Casement remained in his cell, crushed. What could he do? Nothing. He could do nothing.

Casement's legal team was aware of the diaries. A week earlier a female American journalist had tipped off his solicitor, George Gavan Duffy, that correspondents had been shown writings that proved Casement 'to be a moral offender unworthy of public sympathy'. Around the same time a government prosecutor gave the defence a typed copy of diary extracts and suggested a plea of guilty but insane.

It was a double shock to Casement's lawyers and little band of supporters: he was homosexual, and the authorities were busy leaking the fact. Yet no one jumped ship. To spare his anguish they tiptoed around the subject and endeavoured to stop other visitors repeating Morten's gaffe. They would have been reassured to learn that the friend entrusted with concealing Casement's trunks in Antrim burned the contents.

The lawyers doubted an insanity plea would work, or that their client would agree to it. But another tantalising possibility was emerging. The outcry in Ireland and the US over the Dublin executions was unnerving the government. Even if Roger was convicted, with enough pressure the death sentence might be commuted.

The prospect left Casement ambivalent. Perhaps execution would be better than slowly rotting away in prison. In a 14 June letter to lawyers, he predicted government pusillanimity would avert the gallows. 'They are not *men* enough to hang me.'

At the Admiralty, the same thought was creeping over Reginald Hall.

CHAPTER TWENTY-TWO

Trial

Six days before Casement's trial, a rose festival scented London but the city could not shake off the ever-present whiff of death. It was Tuesday 20 June 1916 and Westminster Cathedral was holding a requiem mass for the crew of the *Queen Mary* and others lost at the Battle of Jutland. Reginald Hall's magnificent battlecruiser, which had so impressed the Tsar, took direct hits and sank in a minute, taking 1,200 men to the bottom of the North Sea. They had no chance.

Even Lord Kitchener, the indestructible war minister and recruitment poster talisman, was gone, drowned with his staff when their ship hit a mine. So much death, so many friends and comrades gone, yet as the hymns soared and the bells tolled Hall faced the possibility that Roger Casement might cheat the hangman. He had tracked the scoundrel for 18 months and served him up on a platter, only for the government to now wobble over his comeuppance.

The Irish in America were making a fuss about the executions and 'savage repression' in Dublin, which was to be expected, but normally anglophile US newspapers said the measures had gone far enough and were urging leniency for Casement, deeming him no traitor but a man, in the words of the *New York World*, with a 'screw loose'. The British ambassador in Washington was also advising against execution: 'It is far better to make Casement ridiculous than a martyr.' Hall was not sure Herbert Asquith's cabinet had the resolve to do the right thing.

The director of naval intelligence shared the government's sensitivity to US public opinion. His dearest wish was to enlist America in Britain's fight. Many of his colleagues were sniffy about American military capacity but Hall sensed a vast, dormant power that could tilt the war. So if Americans favoured mercy for Casement, that was no trifle. The challenge was to dispatch the traitor to the next world without alienating the new one.

The trial needed to appear fair even to the dimmest US commentator and congressman. This was in hand. The public and the press would see the Royal Courts of Justice in full legal pomp. The Lord Chief Justice, Rufus Isaacs, would preside. An excellent man, the finest legal mind in the land, and politically sound. Hall had sought Isaacs' advice a year earlier during the Admiralty's Churchill–Fisher ructions.

Despite having hunted and interrogated the defendant, neither Hall nor Basil Thomson would be called to testify. As with the Royal Commission inquiry into the rebellion, the captain and the policeman would remain invisible, ghosts at the feast.

Hall was relying on Sir Roger's diligent record-keeping to avert any clemency nonsense. Word of his diaries continued to waft through London society, a zephyr rippling a pond; once the trial concluded the press could gust up a storm. And that, surely, would settle the matter. Degenerates seldom excited clamours for mercy, not even in America.

. . .

On the cool afternoon of Sunday 25 June, the eve of trial, each side made final preparations.

In his cell Casement's bony hands and long, nicotine-stained fingers rustled through sheets of prison-issue blue foolscap filled with his handwriting – a draft of his speech from the dock. His beard had fully grown back and he looked like his old self. The cockney guard who shared his cell was piping down his tuneless whistling so Casement could concentrate, bequeathing a blessed silence.

After Richard Morten's visit Casement had asked his lawyers to try to retrieve his trunks from Scotland Yard, including 'any papers or documents of mine – diaries, books or anything *not* used at the trial', without result. All he could do now was focus on the trial itself.

In the British public mind he was the rebellion's instigator, wielder of the bloodstained dagger. To reveal he had returned to Ireland to avert the rising conceivably could save his life, but not a word of that was to be breathed in court. Casement would not repudiate his comrades; he would claim the dagger. Duty – and ego – demanded it. He sought to convince himself, and the rest of the world, that he had not been a marginalised, out-of-touch figure but the rebellion's inspiration.

In rewriting his return to Ireland there was a touch of the imposter who in the sixteenth century convinced a French village he was a missing man, Martin Guerre, only to be exposed and executed. Unlike the French imposter, however, Casement was knowingly stepping up to the noose and doing so to serve a cause. The government was depicting the rising as a German-orchestrated confection; he would proclaim it – accurately – as an act of resistance conceived and organised by Irishmen.

The playwright George Bernard Shaw had drafted a fire-and-brimstone text for Casement, for which he was grateful, but if this was to be his final speech, an elegy for what he had tried to do, he preferred to write it himself. Under the cell's bare bulb his pencil hovered over the foolscap.

Alexander Sullivan had his gown, wig and strategy ready. If his doubts about representing Casement still gnawed, it was too late now. The four-day trial would be the biggest test of his professional life. He hoped his nerves would take the strain.

Senior British barristers had rebuffed George Gavan Duffy's requests to take the case so, short of options, he had enlisted Sullivan, his brother-in-law, a Dublin barrister who was licensed to practise in England, though had never done so. In Irish courts Sullivan had a fancy title, the king's serjeant in law, but on this foray to England he would be a junior counsel.

Sullivan was 45, with a sharp mind, a razor tongue and a mindset that sat awkwardly with the defence: he believed the rebels were hooligans and he revered English jurisprudence as the apex of human civilisation. Still, Sullivan was keen to showcase Irish virtuosity in England's most hallowed legal temple.

Prosecutors had repeatedly asked Sullivan to view Casement's diaries but he refused to look at them. It was bad enough that his client, as he later put it, was 'addicted to lamentable practices', and that the Crown possessed this 'horrible' record of erotica, but an insanity plea would merely besmirch, and not save, his client. It was a trap.

Under Duffy's direction, the defence team's response to the rumours was to rubbish them as unworthy of comment – a calculated loftiness that stopped short of confirming the diaries' existence or authenticity – and to avoid the press. In addition to Duffy and Sullivan, the team comprised Artemus Jones, a junior counsel, John Morgan, a constitutional law expert, and Michael Francis Doyle, an American attorney, who had no formal role in the trial.

Sullivan's relationship with Casement was one of mutual exasperation. Convinced his client was a megalomaniac, Sullivan argued against turning the entire trial into a political platform, which the judges would assuredly squash. Casement's oratory would come only *after* the verdict, but before sentencing. The primary legal defence would focus on a potential loophole in the antiquated treason act under which Casement was indicted. Sullivan would try to save his client on the basis of medieval punctuation, specifically, a comma.

Casement's greatest supporters, Alice Green and Gertrude Bannister, dared to hope the whole ordeal would end with Roger incarcerated but alive, despite his insistence he would prefer death. Loving him too much to welcome martyrdom, they had convinced him to fight the case on legal grounds rather than politics and morality.

They formed an indefatigable partnership. Green, nearly 70, was an author and friend who had hosted Casement's gun-running summit at her Grosvenor Road home in 1914. Bannister, 43, had grown up with Roger and viewed him more like an older brother than a cousin.

The two women had criss-crossed London and written letters till their hands ached, eking funds and solidarity from anyone who could help. Donations for legal costs had come from relatives in Antrim and the Cadbury chocolate-making family. In New York the old Fenian John Devoy bitterly wished Casement had stayed in Berlin, as instructed, but now ransacked the Clan's treasury to help him.

Sullivan's narrow, technical legal strategy was a long-shot but had the benefit, if unsuccessful, of leaving the door open to a petition for clemency, and here the omens were promising. Despite the diary rumours, some prominent British and Irish public figures remained sympathetic.

And in America support continued to grow. Irish tricolours were sprouting around New York, eliciting salutes and cheers. On this same Sunday the daughters of Robert Monteith – whose whereabouts remained unknown – were selling tricolour badges on Long Island. Music halls were lauding the rebels. *'If you fought for your country like the Irish did, you're a darned fine man,'* went one song.

For Casement's little team, it all added up to cautious optimism. Despite the newspaper headlines about the traitor knight, and the power arrayed against the defence, on the eve of battle George Gavan Duffy sounded an upbeat note. 'We are not in the least downhearted,' he wrote to a supporter, 'and our friend is in excellent spirits.'

That same night, under the glowing chandeliers of 32 Grosvenor Gardens, the lead prosecutor and attorney general, F. E. Smith, was also feeling confident. Tall, handsome, languorous, he was the most glittering member of government and reputedly the cleverest and rudest man in England. Even his French renaissance-style home, nestled between Buckingham Palace and Casement's former lodgings at Ebury Street, exuded brio. 'A palatial residence . . . which boasted to the world his extraordinary success', noted a biography.

Smith would lead the prosecution and had invited his two junior counsel in the case, Travers Humphreys and Archibald Bodkin, to dinner, after which he produced a typed copy of his opening speech. Their boss seldom bothered to write a full speech in advance, or consult them in this way, but this trial required special care. The text, Smith revealed to his guests, was on its way to New York. 'The whole speech has been cabled to America where it will be published tomorrow morning.'

The initiative bore the hallmark of Reginald Hall. As in naval battle, in public relations it was advisable to strike first.

. . .

Even on the dull, cloudy morning of Monday 26 June the Victorian gothic bulk of the Royal Courts of Justice emitted grandeur, its Portland stone and red brick soaring over the Strand in a swirl of arches and tourelles, a statue of Moses holding the tablets at one apex, a clocktower at another. Inside, marbled mosaics paved the Great Hall that led to oak-panelled courts.

Crowds thronged the street for a glimpse of the defendant but warders hustled Casement through a rear entrance. He would be in the dock alone – his co-accused, Daniel Bailey, was to be tried separately.

It was, as the newspapers said, a sensation: no knight of the realm had faced a treason charge in centuries, now here was one, allegedly spat out from a German submarine on a rocky shore to cleave Ireland from the realm and destroy the United Kingdom amid the most cataclysmic war in history.

The accusations were clamorous yet a calm, ordered hush prevailed as three judges in red robes took their seats in a chamber packed with black-gowned lawyers, guards and members of the public. The only concession to the case's uniqueness was the erection of a new dock to render the defendant fully visible to the jury.

Casement outside the Royal Courts of Justice during the week of his trial.

Green curtains parted and there he was. Dark suit, white shirt and collar, white handkerchief. 'A tall, slender, handsome man, his dark beard helping to emphasise the intellectual cast of his features,' wrote one observer. Another imagined him as a Tudor figure in Elizabethan ruffs stepping into the airplane age. To Gertrude Bannister, he appeared 'dignified and noble ... looking away over the heads of the judges and advocates and sightseers, away to Ireland'.

The usher rose and with an affected air of weariness called out 'Oyez! Oyez! Oyez!', an archaic derivation from Norman French and echo from a more savage era when rebels such as William Wallace, better known as Braveheart, were hanged, cut down while still alive, castrated, disembowelled and beheaded, with the body divided into four quarters 'to be disposed of at the pleasure of the King'.

British law had dispensed with such butchery and prided itself on due process; a solemn tribunal of bewigged gentlemen and evidence-weighing that was – was it not? – stripped of passion and fury, impervious to thunder from the trenches or howls from the mob, an arena of deliberation that was detached, impartial, just. When the usher demanded silence, the court was already silent.

Beneath it all, undercurrents.

The attorney general, who now rose to his feet to make the Crown's opening statement, had himself dabbled in treason. Three years earlier he had conspired to raise a rebel force in Ireland, equipped with German guns, in revolt against His Majesty's government – a perverse symmetry with the man he was prosecuting. It was no secret. But in contrast to the defendant, F. E. Smith had done so as a Conservative MP, on behalf of Ulster unionists, and before the war.

Before he acquired an aristocratic drawl and made his initials a byword for glamour he was Fred Edwin Smith, from Liverpool. Brains got him a scholarship to Oxford and scathing wit turned his provincial law practice into a springboard for a House of Commons seat and a lucrative move to London law courts, where his impudent replies to judges became legendary. When Edward Carson mobilised unionists against Home Rule in 1912, FE, as he became known, was appointed Carson's aide-de-camp, or 'galloper', and made speeches about proud Protestant Ulstermen – armed with German rifles – defying the Liberal government.

In that upside-down time, Casement had railed at F. E. Smith for thwarting British policy. Then came the war, and while Casement was in Germany, Smith joined the coalition government and became attorney general. Despite his record in Ireland it now fell to Smith to prosecute a gun-running rebel, an ironic twist that evoked a Tudor-era epigram: 'Treason doth never prosper; what's the reason? Why, if it prosper, none dare call it treason.'

Two other currents flowed below the trial's surface. Smith and the Lord Chief Justice, Sir Rufus Isaacs, were friends and colleagues. Smith had represented Isaacs when he was charged, three years earlier, with insider trading, and helped save his career, paving Isaacs's rise to the judge's bench and elevation as Viscount Reading. Of the other two judges, Sir Horace Avory was known for ruthlessness and Sir Thomas Horridge for a ferocious facial tic that resembled a macabre grin.

Casement's diaries were the other undertow. The defence had refused Smith's bait of an insanity plea so the diaries were not entered in evidence, but their existence was an open secret.

'The charge upon which the prisoner is arraigned is a very grave one,' Smith began, the voice quiet. 'The law knows no graver.'

The indictment accused Casement of violating the 1351 Treason Act, which dated from Edward III, by suborning soldiers to forsake their allegiance to the King in order to fight against him and his subjects, and alleged Casement had set 'forth from the empire of Germany as a member of a warlike and hostile expedition' with weapons 'intended for use in the prosecution of said war'.

Casement, Smith said, was no life-long rebel but an able, cultivated man who had served the Crown and accepted a knighthood with extravagant expressions of gratitude only to turn against the same Crown amid 'the most prodigious war which has ever tested human fortitude'.

Avoiding looking at the prisoner, Smith described Casement's recruitment efforts in Limburg not as an attempt to suborn the prisoners but 'to seduce and corrupt' them, and said those who refused were punished. Those who were 'seduced' – that word again – were to bring insurrection to Ireland.

The attorney general concluded his opening salvo by describing Casement's voyage to Ireland and capture. 'I have, I hope, outlined these facts without heat and without feeling,' he told the jury. 'Neither in my position would be proper, and fortunately none is required. Rhetoric would be misplaced, for the proved facts are more eloquent than words. The prisoner, blinded by a hatred to this country, as malignant in quality as it was sudden in origin, has played a desperate hazard. He has played it and he has lost it. Today the forfeit is claimed.'

It was a legal masterclass in what one chronicler called 'subtle and restrained invective', and by the time Smith sat down it was all over Manhattan.

Then came the prosecution witnesses. Foreign Office officials testified about Casement's consular career, followed by soldiers from Limburg, returned in prisoner swaps, who described his unsuccessful attempts to enlist them. Next into the stand were the Kerry farmers who found the rowboat and buried pistols at Banna Strand, and the servant girl who spotted Casement. London newspapers revelled in the exotica of their accents and appearance – Ireland might not be a nation but evidently was another world. RIC men recounted catching Casement with German codes, a seaman from the *Bluebell* described intercepting the *Aud* and a diver described retrieving weapons from the seabed.

The testimonies spilled into the second day, layering fact upon fact, some trivial. There was a precise description of a sausage found at McKenna's Fort. In cross-examination, Sullivan's sonorous Dublin tones pinpricked a few holes in the testimonies but the accounts remained solid. The detective who escorted Casement from the train station to Scotland Yard also testified, but of the interrogation, and Casement's plea to try to avert the rising, there was not a word. Reginald Hall and Basil Thomson remained off-stage, beyond cross-examination.

Sullivan's first big moment arrived – his motion to quash the indictment. The statute defined treason as 'levying war against the King or being adherent to the King's enemies in his realm giving them aid and comfort in the realm or elsewhere'. Sullivan argued that this limited treason to acts in the King's realm; to encompass acts outside the realm the wording required a comma after the second 'realm', therefore Casement, who was outside the realm when he tried to recruit the Irish Brigade, was not guilty of treason.

Sullivan's dissection of medieval grammar continued into the third day with help from his constitutional law colleague, John Morgan. The argument was pedantic, arcane, ingenious. And futile. The judges conferred and decided the statute did cover acts outside the realm. Privately, Casement rolled his eyes at his trial's swerve into the abstruse. 'God save me from such antiquaries as these to hang a man's life upon a comma, and throttle him with a semi-colon.'

After Casement made a brief statement to dispute some prosecution claims, Sullivan rose and faced the jury for his closing speech. His heart thumped. Behind the austere facade, he was stressed, sleep-deprived and exhausted. The Crown's evidence stood and his punctuation gambit had failed. This was his last chance to save his client and to prove himself a match for England's law lords. The compromise strategy agreed with Casement now demanded Sullivan alchemise treason against the Crown into patriotism for Ireland. With enough eloquence, perhaps he could win over some members of the jury.

'You represent your country,' Sullivan told them. 'The prisoner is not a countryman of yours. He is a stranger within your gates. He comes from another country where people, though they use the same words, perhaps, speak differently; they think differently; they act differently. It is your duty to demonstrate in the face of the world ... that old virtue for which you have achieved a reputation the world over – the virtue of fair play.'

It was a clever appeal to English pride. Synapses firing, Sullivan spun a narrative that the Irish Brigade's purpose was not to strike at England but to safeguard Home Rule for Ireland. Safeguard it, in fact, against armed Ulstermen who with support from men 'in high position' – a tacit reference to the attorney general – had menaced the British state.

Carried away on his own rhetoric, Sullivan veered into claims not entered into evidence, earning a rebuke from the bench. Rattled, he apologised and paused. The defence barrister had been speaking for two hours. He tried to resume, then stumbled. His train of thought, where was it? His wig felt hot. The court hushed, waiting for him to continue. He apologised again. Random words spilled from his mouth. The courtroom began to blur. Sullivan looked for the clock, it was gone. The Lord Chief justice receded down an infinite vista and became a pin point. 'I regret to say I have completely broken down,' Sullivan managed to blurt before sinking into his seat and burying his head in his hands. He thought he was dying.

Casement's lead barrister did not die but his nervous breakdown abruptly ended proceedings on the third and penultimate day and reinforced a sense of inexorability about where things were headed.

The next morning, Thursday 29 June, Sullivan's colleague Artemus Jones concluded the defence.

F. E. Smith closed the prosecution with a forensic dismissal of the defence arguments and reprised the evidence, including the landing at Kerry. This elicited an exchange with Isaacs about a 'diary' found at McKenna's Fort – it comprised a few pages with coded references to the voyage from Germany – which the Crown said belonged to one of the trio who came ashore.

Lord Chief Justice: 'Is there any evidence as to whose diary it is?'

Smith: 'It was a diary. I will give your lordship the evidence of it. It was a diary found ... I did not say that it was a diary of any particular person. I said "the diary". By "the diary" I mean the diary which was found.'

Clarifying that the prosecution did not claim Casement was the author, Smith moved on with the rest of his speech, but a century later scholars still debate whether the exchange was staged. The pages from McKenna's Fort were unrelated to the sex-filled diaries but the repeated mention of 'diary' – 13 times – may have been the judicial version of a wink.

In his summing up, the Lord Chief Justice told the jury to banish anything they may have heard or read outside the court, and to deliberate dispassionately, but his direction on the meaning of treason in law virtually obliged them to convict.

The jury – a bank clerk, a baker, a tailor, a mechanic and other middle-class Londoners – retired at 2.53 p.m. and returned at 3.48 p.m. A heavy stillness draped the court. In the public gallery people fanned themselves. From the dock Casement surveyed the scene with a slight smile. The court usher asked the jury foreman for the verdict.

'Guilty.'

'And that is the verdict of you all?'

'Yes.'

Asked if he wished to speak before sentencing, Casement removed the foolscap pages from his pocket and began to read. 'I wish to reach a much wider audience than I see before me here,' he said. The voice wavered.

From his seat Smith for the first time looked at the prisoner in the face. Then he leaned back, clasped his hands behind his head and closed his eyes, as if bored, or ready for a siesta.

Casement started by challenging the jurisdiction of a court that tried him under the antiquated statute of a sovereign who was never king of Ireland. 'Today it can still deprive an Irishman of life and honour, not for adhering to the King's enemies, but for adhering to his own people.' Loyalty, he said, was a sentiment, not a law. 'It rests on love, not on restraint.'

Gaining in confidence, his voice rose. 'Ireland has outlived the failure of her hopes – and yet still she hopes. Ireland has seen her sons, aye, and her daughters too, suffer from generation to generation always for the same cause, meeting always the same fate, and always at the hands of the same power.' His finger jabbed the air. 'This surely is the noblest cause men ever strove for, ever lived for, ever died for.'

Moving from history to the present, he said his movement had no quarrel with Ulstermen and wished to win them to the cause of a united Ireland, but that English politicians manipulated and armed Ulster for their own ends, which obliged nationalists to seek weapons. When the war came, his duty was to keep Irishmen at home in the only army – the Irish Volunteers – that could safeguard national existence. 'If small nationalities were to be the pawns in this game of embattled giants, I saw no reason why Ireland should shed her blood in any cause but her own, and if that be treason beyond the seas I am not ashamed to avow it or to answer it here with my life.'

His baritone now filling the court, Casement said he had taken a road he knew must lead to the dock while his opponents – a reference to Smith – chose a form of treason that would smooth professional advancement. 'I am prouder to stand here today in the traitor's dock to answer this impeachment than to fill the place of my right honourable accusers!'

The attorney general stirred from his apparent doze and said in an audible aside: 'Change places with him? Nothing doing.' He then rose to his feet, put his hands in his pockets and sauntered out. Smith's wife, watching from the gallery, remained transfixed by the prisoner. 'His white face and dark, deep-set eyes resembled an Italian's,' she recalled. 'As he spoke, it was as if we were listening to a voice from the grave.'

Leaning across the rail, Casement neared the climax. The British empire sent Irishmen to die in Flanders and Mesopotamia, he said, turning accuser. 'But if they dare to lay down their lives on their native soil, if they dare to dream even that freedom can be won only at home by men resolved to fight for it there, then they are traitors.' Ireland has wronged no man, injured no land, he cried. 'Ireland is treated today among the nations of the world as if she was a convicted criminal. If it be treason to fight against such an unnatural fate as this, then I am proud to be a rebel, and shall cling to my rebellion with the last drop of my blood.'

It was the oratory of his life, and hung in the air. The speech would, in time, reverberate far beyond the court.

The usher again called for silence in a silent court. Attendants stepped forward and placed black caps on the judges' wigs but they ended up askew, adding a rakish air to Horridge's demonic-looking grin.

'Sir Roger David Casement you have been found guilty of treason, the gravest crime known to the law,' intoned Isaacs, the Lord Chief Justice. 'The duty now devolves upon me of passing sentence upon you, and it is that you be taken hence to a lawful prison, and thence to a place of execution, and that you be there hanged by the neck until you be dead . . . may the Lord have mercy upon your soul.'

All eyes turned to the prisoner. He bowed and smiled.

CHAPTER TWENTY-THREE

Erased

In the first days of July 1916, a few days after the trial, Gertrude Bannister waited at a long table in a long room immersed in gloom. Summer blazed outside but a dim bulb condemned the visiting room to perpetual murk. A warder stood vigil by the door. Thick stone walls muffled sounds from the rest of Pentonville Prison. She told herself to not cry.

Boots tramped down the corridor and the door opened, ushering in two warders and Roger. Prisoner 1270 wore the traditional blue convict uniform with broad arrows and a blue cap. The warders seated him at the far end of the table and said the two cousins could not touch. Every word had to be called out. They made the best of it. Roger smiled when she winced at the cap. 'A felon's cap is the brightest crown an Irishman can wear,' he said, quoting an old rebel song.

After sentencing they had brought him to this large, forbidding prison with 40-foot walls in north London. If the execution happened – there was no date yet – it would be here, in the brick shed with a gallows just outside B Block, which housed the condemned cells. He seemed calm, even serene, but Bannister's nerves jangled with all the things that needed to be done to keep him out of the shed, and all the things she needed to say, and not say, to sustain his spirits.

After almost two months of whispers the slander had burst into the open. 'PALTRY TRAITOR MEETS HIS JUST DESERTS ... THE DIARIES OF A DEGENERATE', a *Daily Express* headline shouted on its front page on 30 June, the morning after the verdict. 'It is common knowledge that Sir Roger Casement is a man with no sense of honour or of decency,' said the article. 'His written diaries are the monuments of a foul private life. He is a moral degenerate.'

Details were veiled – even the word 'homosexuality' was too taboo to print – but the declaration of perversion set the tone for other newspapers that let the nation's breakfast tables feast on the revelation that the traitor was a man addicted to unnatural vice. The sort, as Oscar Wilde's lover had put it, that dare not speak its name, and that had condemned Wilde to Pentonville. Bannister could only hope that Roger's isolation – he had limited access to reading material – spared him the press onslaught.

As a convicted traitor he was no longer Sir Roger. Buckingham Palace announced that George V 'had been pleased to degrade Roger David Casement from the Order of Knights Bachelor'. The King also removed him from the roll of the Most Distinguished Order of Saint Michael and Saint George. 'His name shall be erased.'

Bannister seethed. She had grown up with Roger. Whatever the diaries purportedly exposed, or the King did with his honours, she knew the man sitting before her as a champion of the weak and oppressed. As a boy he had defended his sister with fists and head-butts against bullying older brothers. His myriad letters to Bannister from Africa and South America, and his stories on visits home, chronicled lonely quests to protect vulnerable tribes. He was the best man she ever knew – 'the outstanding glorious figure in my life'.

The hate and disdain pouring over him might erase his reputation but need not extinguish his life. The clemency campaign was consuming

Bannister's savings, peace of mind and cherished career – the school where she was acting headmistress was preparing to fire her – but she persisted because there was hope. A reprieve could come via the Court of Appeal, the House of Lords or the cabinet. Despite the diary leaks, the campaign was rallying support in Britain and the US and hoped to enlist President Woodrow Wilson. Each represented a door, a potential exit, along the corridor that led from Casement's cell to the execution shed.

. . .

On Monday 3 July Walter Page, the US ambassador to Britain, sat at his desk, pen in hand, to write a letter in perfect copperplate to his masters in Washington. Originally a journalist and publisher, his balding head, bulbous nose and moustache gave the impression of an old walrus, but he could throw words like a javelin. 'A capital American, ugly, poor, honest, humorous,' noted Margot Asquith, the prime minister's wife.

In the White House, President Wilson faced mounting pressure over Casement. US newspapers leaned towards clemency. Irish-Americans clamoured for it and looming presidential and Senate elections gave them leverage. Eight senators had already called for a reprieve and more were expected to join.

In London, Page had his own view: if the English wanted to hang the man, let them. They had good reason, and he trusted them. The world, he had assured Washington, never saw a finer lot of men than the best of England's ruling class. The war had consummated Page's lifelong anglophilia and left no doubt that the land of Shakespeare and Wordsworth was defending civilisation against Prussian barbarism. The ambassador revered English literature, English customs, English countryside and, above all, Englishmen. If only his fellow Americans could see such patriotism, stoicism and ingenuity.

If only they could meet Reginald Hall.

'The man is a genius – a clear case of genius. All other secret service men are amateurs by comparison . . . I shall never meet another man like him. For Hall can look through you and see the very muscular movements of your immortal soul while he is talking to you. Such eyes as the man has! My Lord!' Page would write this encomium in a letter to Wilson in 1918 but the enchantment began early in the war when the Admiralty captain used all his magnetism to cultivate the diplomat with briefings, secrets and joint enterprises.

Page hoped one day to write Hall's biography but on this July day the more pressing task was his letter to Robert Lansing, the US secretary of state, who had the ear of the president. A US request for clemency would create a very bad impression, the ambassador wrote. 'Not only does Casement, a British subject, stand convicted of treason but I am privately informed that much information about him of an unspeakably filthy character was withheld from publicity.' The British newspaper disclosures were lurid but shy on detail – detail that Page had seen. 'If all the facts about Casement ever became public it will be well that our government had nothing to do with him or his case even indirectly.'

Sharing the full extent of the rogue consul's dark secret with the besotted ambassador was another strand to the rope by which Reginald Hall sought to hang him. It was a small, singular battle but had its place in the wider war. Slaughter at the Battle of the Somme – 57,000 British and Irish men fell dead and wounded on 1 July alone – demanded atonement. Were they to suffer and die, and the nation grieve, while a degenerate traitor lived?

Hall was not relying solely on the ambassador to sway the US. Photographic copies of the diaries were to be transported across the Atlantic, under marine guard, to Washington and New York, where Guy Gaunt, his naval attaché, was already briefing influential figures. A creative rumour flipped Casement's exposure of atrocities in Congo. According to the revisionism, the consul had indeed inspired Joseph

Conrad's novel *Heart of Darkness*, but he was not the hero but the villain, the monstrous Mr Kurtz.

In this contest of storytelling, Casement's campaign had its own assets. John Quinn, a New York lawyer and sympathiser, wrangled a petition of 25 prominent names who demanded clemency. Tammany Hall and Clan na Gael stomped and shouted for the cause. Most importantly Joe Tumulty, the president's private secretary, and an Irish-American, sought to nudge his boss towards an appeal for clemency. On 7 July, Tumulty introduced the president to a journalist who knew Casement and detailed his humanitarian record and nervous breakdown in Germany.

Woodrow Wilson, an enigmatic mix of scholar, puritan and politician, absorbed the competing narratives with minimal comment. The fate of England's famous prisoner mixed morality and political calculation. Wilson did not want to alienate Irish-American voters but had a grievance against some of Casement's Tammany Hall advocates. He ruminated, and kept his thoughts to himself.

On Tuesday 18 July, while Wilson still mulled his verdict, in London five judges in the Court of Criminal Appeal prepared to give theirs.

For two days Alexander Sullivan, recovered from his nervous breakdown, had argued anew that medieval punctuation exonerated his client because the law did not cover acts outside the realm. Two of the judges visited the Public Record Office to inspect the ancient rolls under a magnifying glass to see if a crease in the fabric might be a comma. From the dock Casement observed his counsel's esoteric arguments with barely concealed scepticism. In the public gallery the artist John Lavery sketched the scene in all its claustrophobic stasis. The resulting oil painting showed the clock at five minutes to 12.

After Sullivan concluded, the presiding judge, Sir Charles Darling, dismissed the appeal. 'The subjects of the King owe him allegiance, and the allegiance follows the person of the subject. He is the King's liege wherever he may be.'

Casement's legal team immediately requested an appeal to the House of Lords, where they would stand a better chance. The catch was that such an appeal first required a certificate, which by a quirk of law, or fate, lay in the power of the attorney general. F. E. Smith refused to issue it. There would be no appeal to the House of Lords.

At 4.30 p.m. on Wednesday 19 July, Sir Ernley Blackwell, chief legal adviser to the Home Office, found that for the second time that day he had reason to smile. Another man in his position might have sent an exultant whoop through the marbled corridors of the Home Office, but Sir Ernley was not a whooping or smiling sort. In photos his mouth appeared to curl down and he looked at the camera accusingly. But if ever there was a day to tug those thin lips upwards, this was it.

A lawyer by training, he had risen the civil service ranks by ushering ministers along Whitehall's grooves towards the decisions that wise heads, such as his, deemed optimal. Politicians were a wayward breed and keeping them on track was a grave, delicate responsibility.

In the case of Casement, justice and common decency demanded the ultimate sanction, but from mischief or naivete certain people were badgering the government for a reprieve. Sir Ernley had met the ringleader, Gertrude Bannister – during the trial she buttonholed him for permission to send the prisoner a lunch of roast chicken and bottle of wine and refused to leave until he obliged. He had no desire to meet the woman, or let her prevail, again.

It made the cabinet's position all the more vexing. Several ministers favoured commuting the sentence and sending Casement to a lunatic asylum if he could be deemed insane. The prime minister had hinted agreement. It might infuriate the British public but would avert martyrdom and trouble with the Americans.

Sir Ernley was relieved when doctors who viewed the diaries for the Home Office concluded Casement was 'mentally abnormal' but not certifiably insane, thus closing an escape hatch. To further steel the cabinet's nerve Sir Ernley then wrote two memos. The first, a legal analysis, declared there were 'no possible grounds for interference with the sentence'.

The second considered the diaries. Casement had 'completed the full cycle of sexual degeneracy and from a pervert has become an invert – a woman, or pathic, who derives his satisfaction from attracting men and inducing them to use him', the chief legal adviser wrote. 'It would be far wiser from every point of view to allow the law to take its course, and by judicious means to use these diaries to prevent Casement attaining martyrdom . . . I see not the slightest objection to hanging Casement and afterwards giving as much publicity to the contents of his diary as decency permits.' Leaking the diaries, in other words, meant the prisoner could be safely killed. On the morning of 19 July, the cabinet unanimously agreed: Casement should hang. It gave Sir Ernley his first reason to smile that day.

The job, however, was not complete. Ministers were capricious creatures and could change their minds. Some Casement supporters were claiming he had tried to *avert* the rising, which Sir Ernley considered a nonsense that needed squashing. And despite their man's sodomitic addiction, dozens of prominent figures ranging from Sir Arthur Conan Doyle to the *Manchester Guardian* editor C. P. Scott still lobbied for clemency and hoped to enlist ever grander names.

Lest more evidence of degeneracy were needed, Scotland Yard sent a detective to Norway to interview staff at the hotel where Casement stayed with Adler Christensen. But the existing evidence more than sufficed; it was a matter of targeted dissemination. The King – who was briefed probably by Reginald Hall's royal fixer – did his bit by showing diary extracts to the Bishop of Durham.

Sir Ernley's turn came just hours after his cabinet triumph when John Harris, a representative of the Archbishop of Canterbury, visited the Home Office. The former missionary had worked with Casement in Congo, assumed the diaries were fake and looked forward to assuring the archbishop that he could safely join Casement's campaign.

In his cricketing youth Sir Ernley had bowled out many batters and he would do the same to the traitor's batters. On this Wednesday afternoon he left Harris alone with a diary for an hour, until 4.30 p.m. When the archbishop's envoy emerged he looked like a man who had bitten on an apple filled with maggots. He accepted the wretched diary was genuine – the unfolding, as he put it, of a life 'poisoned by disease'.

In the White House the next day, Thursday 20 July, President Wilson wrote a short note ruling out a clemency request. 'It would be inexcusable for me to touch this. It would involve serious international embarrassment.' There was no elaboration. The matter was closed.

. . .

A week later, on Thursday 27 July, Gertrude Bannister again waited in Pentonville's gloomy visiting room and told herself to not cry. Roger entered, flanked by warders, and gave a thin smile.

Hope had dribbled away. No more appeals, no word from President Wilson, no cabinet reprieve. The petitions had faltered. People dropped out, gave the cold shoulder. Henry Massingham, a radical journalist and ally, had viewed the diaries at the Home Office and confided they were 'as bad as it was possible to conceive'. George Bernard Shaw wrote a brilliant essay on why clemency was in England's interest, but hardly any newspaper would publish it. Instead, a continued drumbeat of excoriation. 'Why Casement must hang; the horrible confessions of his own diary', the *Weekly Dispatch* proclaimed.

Even Ireland was strangely unmoved. Nationalists mourned the 15 leaders executed in Dublin and Cork, but Casement's case seemed disconnected, remote. Some suspected he was a British spy and would be spared. For its part the government concluded that sparing him would do little to stem the growing hostility to British rule.

There was now an execution date: 3 August, seven days away. There remained just the slimmest chance of reprieve.

Under the warders' stony gaze the two cousins feigned cheer, then Roger broke the spell. 'What will you do, Gee, when it is all over?'

'Don't, don't, I can't think of that,' she cried.

He looked at her. 'Go back to Ireland, and don't let me lie here in this dreadful place – take my body back with you and let it lie in the old churchyard in Murlough Bay.'

'I will,' Bannister promised, and for the first time the headmistress persona – authoritative, composed, indefatigable – broke down.

Roger too began to weep. 'I don't want to die and leave you and the rest of your dear ones, but I must.'

In desperation she conjured a fairytale – the petitions, the letters, they might still work, she told him. 'No, Gee, don't delude yourself,' Casement replied. 'They want my death, nothing else will do. And after all, it's a glorious death to die for Ireland. And I could not stand long years in a place like this. It would destroy my reason.'

The warders called time and marched him towards the door. He turned. 'Goodbye, God bless you.'

Bannister abandoned herself to grief and convulsed in sobs. Escorted to the gate, trembling, she asked for a moment to compose herself. A guard pushed her onto the street and locked the gate with a clang.

'I wanted to shriek and beat on the gate with my hands,' she recalled. 'My lips kept saying, "let him out, let him out". I staggered down the road, crying out loud, and people looked at me . . . he was there waiting for death, such a death. I was outside and I wanted to die.'

. . .

Casement recovered his equilibrium the next day, Friday 28 July. He wished to make use of, even savour, the remaining time. He would write, pray, prepare.

In a last letter to Richard Morten, his best friend who had asked about the 'other thing', he reflected with wry humour on his long, winding path to the condemned cell. 'My dear, dear old Dick, I don't want to shut up shop without giving you a farewell word,' he wrote. 'I made awful mistakes, and did heaps of things wrong, confused much and failed at much – but I *very near* came to doing some big things ... on the Congo and elsewhere. It was only a shadow they tried on 26 June; the real man was gone.'

The tone was reflective, wistful. The agitations and doubts that had so long plagued him seemed to fall away as if now, in the shadow of the noose, he had peace. He had never really settled on an identity until African desolation twined around Irish history and launched his voyage from imperialist to rebel, an odyssey buffeted by his mercurial personality, the war and the secret of his sexuality that ended up casting him from honours and palaces to obloquy and this stone cell, with just one journey left to make, an inevitability that now, strangely, instilled tranquillity.

Casement wished to convert to Catholicism but Cardinal Francis Bourne had demanded he first sign an apology for any 'scandal', which Casement refused to do. Sympathetic prison chaplains, however, discovered he had been baptised a Catholic as a child – Casement had not known this – and that they could formally admit him to the church *in articulo mortis*, on the eve of death.

Casement worried about what would become of Gertrude and his far-flung siblings, who relied on him for financial support, and he worried about Robert Monteith, whose fate was unknown. With the war in the balance – a German victory was still possible – he could only wonder about Ireland. Sentiments were shifting, things were changing, but what did it mean? What had the rebellion wrought?

'We reap what we sow,' his letter told Morten. 'Goodbye, dear old Dick, and don't forget me and forgive everything wrong. Always your true friend, Roddie.'

There were six days to his execution.

Two days later, on Sunday 29 July, at 2.08 a.m. Eastern Standard Time, a seed of Irish revolution and German intrigue detonated over New York harbour in a massive explosion that turned the sky orange.

The epicentre was a small island called Black Tom that had stored 2,000 tonnes of munitions destined for Britain's allies, and was now vaporised. Seven people died. The explosion was almost certainly sabotage by German agents carrying on work started a year earlier by Captain Franz von Rintelen and his Clan na Gael helpers.

Uncertainty over the blast's cause averted any backlash against the Irish, or Casement, who continued to gain support. 'The entire Negro race would be guilty of the blackest ingratitude did we not raise our voices on behalf of the unfortunate man,' said the Negro Fellowship League. Senators compared Casement to America's Founding Fathers and passed a resolution asking President Wilson to transmit the plea for clemency. The White House dawdled several days before forwarding it.

On Tuesday 1 August, two days from execution, Herbert Asquith hosted the US ambassador for lunch at Downing Street. The prime minister had lost friends in the war, and worried about a son at the Somme, but he was not a vengeful man. In the House of Commons he had paid a generous tribute to the bravery of the Dublin rebels, and he had initially favoured sending Casement to the lunatic asylum. But when that option closed, political calculation demanded that if Casement went to the gallows, better he do so besmirched.

Under the dining room's chapel-like ceiling, Asquith told the ambassador that despite the shoal of telegrams from the US he could not 'in good conscience' interfere with the sentence. Page sympathised. The US too had a vexing neighbour. 'Ireland and Mexico have each given trouble for two centuries.'

Asquith regarded his guest. 'By the way, have you heard about his diary?'

'I have,' said Page.

'I should like you to see it.'

'I have,' the ambassador replied. Basil Thomson, the assistant commissioner of Scotland Yard, had kindly shown him photographs the previous week.

'Excellent,' said Asquith, 'and you need not be particular about keeping it to yourself.'

The governor of Pentonville Prison had only repugnance for Prisoner 1270, the Irish Judas, so it was not an onerous task to inform him on the afternoon of Wednesday 2 August that there was no eleventh-hour reprieve. The execution would go ahead the next day at 9 a.m.

In the silence of his cell, Casement made final preparations. He wrote a will leaving his meagre estate to Gertrude Bannister, plus certain books to friends. He asked that a roll of Congo tobacco from his trunks be given to Inspector Sandercock, an affable Scotland Yard escort, unaware that the detective had been dispatched to Norway to seek further dirt on him.

'My last message to everyone is *Sursum corda* (lift up your hearts),' Casement wrote in a note to well-wishers. 'My goodwill to those who have taken my life, equally to all those who tried to save it. All are my brothers now.' It was one of the letters to survive Sir Ernley Blackwell's policy of intercepting and eventually burning much of Casement's prison writings.

That afternoon a prison chaplain formally received him into the Catholic Church and heard his first and last confession. His contrition was said to be intense, and afterwards he sobbed like a child.

As evening settled over London, and shadows crept over the prison's vaulted roof, warders escorted Casement to the yard. He lingered in the garden among the hollyhocks, a patch of colour said to be 'the only place of loveliness in that prison', and faced the sun as it sank below the brick horizon. An inmate watching the scene from his cell was struck by Casement's calmness.

The executioner was also probably watching. John Ellis, the state's chief hangman, came to prisons the evening before a job to prepare. He liked to discreetly study a condemned man's physique and in Pentonville did so from a reception room overlooking the yard. Casement's height and leanness required careful calculation, and rehearsals with a bag of equivalent weight, in the execution shed.

Tucked between the northern end of B block and the perimeter wall, it was squat and windowless, with a low slanted roof, and betrayed no outward indication of its purpose. Inside, a beam with what resembled a butcher's hook ran from one whitewashed wall to another. There was no scaffold. The modern method was a trapdoor of two heavy oak leaves over a pit in the floor. A barber by trade, Ellis earned £5 per hanging. After testing the equipment – he lived in terror that an execution would go awry – Ellis retired to a room in the prison to spend the night.

When the sky's glow faded and turned to ink, Casement returned to his cell and asked for pen and paper to compose some final thoughts. These pages too would end up in Sir Ernley's fire but not before a priest managed to make a hasty, secret copy. 'It is a strange, strange fate, and now as I stand face to face with death I feel just as if they were going to kill a boy,' Casement wrote. He was happy to die for Ireland, he declared. 'Surely it is the most glorious cause in history. Ever defeated, yet undefeated.'

As London dissolved into its nightly blackout, friends held a vigil at the house of Alice Green, who had hosted the gun-running meeting two years earlier. 'That remarkable woman continued to speak to us of life and of death with a courage and wisdom beyond all that I have known, unless it be the discourse of Socrates during the hours before his own execution,' one guest recalled.

In his cell, Casement slept until a golden hue announced sunrise. It was, he told the warder, a beautiful morning. Permitted to exchange his convict uniform for a suit, he attended mass at the chapel at 7.30 a.m. and received his first communion, which was also to be his viaticum, spiritual nourishment for the journey to eternity. Back in the cell, he kneeled and prayed with two chaplains. The minutes ticked past 8.30 a.m.

The great metropolis beyond the walls did not come to a standstill or hold its breath for the final act. The war did not pause, or the world stop. Amid millions of deaths, what was this but a footnote to

Armageddon, a flash of foam in the maelstrom? Yet in these final minutes, strands of history strummed and vibrated. The outcast knight's fate threaded empire, nationalism, Victorian morality and twentieth-century state power.

As the climax approached, a crowd of 250 people gathered on Caledonian Road, outside the prison entrance, for a festive countdown, while on a side street a handful of Irish supporters prayed. Across Ireland and Britain those who loved Casement, or reviled him, locked eyes on clocks.

In Pentonville, the tension that precedes execution seeped into every prisoner's cell. Outside, the crowd milled and shuffled. The men sported boaters, as if at a regatta, and women wore munition factory smocks. Children added to the hubbub. There was a hint of impatience.

'He ain't got long now.'

'Serve him right too.'

They turned to gaze up at a newspaper photographer perched above them. Squinting and shielding eyes from the sun, they smiled.

A few minutes before nine the cell door slowly opened and the prison doctor, somewhat nervously, asked if the prisoner required anything. No, Casement replied. On the stroke of the hour the door opened again. Casement stood to let the executioner and his assistant pinion his arms and hands behind his back with leather straps and metal buckles.

Prison officials joined the little procession that marched down the corridor, a priest reciting the litany for the dying, the prisoner towering over them all. His composure and martial tread impressed Ellis. 'Roger Casement,' he recalled, 'appeared to me the bravest man it fell to my unhappy lot to execute.'

Exiting the corridor, sunshine blazed for the few paces to the shed. In the gloom, a noose dangled from the crossbeam.

It happened very fast. Casement positioning his feet on the chalk marks while they pinioned his legs. A white bag over his head. Last words: 'Into thy hands, O Lord, I commend my spirit.' Ellis pulling the lever. The trapdoors opening with a crash. The body falling. The thud-snap of a severed spinal cord.

At seven minutes past nine the prison bell tolled to announce the death. The crowd outside gave a thin cheer; the smaller group on the side street fell to its knees. After a while they all dispersed into the summer morning. Buses and trams rumbled past, another Thursday. In the shed, as was customary, the body hung for an hour.

At the Admiralty's intelligence division it was a day for Willoughby to fetch the rum. The great hunt was over and Captain Reginald 'Blinker' Hall had won, had he not?

CHAPTER TWENTY-FOUR

God Is Not an Englishman

'We venture to assume that you do not wish him to become a national hero. There is, however, one infallible way in which that can be done; and that way is to hang him ... on a British scaffold he will do endless mischief.'

The warning from a clemency petition organised by George Bernard Shaw had not troubled Reginald Hall, not before the hanging, nor in the months since, because cold fact suggested he, and not the author of *Pygmalion*, was the authority on transformation. In the play a professor coaches a flower-girl to pass for a duchess, but it was more potent to turn a knight into a degenerate.

After the execution Casement's supporters had of course made a rumpus, denunciations in the US Senate, laments in South America, scolding from the usual suspects in England and Ireland, all of which changed nothing. The traitor was dead and, to those who mattered, discredited.

There had been some handwringing over the method. A *Times* editorial endorsed the execution but protested at the 'inspired innuendos which, whatever their substance, are now irrelevant, improper, and un-English'. A lofty sentiment, but the fact remained Casement faced justice with martyrdom neutralised. At the end of *Les Misérables*, Inspector Javert let his quarry escape; Blinker Hall chased his into the grave and beyond.

Care was still required. Casement's lawyers had requested the body on behalf of Gertrude Bannister, who was said to be 'sorrowing under a sorrow almost too grievous for any man or woman to bear', but the Irish flair for funerals and shrines ruled this out. The corpse had been stripped, doused in quicklime and put in an unmarked hole in Pentonville graveyard, alongside executed murderers, and there it would remain.

Before burial an autopsy identified 'unmistakeable evidence' of addiction to sodomy. Lest needed, other evidence was gathered: the army intelligence agency, MI5, identified a 26-year-old Belfast bank clerk as the 'Millar' named in the diaries.

Hall's attaché in New York continued to show extracts, but by autumn 1916 there was no longer need to do so in England, and the diaries vanished into the bowels of the Home Office. The Casement affair bequeathed mementos – ministers received rifles from the wreck of the *Aud* and Scotland Yard's private museum obtained the consul's ceremonial sword and uniform.

As the first frosts of November 1916 coated Horse Guards Parade, Reginald Hall appeared vindicated and Shaw's warning, or prophecy, withered. Casement was no hero, no mischief-maker, he was just dead. There were loose ends. Robert Monteith remained a fugitive. And the Sinn Féiners – the 'festering sore' Hall had hoped to extirpate – were crawling back out of the woodwork. But that was more nuisance than threat. The Admiralty captain's gambles had paid off. Across Europe the war continued to rage, its outcome uncertain, but at least Ireland, like Casement, was contained.

· · ·

On a cold, foggy morning a few weeks later, in early December 1916, a stocky, bearded man in overalls, boots and cap tramped aboard the SS *Adriatic*, a White Star liner moored at Liverpool docks. He made his way to the stokers' quarters and reported for duty. The ship was bound for New York, and Robert Monteith was going home.

Eight months had passed since he landed with Casement at Banna strand and left him at McKenna's Fort, a parting he bitterly regretted and grieved, for it paved the chief's death and desecration. Monteith had eluded the police and army searchers by wading rivers and hiding in glens like a Gael outlaw fleeing the redcoats. He had lived with a hermit, posed as a farmer, hidden in holes, run from dogs and clambered over moonlit peaks, all with the one thought of reuniting with Mollie and his daughters.

Luck, grit and help kept him free. The British thought the Irish were cowed, but a network of sympathisers sheltered him – IRB men, priests, farm girls, middle-class families, outwardly respectable folk who channelled the rebellion's spirit to protect and deliver him, with fake documents, to Liverpool.

Before departure, police lined up and inspected the stokers but did not discover the imposter. When the *Adriatic* steamed out of the Mersey her splendour belied the Dantean conditions of the soot-blackened 'firemen' who hurled coal into her boilers. The speed needed to outrun suspected German submarines demanded paroxysms of effort that left Monteith a wheezing wreck with a burst blood vessel, and still he shovelled.

On 18 December the towers of Manhattan appeared, and the next day the liner chugged up the Hudson. It was snowing. Monteith slipped ashore with a seaman's pass, a few dollars and a scrap of paper with his family's new address. He caught the crosstown trolley, changed to an elevated train and got off at 116th Street. Christmas lights glowed from apartments.

He entered a tenement and asked children on a staircase if Mrs Monteith lived there. A small girl nodded, but looked fearfully on the visitor. The grimy scarecrow was barely recognisable from the strapping drill sergeant who had left 14 months earlier. 'Will you show me the way?' he asked. From the gloom or weakened eyes, he did not recognise her.

On the third floor, while Monteith gripped a rail and struggled for breath, the girl opened an apartment door and called out. 'Mammy, there's a man here.' Mollie emerged and caught her husband as he collapsed. Ruined but alive, the rogue knight's loyal lieutenant had made it home.

Six weeks later, at 2 p.m. on Monday 5 February 1917, an official clutching voting tallies emerged from the courthouse at Boyle, a town in County Roscommon in the heart of Ireland, to inform the waiting crowd of an electoral earthquake.

The sentiment of defiance that had assisted Monteith was now producing a seismic result in a rural by-election. By an overwhelming margin voters rejected the candidate of the Irish Parliamentary Party, the behemoth that for decades had sent MPs to Westminster. Instead, they elected an elderly man with a flowing beard and electric name: Plunkett.

Count George Plunkett, a blow-in from Dublin, a stiff speaker and awkward campaigner, a scholar more interested in Botticelli than the affairs of North Roscommon, yet none of that mattered because he was the father of Joe, executed nine months earlier, and electing him honoured the rebels and sent a message to London that this patch of Ireland no longer accepted British parliamentary sovereignty.

'My place henceforward,' the papal count told the cheering crowd in sonorous tones, 'will be beside you in our own country, for it is in Ireland, with the people of Ireland, that the battle for Irish liberty is to be fought.' The new MP would boycott Westminster, a 'foreign parliament'.

News of his victory – officially he was an independent but de facto Sinn Féin – flashed around the country. 'In Dublin the result was awaited with feverish anxiety,' said the *Evening Herald*. 'The newsboys were almost torn to pieces in the rush to secure copies.' In the Dublin Corporation chamber people cheered and waved their hats. In Mayo people held a torchlit procession.

Plunkett's victory was just one constituency but an ominous portent for the incumbent nationalist party that played by England's rules and a breakthrough for its tiny, radical rival that said enough of England, by God, enough.

Despite British denunciations Sinn Féin had nothing to do with the rising, but the party now absorbed burgeoning separatist sentiment. People were praying not only for but *to* the executed leaders and treated their writings as quasi-sacred texts. The Irishmen fighting and dying in the trenches, in contrast, went from gallant heroes to patsies of empire, bleeding for the wrong cause. The song that set pulses racing at pubs and fairs was titled 'Who Fears to Speak of Easter Week?'

On the eve of his execution Tom Clarke, the rising's architect, had predicted an awakening, and British blunders, like continued martial law, were making a seer of the shopkeeper. To undo the damage, the government tried to reform the Irish administration and accelerate Home Rule for the south of Ireland but gave up in the teeth of unionist resistance, and policy drifted.

W. B. Yeats completed his poem, 'Easter, 1916', about the exaltation of the dead rebel leaders and the unfolding, ambiguous consequences, with a refrain that would become famous:

All changed, changed utterly:
A terrible beauty is born.

The talk was of political mobilisation, not another insurrection, but the young rebels released from internment camps had a swagger. Reginald Hall had hoped to cow Ireland's troublemakers but they were emboldened and restless. The rising, a historian wrote, had 'burst the limits of what could be imagined'. It would require British finesse to win back Irish hearts and stop dangerous dreams.

. . .

Reginald Hall's agony of suspense at the end of February 1917 had nothing to do with Ireland. He had thrown a hand grenade into history and was awaiting the detonation.

In January, Room 40 had intercepted and deciphered an extraordinary message. The German foreign minister, Arthur Zimmermann, told Mexico that in the event of war between Germany and the US, Germany would help Mexico reconquer Arizona, Texas and New Mexico. If ever US neutrality was going to snap, Berlin wanted a contingency plan to divert American efforts to the Rio Grande.

Handled correctly, the provocative message could rouse the US from its slumber and save the Allies. Britain was running out of men and money, France was drained, Russia shattered. Germany too was down to its bones but might outlast its foes – unless drowned by a gush of American money, ships and men.

But the gift came with dangers. By sharing it with the Americans, Hall risked exposing the fact he was also intercepting their messages. It might also alert the Germans to Room 40's eavesdropping. Painstakingly, Hall moved his pieces into place to allay each possibility before passing the message to the Americans and now, in the waning days of February, he was awaiting President Wilson's response. 'I lived in a kind of nightmare,' he recalled.

It ended on 1 March with deafening outrage on the front page of every major American newspaper. 'GERMANY SEEKS AN ALLIANCE AGAINST US . . . FULL TEXT OF HER PROPOSALS MADE PUBLIC'. Colossus was awakening. With Hall's connivance the Americans claimed they had intercepted the Zimmermann telegram, as it came to be called, and the Germans swallowed the cover story. America entered the war on 6 April. Hall celebrated with champagne.

By the end of 1917 – now a knight and promoted to rear-admiral – Hall's gaze returned to Ireland, and immediately his vision blurred, as if a mist coated the island. It was uncanny. The mastermind who could read the US and Germany and pull off the war's greatest intelligence coup, and tilt the world on its axis, became a bumbler.

Hall was convinced that Germany sought to orchestrate another rebellion in Ireland – that U-boats were exchanging coded messages with Irish militants and were landing arms, ammunition and propaganda leaflets. Back in February, an intercepted Clan na Gael message had suggested such a plot. Then the US cut ties with Berlin, ending the flow of telegrams. Deprived of his best information source, Hall fell for rumours and gossip and told the government that the largely imaginary intrigues were real.

Blinded to the real threat of growing support for Sinn Féin, the authorities floundered. In April 1918, they tried to extend conscription to Ireland, which united and radicalised all shades of nationalism into a furious, successful campaign to block it. The government compounded the debacle by appointing a hardline Lord Lieutenant and then dug a deeper hole by heeding Hall's urging to arrest Sinn Féin leaders and publicly reveal their supposed conspiracy with Germany. The evidence fell flat and Sinn Féin emerged even stronger.

By November 1918 none of this seemed to matter because Germany surrendered and the war ended. Four years of unprecedented carnage had left more than 20 million dead, toppled empires, remade Europe's map, turned the US into a global power and left an exhausted Britain clutching victory – and its empire.

The audacity and imagination of the little naval officer with the staccato bark and blinking eyes had helped to deliver his country from its greatest test. Admirers expected him to be made a full admiral, and perhaps a baron, but instead of promotion Hall ended up resigning from the navy without further honours. It was a legacy of Admiralty in-fighting and, some said, the Casement diary business, which left a whiff of sulphur.

Still, Room 40 colleagues staged a farewell concert for their beloved chief on 11 December. A caricature on the programme cover showed Hall grinning as he eavesdropped on two quarrelling German admirals. There were reminiscences, poems and songs, including one adapted from an old folk song:

They call me Blinker Hall,
Damn their eyes.
My name is Captain Hall,
I adore you one and all ...
They say I stuffed the press,
Damn their eyes;
'Twas the gospel, more or less ...
Damn their eyes ...
And now in peace I dwell,
Damn your eyes;
Though there isn't much to tell.

There was, of course, much to tell, secrets from his underworld, not least his role in the hunt for Casement and the Easter rising, but some details were best left buried. Leaving the Admiralty and heading into the winter dark that night, Reginald Hall began to fade from history's stage. He had seen the war, the world's greatest, bloodiest drama, to its conclusion. Ireland, however, was days away from raising the curtain on a final act he did not see coming.

. . .

In the general election held across the UK on 14 December 1918, Sinn Féin all but extinguished the Irish Parliamentary Party by winning 73 seats, while unionists won 22 seats in the north. A few weeks later, on 21 January 1919, a Sinn Féin assembly in Dublin declared an independent Irish republic and set up a Dáil, a breakaway parliament. In just three years, the fever dream of the dead rising leaders had become the popular will.

Britain could not permit it. Ireland was the first colony – Dublin Castle's ceiling still depicted the submission of chieftains to Henry II in 1171 – and the foundation stone of empire. The navy ruled the oceans via Irish waters. To let the Irish break free would seed dangerous notions among Indian and African subjects. There could be no independence, no republic. In any case, Sinn Féiner rabble were no match for state might.

Michael Collins thought otherwise. Joe Plunkett's former aide-de-camp had emerged as a senior figure in Sinn Féin and a reconstructed Irish Republican Brotherhood. While the party established a would-be government, his gunmen started shooting police and burning their barracks. Learning from the mistakes of 1916, the rebels waged this new conflict through public opinion, intimidation and guerrilla attacks.

Collins 'put out the eyes of the British' by identifying and executing their spies while running his own informants in Dublin Castle. Lloyd George, who had replaced Asquith as prime minister, ruefully acknowledged this young opponent had 'a bellyful of fire and a head that was ice cold'.

As chaos escalated, London unleashed a brutal paramilitary force of war veterans dubbed the 'Black and Tans'. The Irish Republican Army, or IRA as the rebel force became known, was equally ruthless. The result, by summer 1921, was 2,300 dead, scorched towns, a paralysed administration and military stalemate, neither side able to vanquish the other. A truce led to peace talks.

During negotiations in London a spectral presence hovered: Roger Casement. His lawyer, George Gavan Duffy, was part of the Irish delegation and his courtroom nemesis, F. E. Smith, now ennobled as Lord Birkenhead, was on the British side. Smith was unrepentant about Casement's execution – 'nothing ever gave me greater delight' – and arranged for Collins to view the notorious diaries.

It made no difference because nationalist fervour had already extracted the ghost of Pentonville from the pit of disgrace and installed his spirit, if not his body, in Ireland's rebel pantheon. Parades in Kerry marched to the area where he was captured, renamed it Casement's Fort and proclaimed a liberator who 'brought no great powers... but a loving heart and undaunted spirit'. Ballads celebrated Casement's life, mourned his end and ignored the diaries or implied they were slander:

> O lordly Roger Casement,
> You gave all a man could give...
> They tried to foul your memory
> As they burned your corpse with lime,
> But God is not an Englishman, and truth will tell with time.

The wonder was not just that Casement's spirit was being invoked, but that it was being done so in a rebellion that fought the British to a standstill. In the tropics, Casement had likened England's relationship with Ireland to *sipo matador*, the parasitic vine, but he also found a metaphor for Irish resistance: when swallowed by a shark the diodon, a small, spiny fish, reputedly could gnaw its way out of the stomach to freedom, killing the shark in the process.

The Anglo-Irish Treaty of December 1921 delivered conditional freedom and a partitioned island. The rebels won not an independent republic but a Free State, equivalent to Canada's dominion status, which meant Ireland could exit the United Kingdom and run its own affairs, but cede control of naval ports and remain part of the British empire. And this applied only to 26 counties; six northeastern counties would form Northern Ireland, under unionist control, and remain in a shrunken UK.

Even with those caveats, for a ragtag rebel force facing overwhelming odds it was a stunning feat to obtain an Irish state and a stepping stone to a republic. For hardliners it was not enough; they rejected the treaty, sparking a bitter civil war between former comrades, which claimed Collins's life. But his pro-treaty side gradually prevailed and on 6 December 1922 the Irish Free State was formally established.

Eleven days later, on 17 December, an early winter dusk was creeping over Dublin when the polished, laced-up boots of General Nevil Macready stepped aboard the Royal Navy cruiser in Kingstown harbour that was to take him, the last commander of British forces in Ireland, away from the island that caused so much trouble. He was relieved to leave, he loathed Ireland and loathed the Irish, but could not deny the draught of history in the evening chill.

This was the final evacuation of British troops from southern Ireland. Earlier that day the khaki-clad garrison handed over its remaining barracks to the green-uniformed national army of the new state, then marched away to waiting ships. In place of the union jack an Irish tricolour flew from Dublin Castle. A newspaper reporter felt awed at what he was witnessing. 'What generations of Irishmen have fought, suffered and died for down through the centuries: the departure of England's garrison from our midst.'

Questions hovered. What would the Irish do with this freedom? Could a unified state have emerged if the rebels let Home Rule run its course? Would the Irish example send cracks spidering through the empire? There were no answers this night, just a sense that a story begun eight centuries earlier with Henry II's knights clanking ashore was reaching an end.

The quixotic life of Roger Casement, the knight who strode into the twentieth-century chapter, framed the denouement. He was born in Kingstown and left Ireland for the last time from here, sailing through a darkened bay. Now it was the turn of the British to sail away and not return.

Engines throbbing, the hulking grey warships steamed out of the harbour into the gathering gloom, dwindled to specks, and disappeared over the horizon.

EPILOGUE

Reginald Hall slipped from Irish history but he was not done with intrigue. After leaving the Admiralty he was elected to parliament for the Conservatives – inheriting the seat vacated by F. E. Smith – and in 1924 played a role in the 'Zinoviev letter', an attempt to discredit the Labour government by leaking a purported Soviet document.

The charisma that had crackled through his warships, and the Admiralty, faltered in politics. Hall made little impact in the Conservative party or the House of Commons. He tried in vain to save the career and reputation of his old friend and fellow Casement-hunter, Basil Thomson, who was ousted from Scotland Yard in a dispute with the government, then convicted of gross indecency in a London park with a young woman named Thelma de Lava.

Hall retired from politics in 1929 and moved to Hampshire, where he discovered a passion for gardening. He lost his beloved wife to a heart attack but sustained a wide range of friendships, including an unexpected rapprochement with Franz von Rintelen, the German spy. Citing security concerns, the Admiralty vetoed Hall's request to publish his memoirs, though part of his unfinished, unpublished draft survived.

When war came in 1939 he became an unofficial adviser to Admiralty intelligence and had the satisfaction of seeing remnants of his Room 40 team help to birth a new codebreaking centre at Bletchley Park that played a pivotal role against Hitler – it was some consolation for losing a son, a naval officer, in a German air raid.

Hall would stand in his garden amid rose bushes, watching British and American bombers fly towards the enemy, but did not live to see the war's outcome. His chronic chest ailments turned terminal in October 1943. His spirit remained unbroken. A repairman who visited to fix a plumbing problem, and wore all black and a lugubrious air, elicited a peppery riposte from the deathbed. 'If you're the undertaker, my man, you're too early.'

Hall died soon after, aged 73. He would be remembered, and celebrated, as the wily intelligence chief who helped to turn the tide of the First World War.

. . .

On the winter evening of 22 February 1965, a team of prison officials with shovels and picks started to hack at the cold earth of Pentonville's graveyard. Irish diplomats and British government officials stood to the side, watching. Successive Irish governments had requested Roger Casement's remains, in vain, but the death of Winston Churchill several weeks earlier removed the most obdurate opponent and London agreed to repatriate what was left of the rogue knight.

Illuminated by floodlights, the diggers reached a layer of lime. Beneath it was a mush of mud and water with two small black objects floating on the surface – thumb bones. Soil-encrusted arm bones emerged, then a pelvis, ribs and vertebrae. Eventually, some of the skull. The bones were washed and placed in a coffin. Forty-nine years after the prison bell tolled for his death, Casement's remains were returning to Ireland.

In Dublin hundreds of thousands queued to see and pray at the relics as they lay in state at a Catholic church. To the sound of muffled drums and the 'Dead March' an army gun carriage carried the tricolour-draped casket past the rebuilt General Post Office on what was no longer Sackville but O'Connell Street.

Despite snow and lightning at Glasnevin cemetery, it was Ireland's biggest funeral since that for Jeremiah O'Donovan Rossa in 1915, when Patrick Pearse's oration mesmerised the crowd. After rifle volleys and clarion bugles the president, Éamon de Valera, a veteran of the rising, gave the oration. 'As long as this nation exists and Irish men live, his sacrifice will be recalled and his memory revered,' he said. 'We claim him, and we are glad to have him back among us.' Then they lowered the casket and put two tonnes of earth over it.

Ireland believed, or affected to believe, that the diaries were dastardly British forgeries – an infamy of slander cooked up in Scotland Yard. Few, after all, had actually seen what were now called the Black Diaries: after decades of refusing to admit their existence, the British government restricted viewings to academics and a handful of others at the Public Records Office at Kew.

The forgery thesis facilitated Casement's sanctification in what was now an independent republic steeped in conservative Catholicism, proudly sovereign but patriarchal and economically stunted. When Ireland commemorated the rising's 50th anniversary in 1966, the returned martyr slotted in. Poems and ballads saluted the noble, defamed knight. The government invited and feted surviving crew members of *U-19*, who recounted the fateful journey to Tralee Bay. Kerry folklore tweaked details of Casement's arrest to atone for the county's shame in delivering him to his enemies. His speech from the dock was credited with helping to inspire independence movements that were dismantling Britain's empire.

But even from under a mound of consecrated Dublin soil, Casement's relics emitted a troublesome rattle: some accepted that the diaries were authentic, others feared they might prove to be. Hymns and eulogies sought to muffle the dreaded word, 'homosexual', but still it was whispered.

For nationalist Ireland, the other problem was that it could not grant Casement's wish to be buried in Antrim, which was in Northern Ireland. Britain had released the remains on condition they be buried south of the border. The rebels of 1916 did not create the division, but by forsaking constitutional methods they made partition more likely.

They also legitimised a subculture of political violence. Hardline republicans launched sporadic attacks on the border in the 1940s and 1950s, and then from 1969 the Provisional IRA waged a 30-year campaign of bombings and shootings. They lacked a popular mandate but so, after all, had the republic's founding fathers. The 1998 Good Friday agreement drew a line under the Troubles, but shadowy groups continue to trace their lineage back to 1916, a Pandora's Box that has complicated Ireland's veneration of the rebel leaders.

Even so there is enduring gratitude for their sacrifice. Streets and train stations are named after the rising leaders. The tragic romance of Joe Plunkett and Grace Gifford continues to bewitch.

Casement's sexual identity, meanwhile, has shed secrecy and shame. British and Irish scholars and forensic scientists who studied the diaries found they were authentic. (Not all accept that conclusion – see a note on the forgery thesis after the epilogue and acknowledgements.) But there is now widespread acceptance that he was gay. And Ireland – which has voted for a gay taoiseach (prime minister) and same-sex marriage – is OK with that. In fact, the queer knight has become an LGBTQ symbol on a par with Oscar Wilde and the Bletchley Park codebreaker Alan Turing. This latest sanctification tends to overlook the youth of Casement's partners.

Artists and writers have gravitated to a life, and elusive nature, on which almost any narrative can be projected. One called Casement a 'memory in motion'. A 1934 Hollywood screenplay, never made, envisaged a traditional hero. 'In a small room of a dingy boarding house in Liverpool, Roger Casement spends his last evening with his girlfriend, Mary, before going to Africa,' it begins. 'She is a pretty, young blonde. She loves him passionately but he is not aware of this.'

T. E. Lawrence, seeking a project after his adventures in Arabia, and perhaps impelled by his own ambiguous sexuality, considered penning a biography. 'I should like to write upon him subtly, so that his enemies would think I was with them till they had finished reading it and rose from my book to call him a hero. He had the appeal of a broken archangel.'

There are references to Casement in James Joyce's *Ulysses*, an Agatha Christie mystery, a W. G. Sebald novel and a full-fledged imagining in Mario Vargas Llosa's *The Dream of the Celt*. He is the subject of countless biographies, plays, documentaries and symposiums, including a summer school in the Dublin suburb of Dun Laoghaire, formerly Kingstown. In 2022 its council erected a bronze statue over the bay. His back turned to Britain, Casement faces the centre of Dublin and from a distance appears to be stepping ashore, suspended between sea and sky.

Statue of Roger Casement at Dun Laoghaire, formerly Kingstown, in Dublin Bay.

He hovers, too, in history, defying categorisation. Just sometimes, the story raises a question that yields an easy answer. 'Don't forget the Old Cross at Broughanlea!' Casement wrote to relatives from prison. 'Is it still on the fence or has it slipped into oblivion?' He was referring to a fifth-century stone cross on a roadside near his childhood home in Antrim, and he went to the noose before getting a reply. More than a century later his grandnephew, Patrick Casement, lives in the great grey house overlooking Murlough Bay, and on occasion takes visitors to the spot mentioned in Roger's letter. There by the roadside, half concealed by yellowed, wind-bent grass, impervious to time or oblivion, sits the cross.

ACKNOWLEDGEMENTS

There was no time machine to spirit me to the vanished worlds of Ireland, England, Germany and America a century ago, but I had the next best thing: help from researchers and scholars who knew their stuff.

Steve Ramsey is a researcher of uncommon skill and resourcefulness. He combed archives, hunted memos and newspaper cuttings, trawled second-hand bookshops, parsed weather reports and train timetables, deciphered German gothic script, intuited narrative connections and fact-checked the manuscript – all with enthusiasm and dry humour. When I was ready to abandon pursuit of some arcane point, Steve would persist and find it in a faded document or forgotten memoir. A thousand times, thank you.

In a work of history it was a privilege to meet and connect with descendants of those mentioned in these pages. Patrick Casement – Roger's grandnephew – and his wife Anne were gracious hosts at Magherintemple, the imposing, austere house in Antrim, which was the closest thing young Roger had to a home. In Dublin Honor O Brolchain, a historian and Joseph Plunkett's grandniece, shared her research and family lore in a home jammed with documents, photographs and books related to 1916. Maureen Waugh, the great-grandniece of

Cleland Hoy, Reginald Hall's private secretary, shared the results of her dogged investigation into Hoy family secrets and Admiralty tales. I have Caroline Mullan, Blackrock College's former archivist, to thank for the introduction to Maureen, and much else besides.

Helen McAlister, a retired librarian and oracle of the Antrim glens, produced details, including a hand-drawn map, that breathed life into early sections of the book. Thanks also to Katy English, who inhabits Ada McNeill's former home in Cushendun, and Roland Spottiswoode, another Antrim history custodian.

In Belfast Jeffrey Dudgeon, who wrote a magisterial Casement biography, was generous with his time and expertise. Being a Northern Ireland unionist and trailblazing gay activist gives Dudgeon a unique perspective, and he is – above all – a details man, who has transcribed, edited, annotated and analysed Casement's 'black' and German diaries, a precious resource for scholars.

At Trinity College Dublin Eunan O'Halpin, emeritus professor of contemporary Irish history and the leading authority on British intelligence operations in Ireland, gave valuable insights and material, some not previously published, and critiqued a draft of the manuscript.

Bjørn Godøy shared his biography of Adler Christensen, a valuable work that illuminates the psychology of one of the story's most enigmatic characters. Steve Fielding, an authority on British prison executions, helped me to reconstruct Casement's final days.

In Tralee I visited the Kerry County Museum exhibition on Casement's landing and arrest, and I relied on the curator, Helen O'Carroll, to set me straight on the timeline and other details. At Dublin Castle Paul O'Brien, a military historian, gave me a vivid tour of the seat of British rule.

For filling narrative gaps in Casement's time in Berlin my thanks to the scholars Ralf Dose, Jeannot Fritschen and Manfred Herzer-Wigglesworth. For making the Bavaria section such a joy to research I will forever owe Martin Zimmerman, Naomi Pérez-Fu and their boys Arthur and Adrian, who showed me Munich and the villages around Lake Ammer. Their payment was coffee, hot chocolate and cake at the Luitpold café, where Casement used to sit in a corner, chain-smoking and writing.

Back in Dublin I benefited from the tenacity of Dave Alvey, who has almost single-handedly sustained the Roger Casement Summer

School, which hosts talks and essay competitions and has brought Congolese drumming, capoeira displays and wreath-laying to the Casement statue in Dun Laoghaire.

The bibliography on Casement is vast but I must single out the works of Angus Mitchell, a guardian of the flame, as well as biographies by Roland Phillips and Séamas Ó Síocháin, older biographies by B. L. Reid, Brian Inglis, Roger Sawyer and René MacColl, and essays by Lucy McDiarmid, Frank Callanan, Conor Gearty and Margaret O'Callaghan.

For the life and career of Reginald Hall I am indebted to works by Philip Vickers, David Ramsay, William James, Patrick Beesly, Barbara Tuchman, Christopher Andrew, Eunan O'Halpin, Paul Gannon and Paul McMahon. For wider context and other characters, I mined books by Roy Foster, Charles Townshend, Xander Clayton, Padraig Yeates, Michael Foy, Sinéad McCoole, F. X. Martin, Terry Golway, Michael Laffan, Piaras Mac Lochlainn, Ruth Dudley-Edwards, W. J. McCormack and many others, all cited in the endnotes.

To the unsung staff who preserve memory at the National Library of Ireland, Dublin City Library and Archive, Trinity College Dublin Library, National Maritime Museum of Ireland, Dun Laoghaire LexIcon, Public Record Office of Northern Ireland, Churchill Archives Centre at the University of Cambridge and the UK National Archives at Kew, thank you.

This book would not exist without navigation by my brilliant, indefatigable, longstanding agent Will Lippincott, who yet again took a vaporous idea and with Vanessa Kerr, Allison Warren and others at Aevitas Creative steered it to reality. Joel Simons at Mudlark championed the story from the outset and with deft, inspired interventions made everything better. My appreciation too to Isabel Prodger, Orlando Mowbray, Simon Gerratt, Gaurika Kumar, Liane Payne, Ben Hurd, Patricia McVeigh, cover designer Claire Ward and the rest of Joel's team at Mudlark and HarperCollins Ireland and UK.

Lastly, a big thanks to my parents Joe and Kathy and my sisters Karina and Mandy for the encouragement and critiques, and above all to my wife Ligi and daughter Alma, loves of my life. Their curiosity and enthusiasm made the vanished world of Roger Casement and Reginald 'Blinker' Hall feel alive and urgent.

PICTURE CREDITS

While every effort has been made to trace the owners of copyright material reproduced herein and secure permissions, the publishers would like to apologise for any omissions and will be pleased to incorporate missing acknowledgements in any future edition of this book.

Pages 5, 194, 209 (maps) © Collins Bartholomew 2026

Page 17 (Roger Casement, c. 1910) Alamy Stock Photo

Page 23 (Casement with Juan Tizon, 1912) Daily Mirror/Mirrorpix via Getty Images

Page 37 (Reginald 'Blinker' Hall aboard his battlecruiser HMS *Queen Mary* in 1914) Penta Springs Limited/Alamy Stock Photo

Page 46 (Winston Churchill, as First Lord of the Admiralty) Popperfoto via Getty Images

Page 47 (Roger Casement and John Devoy, NY 1914) Pictorial Press Ltd/Alamy Stock Photo

Page 51 (Tom Clarke outside his shop) Courtesy of the National Library of Ireland

Page 77 (Adler Christensen, 1915) Courtesy of the National Library of Ireland

Page 98 (Basil Thomson) Photo by General Photographic Agency/Hulton Archive/Getty Images

Page 100 (Anthony Drexel's steam yacht *Sayonara*, 1912) The Print Collector/Alamy Stock Photo

Page 117 (Joseph Plunkett, 1915) Courtesy of the National Library of Ireland

Page 153 (Captain Robert Monteith) Courtesy of the National Library of Ireland

Page 154 (NCOs of Casement's Irish Brigade, 1915) The Royal Irish/https://creativecommons.org/licenses/by-sa/4.0/

Page 183 (Casement and German crew members aboard *U-19*) © Tom Graves Archive / Bridgeman Images

Page 223 (Belfast mural of Casement and members of the doomed radio team) Courtesy of the author

Page 252 (Casement's diaries and ledgers) Hulton Archive/Getty Images

Page 261 (Eden Quay and the GPO from Abbey Street, 1916) Both images by permission of the Royal Irish Academy © RIA

Page 287 (Casement during the week of his trial) Hulton Archive/Getty Images

Page 327 (Roger Casement statue in Dublin Bay) © Thilo Rusche

THE FORGERY THESIS

Almost all modern scholarship accepts that Casement's diaries are authentic. The five volumes are held at the UK's National Archives at Kew, in London, and are available to researchers. They comprise hundreds of pages and thousands of entries from 1903 and 1910–11. The paper and bindings have been analysed, the handwriting inspected and the contents parsed for corroboration or contradiction against other writings by Casement as well as those of his friends and colleagues during those years. Most historians, biographers and scientists take as given that the diaries are genuine.

However, some believe the diaries are forged, a theory that has waxed, waned and evolved over a century and in recent years found new adherents. They assert that British intelligence agencies confected the diaries to destroy Casement's reputation and enlisted other branches of the British state to perpetuate the duplicity in a conspiracy that continues to this day.

The bibliography on this subject is vast and I shall not reprise it here except to briefly explain why I accept the mainstream view.

The evidence for authenticity is overwhelming – forensic analysis, cross-referenced historic records and what we know of Casement's personality and habits all indicate that he wrote the diaries.

Common sense also points towards authenticity. A few fake letters would have sufficed to smear Casement as a homosexual, so why fabricate voluminous, intricate diaries requiring painstaking cross-referencing with other published material? There was little time for such mammoth effort and the result, involving countless fabrications, would have been far more vulnerable to exposure. If the diaries were fake, why did prosecutors give copies to Casement's lawyers, who could then have blown the whistle? If the diaries were fake, why not, after they had served their purpose, destroy them?

Forgery theorists have produced a range of answers. They draw on inconsistencies in British accounts, such as when Scotland Yard obtained the diaries, and the fact that after Casement's execution the authorities for decades refused to acknowledge the diaries' existence or whereabouts. Public pressure forced the government to admit their existence, and to make them available to researchers, from 1959.

That dented but did not stop allegations of forgery. One theory suggests Scotland Yard started work on the diaries in 1914, providing sufficient time to have the fake volumes ready by Casement's capture. Another suggests only typescripts were ready in 1916 and that the actual handwritten diaries were created years later, a delicate labour finally unveiled in 1959. Another version says the diaries were genuine but that the sexual elements were interpolated.

What the rival explanations have in common is an all-powerful British state that has sustained the deception generation after generation. Scholarly near-consensus and forensic evidence will not quench the dispute. Belief in forgery may ebb but never vanish. It is an act of faith.

ENDNOTES

PROLOGUE

7. **U-19 cut its electric motors:** *U-19* logbook, cited in John de Courcy Ireland, *The Sea and the Easter Rising 1916*, Maritime Institute of Ireland, first edition 1966, 2016 edition.
7. **It was 12.15 a.m.:** *U-19* logbook, de Courcy Ireland.
8. **singing ballads about his homeland:** Otto Walter, *U-19* crew member, *Die Seeoffizierjahrgang 1911* (The Naval Officer Class 1911), 1921, cited in Clayton, *Aud*.
8. **preferred Schubert:** Clayton, 'Playing pieces by Mozart and Schubert were his greatest of pleasures and he practised daily.' *Aud: The true and in-depth history of the German arms ship which battled way into Tralee Bay for the 1916 Easter Rising*, GAC, 2007.
8. **'Only my shroud.':** Basil Thomson, assistant commissioner of Scotland Yard, cited Casement's comment in his memoir, *Odd People: Hunting Spies in the First World War*, Biteback Publishing, 2015, first published in 1922 by Hodder & Stoughton.
9. **line of white foam:** Robert Monteith, *Casement's Last Adventure*, revised edition, Michael F. Moynihan Publishing, 1953, first edition Chicago, USA, 1932.
9. **'Only two hundred yards more,':** Monteith, *Casement's Last Adventure*.

CHAPTER ONE: OBEDIENT SERVANT

13. **damp, grey morning:** UK National Meteorological Library and Archive.
13. **hole in his boot:** Darrell Figgis, *Recollections of the Irish War*, Ernest Breen, 1927. Figgis records meeting Casement later that day and noted his left boot 'was torn in a great hole'.
13. **cheesemonger, a fishmonger and sour milk:** Post Office London street directory, 1914.
13. **brightly painted doorways:** Nikolaus Pevsner, *London 1: The City of London*, 1957.
14. **errand boy named Cyril Ellis:** *Daily Mirror*, 9 May 1914.
15. **'Flying without wings,':** *The Globe*, 8 May 1914.
15. **'But he felt fresher':** *Daily Mirror*, 8 May 1914.
16. ***The Dangerous Age* ... at the Vaudeville:** *The Standard*, 8 May 1914.
16. **assemblage of horses:** *Pall Mall Gazette* (extra late edition), 8 May 1914.
16. **Wreaths of white blooms:** *Pall Mall Gazette* (extra late edition), 8 May 1914.
17. **Royal Commission House ... ink pots:** Photograph of Royal Commission meeting, *Leeds Mercury*, 1 April 1911.
18. **'One of the finest-looking creatures':** Memoir of Stephen Gwynn, cited by Brian Inglis, *Roger Casement*, Hodder & Stoughton, 1973.
18. **'Magnificent-looking ... fastened on him':** Mary Colum, *Life and the Dream*, Dolmen Press, revised edition 1966.
18. **stepped from a Velázquez painting:** Louis McQuilland in *The Sunday Herald*, 30 October 1916, quoted by Geoffrey Parmiter, *Roger Casement*, Arthur Barker, 1936.
18. ***Swami*** **(Woman's God) and *Monafuma*:** Fred Puleston, *African Drums*, Victor Gollancz Ltd, 1930, cited by Inglis, *Roger Casement*.
18. **sailed to Africa in 1883:** Roger Sawyer, *Casement: The Flawed Hero*, Routledge & Kegan Paul, 1984.
18. **touch of the conquistador:** Joseph Conrad letter to Robert Cunninghame Graham, 26 December 1903, National Library of Ireland (NLI), MS 17,601/2/1.
19. **tendency to hypochondria:** medical reports suggest Casement had genuine chronic and recurring illnesses but also a tendency, at times, to exaggerate their extent.
19. ***Force Publique*, were using whips:** Adam Hochschild, *King Leopold's Ghost: A Story of Greed, Terror and Heroism in Colonial Africa*, 1998.
19. **steamer into the Amazon:** *The Amazon Journal of Roger Casement*, Anaconda Editions, 2000, edited and with an introduction by Angus Mitchell.

20. **'Nobody in the Foreign Office'**: Casement quoted in Inglis.
21. **Morton Stanley had called him 'a good specimen**: Stanley's journal, quoted in Hochschild, *King Leopold's Ghost*.
22. **epiphany. 'I had accepted imperialism,'**: Casement letter to Alice Stopford Green, 20 April 1907, NLI, MS 10,464/3/1.
23. **identified a metaphor ... *sipo matador***: Casement's Amazon journal, cited by Angus Mitchell, *16 Lives: Roger Casement*, O'Brien Press, 2016.
24. **Number 36 was a gaunt, narrow house**: R. B. McDowell, *Alice Stopford Green: A Passionate Historian*, Allen Figgis, 1966. Green was an author and Irish nationalist with connections across British society and politics. Casement, a close friend, often visited her London home.
24. **spring mist shrouded the warehouses**: Darrell Figgis, *Recollections of the Irish War*.

CHAPTER TWO: CHIEFTAINS

25. **Golden Sturgeon cafe**: Frederic Morton, *Thunder at Twilight: Vienna 1913–1914*, Methuen, 1989.
25. **haunting Belgrade cafes**: Tim Butcher, *The Trigger: the Hunt for Gavrilo Princip, the Assassin who Brought the World to War*, Penguin Random House, 2014.
26. **oil painting on the ceiling of Dublin Castle**: one of three paintings on the ballroom ceiling by Italian artist Vincent Waldré. Author visit, September 2024.
26. **showed King Henry II**: the *Dictionary of Irish Biography* and other modern sources agree it is Henry, but some older sources identify the figure receiving homage as the Earl of Pembroke.
27. **Spain and France, sent ships to aid the rebels**: Spanish expeditions arrived in 1601 and 1602 and French expeditions in 1796 and 1798.
28. **Treasury mandarin in charge of famine relief**: Sir Charles Trevelyan, assistant secretary to the Treasury, supervised relief efforts during the famine.
28. **'second city of the empire'**: informal title also claimed by Glasgow and Birmingham.
29. **aroma of filth**: Padraig Yeates, *A City in Wartime: Dublin 1914–18*, Gill & Macmillan, 2012.
29. **Europe's worst child mortality rates**: Yeates, *A City in Wartime*.
29. **Members of Dublin corporation were slum landlords**: Roy Foster, *Modern Ireland, 1600–1972*, Penguin, 1990, first published 1988.
30. **King Carson ... mobilised huge rallies**: H. Montgomery Hyde, *Carson: The Life of Sir Edward Carson, Lord Carson of Duncairn*, Constable, 1974, first published William Heinemann, 1953.

31. **F. E. Smith, a party darling:** Roy Jenkins, *Asquith*, Papermac, 1994, first published 1964.
31. **Several times Birrell tried to quit:** Eunan O'Halpin, *Augustine Birrell*, profile in Lawrence William White and James Quinn, *1916 Portraits and Lives*, Royal Irish Academy, 2015.
31. **army officers said they would ignore:** The so-called Curragh mutiny of March 1914. Well-analysed in Foster's *Modern Ireland*.
31. **militia obtained 25,000 rifles:** Most landed at Larne, County Antrim, on 23 and 24 April 1914.
31. **Berlin's calculus, England was too sunk ... Irish quagmire:** Winston Churchill, *The World Crisis 1911–1918*, Penguin, abridged version, 2007. First published 1923–31.
31. **Birrell braced for another Irish Sea:** *Yorkshire Post*, 3 June 1914.
32. **took a train to Koviljača:** Butcher, *The Trigger*.
32. **pipers leading the way:** *Ballymoney Free Press*, 9 July 1914.
32. **criss-crossed Ireland making recruiting speeches:** *Irish Weekly and Ulster Examiner*, 23 May 1914, *Belfast News Letter*, 25 May 1914, *Derry Journal*, 25 May 1914, *Strabane Chronicle*, 30 May 1914, *The Weekly Freeman*, 13 June 1914
34. **an eccentric wanderer ... Hindu mysticism:** Roland Philipps, *Broken Archangel: The Tempestuous Lives of Roger Casement*, Bodley Head, 2024.
34. **Anne Jephson, who converted to her husband's faith:** Jeffrey Dudgeon, *Roger Casement: The Black Diaries, with a Study of his Background, Sexuality, and Irish Political Life*, Belfast Press, 2002.
34. **liver cirrhosis, suggesting alcoholism:** Dudgeon, *Roger Casement: The Black Diaries*.
34. **Magherintemple, an uncle's dark, forbidding house:** Casement's grand-nephew, Patrick Casement, gave the author a tour of the house in July 2024.
34. **fractured identity:** Some biographers who have explored this aspect in depth include Inglis, Dudgeon, Philipps and B. L. Reid, *The Lives of Roger Casement*, Yale University Press, 1976.
34. **Ada McNeill was tall, smart, attractive:** *Feis na nGleann: a Century of Gaelic Culture in the Antrim Glens*, Ulster Historical Foundation, 2005, edited by Eamon Phoenix, Padraic O Cleireahain, Eileen McAuley and Nuala McSparran.
34. **'poor old soul ...':** Casement January 1913 letter to Gertrude Bannister, NLI, 13074/8.
35. **gave him a rose:** 'Ada McNeill's recollections of Roger Casement', 1929, article in *Feis na nGleann*.
35. **'It is nothing,' he murmured:** Butcher, *The Trigger*.

CHAPTER THREE: GUNS

36. **10 p.m., ... Russians thronged the embankment:** Harold Tennyson, *The Story of a Young Sailor Put Together by a Friend*, MacMillan, 1918. This posthumous volume, based on sub-lieutenant Tennyson's journal and letters to his family, gives a detailed, vivid sense of life aboard the *Queen Mary* and Hall's captaincy.

36. **goodwill visit of the Royal Navy's 1st Cruiser Squadron:** Tennyson, *The Story of a Young Sailor*.

37. **sailed to a coaling station at Bjorko Sound:** Tennyson, *The Story of a Young Sailor*.

37. ***Queen Mary* was pride of the fleet:** 'the finest ship, taking everything into consideration, on the Seven Seas before the war ... heavier, faster, and more costly than the great battleships.' *Evening Standard*, 3 June 1916.

36. **toast between his nose and chin:** Hall's grandson, Timothy Stubbs, cited in Admiral Sir Reginald 'Blinker' Hall, *A Clear Case of Genius: Room 40's Codebreaking Pioneer*, with commentary by Philip Vickers, The History Press, 2017. This volume published for the first time the surviving fragments of Hall's autobiography. He started work on it in 1926 and stopped in 1933 when the Admiralty objected to publication, citing security concerns. Most of the material was destroyed, but seven of 30 chapters survived. Vickers published them in 2017, along with commentaries and notes, with support from Hall's literary estate and the Churchill Archives. The title – almost certainly not Hall's choice – is drawn from a description of Hall by the US ambassador, Walter Hines Page.

37. **twitch possibly caused by dry-eye syndrome:** David Ramsay, *'Blinker' Hall, Spymaster: The Man Who Brought America Into World War 1*, History Press, 2009.

38. **dragon tattoos on his arms:** Timothy Stubbs, cited in Hall, *A Clear Case of Genius*.

38. **newspaper interviewer wrote in 1911:** *Liverpool Journal of Commerce*, 2 August 1911. The article recorded a civic reception to thank Hall for his daring the previous February when as commander of the Royal Navy's HMS *Natal* he extracted a stricken ship, *Celtic Race*, from a storm. The full description: 'A dapper, alert figure, clean-shaven, with perfectly domed head (compensation for premature baldness), large hooked nose, the strong cleft chin of character beloved of lady novelists, eyes of hypnotic force – dark, penetrating, index of an indomitable soul – a personality; a Man, and you may grasp something of the appearance of Captain W. R. Hall.'

38. **'damned foolish thing in the Balkans,':** There is dispute over when or whether Bismarck said this.

38. **'zealous, promising, smart and intelligent':** Cited in Ramsay, *'Blinker' Hall, Spymaster*.
39. **broke gunnery records:** Ramsay, *'Blinker' Hall, Spymaster*.
39. **cold roast partridge:** Timothy Stubbs, cited in Hall, *A Clear Case of Genius*.
39. **a historian would note ... nerved in men an impulse:** Barbara Tuchman, *The Zimmermann Telegram: How the USA Entered the Great War*, Papermac, 1981. First published 1959. Tuchman interviewed Hall's colleagues and created a vivid portrait of his personality.
39. **resembled a crazed Mr Punch:** Tuchman, *The Zimmermann Telegram*.
39. **abolished the Queen Mary's naval police:** Admiral Sir William James, *The Eyes of the Navy: A Biographical Study of Admiral Sir Reginald Hall*, Methuen & Co., 1956. James served under Hall as the *Queen Mary's* executive officer and later joined the Admiralty, where he helped to run Room 40.
40. **There wasn't a cloud:** Tennyson, *The Story of a Young Sailor*.
40. **SS *Cassandra* ... River Clyde:** Shipping intelligence report, *The Journal of Commerce*, 6 July 1914.
40. **second-class emigrant under the name R. D. Casement:** Casement recounted this journey in a commentary written in Berlin in November 1914. Charles Curry, an Irish-American who befriended Casement in Munich during the war, later edited and published papers from Casement's time in Germany: *Sir Roger Casement's Diaries – His Mission in Germany and the Findlay Affair*, Arche, Munich, 1922. The NLI has an extensive collection of Curry's papers, MS 17,000–17,032.
Jeffrey Dudgeon, drawing on the NLI archives, edited and published the full text of Casement's German diaries and commentaries: *Roger Casement's German Diary 1914–16, Including 'A Last Page' and associated correspondence*, Belfast Press, 2016.
40. **1798 rebellion's last stand:** English ships defeated a French squadron in a battle off the island in October 1798, ending French attempts to aid Irish rebels.
40. **most identified with Wolfe Tone:** Casement's friend Alice Stopford Green, and several biographers, believed he wished to emulate Tone in uniting Irish Catholics and Protestants in a rebellion, and seeking foreign aid.
41. **'Great Arctic palaces':** Casement commentary, cited by Curry and Dudgeon.
41. **same city he had visited before:** In 1911, en route back to Europe from South America.
41. **insomnia that rendered him a 'sleepless demon':** Description of Devoy by his contemporary Patrick Egan, quoted by Terry Golway, *Irish Rebel: John Devoy and America's Fight for Ireland's Freedom*, Merrion Press, 1998.
42. **Devoy resembled Sigmund Freud:** Mary Colum, who met Casement in New York in 1914, noted: 'A powerful head with thick grey hair that gave

him a strong resemblance to Sigmund Freud, but beside the aristocratic figure and face of Roger Casement, all the people in the office ... looked plebian.' *Life and the Dream*, Dolmen Press, revised edition 1966. First published 1958.

42. **building America's first exile political movement:** Well documented by Golway in *Irish Rebel*, and Devoy himself in *Recollections of an Irish Rebel*, Irish University Press, Shannon, Ireland, 1969, first edition 1929.

42. **spartan hotel room, $1.50 a night:** Ennis hotel on 42nd Street, Golway, *Irish Rebel*.

43. **assumed he was English:** Henri Le Carron, born Thomas Billis Beach, was an English informer who infiltrated the Fenians in the US in the 1860s and 1870s. *Dictionary of Irish Biography*.

43. **Dublin counselled wariness:** Tom Clarke did not trust Casement and suspected he was a spy. Reid, *The Lives of Roger Casement*.

43. **moderate nationalists to join the Volunteer Committee:** Casement and other committee members had voted to let representatives of the Irish Parliamentary Party (IPP) join the committee, a decision that Devoy feared would undermine the Irish Volunteers' revolutionary potential.

43. **a letter reiterating his case:** In *Recollections of an Irish Rebel*, Devoy said he was struck by Casement's sincerity.

43. ***Asgard* took 900 rifles and 29,000 rounds:** *The Howth Gun-running and the Kilcoole Gun-running 1914, Recollections and Documents*, edited by F. X. Martin with a foreword by Éamon de Valera, Browne and Nolan, 1964. A thorough compendium that draws on diaries, letters and other material from key participants. Mary Spring-Rice's diary during the voyage was especially informative.

43. **members of Anglo-Irish society:** Erskine Childers, author of *The Riddle of the Sands*, owned and captained the *Asgard*; Mary (Molly) Childers, American-born author and wife of Erskine; Mary Spring-Rice, nationalist activist and cousin of Cecil Spring-Rice, Britain's ambassador to the US; Gordon Shephard, a British sailor and aviator. Two Donegal fishermen, Patrick McGinley and Charles Duggan, completed the crew.

44. **later declare, immodestly but probably accurately:** Churchill, *The World Crisis 1911–1918*.

44. **floated Reginald Hall:** The *Queen Mary* had special reason to be busy – it was preparing to host a visit from King George V, who inspected the ship (that was named after his wife) on 19 July 1914.

45. **female crew member on deck wearing a red skirt:** Mary Spring-Rice, recorded in her diary.

45. **in apparently futile tramping:** Casement entrusted his friend and fellow Irish Volunteer committee member, Bulmer Hobson, to land the arms. He first lulled the police into complacency by arranging weeks of long, eventless marches so that the police gave up surveillance. Then Hobson turned

the *Asgard* shipment into a propaganda spectacle by landing the weapons in broad daylight, an operation he detailed in his memoir *Ireland Yesterday and Tomorrow*, Anvil Books, 1967.

Dynamic and able, Hobson was also an IRB leader and with Tom Clarke had revived the organisation. But after a dispute in summer 1914, Clarke excluded Hobson from the rising conspiracy, the start of Hobson's marginalisation and virtual erasure from Irish history.

45. **killed four unarmed people:** Taunted by a crowd hours later, a detachment of the King's Own Scottish Borderers opened fire, killing four and wounding dozens in what became known as the Bachelor's Walk massacre. Vast funerals for the victims further galvanised nationalist sentiment.
45. **newspapers clamoured for interviews. 'Utter kindliness ... radiates:** Dudgeon cites NLI, 13173.
45. **Casement wrote to a friend on 29 July:** Alice Stopford Green, who hosted the first gun-running meeting at her London home in May 1914.
45. **Fleet had left Portland at 7 a.m.:** Tennyson, *The Story of a Young Sailor*.
45. **Churchill was preparing his navy for war:** Churchill, *The World Crisis 1911–1918*.
46. ***Queen Mary* arrived at 6.45 a.m. on 30 July:** Tennyson, *The Story of a Young Sailor*.
47. **in Philadelphia ... tried to shield his face:** On 2 August 1914, according to Devoy, *Recollections of an Irish Rebel:* 'In the procession he and I were placed in the same open carriage and the reporters, who were out in force, took a snapshot of us. Casement tried to hide his face, but was not quick enough to evade the photographer, and the result was that copies of the picture were put in circulation. This made his features very familiar to a portion of the public and caused him to fear that it would lessen his chances of escaping detection by the English in case he wanted to go any mission unknown to them. He was evidently, even then, thinking of going to Germany, although he had not mentioned it up to that time.'

CHAPTER FOUR: ENGLAND'S DIFFICULTY

48. **Shells scrawled with messages:** Memoir from crewman on the accompanying battlecruiser *Lion*, cited in *The Battle of Jutland Crew Lists Project*, an online collaboration that includes accounts from participants in earlier battles, including Heligoland Bight. https://www.jutlandcrewlists.org/.
49. **12.04 p.m. the leviathans steamed towards the kill zone:** Archibald Hurd and H. H. Bashford, *The Heroic Record of the British Navy: A Short History of the Naval War 1914–18*, Doubleday, 1919.
49. **'Like elephants walking through a pack of dogs':** Lieutenant Oswald Frewen, cited in *The Battle of Jutland Crew Lists Project*.
49. ***Cöln* shattered. Her stern rose:** Tennyson, *The Story of a Young Sailor*.

50. **Kaiser ... chained his admirals:** Barbara Tuchman, *The Guns of August: the Outbreak of World War 1*, Penguin, 1994, first edition 1962: 'He could not bear to think of his "darlings" ... shattered by gunfire, smeared with blood or at last, wounded and rudderless, sinking beneath the waves.'
50. **began to wheeze:** North Sea cold worsened Hall's chronically weak chest and lungs. James, *The Eyes of the Navy*: 'He had not been in good health for some weeks and had been put on low diet.'
50. **newspapers to his little shop at 75a Parnell Street:** Michael Foy, *Tom Clarke: The True Leader of the Easter Rising*, Ireland History Press, 2014. A comprehensive, unromanticised biography.
51. **interior was narrow, spotless and brightly lit:** Louis Le Roux, *Tom Clarke and the Irish Freedom Movement*, Talbot Press, 1936.
51. **on a stool, trunk erect, hands on knees:** Le Roux, *Tom Clarke*.
52. **cold fury of a patient man:** Foy, *Tom Clarke*: 'His fierce simplicity caused him to focus on one dream with a revolutionary fervour that never dimmed ... personified the dictum that one should beware the fury of a patient man.'
52. **renditions of 'Let Erin Remember':** Sean O'Casey, *Autobiographies: Drums Under the Window*, Macmillan, 1981, first edition 1945.
52. **prisoner J464, selected for special punishment:** Clarke detailed this bleak existence in his memoir *Glimpses of an Irish Felon's Prison Life*, Maunsel, 1922.
53. **Irish Republican Brotherhood:** John O'Beirne Ranelagh, *The Irish Republican Brotherhood 1914–1924*, Irish Academic Press, 2024.
53. **atrophied into an old boys' club:** Bulmer Hobson, *Ireland Yesterday and Tomorrow*.
53. **'the old chap' had an aura:** His widow Kathleen Clarke, quoted in Sinéad McCoole, *Easter Widows: Seven Irish Women who Lived in the Shadow of the 1916 Rising*, Doubleday, 2014.
53. **recalled Sean O'Casey, a writer who knew him:** O'Casey, *Autobiographies*.
53. **1,600 committed members:** John O'Beirne Ranelagh, *The Irish Republican Brotherhood*.
54. **suspected the former consul was a British spy:** McCoole, *Easter Widows*.
54. **slip the key into his pocket:** O'Casey, *Autobiographies*.
54. **IRB men and representatives of other groups:** Foy, *Tom Clarke*.
55. **For John Devoy, Clan na Gael's duty:** Devoy, *Recollections of an Irish Rebel*.
55. **sought to stifle her Teutonic rival:** Casement laid out his thesis in a series of articles first published anonymously in the Dublin journal *Irish Review*, which were later gathered in a single pamphlet titled *Ireland, Germany and the Freedom of the Seas*.
55. **some historians – not many – would share this view:** No mainstream historian fully endorses Casement's critique, but some, such as John Charmley, *Splendid Isolation? Britain and the Balance of Power 1874–1914*, Sceptre,

	2000, and Christopher Clark, *The Sleepwalkers: How Europe Went to War in 1914*, Allen Lane, 2012, posit British overreaction to German rivalry.
55.	**Germany's massacres of the Herero:** German troops and colonisers killed tens of thousands of Herero and Nama people, more than half of the population, between 1904 and 1908 in German South West Africa. Casper Erichsen 'German-Herero conflict of 1904–07' (African history), *Encyclopædia Britannica*.
55.	**idea for a novel, which he never wrote:** A 1908 letter to Gertrude Bannister outlined the plot in which German troops landed in Ireland. 'Advanced rapidly on Dublin, received everywhere as deliverers and friends … the Irish flag had been hoisted on Dublin Castle and in all the cities of the land. The terrified unionists everywhere accepted the inevitable and a stable government had been ably got together under German direction.' It could be 'awfully funny', he wrote. Cited in René MacColl, *Roger Casement: A New Judgment*, Four Square Press, 1960. First published 1956.
56.	**'this cauldron of hatred and murder,' he wrote to a friend:** Letter dated 12 October 1914 to Gertrude Bannister. 'I sorrow for the Belgians – but I cannot blame the Germans. They offered fair terms and did it openly and above board. If England has refused to cooperate with France and Russia the war would never have come – that is the grief of it all … I feel despair often … I cannot bear to think of Ireland in this cauldron of hatred and murder.' NLI, MS 13074. Also cited by Séamas Ó Síocháin, *Roger Casement: Imperialist, Rebel, Revolutionary*, Lilliput Press, 2008.
56.	**sentiment of a Bronx precinct sergeant:** MacColl, *Roger Casement: A New Judgment*: 'As tough as a precinct station-sergeant and about as romantic as a Jersey City petty politician.'
57.	**'As trustful as a child', he later noted:** Devoy, *Recollections of an Irish Rebel*.
57.	**hired a private detective to watch Casement:** Colum, *Life and the Dream*.
57.	**'Oscail an doras,' he told her:** Colum, *Life and the Dream*.
57.	**German ambassador, Johann Heinrich von Bernstorff:** Devoy, *Recollections of an Irish Rebel*.
57.	**washed his own underwear:** Inglis, *Roger Casement*. 'After some hesitation the Clan executive decided to let Casement go, and to pay his expenses – Devoy having found that Casement was both meticulous in his accounting and frugal in his habits; although short of money, he always insisted on paying for his own meals ('he was very sensitive on this point') and on washing his underclothes, which few people of his background would have thought of doing.'
58.	**took counter-surveillance precautions:** Devoy, *Recollections of an Irish Rebel*.
58.	**palatial home of Daniel Cohalan:** Golway, *Irish Rebel*.

58. **cruised confidently through the shadows**: Dudgeon, *Roger Casement: The Black Diaries*: 'The series of London lodging rooms may have made the youngster streetwise, giving him the later adult confidence to cruise effortlessly around the cities of three continents and operate two separate lives – one as a sexual being, and the other as a gentleman and British diplomat.'

59. **'The Nameless One', a poem**: Casement wrote two poems with this title. The first, in 1898, dwelt on massacres in Armenia. The second, partially quoted in the text, is a seven-verse meditation on homosexuality and loneliness. Jeffrey Dudgeon settled a dispute over whether Casement really wrote this when he tracked down a copy at the New York Public Library. On the back of the page Casement wrote 'Lines written in very great dejection at Genoa November 15 1900 before sailing on "Sirio" for Barcelona.' Dudgeon, *Roger Casement: The Black Diaries*.

59. **former ship's stoker was 24**: Bjørn Godøy, *Dobbeltspill: Kjærlighet og forræderi i skyggen av første verdenskrig* (Double play: Love and betrayal in the shadow of the First World War), Spartacus Forlag, 2016. A Norwegian biography of Adler Christensen. Translated with artificial intelligence.

60. **engagements for Casement in Chicago**: Dudgeon, *Roger Casement's German Diary 1914–16*.

60. **the bitterest moment of his life**: James, *Eyes of the Navy*.

60. **acidic ditty about the outpost**: Cited by Malcolm Brown and Patricia Meehan in *Scapa Flow: The Reminiscences of Men and Women Who Served in Scapa Flow in the Two World Wars*, Pan, 2002.

61. **chest, which was prone to infection**: Ramsay, *'Blinker' Hall, Spymaster*.

61. **Admiral David Beatty, wrote in alarm**: Ramsay, *'Blinker' Hall, Spymaster*, quotes from Beatty's letters to his wife. 'He looks so terribly grey and tired . . . I am sorry to lose him (to the Admiralty in London) but it will save his life. He could not last if he continued as he gets no better, in fact worse and looks an awful colour.'

61. **cheers were deafening**: Tennyson, *The Story of a Young Sailor*: 'As he went away the ship's company, of their own accord, gave three tremendous cheers, and I shall always remember seeing the little figure, with his head bared, standing in the sternsheets of the picket-boat as she was rushing away.'

61. **now they loved him,' one officer recalled**: Admiral William James, in his memoir *The Sky Was Always Blue*, Methuen, 1951: 'The ship was plunged in gloom when they heard he was leaving; they had begun by fearing him, now they loved him. I was losing not only the finest officer I had yet met, but a friend whom it had been a joy to serve.' Hall had been close to death, said James. 'I believe the new appointment saved his life.'

61. **Shortly after 5 p.m. Hall left the *Queen Mary***: Midshipman Bagot cited in *The Battle of Jutland Crew Lists Project*.

CHAPTER FIVE: SHARK'S JAWS

62. **wettest week of the year:** UK National Meteorological Library and Archive.
62. **enthralled pensioners and terrorised squirrels:** *Bristol Times*, 19 October 1914.
62. **Hodson caught the mood in an ode:** *The London Evening News*, 6 October 1914.
63. **Refugees from Belgium:** *Manchester Courier*, 19 October 1914.
63. **Government restrictions multiplied, with little dissent:** A. J. P. Taylor, *English History 1914–45*, Oxford University Press, 1965.
63. **Big Ben was muffled:** Michael MacDonagh, *In London During the Great War: The Diary of a Journalist*, Eyre and Spottiswoode, 1935.
63. **blackout. Headlights, lanterns and street lamps were dimmed:** MacDonagh, *In London During the Great War*.
63. **Buckingham Palace, were boarded up:** *Manchester Courier*, 19 October 1914.
63. **invisible,' one visitor noted:** Alice Ziska Snyder and Milton Valentine Snyder, *Paris Days and London Nights*, E. P. Dutton, 1921.
63. **Northcliffe, a press magnate, believed Britons liked a 'good hate':** Christopher Andrew, *Secret Service: The Making of the British Intelligence Community*, Viking, 1986.
63. **Spy mania gripped the public:** Andrew, *Secret Service*.
64. **German troops had massacred civilians … reprisals:** Tuchman, *The Guns of August*.
64. **active citizens, the historian A. J. P. Taylor later wrote:** *English History*.
64. **tin and iron structures:** Hugh Cleland Hoy, *40 O.B. or How the War Was Won*, with foreword by Sir Basil Thomson, Hutchinson, 1935.
64. **1723, the Admiralty complex:** Colin Brown, *Whitehall: The Street that Shaped a Nation*, Simon & Schuster, 2009.
65. **displayed prows of sailing ships:** Brown, *Whitehall*.
65. **Kitchener would crunch:** *Bristol Times*, 12 December 1914.
65. **'I knew little enough about politicians':** Hall, *A Clear Case of Genius*.
66. **'Take the damned thing away at once!':** Hoy, *40 O.B.*
66. **Hall ordered a brush and ink:** Hoy, *40 O.B.*
66. **small department with 29 staff:** Ramsay, *'Blinker' Hall, Spymaster*.
66. **William Hall, had been appointed to set up the unit:** Ramsay, *'Blinker' Hall, Spymaster*.
66. **his ship, HMS *Cornwall*, to Kiel:** Hall, *A Clear Case of Genius*.
67. **endorsed the plan with a cry of 'Rule Britannia!':** Hall, *A Clear Case of Genius*.
67. **Rear-Admiral Henry Oliver … was promoted:** Patrick Beesly, *Room 40: British Naval Intelligence 1914–18*, Hamish Hamilton, 1982.

67. codebreakers. A handful had already been recruited: Beesly, *Room 40*.
67. blockade that controlled entry to the North Sea: Churchill, *The World Crisis*.
68. 'Well, I guess I don't,': The account of Casement's departure from New York and journey to Norway aboard the *Oscar II* comes mainly from a 44-page letter Casement started writing on 28 October 1914, while still aboard the ship, and completed in Berlin on 1 November 1914. It was addressed to his sister, who was then living in England. To pass any British censor Casement wrote in the persona of a woman, referred to Adler Christensen as a servant girl, and disguised other details. For unknown reasons Casement never sent the letter. It is included in the book Curry edited, *Sir Roger Casement's Diaries – His Mission in Germany and the Findlay Affair*.
68. captain announced they would veer north: Curry, *Sir Roger Casement's Diaries*.
68. James Landy, an estate agent, lent his identity: Golway, *Irish Rebel*.
68. Austro-Hungarian consulate booked: Reinhard Doerries, *Prelude to the Easter Rising: Sir Roger Casement in Imperial Germany*, Frank Cass, 2000. Doerries mined the political archive at the German Foreign Office, which survived two world wars.
68. registered as 'Mr R. Smythe': Parmiter, *Roger Casement*.
68. emotional farewell letter to John Devoy: William O'Brien and Desmond Ryan, editors of *Devoy's Post Bag, Volume II 1880–1928*, Fallon, 1970. First published 1948.
69. a vessel laden with coffee and bananas: A United Fruit steamer, *Matapan*, collided with the SS *Iowan* in dense fog in the Ambrose Channel. *Bennington Evening Banner*, 17 October 1914.
69. hacking off people's hands … claims were never corroborated: Taylor, in *English History*: 'The violated nuns and babies with hands cut off were never found.'
70. enciphered letter from Germany's ambassador: Doerries, *Prelude to the Easter Rising*.
70. memo to Berlin the military attaché, Franz von Papen: Doerries, *Prelude to the Easter Rising*.
70. ambassador said in a coded message to Berlin: Doerries, *Prelude to the Easter Rising*.
71. lifted Germany's trans-Atlantic cables: Tuchman, *The Zimmermann Telegram*, has an evocative description of the ship *Talconia* hauling up and slicing the cables.
71. most powerful transmitter at Nauen: Tuchman, *The Zimmermann Telegram*.
71. Scottish engineer named Alfred Ewing: Beesly, *Room 40*, and Paul Gannon, *Inside Room 40: The Codebreakers of World War 1*, Ian Allan, 2010.

71. **a sinking German cruiser:** The Russians retrieved three codebooks from the *Magdeburg*, a German cruiser that ran aground off the coast of what is today Estonia, on 26 August 1914. They passed one to the British, which reached Winston Churchill in October. In *World Crisis* he embroiders the story: 'The body of a drowned German under-officer was picked up by the Russians. Clasped in his bosom by arms rigid in death were the cipher and signal books of the German navy.' Historians agree the code was invaluable but doubt Churchill's macabre colour.

72. **soon sight the Faroes:** Casement letter, in Curry, *Sir Roger Casement's Diaries*.

72. **granite battery ... shark's jaws:** Casement letter, in Curry, *Sir Roger Casement's Diaries*.

73. **codebreakers worked seven days a week, a night shift and day shift:** according to Beesly, at this stage naval intelligence had just seven codebreakers, four working by day, three by night.

73. **'Open Letter to Irishmen':** Casement wrote it in the US on 17 September 1914 and the *Irish Independent* published it on 5 October.

73. **jolted his former employers at the Foreign Office:** Arthur Nicolson, the department's under-secretary, wrote to Casement to ask if he was indeed the author of the letter.

73. **British agents in New York visited:** Devoy, in *Recollections of an Irish Rebel*: 'They missed him after he left and made inquiries at the hotel.'

73. **guards hauled away six Germans:** Casement letter, in Curry, *Sir Roger Casement's Diaries*.

74. **board dissolved. There was laughter:** Casement letter, in Curry, *Sir Roger Casement's Diaries*.

74. **at 10 a.m. they stepped out:** As part of Casement's later effort to expose what became known as the 'Findlay affair', on 9 April 1915 Adler Christensen made a statement at the US consulate in Berlin about their experiences in Norway the previous October. Much must be taken with doses of salt, but certain details, such as the timeline, are credible. Included in Curry, *Sir Roger Casement's Diaries*.

74. **enter Germany. The ambassador:** The head of legation was technically a minister but for clarity the term 'ambassador' is used.

74. **regard Adler as a 'treasure':** Dudgeon, *Roger Casement: The Black Diaries*.

74. **headed up Karl Johans gate:** Godøy, *Dobbeltspill* (Double play).

CHAPTER SIX: OPEN TREASON

75. **Lindley, short, balding, son of a baron:** *Oxford Dictionary of National Biography*.

75. **audience in an upstairs study:** Adler Christensen written statement of 9 April 1915, cited in Curry, *Sir Roger Casement's Diaries*.

75. **English nobleman – he withheld the name:** Letter from Mansfeldt de Cardonnel Findlay, head of Britain's legation at Christiania, to the foreign secretary, Sir Edward Grey, 31 October 1914. It cited Lindley's meeting with Christensen on 29 October and outlined Findlay's meetings with Christensen on 30 and 31 October. The (UK) National Archives (TNA) at Kew. MEPO 2/10660.

75. **unnatural relations:** Findlay wording: 'He implied that their relations were of an unnatural nature and that consequently he had great power over this man who trusted him absolutely.'

76. **admired Norwegian men as hearty, wholesome:** Godøy, *Dobbeltspill* (Double play).

76. **tallest Englishman in diplomacy, 6 ft 9 in.:** In *Memoirs of a British Agent*, Putnam, 1932, R. H. Bruce Lockhart described meeting Findlay in 1918: 'One of the tallest Englishmen in the world and certainly the tallest man in diplomacy. He was a good organiser and ... ran his huge legation with great efficiency. In his political views he was an extreme Conservative, who would rather have lost the war than run the risk of social upheaval in England.'

76. **'fleshy, dissipated appearance':** Findlay made this observation about Christensen in a note to the Foreign Office on 3 January 1915. TNA, FO 337/107.

76. **Assuring the visitor that the British indeed paid:** Findlay letter to Grey, 31 October 1914.

76. **Born in 1890, he was the eldest of five children:** Godøy, *Dobbeltspill* (Double play).

77. **stole cash, beer, boots, food, horseshoes:** Godøy, *Dobbeltspill* (Double play).

77. **In the US he acquired a wife:** Sadie Weaver, a member of the Nansemond Indian Nation in Virginia. Dudgeon, *Roger Casement: The Black Diaries*.

77. **evidence they met several years earlier in South America:** a note in Casement's handwriting from 1915 refers to meeting Christensen in South America, before their 1914 encounter in New York. In a statement to British authorities in May 1916, Christensen said he met Casement about 10 or 11 years earlier in Montevideo, Uruguay, and that they had a brief relationship.

78. **buffeted by life, and was sexually versatile:** Dudgeon, *Roger Casement: The Black Diaries*.

78. **tell people to go fuck themselves:** Godøy, *Dobbeltspill* (Double play).

78. **an immobile face:** Joe Plunkett remarked on his 'curiously immobile face, not easy to decipher'.

78. **fallen for a sociopath:** Dudgeon, *Roger Casement: The Black Diaries*: 'The evidence suggests that Adler had a pathological personality. Indeed he was

a sociopath, entirely self-interested but not averse to becoming emotionally involved in whatever scheme he had in progress.'

In *Dobbeltspill* (Double play) Godøy suggests an amoral opportunist: 'Christensen developed an early taste for easy money and quick pleasure. His conscience doesn't seem to have bothered him, neither when he stole wallets in Moss nor when he offered to sell Casement in Christiania. Or are we wrong? Perhaps there was a core of warmth and . . . he was just helpless in his day-to-day existence, and ruined every opportunity he had in life. The result was that he constantly had to run away from his enemies. He often succeeded. But in the end, he had to give in to the one enemy he could never escape – himself.'

78. **Casement's room with a breathless story:** Casement 'memorandum', written in Berlin and dated 16 November 1914. Included in Curry, *Sir Roger Casement's Diaries*.
78. **said whoever 'knocked him on the head':** Adler Christensen written statement of 9 April 1915.
78. **'monstrous bribes' to commit a 'dastardly:** Casement's open letter to the British foreign secretary, Sir Edward Grey, dated 1 February 1915.
79. **letters to Herr Sigvald Wiig, a legation clerk:** Casement's 'memorandum', 16 October 1914.
79. **'My dear Sir Edward Grey:** Findlay letter to the foreign secretary, 31 October 1914.
79. **triumph of Norwegian integrity,':** Casement's open letter to Sir Edward Grey, 1 February 1915.
80. **Consett . . . Casement as 'distinguished looking':** Findlay letter to Grey, 31 October 1914.
80. **By 7.45 p.m. he was in Berlin:** Casement's 'memorandum', 16 November 1914.
80. **Brandenburg Gate in the heart of the city:** Karl Baedeker, *Berlin and its Environs: Handbook for Travellers*, Charles Scribner, 1912.
80. **new alias, Mr Hammond of New York:** Dudgeon, *Roger Casement's German Diary*.
81. **diners filled restaurants:** *Grand Forks Daily Herald*, quoting US visitor to Berlin, 5 October 1914.
81. **Women . . . tram conductors:** *Northern Daily Telegraph*, citing visitor to Berlin, 24 October 1914.
81. **Music hall comedians made bleak jokes:** Detailed account of the mood in Germany's capital from an unnamed citizen of a neutral country, in 'Civil life in Berlin', *The Times*, 17 October 1914.
81. **'Nicht zu Laut':** unnamed observer from neutral country cited in *The Times*, 17 October 1914.

82. **Teutonic moral and military superiority:** Tuchman, *The Guns of August*, on the decision to attack France via neutral Belgium: 'A hundred years of German philosophy went into the making of a decision in which the seed of self-destruction lay embedded, waiting for its hour.'
82. **hierarchy of enmity:** James Gerard (the US ambassador to Berlin), *My Four Years in Germany*, Hodder & Stoughton, 1917. 'At first, with the coming of the war, the concentrated hate of the German people seemed to be turned upon the Russians ... but later, and directed by the master hand of the governing class, all the hatred of the Germans was concentrated upon Great Britain.'
82. **'If my grandmother had been alive':** Tuchman, *The Guns of August*.
82. **'almost a state prisoner,':** Casement diary entry, 1 November 1914. Dudgeon, *Roger Casement's German Diary*.
83. **'If I win all it is national resurrection:** Casement diary entry, 2 November 1914. Dudgeon, *Roger Casement's German Diary*.
83. **Zimmermann accepted with a smile:** Casement diary entry, 2 November 1914. Dudgeon, *Roger Casement's German Diary*.
84. **Unter den Linden less impressive than expected:** Casement diary entry, 2 November 1914. Dudgeon, *Roger Casement's German Diary*.
84. **shake hands with a German spy?':** 'MI5's early years', MI5 official history. https://www.mi5.gov.uk/history/mi5s-early-years/carl-hans-lody.
84. **Lody walked steadily and stiffly:** John Fraser, a Yeoman Warder in 1914, quoted in BBC article. 'World War One: eleven shot at dawn in Tower of London', 26 February 2014.
85. **he looked right through me,':** *South Wales Evening Post*, 28 October 1943, cites the quote from an obituary of Hall by Admiral Algernon Walker-Heneage-Vivian.
85. **'Fire!' Eight shots rang out:** 'Carl Lody's End', *Derby Daily Telegraph*, 11 November 1914.
85. **home at 53 Cadogan Gardens:** Hall, *A Clear Case of Genius*.
85. **Hugh Cleland Hoy, recorded:** Hoy, *40 O.B.*
85. **'crackling breeze' ... a historian noted:** Tuchman, *The Zimmermann Telegram*.
85. **cryptographers would move to a new home:** Beesly, *Room 40*.
86. **'miraculous draught of the fishes':** Gannon, *Inside Room 40*.
86. **'Ring bell,':** Penelope Fitzgerald, *The Knox Brothers*, Fourth Estate, 2013. First published 1977.
86. **card index of suspicious persons ... scale from AA to BB:** Andrew, *Secret Service*.
87. **Why? That question can never be fully answered:** However, biographers tend to agree that a key motive was to revisit the encounters. Reid, *The*

Lives of Roger Casement: 'A kind of afterglow or second experience of the event that then made it vicariously repeatable, to be savoured at will.'

Inglis, *Roger Casement*: 'So that he could again savour the pleasure when re-reading them (he would sometimes add an exclamation of delight in the margin, later).'

87. **'like the shell on a snail's back'**: Dudgeon, *Roger Casement: The Black Diaries*.
88. **6 November ... message across the Atlantic**: Message from the German Foreign Office to the Germany embassy in Washington. 'Casement begs that the following intelligence be transmitted ... : [the enemy] are ignorant true purpose my coming Germany but seek evidence at all cost. Here everything favourable, authority helping warmly. Send messenger immediately to Ireland ... let him tell Bigger solicitor Belfast to conceal everything belonging to me. Roger.' The message was intercepted and later published in *Documents Relative to the Sinn Féin Movement*, British government command paper 1108, published 1921, that included intercepted and decrypted messages and letters between the German embassy in Washington and Casement. Perhaps deeming it a low priority, the British did not search the house of Francis Joseph Bigger, Casement's friend and host in Belfast.
88. **Five days later Casement ... lamenting he had left 'papers'**: Casement letter dated 11 November 1914 to Clan na Gael member Joseph McGarrity. 'My chief concern is for my sister in Ireland & for my papers with Bigger and at the agent's in London. How foolish of me not to have got them over to the USA. Now the enemy will get them I fear. They are in a state of mind that sticks at nothing.' Casement had left trunks at his shipping agent, W. J. Allison, at Farringdon Road, but it was the trunks at his lodging house at Ebury Street that contained sensitive papers.
88. **20 November ... official German government statement**: Casement diary entry, 24 November 1914. Dudgeon, *Roger Casement's German Diary*.
89. **must have gone mad**: Arthur Conan Doyle believed his friend was 'a sick man ... worn by tropical hardships' and 'not in a normal state of mind'. Letter to E. D. Morel, cited in Philipps, *Broken Archangel*.

CHAPTER SEVEN: SAYONARA

93. **Reginald McKenna, stood by the fireplace**: Hall, *A Clear Case of Genius*, depicts the scene in detail. Hall co-wrote his incomplete autobiography with a ghost writer, Ralph Straus, which may account for literary flourishes in certain sections, such as the encounter with McKenna. When the

Admiralty kiboshed the autobiography, Straus suggested doing it as a novel but Hall declined.

94. **MP was kicking up hell about it:** Hall, *A Clear Case of Genius*, does not name the MP but explains the background. The new censorship system had initially worked smoothly and unnoticed – the censors steamed open letters and copied or photographed the contents. Some letters were retained but most were re-sealed and resumed their journey to the intended recipient. For their records the censors made a note of each letter on a slip of paper. One note was accidentally included in a re-sealed letter to an MP, who was outraged to discover the authorities were tampering with his mail and threatened to ask awkward questions in the House of Commons.

95. **Wrangling £1,600 of funding from Churchill:** Hall, *A Clear Case of Genius*.

95. **no slavish regard for peacetime precedents:** Hall, *A Clear Case of Genius*, expands on his mindset: 'I had taken the law into my own hands. True, there had been no ill purpose on my mind, but would that be accounted sufficient excuse? Had the government yet realised the nature of its colossal task? . . . it seemed that except for Kitchener himself, and possibly the First Lord [Churchill], no member of the cabinet was yet prepared to forget his peace-time principles and fight with new and if necessary undemocratic weapons.'

95. **Hall was invited to Downing Street:** Hall, *A Clear Case of Genius*.

95. **employed thousands of postal censors:** Andrew, *Secret Service*: 'In April 1915 the postal censors were formally reconstituted as a new department at the War Office ... their numbers grew steadily from the original single censor in August 1914 to 170 at the end of the year and 4,861 (of whom three-quarters were women) by the armistice.'

96. **birth of Britain's modern secret service:** Vickers, in his commentary in *A Clear Case of Genius*: 'The ID [naval intelligence division] and WTID [War Trade Intelligence Department] saw the birth of the modern, and present day, secret intelligence and espionage service in Great Britain.'

96. **their complete confidence,' a biographer noted:** James, *The Eyes of the Navy*.

96. **hiring Lord Richard Herschell ... and Claude Pearce-Serocold:** Ramsay, *'Blinker' Hall, Spymaster*.

96. **25 November the Foreign Office cabled:** The message to diplomatic missions in Christiania, Stockholm, Copenhagen, the Hague, Rome and Berne: 'Private and secret: Sir Roger Casement against whom there is strong evidence of high treason is believed to be at present in Germany whence he may at any moment leave for America. Please telegraph at

once if he enters country in which you reside, giving earliest possible warning of departure with details as to route, destination etc. He may be travelling under his own name or that of James Landy.' TNA, FO 95/776.

96. **Findlay ... cabled London with a dramatic update:** TNA, FO 95/776.
97. **authorised ... to pay the informer up to £5,000:** Foreign Office under-secretary Arthur Nicolson telegraphed Findlay on 28 November 1914: 'You may promise informer £5,000 in the event of his supplying information leading to the capture of C. and his accomplices.' TNA, FO 95/776.
97. **ambassador in Madrid reported ... *Manuel Calvo*:** TNA, FO 95/776.
98. **if you believed Thomson's memoirs:** By 1914 Thomson had published articles and three books about his stints as a colonial administrator in Fiji and the South Sea islands: *South Sea Yarns*, William Blackwood and Sons, 1894, *The Diversions of a Prime Minister*, Blackwood, 1894 (about Thomson becoming de facto premier in Tonga) and *The Indiscretions of Lady Asenath*, A. D. Innes and Company, 1898. Some of the stories reappeared in *An Autobiography: The Scene Changes*, Doubleday, 1937. Thomson's sense of marketing is evident in the cover's blurb. 'This book covers forty danger-filled and achievement-crowned years in the life of one of the world's greatest detectives.' He published other memoirs, notably *Queer People: Hunting Spies in the First World War*, Hodder & Stoughton, 1923. It was renamed *Odd People* in Biteback Publishing's 2015 edition.
98. **boulevardier than a detective,' one historian observed:** Adam Hochschild, *To End All Wars: How the First World War Divided Britain*, Pan, 2011.
98. ***Koe tangata Fakahinohino*:** Thomson, *An Autobiography*.
98. **long-haired sexless men,' he wrote:** Thomson, *An Autobiography*.
99. **placed them in a low armchair:** Thomson, *Odd People*.
99. **tweaked to combine another, bolder objective:** Hall, *A Clear Case of Genius*.
100. **American drawl was Lieutenant Simon:** Hall, *A Clear Case of Genius*.
100. **at the Continental hotel in Berlin:** Casement moved to the Eden hotel on 11 December 1914 and returned to the Continental on 15 December, the day the *Sayonara* sailed, to retrieve a trunk. Adler Christensen arrived at 7 p.m., just back from Christiania, and briefed Casement about his meetings with the British ambassador. 'He says that if I go to Norway, Findlay will "go bug house" (an American euphemism, I believe, for "going off his chump").' Casement diary entries 11 and 16 December 1914.
101. **'disquieting' misbehaviour in Berlin:** Casement recorded that Professor Theodor Schiemann, an academic who liaised with the German Foreign

Office, relayed 'disquieting statements about Adler that were unwarranted and malicious'. Casement did not specify the accusations but sided with his servant. 'Poor Adler! God knows he is bad enough without these professional inquests on him. I was annoyed beyond words – and disgusted.' Casement diary entry, 3 December 1914, Dudgeon, *Roger Casement's German Diary*.

101. ***Manchester Guardian*** **condemned ... 'monstrous baseness:** Casement diary entry, 18 December 1914, and Angus Mitchell, *One Bold Deed of Open Treason: The Berlin Diary of Roger Casement, 1914–16*, Merrion Press, 2016.

101. **Questions in the House of Lords about what punishment:** The Marquis of Crewe, in reply to a question from Earl Curzon, 8 January 1915, *Hansard*: 'I entirely agree with the noble Earl that such an action as he is reported to have taken is one which not only is subject to the most severe blame but which also ought to be followed, so far as possible, by the infliction of severe penalties; and it is a melancholy reflection that a man who did some good service in the past should, assuming him to be in the possession of all his faculties, have fallen so low as he appears to have done.'

102. **risked sending a letter, via neutral Holland:** the letter to Alice Stopford Green included a copy of the German government's declaration about Ireland. The letter inside, intended for Eoin MacNeill, the head of the Irish Volunteers, averred: 'If Ireland will do her duty, rest assured Germany will do hers towards us, our cause and our whole future ... Tell all to trust the Germans – and to trust me.' Casement sent it via an intermediary in Rotterdam, who was said to be able to get letters to England unopened. Reginald Hall's censorship system intercepted it. Casement diary entry, 1 December 1914, and *Documents Relative to the Sinn Féin Movement*, British government command paper 1108.

102. **In December he met some Irish prisoners-of-war:** Casement's 5 December 1914 diary entry: 'I saw about 20 non-commissioned officers first in their room and spoke to them alone. O poor lot – more English than the English themselves – he talked of "getting back to England" – of "squaring it with the Germans when we get them to England" and so forth. Others and the Irish face & eye – & (mostly young men) they had horrid beards. The men outside looked even worse than the non-coms and very unpromising material to work on I felt. The scum of Ireland – literally.'

102. **'splendid calves and the figure of a young Hercules':** Spotted during a tour of a POW camp kitchen: 'One of the young French soldiers cooking was a splendid young fellow – about 6 feet, fair, strong – in blue puttee's showing

splendid calves & with the figure of a young Hercules. His face was fixed, no smile.' Casement diary entry, 5 December 1914.

102. **about the war, British skullduggery:** Casement told Bethmann Hollweg: 'Individually the Englishman is a gentleman often and frequently very charming – collectively they're a most dangerous compound and form a national type that has no parallel in humanity. Like certain chemicals – apart harmless, brought together you get an infernal explosive or a deadly poison.' Casement diary entry, 18 December 1914.

102. **black mourning ribbons hung from Christmas trees:** 'Germany's mournful Christmas', *Evening Post*, 26 December 1914, citing Copenhagen correspondent of the *Star*.

103. **collapsed a recruiting tent:** *The Times*, 30 December 1914. 'The weight of the snow caused the top sheets of the recruiting tents on the Horse Guards Parade to sag and the big tent was thrown down. A second tent nearly collapsed also.'

103. **'Maskell, that's wanted here.':** Hoy, *40 O.B.*

103. **Hall's temper was legendary:** Ramsay, *'Blinker' Hall, Spymaster*. 'He normally had this trait well under control but there were occasions when it could explode into bursts of startling anger.'

103. **40 OB ... giving the Admiralty advance warning:** It intercepted and swiftly deciphered German naval messages on 14 December 1914 about an impending German raid on England's east coast, giving the Royal Navy time to scramble ships to intercept the raiders. However, poor visibility and British miscommunications allowed the Germans to escape. Gannon, *Inside Room 40*. Churchill, *The World Crisis*, evokes the tense atmosphere in the Admiralty.

103. **Recalling a fragment from Kipling's *Kim*:** Hall, *A Clear Case of Genius*.

104. **juggling bribery in Turkey, propaganda in the US:** Hall, *A Clear Case of Genius*.

104. **Marquess of Sligo, who came to London:** Hall, *A Clear Case of Genius*.

104. **the Great Game ... deception, bribery:** Beesly, *Room 40*.

104. **'half Machiavelli and half schoolboy':** Observation by James Bone, the *Manchester Guardian*'s London correspondent, to Hall's secretary, Ruth Skrine, cited in James, *The Eyes of the Navy*.

104. **to the cottage of Darrell Figgis, a writer:** Figgis, *Recollections of the Irish War*.

105. **expected Casement to depart Germany on 8 January:** Hall, *A Clear Case of Genius*, includes an excerpt of his 4 January 1915 message to the *Sayonara* skipper. 'It is anticipated Casement will arrive in the Danish steamer Mjölnir ... with Casement will be Adler Christensen, age 24, height 6ft, strongly made, clean-shaven, gap in front teeth, wears thick double-

breasted greatcoat and soft dark hat ... I feel that you are just about at the best place round the coast from Cashel to Achill.'

105. **'I deeply regret failure ... a mind absolutely unregulated**: Findlay letter to under-secretary Arthur Nicolson, 14 January 1915, TNA, FO 95/776. 'I need hardly say that the failure of the coup we had hoped to bring off in the Casement case has distressed me greatly ... it is impossible to follow the workings of a mind [that of Adler Christensen] absolutely unregulated by any rules of morality or intelligence, but subject to intense suspiciousness and guided by low cunning.'

105. *Sayonara* **was recalled**: Hall's autobiography depicted the debacle as a success. Andrew, *Secret Service*: 'Curiously, Hall remained quite proud of the whole farcical episode. He later claimed, without much justification, that intelligence obtained by the *Sayonara* had proved very valuable during the Irish Easter rising of 1916. For the remainder of the war Hall tended to confuse good Irish intelligence from Room 40 (which included intercepts dealing with the movements of Sir Roger Casement) with far less reliable agent reports on sometimes mythical German intrigues.'

105. **table and stomped out**: Mentioned in Vickers introduction, Hall, *A Clear Case of Genius*.

CHAPTER EIGHT: BROTHERHOOD

106. **headed up, towards the camp**: Casement diary entry, 8 January 1915, relates his grim trip to the POW camp at Limburg three days earlier.

106. **infantry into frontal attacks**: Churchill, *The World Crisis*, decried the generals' lack of imagination. 'The centre could not be pierced, and there were no flanks to turn. Confronted with this deadlock, military art remained dumb; the commanders and their general staffs had no policy except the policy of exhaustion ... the military authorities of France and Britain consumed, during three successive years, the flower of their national manhood.'

107. **worth 10 army corps to Germany, an official told Casement**: Richard Meyer, a German Foreign Office official, cited in Casement diary entry, 2 November 1914.

107. **South Africa scores defected from the British army:** They joined the Irish Transvaal Brigade, also known as the Irish Commando, formed under Major John MacBride, an Irish emigrant from County Mayo. Casement, in contrast, supported the British during the Boer war but a decade later, in 1913, he told MacBride the story of South Africa's Irish Brigade 'was a fine fight and should be told'. Casement letter to Alice Stopford Green, 30 May 1915, NLI, MS 10646.

107. **an agreement with the Germans, which he called a 'treaty':** 10-article agreement detailed the terms for the Irish Brigade, 'with a view to securing the national freedom of Ireland'.
107. **brigade's expenses, which jolted John Devoy:** In *Recollections of an Irish Rebel*, Devoy said Clan na Gael had assumed the Germans would supply any force raised from Irish POWs. 'It never occurred to us that we would be expected to send money to Germany for that purpose.'
108. **listeners grew restless … hissing, boos:** Parmiter, *Roger Casement*. Casement's diary entry recorded a hostile response: 'Some of them insulted me … I came down from the camp at 6.16pm in dark and mud – in a very despondent mood after the revelation of Irish depravity I had witnessed.' Parmiter and other authors depicted an even rougher reception based on POW testimony.
108. **sergeant-major of the Dragoon Guards:** Parmiter, *Roger Casement*.
108. **'How much are they paying you?':** Bryan Kelly statement to under-secretary Matthew Nathan, 8 February 1915. NLI, MS 31783. Background to Kelly's statement explained in Chapter 9.
108. **honour to be British soldiers,':** Fuller quote from NCOs' letter to the Kaiser: 'We fully appreciate the kindness extended in (1) grouping us together under one roof; (2) assuring us of better food; (3) decreasing the amount of fatigue work to be performed; but we regret we must beseech His Imperial Majesty to withdraw these concessions unless they are shared by the remainder of the prisoners, as, in addition to being Irish Catholics, we have the honour to be British soldiers.' Copy included in Peter Singleton-Gates, *Casement – A Summing Up*, draft manuscript, NLI, MS 46064.
109. **rain bounced off the town's cobbles and his teeth ached:** Casement diary entry, 15 January 1915, and Dudgeon, *Roger Casement's German Diary*.
109. **wrangled from the ambassador a note … £5,000:** Findlay gave the written promise to Christensen on 3 January 1915. It stated that if information supplied by Christensen helped to capture Casement he would be paid £5,000 and 'enjoy personal immunity and be given a passage to the United States should he desire it'. NLI, MS 13,084/1/12.
109. **3,000-word open letter to his former boss:** Curry papers, NLI, MS 17000/2.
110. **accent from his New York days, 'moidered':** Clarke's IRB duties left him drained even before the war and the conspiracy. In a 3 June 1914 letter to John Devoy he wrote: 'Everything goes well here, but old age appears to be creeping up on me. Most of the time I feel "moidered" and can't cope with all the work that is crying out to be attended to on my doorstep. But I'll peg away at any case.' *Devoy's Post Bag, Volume II 1880–1928*, edited by William O'Brien and Desmond Ryan.

110. **Gardening brought him solace:** Le Roux, *Tom Clarke*.
111. **few months earlier to a fancier house:** The most desirable residence on Richmond Avenue in Fairview, according to Foy, *Tom Clarke*.
111. **When fellow radicals baulked at the implications:** Foy, *Tom Clarke*.
111. **staked out a property overlooking his shop:** Le Roux, *Tom Clarke*.
111. **gold sent by John Devoy:** Hidden in the basement of the Limerick home of John Daly, the father of Clarke's wife, Kathleen. Foy, *Tom Clarke*.
111. **muddled the IRB with Sinn Féin:** Some IRB members joined Sinn Féin but did not control it. According to O'Beirne Ranelagh, *The Irish Republican Brotherhood*: 'They hoped that Sinn Féin might become an IRB front but Arthur Griffith policed his party and prevented any takeover.'
112. **Arthur Griffith, advocated non-violent means:** Griffith founded Sinn Féin in 1905 to unite different strands of nationalism. He favoured independence but not necessarily a republic and proposed a dual monarchy system under which Ireland would have a royal figurehead. Sinn Féin remained a minnow compared with the Irish Parliamentary Party (IPP), which sought the limited autonomy of Home Rule, not independence. Griffith had amicable relations with Tom Clarke and other IRB leaders but opposed seeking independence by force. *Dictionary of Irish Biography*.
112. **outmanoeuvre dissenters:** Foy, *Tom Clarke*, depicts a single-minded plotter who judged a person based on revolutionary commitment. 'If he was not on Tom's side, then nothing else mattered, not past friendships, shared history, sentimental attachments or political partnerships. Unburdened by emotional constraints, Clarke could clinically dispose of even long-standing associates, comforted no doubt by a belief that history demanded he harden his heart and think only of Ireland. Tom had long ago learned to bury his emotions deep.'
112. **original 130,000-strong force had split:** The great majority broke away to form the National Volunteers, which had the blessing of the IPP and backed Britain's war effort. As the war progressed, the National Volunteers atrophied into irrelevance while the smaller, more radical group, which retained the name Irish Volunteers, gained support and momentum.
113. **growing doubts about the envoy:** Foy, *Tom Clarke*.
113. **came out thin and scraggly:** Honor O Brolchain, *16 Lives: Joseph Plunkett*, O'Brien Press, 2012. O Brolchain is a grand-niece of Plunkett and mined family lore, archives and memorabilia to produce an intimate biography. O Brolchain grew up hearing stories from her great-aunt Geraldine Plunkett, who was Joe's sister and aide, and O Brolchain edited *All in the Blood: A Memoir of Geraldine Plunkett-Dillon*, A. & A. Farmar, 2006.
113. **moving to Jersey in the Channel Islands, for his health:** O Brolchain, *16 Lives: Joseph Plunkett*.

113. **two years old ... bovine tuberculosis:** O Brolchain, *16 Lives: Joseph Plunkett*.
114. **George ... preferred Botticelli to parenting:** George Plunkett was a director of the National Museum of Ireland and wrote scholarly pamphlets and books including *Sandro Botticelli*, a biography of the Italian painter. Pope Leo XIII made him a papal count in 1884 after he donated funds and property to an order of nuns. *Dictionary of Irish Biography*.
114. **Josephine Mary, was a former society beauty:** O Brolchain's two books about the Plunketts depict the matriarch with innate creativity and talent but meagre education and a wild temper who terrorised her children while her husband turned a blind eye and hibernated in his study.
114. **dictatorial with her seven children:** Ruth Dudley Edwards, *The Seven: The Lives and Legacies of the Founding Fathers of the Irish Republic*, Oneworld, 2016, stresses the impact on Joe Plunkett. 'Tormented throughout his short life by a maternal monster.'
114. **loathed most of the guests ... including Casement:** Plunkett-Dillon, *All in the Blood*: 'After Ma's freezing reception, few of them ever came again.'
114. **'youth of that period were like the 1960s:** Roy Foster interview, 'Irish unification "is nearer than I would have thought it a couple of decades ago",' *The Irish Times*, 18 November 2023.
115. **Clarke ... saw value for the IRB in young poets:** Foy, *Tom Clarke*: 'Clarke realised that one day soon the IRB would finally emerge from the shadows and stand in judgement before not only the Irish people but history itself. To avoid being classed as the underbelly of society, the organisation needed eloquent poets and playwrights like [Patrick] Pearse and Plunkett in its ranks ... However, this was to be no revolution of the intellectuals but in which men of proletarian origin who disdained theorising would control the intellectuals.'
115. **verse, turned out to be a police spy:** Plunkett-Dillon, *All in the Blood*: 'A dull nonentity of a man who produced some bad poetry and professed great interest in literature came again and again to Marlborough road. We didn't know until after the rising that he was a spy from Dublin Castle.'
115. **enthusiasm for subterfuge:** W. J. McCormack, *Enigmas of Sacrifice: A Critique of Joseph M. Plunkett and the Dublin Insurrection of 1916*, Michigan State University Press, 2016. McCormack suggests Plunkett used conniving as a screen to explore his emotions. 'Plunkett flourished in hide-and-seek conditions whether behind an editor's desk or clandestine military planning.'
115. **mummeries of dusty conspiracies,' said one historian:** Desmond Ryan, *The Rising: The Complete Story of Easter Week*, Golden Eagle, 1966. First published 1949.
115. **read Clausewitz and played *Little Wars*:** O Brolchain, *16 Lives: Joseph Plunkett*.
116. **taught his sister Geraldine a cipher:** Plunkett-Dillon, *All in the Blood*.

116. *My hour is not yet come*: Draft dated 17 February 1915, NLI, 10,999/17/1/6.
116. **Dublin's North Wall port on the SS *Carlow***: O Brolchain, *16 Lives: Joseph Plunkett*.
117. **England, France, Spain ... odyssey**: O Brolchain, *16 Lives: Joseph Plunkett*.

CHAPTER NINE: LOVE YOUR ENEMIES

118. **Claude Pearce-Serocold, made two phone calls from the Admiralty**: Hall, *A Clear Case of Genius*.
118. **secretary, Ruth Skrine, recalled. 'The fun and hazard**: James, *The Eyes of the Navy*.
119. **hosted British and American correspondents ... Wednesday**: James, *The Eyes of the Navy*.
120. **Room 40 – technically a separate department**: Naval historians fault Churchill for tangling the chain of command by leaving Room 40 under the ostensible control of Alfred Ewing, who answered to Rear Admiral Henry Oliver, an arch-centraliser who did not grasp Room 40's full potential. As the director of naval intelligence, Hall was included in Room 40 deliberations but he needed sharp elbows to gradually take control. Beesly, *Room 40*, and Ramsay, *'Blinker' Hall, Spymaster*.
120. **'His charm would carry everything before it,' Skrine**: James, *The Eyes of the Navy*.
120. **'We thought him the real Sherlock Holmes,'**: James Bone, article in the *Guardian*, quoted in James, *The Eyes of the Navy*. The quote in full: 'We thought him the real Sherlock Holmes with just a touch of Watson's naivety and a bit of Somerset Maugham's disconcerting realism. He never overplayed his hand.'
120. **'The world's super spy,'**: 'Super-spy bereaved', *Derby Evening Telegraph*, 29 December 1932, reporting the death of Hall's wife.
120. **wizard of Whitehall'**: 'Britain's chief spy catcher in 1914–18', *Belfast News Letter*, 23 October 1943.
120. **mystery or suppressed excitement'**: *Daily Arkansas Gazette*, 16 July 1922. A fuller quote: 'What "Blinker" Hall didn't know about what was going on – in all parts of the world including Germany – wasn't worth knowing. "Blinker" was a great favourite with all the American correspondents ... and the Wednesday afternoons spent with him at the Admiralty over tea and cigarettes were a real delight. He thoroughly enjoyed the cross-examinations we used to put him through ... the sacred precincts of his office which always had an air of mystery of suppressed excitement about it.'
121. **fictitious gold shipment ... to lure a German ship**: The *Kronprinz Wilhelm*, an armed German merchant ship that was raiding British vessels off Brazil. Hall, *A Clear Case of Genius*.

121. **within the bounds of reason,' he later wrote:** Hall, *A Clear Case of Genius.*
121. **tongue strings were loosed,' Hall wrote:** Hall, *A Clear Case of Genius.*
121. **left on his desk a fake Admiralty telegram:** Hoy, *40 O.B.*
121. **Franklin Roosevelt still believed:** James, *The Sky Was Always Blue*, and Andrew, *Secret Service.*
122. ***New York World* ... Berlin correspondent:** Casement learned of the report on 15 March 1915 and was furious. He asked New York-based attorneys to sue, saying he had never received a cent from the German government. Ó Síocháin, *Roger Casement*, and Inglis, *Roger Casement*, which speculates that the article was placed in the *New York World* 'in all probability by the British agency which was busy feeding such material to the press in America'.
122. **message: 'Love your enemies.':** 'How I entrapped Germany's Cleverest War Spies,' *San Francisco Examiner*, 6 July 1924, article by Evelyn Knight.
122. **army medic cousin, Frank ... poet Rupert Brooke:** Dudgeon, *Roger Casement: The Black Diaries.*
122. **journalist who knew Thomson later wrote:** Peter Singleton-Gates and Maurice Girodias, *The Black Diaries: An Account of Roger Casement's Life and Times with a Collection of His Diaries and Public Writings*, Grove Press, 1959.
123. **Mr Doubleday piqued interest:** Dudgeon, *Roger Casement: The Black Diaries*, and TNA, KV2/6-3.
123. **statement about the fugitive from Bryan Kelly:** NLI, MS 31783.
123. **young Hoy betrayed his benefactor:** Hoy, *40 O.B.*, does not identify the informant as the author's nephew, Gerald Hoy. The Hoy family learned of Gerald's cooperation with Casement's hunters and hushed it up as a shameful family secret. Decades later Gerald's granddaughter, Maureen Waugh, investigated family lore about Gerald's statement to Reginald Hall, which she viewed at the National Archive. She concluded that Gerald was a charming but weak man who caved under pressure from his uncle Hugh – Hall's secretary – to share information about Casement, and padded out the little he knew with fictions. In an April 2024 interview with this author, Waugh said: 'My grandfather's statement wasn't worth a hill of beans. He did give away where Casement was staying in Berlin – the Avalon hotel, and his alias – but British intelligence already knew that.' Waugh considers it rather harsh to say Gerald betrayed Casement.
123. **topic to ask if sodomy:** Findlay letter to Arthur Nicolson, 21 February 1915, TNA, FO 95/776.
124. **of little use at the time,' he later wrote:** Hall, *A Clear Case of Genius.*
124. **Germans had ... six submarines:** Erik Larson, *Dead Wake: The Last Crossing of the Lusitania*, Doubleday, 2015.

124. **neutral shipping in the danger:** Churchill letter dated 12 February 1915 to Walter Runciman, president of the Board of Trade, cited in Diana Preston, *Wilful Murder: The Sinking of the Lusitania*, Doubleday, 2015. First published Great Britain, 2002.
125. **sacrifice of 100,000 men,':** 'Remembering the *Lusitania*: one passenger's remarkable story of survival,' BBC, 6 May 2015, https://www.bbc.com/news/uk-northern-ireland-32591594.
125. **Suspicion lingers to this day:** Beesly and Preston are among historians who lean towards belief in a British Admiralty conspiracy to expose the *Lusitania* to sinking.
125. **admirals asked their junior:** Hall, *A Clear Case of Genius*.
126. **expanding network of signal stations:** Gannon, *Inside Room 40*.
126. **them up with a *fwump*:** Larson, *Dead Wake*, uses the word and I cannot improve on it.
126. **typists nicknamed 'Blinker's beauty chorus':** James, *Eyes of the Navy*.
126. **Hambro, who was assigned her own nickname, Big Ben:** Andrew, *Secret Service*.
126. **art expert, a dress designer:** James, *Eyes of the Navy*, and Ramsay, *'Blinker' Hall, Spymaster*.
126. **'vibrating with excitement, expectation:** James, *Eyes of the Navy*.
126. **invalided home from the Persian:** Beesly, *Room 40* and Ramsay, *'Blinker' Hall, Spymaster*.
127. **All costs? A touch of vanity:** Hall, *A Clear Case of Genius*: 'That we were highly interested in Casement's movements at this time was true, though the "at all costs" was an addition which personal vanity must have prompted.'

CHAPTER TEN: THE FOOLS, THE FOOLS, THE FOOLS

128. **renewed recruitment efforts:** O Brolchain, *16 Lives: Joseph Plunkett*, draws on Plunkett's diary – at times written in Irish and in contracted form for security – spanning March to June 1915. Rather than risk taking the diary back to Ireland he left it with the German Foreign Office, where it was retrieved after the war and now forms part of the Joseph Plunkett papers at the NLI. O Brolchain also drew on conversations with her great-aunt Geraldine Plunkett-Dillon, Joe's sister and aide, and from Geraldine's memoirs, *All in the Blood*, which she edited.
129. **visited the former home of Charlemagne:** O Brolchain, *16 Lives: Joseph Plunkett*.
129. **'folly' and 'criminal stupidity':** Casement diary entry 28 March 1916. Dudgeon, *Roger Casement's German Diary*, and NLI, MS 5244. After

abandoning diary writing in February 1915, Casement resumed 13 months later and summarised events during the interregnum, including his dismissal of Plunkett's 'great tale of the planned revolution' in Ireland. 'I discounted all that – and sat on it and him as vigorously as was possible. I told him … no rebellion or rising in Ireland could possibly succeed of its own unaided effort. The *sine qua non* … was the military (and naval) support of a great continental power. To attempt a rising in the streets of Dublin in 1915 I held was worse than folly – it was criminal stupidity. But I said 'if you do it – if you are bent on this act of idiocy I will come and join you (if the Germans will send me over) and stand and fall beside you.'

129. *Ireland Report*, **a 32-page analysis:** Charles Townshend, *Easter 1916: The Irish Rebellion*, Penguin, 2015, first published 2005, says it mixed plausible strategy with window-dressing. 'Designed to put the rosiest colouring on what were in many cases very remote possibilities.'

130. **Norwegian had a 'curiously immobile face:** O Brolchain, *16 Lives: Joseph Plunkett*.

130. **selling vacuum cleaners:** Godøy, *Dobbeltspill* (Double play*)*.

130. **film of the Findlay affair:** Franz Rothenfelder, *Casement in Deutschland* (Casement in Germany), with a foreword by Ferdinand Hansen, Augsburg, 1917.

130. **kidnap them,' Plunkett declared:** Casement diary entry, 28 March 1916.

130. **beer and Bulgarian sour milk:** Plunkett-Dillon, *All in the Blood*.

130. **manager in Milwaukee, Boehm:** Michael Keogh, *With Casement's Irish Brigade*, compiled by Kevin Keogh, edited by Brian Maye, Choice Publishing, 2010. Keogh was the brigade's sergeant-major. He retrieved his father's unpublished manuscript many years after his death in 1964.

130. **theatrical, but certainly effective!':** Godøy, *Dobbeltspill* (Double play).

131. **his rented apartment:** 42 Hardenbergstrasse. O Brolchain, *16 Lives: Joseph Plunkett*.

131. **decided to fight to die,' said a biographer:** Dudley Edwards, *The Seven*.

131. **an unidentified bearded man:** O Brolchain, *16 Lives: Joseph Plunkett*.

131. **a spa in Bavaria:** in Grünwald, a scenic area southwest of Munich.

132. **But he was a liability:** O Brolchain, *16 Lives: Joseph Plunkett*.

132. **recognised him on a tram:** The friend was John MacDonagh. 'Joe nearly jumped out of his skin.' O Brolchain, *16 Lives: Joseph Plunkett*.

132. **Alps soared in the distance:** Author visit to Casement's Bavarian haunts in August 2024.

132. **humid, sultry Sunday:** Rothenfelder, *Casement in Deutschland*. Rothenfelder in 1916 and 1917 retraced Casement's steps and interviewed people who had known him.

132. **To escape he proposed a bet:** Rothenfelder, *Casement in Deutschland*.

133. **'campaign of infamy':** Casement letter to E. D. Morel, 7 August 1915, MacColl, *Roger Casement*.

133. **a terrier he named Rebel:** Keogh, *With Casement's Irish Brigade*.
133. **liberating cows from a paddock:** Keogh, *With Casement's Irish Brigade*.
133. **'ausgeschlossen' – out of the question:** 'The Prussian official's favourite word,' Tuchman, *The Zimmermann Telegram*.
133. **not written by John Devoy:** George Freeman, an associate of Devoy in New York, said in a letter to a German Foreign Office official that Clan na Gael regretted sending Casement. Devoy later disowned the statement. Doerries, *Prelude to the Rising*, and Ó Síocháin, *Roger Casement*.
133. **terrible place,' Casement lamented:** Cited by Gilbert Hirsch, who interviewed him in Berlin, in the *Evening Post*, 1 May 1916, 'Casement won trust of German officials'.
133. ***Lusitania* was further folly – he warned his hosts:** Rothenfelder, *Casement in Deutschland*.
134. **Adler had acquired a German girlfriend:** Margaretta Werschmidt, daughter of a Berlin businessman. Godøy, *Dobbeltspill* (Double play).
134. **advice from Magnus Hirschfeld:** The German sexologist and homosexual rights activist cited the meeting in a brief reference in *Von einst bis jetzt: Geschichte einer homosexuellen Bewegung 1897–1922*, a collection of his writings published by Verlag Rosa Winkel in 1986. The full reference: 'In a similar state [on the verge of a nervous breakdown], the great English [sic] patriot Sir Roger Casement once came to me during the World War. One night, he was sitting on a Tiergarten bench, engaging in harmless conversation with a soldier, when suddenly an electric lantern lit up over his lap. Although nothing suspicious arose, his name was recorded, and the extremely sensitive man suffered a shock.'
German scholars told the author that they interpret this as meaning a park guard, or policeman, confronted Casement and his companion. According to other writings by Hirschfeld, such as the 1904 booklet *Berlins Drittes Geschlecht*, the Tiergarten was a well-established cruising spot for sex, with homosexuals using the southern section while heterosexual prostitutes frequented the eastern section.
134. **pro-German expats welcomed Ireland's rebel envoy:** Thomas St John Gaffney, *Breaking the Silence: England, Ireland and the War*, Horace Liveright, 1930, and Charles Curry, *Sir Roger Casement Diaries*.
134. **cavernous Luitpold cafe:** Rothenfelder, *Casement in Deutschland*. The cafe is still thriving.
134. **Curry, another leading:** Charles Curry, who edited and first published Casement's German diary.
135. **correspondence with a teenager, Max Zehndler:** The NLI has eight letters and eight postcards from Casement to Zehndler spanning 28 July 1915 and 4 April 1916.
135. **writer interviewed locals:** Rothenfelder, *Casement in Deutschland*.
135. **Sacrifice Day, 1 August 1915'.:** Rothenfelder, *Casement in Deutschland*.

135. **Tom Clarke . . . closed the lid:** Foy, *Tom Clarke*.
136. **'die at the most opportune time:** Foy, *Tom Clarke*. John Devoy made the same point in his memoirs: 'In dying when he did and at the age he did Rossa performed his last and perhaps greatest service to the Fenian cause.'
136. **steered the Gaelic League:** Clarke ousted the League's president, Douglas Hyde, in July 1915 and installed IRB men in key posts. O'Beirne Ranelagh, *The Irish Republican Brotherhood*.
136. **Plunkett's news, when he returned:** In the absence of surviving written records, accounts differ over what Plunkett told his IRB comrades about German aid. The balance of evidence suggests he expressed optimism about obtaining weapons.
136. **Lord Kitchener, refused to create:** Inglis, *Roger Casement*, and Townshend, *Easter 1916*.
137. **form of disloyalty to Ireland,' a chronicler wrote:** James Hannay, who used the pseudonym George Birmingham, quoted in Townshend, *Easter 1916*.
137. **satirical song captured:** Quoted in Philipps, *Broken Archangel*.
137. **funeral committee with 11 sub-committees:** Le Roux, *Tom Clarke*.
138. **ferried to Dublin on 17 special trains:** Foy, *Tom Clarke*.
138. **Birrell let Tom Clarke:** León Ó Broin, *Dublin Castle and the 1916 Rising: The Story of Sir Matthew Nathan*, Helicon, 1966, gives an almost fly-on-the-wall account of decision-making by Birrell and his under-secretary, Nathan.
138. **pickets of Volunteers, among them Joe Plunkett:** O Brolchain, *16 Lives: Joseph Plunkett*.
138. **Mayo man whispered to a companion:** The companion was Darrell Figgis, an exchange he recounted in *Recollections of the Irish War*.
139. **'Make it hot as hell,' Clarke replied:** Le Roux, *Tom Clarke*.
139. **embodied 'enough material:** Dudley Edwards, *The Seven*. Edwards gives a fuller portrait in *Patrick Pearse: The Triumph of Failure*, Irish Academic Press, 2006. First published 1977.
139. **droopy eye and slight stutter:** Dudley Edwards, *The Seven*.
139. **five minutes of propagandistic brilliance:** Townshend, *Easter 1916*: 'A major watershed in public attitudes . . . it set the Volunteers at the centre of an evolution in which it became clear that the Catholic clergy were ready to be identified with a large-scale celebration of the physical force idea.'

CHAPTER ELEVEN: BLINKER'S WEB

141. **paranoia or foreboding:** *The Dark Invader: War-Time Reminiscences of a German Naval Intelligence Officer*, Captain Franz von Rintelen, Penguin, 1936. A colourful and at times implausible memoir that includes a letter

from Reginald Hall, who struck up a remarkable friendship with Rintelen after the war.
141. **audacious and successful spy:** Tuchman, *The Zimmermann Telegram*: 'Possessor of intelligence, daring and that streak of megalomania ... that may be the secret agent's most important qualification.' The verdict of Guy Gaunt, who hunted Rintelen, *The Yield of the Years: A Story of Adventure Afloat and Ashore*, Hutchinson, 1940: 'He achieved sensational success – for a time.'
142. **produce enough artillery shells:** An outcry over the British army's shell shortage contributed to the collapse of Herbert Asquith's Liberal government in May 1915.
142. **gap by buying ... American munitions:** Tuchman, *The Zimmermann Telegram*.
142. **'I'll buy up what I can, and blow up:** Rintelen, *The Dark Invader*.
142. **Clan na Gael enlisted Irish stevedores:** Rintelen, *The Dark Invader*: 'My most fanatical helpers in this way were the Irish. They swarmed about the various ports with detonators in their pockets.'
142. **fires, diversions and sinkings:** According to Rintelen, the main targets were Russia-bound ships.
143. **'Do you know a Captain Rintelen?':** Rintelen, *The Dark Invader*.
143. **one estimate ... Room 40 handled 37,000:** Gannon, *Inside Room 40*.
143. **unparalleled intelligence feat, wrote one historian:** Gannon, *Inside Room 40*.
143. **dogs who can hear high-pitched sounds:** Tuchman, *The Zimmermann Telegram*.
143. **without Basil Thomson, who was away:** Thomson, *The Scene Changes*.
144. **chain of command ... bureaucratic mess:** issue addressed in Chapter 9 endnote citing Churchill.
144. **'If ever we dug out anything:** Nigel de Grey, a codebreaker, quoted in Gannon, *Inside Room 40*.
144. **Of 30,000 diplomatic messages:** Gannon, *Inside Room 40*.
144. **Sir Edward Grey's second-storey window:** Tuchman, *The Zimmermann Telegram*.
145. **relished the responsibility of sole command.':** Tuchman, *The Zimmermann Telegram*.
145. **10,000 diplomatic decrypts in his basement:** Hall, *A Clear Case of Genius*.
145. **a Munich artist:** Ramsay, *'Blinker' Hall, Spymaster*. The artist, Karl Goetz, intended to highlight alleged British cynicism in ignoring German warnings and sending the *Lusitania* to its doom.
145. **'Maskell, steal petrol.':** Hoy, *40 O.B.*
145. **orchestrating a Zeppelin raid ... recounted it with relish:** Beesly, *Room 40*.

145. **ordered the killing of a spy**: Alexander Szek, a radio operator in Belgium, vanished after passing German codes to the British. Henry Oliver, Hall's boss at the Admiralty, later claimed he paid £1,000 to have Szek killed. More recently the historian Alexander Rose argues the Germans shot Szek. https://alexanderrose.substack.com/p/the-search-for-szek.
145. **serve under the devil if he was proficient,'**: Hall, *A Clear Case of Genius*.
146. **'Willoughby, fetch the rum.'**: Ramsay, *'Blinker' Hall, Spymaster*.
146. **Ed Bell ... 'A perfectly marvellous**: Handwritten note, Reginald Hall papers, Churchill archives, Cambridge, 2/2.
146. **'They were a little frightened of him**: James, *The Eyes of the Navy*.
146. **compared the DNI to Sir Francis Walsingham**: Gannon, *Inside Room 40*.
146. **John started his last phase**: John Abney Hall naval record, TNA, ADM 196/123/136.
146. **naval attaché, Guy Gaunt, teamed up with a Bohemian émigré**: Guy Gaunt, *The Yield of the Years*, and Tuchman, *The Zimmermann Telegram*.
147. **Immigration officials ... Plunkett's swollen glands**: Devoy, *Recollections of an Irish Rebel*.
147. **hollowed walking stick**: O Brolchain, *16 Lives: Joseph Plunkett*.
147. **worked his political contacts**: Devoy, *Recollections of an Irish Rebel*.
148. **unrequited ardour**: O Brolchain, *16 Lives: Joseph Plunkett*.
148. **Ma, who was visiting**: Oliver beatified in 1920 and canonised in 1975, becoming a saint.
148. **bankrupt, with just $22**: Golway, *Irish Rebel*.
149. **Casement sent Devoy bulky packages**: Devoy, *Recollections of an Irish Rebel*.
149. **chafed at untrue press reports**: Devoy, *Recollections of an Irish Rebel*.
149. **entrusted with escorting Monteith**: Robert Monteith, *Casement's Last Adventure*, Michael Moynihan, 1953. First edition 1932. Vivid memoir chronicles Monteith's service in the Irish Volunteers, his move to New York, mission to Germany and return to Ireland with Casement.
150. **stowed on the SS *United States***: Monteith, *Casement's Last Adventure*.
150. **Plunkett followed ... in the SS *New York***: O Brolchain, *16 Lives: Joseph Plunkett*, cites the licence to import arms under the Defence of the Realm regulations: 'Mr J Plunkett ... is hereby authorised to bring into the United Kingdom ... 2 swords each marked US 1865.'
150. **dragged 24 captured German field guns**: 'The Captured German Guns', *The Times*, 27 October 1915, and images in 'London's New Battle Trophies', *The Illustrated War News*, 3 November 1915.
150. **growing support for Sinn Féiners**: O'Broin, *Dublin Castle and the 1916 Rising*.
151. **'What did you discuss with the Irish leaders**: Rintelen, *The Dark Invader*.
151. **scornfully of the traitor's 'temptations'**: *Daily Telegraph*, 8 October 1915.
151. **St John Gaffney, was fired**: Gaffney, *Breaking the Silence*.

152. **secret coast-watching network:** Paul McMahon, *British Spies and Irish Rebels: British Intelligence and Ireland, 1916–1945*, Boydell, 2008.
152. **point at the Foreign Office:** They were trained on St James's Park, just beyond the Foreign Office.

CHAPTER TWELVE: WE HAVE DECIDED TO ATTACK

153. **14 December 1915, a crisp, beautiful day:** Monteith diary entry cited in Florence Monteith Lynch, *The Mystery Man of Banna Strand: The Life and Death of Captain Robert Monteith*, Vantage, 1959. Written by Monteith's daughter, it includes extracts from his diary and letters to his wife Mollie.
154. **Trees with gaunt, naked branches:** Monteith, *Casement's Last Adventure*.
154. **talk about the men, the war, Ireland and Africa:** Monteith, *Casement's Last Adventure*.
154. **Michael Keogh, puffing. 'Aw, Sir Roger:** Monteith, *Casement's Last Adventure*.
154. **would sing 'Clare's Dragoons':** Keogh, *With Casement's Irish Brigade*.
155. **Monteith would give a silent thanks:** Monteith, *Casement's Last Adventure*.
155. **Ordnance Survey job:** Monteith was also deported from Dublin and relocated to Limerick in November 1914.
155. **British agents monitored Monteith:** Monteith Lynch, *The Mystery Man of Banna Strand*.
155. **detour to visit his family in Moss:** Monteith, *Casement's Last Adventure*.
155. **'despondent and nervous:** Monteith diary entry, 24 October 1915, cited in Monteith Lynch, *The Mystery Man of Banna Strand*.
156. **Putumayo,' he later wrote:** Monteith, *Casement's Last Adventure*.
156. **wrote to Mollie:** Letter dated 30 November 1915, Monteith Lynch, *Mystery Man of Banna Strand*.
157. **camp they called the Birdcage:** article by Quinlisk, brigade member, originally in the magazine *Land and Water*, retrieved through republication in the *South Bend News-Times* (of Indiana, US): 'The German Irish Brigade: An Inside Story From the Diary of One of Sir Roger Casement's Chief Lieutenants Showing How the Kaiser Tricked Men He Made Traitors', 25 January 1920.
157. **five marriage requests:** Monteith, *Casement's Last Adventure*.
157. **urgent summons to the Golden Lion:** Monteith, *Casement's Last Adventure*.
157. **sanatorium outside Munich:** Kuranstalt Neuwittelsbach resembled a hotel but treated patients with mental health issues. 'A variety of treatments, all useless (massages, baths, and so on)', according to Élisabeth Roudinesco, *Freud: In His Time and Ours*, Harvard University Press, 2016.
158. **gland on his right cheek throbbed:** O Brolchain, *16 Lives: Joseph Plunkett*.

158. **never meant to be so happy:** Plunkett letter to Gifford dated 2 December 1915: 'Darling Grace, you will marry me and nobody else. I have been a damned fool . . . but thank God I see. I love you and only you and will never love anyone else . . . I was never meant to be so happy . . . I love you a million million times.' O Brolchain, *16 Lives: Joseph Plunkett.*
158. **tried talking sense into the man:** Ryan, *The Rising.*
158. **semi-abandoned house:** precise address is not known but most accounts place the encounter in Dolphin's Barn, a neighbourhood just over a mile from Larkfield, the Plunkett family estate.
158. **ardour for Grace Gifford:** Letter to Gifford dated 4 December 1915: 'You have taken the harm out of all my troubles and made the whole world beautiful for me. You have made me happy – never forget that whatever happens because it's a kind of miracle.' O Brolchain, *16 Lives.*
158. **biting, mordant wit:** Sidney Gifford Czira, *The Years Flew By: The Recollections of Madame Sidney Gifford Czira,* edited by Alan Hayes, foreword by Gifford Lewis, Arlen House, 2000. First edition 1974. Lewis's foreword makes the reference to mordant wit. And Marie O'Neill, *Grace Gifford Plunkett and Irish Freedom: Tragic Bride of 1916,* Irish Academic Press, 2000.
158. **domineering mother:** Isabella Julia Gifford was by all accounts a strong personality and staunch Protestant who insisted, among other things, that certain daughters wear hats to conceal the shame of having red hair. Gifford Czira, *The Years Flew By,* and O'Neill, *Grace Gifford Plunkett.*
158. **physical consummation:** Undated poem titled *New Love,* included in *The Poems of Joseph Mary Plunkett,* Talbot Press, 1916.
159. **biographer put it, the 'repeated:** McCormack, *Enigmas of Sacrifice.*
159. **rainwater piping:** Max Caulfield, *The Easter Rebellion,* Gill and Macmillan, 1995. First published 1963.
159. **returned emigrants . . . Michael Collins:** Plunkett-Dillon, *All in the Blood.*
160. **Other IRB leaders . . . visited Larkfield:** Plunkett-Dillon, *All in the Blood.*
160. **bow-legged gait unmistakeable:** Dudley Edwards, *The Seven.*
160. **Irish habit of procrastinating:** Dudley Edwards, *The Seven.*
160. **Connolly's experiences in the British army:** Foster, *Modern Ireland.*
161. **socialist, which he rendered 'solist':** Gifford Czira, *The Years Flew By.* Her affectionate portrait says Connolly had a quiet courtesy and dignity. 'Short, stout, clear, healthy complexion, with keen, shrewd intelligent eyes . . . [you] could imagine him in a pub but he didn't smoke or drink.'
161. **'throw off gloom like a cloak:** Figgis, *Recollections of the Irish War.*
161. **'The time for Ireland's battle is NOW:** Published in *Worker's Republic,* Connolly's weekly newspaper, on 22 January 1916, but believed to have been written before his marathon encounter with the IRB. A fuller quote: 'The time for Ireland's battle is NOW, the place for Ireland's battle is

HERE; that a strong man may deal lusty blows with his fists against a host of surrounding foes, and conquer, but will succumb if a child sticks a pin in his heart.'

162. **lying on a bare iron bedstead:** Plunkett-Dillon, *All in the Blood*.
162. **women. They played key roles:** McCoole, *Easter Widows*.
162. **Plunkett... a letter on 27 January:** O Brolchain, *16 Lives: Joseph Plunkett*.
163. **Harold Tennyson... on another ship:** Killed when HMS *Viking* hit a mine on 29 January 1916. 'Naval news', *The Globe*, and 'Funeral of Lt Tennyson', *The North Star*, 2 February 1916.
163. **'He never failed me...,' Hall wrote:** Letter to Harold's mother, 30 January 1916, included in Tennyson, *The Story of a Young Sailor*.
163. **Lady Tennyson later said:** Tennyson, *The Story of a Young Sailor*.
163. **intrigues in the US:** Gaunt, *Yield of the Years*, and Tuchman, *The Zimmermann Telegram*.
163. **discovering the cypher key:** James, *The Eyes of the Navy*.
164. **messenger... crossword puzzles:** Hoy, *40 O.B.*
164. **temperatures gripped Manhattan:** A week of snow, hail and ice, according to the Record of Climatological Observations for New York's Central Park weather station.
164. **contracted the Norwegian to smuggle men:** Devoy, *Recollections of an Irish Rebel*.
164. **Haan's on Park Row... East Side streetcar:** Golway, *Irish Rebel*.
165. **accepted the home organisation's right:** Devoy, *Recollections of an Irish Rebel*.
165. **communication numbered 79:** Doerries, *Prelude to the Easter Rising*.
165. **Sayville radio station on Long Island:** Gaunt, *Yield of the Years*.

CHAPTER THIRTEEN: CONJURER'S BOX

166. ***Abteilung IIIb*... military intelligence:** Doerries, *Prelude to the Easter Rising*.
167. **Captain Rudolf Nadolny:** Doerries, *Prelude to the Easter Rising*.
167. **Allied shipments... anthrax:** 'First shots fired in biological warfare', *Nature*, 17 September 1998.
167. **message to John Devoy on 1 March:** Doerries, *Prelude to the Easter Rising*.
167. **At first he welcomed the news:** Casement diary entry titled 'A Last Page', a 134-page narrative written mostly in Berlin between 17 March and 8 April 1916. Spans events from several months earlier and continues to the eve of Casement's departure from Germany. Included in the volumes of *Casement's German Diary* separately edited by Curry, Dudgeon and Mitchell.
167. **arrived in Berlin on the 8.40 a.m. train:** Casement diary entry, 'A Last Page', 17 March 1916.

168. **loathed for its heel-clicking officials:** By now Casement also hated Berlin's statues of Hohenzollern aristocrats. 'Grotesque and ponderous monstrosities in marble – fitting types of the line of coarse and selfish heads of this Prussian abortion.' Casement, *'A Last Page'*.
168. **Nadolny and two other officers:** Captain Bernhard von Hülsen and Count Kurt von Haugwitz-Hardenberg-Reventlow.
168. **'stupendous idiocy' and 'foredoomed failure':** Casement, *'A Last Page'*.
168. **'The Dream of the Celt':** Poem about Ireland's subjugation that Casement completed in 1903.
169. **Casement projected enthusiasm:** 'I listened, smiled and looked at Monteith across the table. I even pretended to concur in these manifestations of lunacy ... what else could I do? The guns were of service.' Casement, *'A Last Page'*.
169. **'Of course it is impossible ...':** Casement, *'A Last Page'*.
169. **Karl Spindler tramped into his quarters:** Karl Spindler, *Gun Running for Casement in the Easter Rebellion, 1916*, translated by W. Montgomery, W. Collins Sons, 1921. Later edition with minor changes published under the title *The Mystery of the Casement Ship*, Anvil, 1965. Vivid account of Spindler's mission to Ireland and the aftermath.
170. **lacked the connections and aristocratic pedigree:** Clayton, *Aud*. Clayton served in the Irish and British navies and worked for the Irish Underwater Archaeological Research Team before turning a fascination for the gun-running mission into this 895-page book. It draws on German, British and Irish archives and other sources, including Clayton's exploration of the *Aud* wreckage, to produce an exhaustive analysis of crews, vessels, cargo, routes, tides and weather.
170. **'command of this expedition:** Spindler, *The Mystery of the Casement Ship*.
170. **billowing across Horse Guards Parade:** Weather reports in *Westminster Gazette*, 21 March 1916, and *London Daily News*, 23 March 1916.
170. **Room 40 had intercepted and deciphered:** *Documents Relative to the Sinn Féin Movement*, British government command paper 1108.
171. **BRAN. FINN means that the cargo:** *Documents Relative to the Sinn Féin Movement*, British government command paper 1108.
171. **'covering up all tracks:** Hall, *A Clear Case of Genius*.
171. **withheld sensitive political information ... from Arthur Balfour:** Andrew, *Secret Service*.
171. **Vice-Admiral Lewis Bayly ... was told:** O'Broin, *Dublin Castle and the 1916 Rising*, and Eunan O'Halpin, 'British Intelligence in Ireland, 1914–1921', a chapter in *The Missing Dimension: Governments and Intelligence Communities in the Twentieth Centuries*, edited by Christopher Andrew and David Dilk, Palgrave Macmillan, 1984.

172. **Major-General Lovick Friend ... 'absolutely reliable source':** O'Broin, *Dublin Castle and the 1916 Rising*, and O'Halpin, *British Intelligence in Ireland*.
172. **Lacking Room 40's information:** George Dangerfield, *The Damnable Question: A Study in Anglo-Irish Relations*, Quartet, 1979. First published 1976. And O'Halpin, *British Intelligence in Ireland*.
172. **Granite and Chalk:** O'Halpin, *British Intelligence in Ireland*, and McMahon, *British Spies and Irish Rebels*.
172. **Joe prepared a defence:** O Brolchain, *16 Lives: Joseph Plunkett*.
172. **In the stairwell, maids screamed:** Plunkett-Dillon, *All in the Blood*.
172. **estate had become increasingly militarised:** Joe Good, *Inside the GPO: A First-Hand Account*, O'Brien Press, 2015. First published 1946.
173. **Mimi, had couriered:** Plunkett-Dillon, *All in the Blood*, and Devoy, *Recollections of an Irish Rebel*.
173. **chamois bag strapped to her thigh had $2,000:** Plunkett-Dillon, *All in the Blood*.
173. **mission for his father, the papal count:** O Brolchain, *16 Lives: Joseph Plunkett*.
174. **Pearse ... condition Volunteers:** Foy, *Tom Clarke*, and Dudley Edwards, *Patrick Pearse*.
174. **history professor still believed:** Michael Tierney, *Eoin MacNeill: Scholar and Man of Action, 1867–1945*, Oxford University Press, 1980.
174. **'running a revolution:** Grace Gifford statement to Irish Bureau of Military History, 1 June 1949.
174. **steered a course out of Wilhelmshaven:** Spindler, *The Mystery of the Casement Ship*.
174. **Summoned to Hamburg docks:** Spindler, *The Mystery of the Casement Ship*.
175. **hauling cargo off the coast of Spain:** Clayton, *Aud*.
175. **similar dimension and shape:** Clayton, *Aud*.
175. **nicknamed the conjurer's box:** Spindler, *The Mystery of the Casement Ship*.
176. **taken a liking to the genial lieutenant:** 'A fine young fellow.' Casement, *'A Last Page'*.
176. **Nadolny ... Dropping any pretence of fraternity:** Casement, *'A Last Page'*.
177. **tried and failed to bribe Robert Monteith:** Monteith, *Casement's Last Adventure*: 'He offered me a considerable sum of money ... I really was sorry for this man, his whole attitude showed me that the job of bribing me had been forced upon him, and that he was thoroughly ashamed of it.'
177. **brigade volunteer called Daniel Bailey:** A Dubliner who used Julian Beverley as a *nom de guerre*.
177. **'Only God can save the situation,':** Casement, *A Last Word*, diary entry, 6 April 1916.

177. **a government intermediary:** Jacob Noeggerath, a politically connected German-American.
177. **church tower clanged over Lübeck:** Spindler, *The Mystery of the Casement Ship*.
177. **bear of a mongrel called Hector:** Spindler, *The Mystery of the Casement Ship*.

CHAPTER FOURTEEN: CALM LIES THE SEA

178. **completing the ship's metamorphosis:** Spindler, *The Mystery of the Casement Ship*.
178. **fake Norwegian families:** Spindler, *The Mystery of the Casement Ship*.
179. **wild with delight,' he later wrote:** Spindler, *The Mystery of the Casement Ship*.
179. **2,000-mile route ... wide loop around Scotland:** The alternative was to go south, via the English Channel, but Royal Navy patrols and minefields made this all but impassable.
179. **sink the genuine *Aud*:** It was en route from Cardiff to Lisbon with 1,213 tonnes of coal when intercepted and sunk by *U-18* off Cornwall on 30 November 1916.
180. **towards the Arctic Circle:** Spindler, *The Mystery of the Casement Ship*.
180. **Casement ... breakfast on *U-20*:** Monteith, *Casement's Last Adventure*.
180. **Usually entailed jamming:** A description of *U-20* in 1915 in Preston, *Wilful Murder*: 'Crammed with supplies, from butter under the bunks to sausages next to the grenades.' One crewman shared his bunk with a torpedo: 'At first I was kept awake a bit by the thought of having so much TNT in bed with me. Then I got used to it.'
180. **From Zoo station at Kurfürstendam:** Monteith, *Casement's Last Adventure*, and Bailey statement to police after his arrest, cited in appendix of Parmiter, *Roger Casement*.
181. **confidential German Admiralty order:** Spindler, *The Mystery of the Casement Ship*.
181. **Schwieger ... had charm:** Larson, *Dead Wake*: 'Known for kindness and good humour and for maintaining a cheerful atmosphere aboard.'
181. **recoiling from actual bloodshed ... bombs, which seemed unchivalrous:** Casement note to defence counsel, NLI, 13088, and B. L. Reid, *The Lives of Roger Casement*: 'In view of his enthusiasm about the rifles and machine guns, the distaste Casement showed for the idea of the explosives was curious. Apparently he was offended by the destructive and aggressive quality of such instruments. He seems hardly to have thought of the rifles as dealing death: they were symbolic or at worst defensive; mainly they were emblems to be waved at the British in token of Irish manliness and readi-

ness for independence. But dynamite was hard to sublimate and Casement did not like to associate it with his friends or his movement. He thought perhaps the Irish could "refuse" the explosives when they unloaded the *Aud*.'

181. **not resist bragging:** Monteith, *Casement's Last Adventure*.
181. **John Philip Holland:** Born 1841 in County Clare, died in Newark, New Jersey, 1914. *Britannica* calls him 'the father of the modern submarine'.
182. **limped to a naval base at Heligoland:** Doerries, *Prelude to the Easter Rising*.
182. ***U-19* left Heligoland at 1.26 p.m.:** Clayton, *Aud*.
182. **9 p.m. made its first dive:** Clayton, *Aud*.
182. **expression of childlike wonder:** Monteith, *Casement's Last Adventure*.
182. **rip off fingernails scrabbling at hatches:** Larson, *Dead Wake*.
182. **Crews called it 'the blind moment':** Larson, *Dead Wake*.
183. **'to humiliate and degrade me:** Curry papers, NLI, MS 17,026/1.
184. **'By assailing me ... blacken my cause too.':** Curry papers, NLI, MS 17,025/1.
184. **temperature rose and so did the reek:** Larson, *Dead Wake*, on the interior of a typical U-boat: 'The odour of diesel fuel infiltrated all corners . . . when deep underwater the boat developed an interior atmosphere akin to a tropical swamp.'
184. **At 11.20 p.m. *U-19* climbed and broke to the surface:** Clayton, *Aud*.
184. **Another fragment enquired 'whether German auxiliary:** Beesly, *Room 40*.
185. **notify Vice-Admiral Bayly:** O'Broin, *Dublin Castle and the 1916 Rising*, Andrew, *Secret Service*, and O'Halpin, *British Intelligence in Ireland*.
185. **Bayly sent his commanders:** Clayton, *Aud*, publishes the message in full.
185. **tipped off Brigadier-General William Stafford:** O'Broin, *Dublin Castle and the 1916 Rising*, and Andrew, *Secret Service*, and O'Halpin, *British Intelligence in Ireland*.
186. **Castle's puddle of rumours:** According to O'Broin, *Dublin Castle and the 1916 Rising*, Matthew Nathan was 'doubtful whether there was any foundation for the rumour' but urged RIC county inspectors in southern and southwestern counties to be on their guard.
186. **Plunkett ... cheek and neck had been operated on:** O Brolchain, *16 Lives: Joseph Plunkett*.
186. **music hall troupe from England:** Lawrence Wright Company, *Dublin Daily Express*, 17 April 1916, billed the show as a 'musical ecstasy ... of operatic selections, ballads and choruses'.
186. **looking forward to tea with milk:** O'Casey, *Autobiographies*.
186. **Jennie Wyse-Power ... meet at her premises:** Le Roux, *Tom Clarke*.
186. **bandoleers, belts, haversacks:** Ryan, *The Rising*.
187. **Fred Hanna, a bookseller:** L. G. Redmond-Howard, *Six Days of the Irish Republic*, Aubane Historical Society, 2006. First published 1916.

187. **melting lead into bullets:** Gene Kerrigan, *The Scrap: A True Story from the 1916 Rising*, Doubleday, 2015.
187. **'Please keep to the right.':** Kerrigan, *The Scrap*.
187. **basement of Liberty Hall:** Yeates, *A City in Wartime: Dublin 1914–18*.
187. **piccolo player ... 'The Deep Blue Sea':** *Dublin Daily Express* review of the show, 17 April 1916.
188. **papal count, had returned from Rome:** O Brolchain, *16 Lives: Joseph Plunkett*.
188. **'Castle document', ... fabrication:** Honor O Brolchain, Plunkett's biographer and grand-niece, believes the document was authentic but most historians think it was forged or embroidered – 'sexed up', in contemporary parlance.
188. **Volunteers' chief-of-staff, believed it:** *Eoin MacNeill: The Pen and the Sword*, edited by Conor Mulvagh and Emer Purcell, Cork University Press, 2022.
188. **alderman bypassed censorship:** Tom Kelly, a Sinn Féin stalwart. Yeates, *A City in Wartime*.
188. **scrapped when the organiser:** Alfred Cotton held sports-themed training camps near Banna Strand to give Volunteers a pretext to be in the area, without arousing suspicion, when the arms ship arrived. However, on a visit to Belfast in March, police prohibited Cotton from returning to Kerry. Fearful of arousing scrutiny, the IRB abandoned the camps, adding another what-if to the arrival of the arms ship and Casement. Donal O'Sullivan, *District Inspector John A. Kearney*, Trafford, 2005.
189. **control telephone and telegraphy lines:** Ryan, *The Rising*.
189. **marry Grace Gifford:** O Brolchain, *16 Lives: Joseph Plunkett*.
189. **Weisbach ... ceiling of black clouds:** John de Courcy Ireland, *The Sea and the Easter Rising 1916*.
189. **played Schubert and Mozart on his violin:** Clayton, *Aud*.
190. ***U-19*, the navy's first diesel submarine:** 'A pioneer vessel', according to De Courcy Ireland.
190. ***Kleinerlöwe*, Little Lion:** Clayton, *Aud*.
190. **Irish ballads:** Walter, *Die Seeoffizierjahrgang 1911*: 'Casement sang very sad Irish songs.'
190. **neutral flag but why no checks?:** Spindler, *The Mystery of the Casement Ship*.
190. **playing 'Calm Lies the Sea' on the gramophone:** Spindler, *The Mystery of the Casement Ship*.
191. **business began to look queer,':** Spindler, *The Mystery of the Casement Ship*.
191. **testing a new tracking system:** Clayton, *Aud*.
191. **coastal patrols had no description:** *Pull Together! The Memoirs of Admiral Sir Lewis Bayly*, Harrap, 1939: 'The Admiralty also informed me a

disguised German ship was believed to be on the way to the coast of Ireland loaded with war munitions, and in view of the wonderful correctness of the Admiralty intelligence a good lookout was kept for her, though no one knew where she would be met with, and whether she would get through the north sea patrol.'

- 192. **steam-winches and unloading tackle:** Spindler, *The Mystery of the Casement Ship*.
- 192. **carpeted in daisies:** 'The islands of Ireland: a Rising tide and the arrival of the *Aud* at Illauntanning', *Irish Examiner*, 27 November 2017.
- 193. **coated in soot to dim the beam:** Spindler, *The Mystery of the Casement Ship*.
- 193. **noticed her in the bay:** Mortimer O'Leary quoted in *An Phoblacht*, 13 September 1930, cited in Clayton, *Aud*.
- 193. **captain of his Volunteer company:** Tadhg Brosnan.
- 194. **'All right,' Mort replied:** O'Leary statement to *An Phoblacht*, cited in Clayton, *Aud*.

CHAPTER FIFTEEN: GOOD FRIDAY: IN THE NAME OF KING GEORGE

- 195. ***U-19* slid into Tralee Bay:** *U-19* log: de Courcy Ireland, *The Sea and the Easter Rising 1916*.
- 195. **behind Mount Brandon:** Clayton, *Aud*, details Kerry topography and lunar records.
- 195. **water was whispering:** Monteith, *Casement's Last Adventure*.
- 195. **gold-rimmed watch:** On display at the Kerry County museum in Tralee, where an exhibition titled 'Casement in Kerry: a revolutionary journey' has run since 2016.
- 196. **prophecy about a mystical liberator:** Angus Mitchell, *16 Lives: Roger Casement:* 'An extremity of Ireland infused with the mysticism associated with the land of saints and scholars . . . a profound symbolism of landing here.'
- 196. **A twinkle! It disappeared:** Monteith, *Casement's Last Adventure*.
- 196. **Spindler's ship was swallowed in blackness:** Clayton, *Aud*.
- 197. **pistol, Casement demurred:** Monteith, *Casement's Last Adventure*.
- 197. **going ashore in this cockle shell.':** Monteith, *Casement's Last Adventure*.
- 197. **sink a British cargo ship:** SS *Feliciana*, a London-registered 4,200-tonne steamer.
- 198. **Only two hundred yards more,':** Monteith, *Casement's Last Adventure*.
- 198. **skylarks were launching:** Casement letter from Pentonville prison to his sister Nina, 25 July 1916. NLI, MS 17,409.
- 198. **resembled a sleeping child:** Monteith, *Casement's Last Adventure*.

198. **buried pistols and ammunition:** Monteith, *Casement's Last Adventure*. Inventory of what police retrieved – the list includes electric lamps, cuff links, a fountain pen – at TNA, KV 2/8.
198. **5.20 a.m. they passed a low wall:** Kerry County museum timeline.
199. **Royal Navy visitors a tour of the *Aud*:** Spindler, *The Mystery of the Casement Ship*.
199. **Sybil Head signal station:** Vice-Admiral Bayly report to the Admiralty, 4 May 1916, credited the signal station crew with 'intelligent observation and report of a suspicious vessel', cited in Clayton, *Aud*.
199. **guise of Niels Larsen:** Spindler, *The Mystery of the Casement Ship*.
200. **John Donaldson ... not a full Royal Navy officer:** Clayton, *Aud*.
200. **glow of White Horse whisky:** Spindler, *The Mystery of the Casement Ship*.
200. **escape, perhaps to Spain:** Spindler, *The Mystery of the Casement Ship*.
201. **seated on a wall by a bridge:** Monteith, *Casement's Last Adventure*.
201. **'You sell the right sort of papers,':** Monteith, *Casement's Last Adventure*.
201. **Austin Stack, a 36-year-old:** A solicitor's clerk, his role in the Kerry rebels' 1916 debacle remains disputed. One version portrays a dynamic leader who made detailed plans and was undone by circumstance; another version suggests he was lazy and out of his depth. Stack played a significant role in the 1919–21 War of Independence and fledgling Irish state. *Dictionary of Irish Biography*.
202. **stored in Stack's head:** Townshend, *Easter 1916*.
202. **cream of Irish manhood: that's how the RIC billed itself:** Donal O'Sullivan, *District Inspector John A. Kearney*, a biography of the DI who was in charge of the RIC barracks at Tralee.
203. **'If a cow farted, the RIC knew,':** Eunan O'Halpin, in an interview with the author, 2023.
203. ***Lusitania* victims washed ashore months:** Larson, *Dead Wake*.
203. **Pat O'Driscoll rode into Ardfert:** Constable Bernard Reilly witness statement to Irish Bureau of Military History, 2 February 1950.
203. **unclear why McCarthy:** At Casement's trial McCarthy said he rose at 2 a.m. to pray at a holy well a mile from his home but that he had not done so before and could not remember its name.
203. **speculation authorities paid him:** According to Parmiter, *Roger Casement*, 'many peasants living on the coast' earned extra money this way, but the claim has not been verified.
203. **Reilly ... phone Ballyheigue barracks:** An anonymous and apparently well-informed correspondent using the pseudonym 'Magna est veritas' narrated Reilly's role in the hunt and capture in a letter published in *The Constabulary Gazette*, 30 September 1916.
204. **labourers cutting peat:** Letter published in *The Constabulary Gazette*.

204. **Daniel Crowley was quizzing Stack:** Kerry County museum exhibition, and Singleton-Gates and Maurice Girodias, *The Black Diaries: An Account of Roger Casement's Life and Times*.
204. **spotted a finger of smoke:** Spindler, *The Mystery of the Casement Ship*.
204. **crackled through the voice pipes:** Spindler, *The Mystery of the Casement Ship*.
205. **McKenna's Fort, a rather grand:** Named after Patrick McKenna, owner of an adjoining farm.
205. **Hearn dawdled on the perimeter:** Reilly witness statement to Irish Bureau of Military History.
205. **'If you move hand or foot:** H. Montgomery Hyde, *Famous Trials 9: Roger Casement*, Penguin, 1964. First published 1960.
205. **'Richard Morten.':** the name of his best friend, who appears in Chapter 21.
206. **papers in rabbit holes:** Gerard Lyne, 'New Light on Material Concealed by Roger Casement Near Banna Strand', Series 1, Vol. 20, Kerry Archaeological and Historical Society, 1987.
206. **ticket for Berlin to Wilhelmshaven:** Many accounts assume the ticket was in Casement's coat, but it may have been in that of Monteith or Bailey.
206. **servant girl to identify him:** Mary Gorman, who worked on the Allman farm. Reilly witness statement to Irish Bureau of Military History.
206. **boy who was passing:** Martin Collins. Reilly witness statement to Irish Bureau of Military History.
207. **billiards room:** O'Sullivan, *District Inspector John A. Kearney*.
207. **scrutinising this fellow:** O'Sullivan, *District Inspector John A. Kearney*.
207. **wailed that the boilers would burst:** Spindler, *The Mystery of the Casement Ship*.
207. **Royal Navy sloop:** Bayly's memoir, *Pull Together!*, implies he guessed the *Aud*'s real identity. 'They received a wireless from me to escort her into Queenstown, and, if she resisted, to sink her.'
207. **HMS *Bluebell* . . . raised a signal flag:** Spindler, *The Mystery of the Casement Ship*.
208. **Doctor Michael Shanahan:** MacColl interviewed Shanahan for MacColl, *Roger Casement*.
208. **The patient whispered he was Sir Roger:** MacColl, *Roger Casement*.
208. **paper to cover the beard:** O'Sullivan, *District Inspector John A. Kearney*.
208. **fobbed him off:** MacColl, *Roger Casement*.
208. **Con Collins were detained:** O'Sullivan, *District Inspector John A. Kearney*.
209. **'bring God's blessing:** O'Sullivan, *District Inspector John A. Kearney*.
209. **pier at Ballykissane:** *The Men Will Talk to Me: Kerry Interviews* by Ernie O'Malley, edited by Cormac O'Malley and Tim Horgan, Mercier Press, 2012.

CHAPTER SIXTEEN: HOLY SATURDAY: THE PROFESSOR

213. **News of Casement's capture:** Ryan, *The Rising*.
213. **the drowned radio team:** Charlie Monahan, Daniel Sheehan and Con Keating died. The surviving two members of the team abandoned the mission.
214. **sober, cerebral, dithering Eoin MacNeill:** Michael Foy and Brian Barton, *The Easter Rising*, History Press, 2011, say the Volunteers' leader 'made Hamlet seem the embodiment of ruthless decision'. MacNeill's deputy, Bulmer Hobson, said it was easier to persuade him to take no action than to take action. Irish Bureau of Military History.
214. **distinguished Irish language scholar:** Reared in a Catholic enclave in the Antrim glens, MacNeill served as a clerk in Dublin law courts, championed the Irish language and was chair of early Irish history at University College Dublin (UCD). According to Tierney, *Eoin MacNeill*, he 'dragged Celtic Ireland from antiquarian mists' into the light of history.
214. **Thomas MacDonagh, a fellow conspirator:** MacDonagh lectured in English at UCD but gave his primary loyalty to his fellow poet and IRB member, and close friend, Joseph Plunkett.
214. **imposing Victorian villa:** MacNeill recorded the visit in a handwritten memorandum for his court martial after the rising. NLI, Eoin MacNeill papers, MS 43,228/1-30.
214. **fight a guerrilla campaign:** MacNeill was no 'dotty professor' and was 'prepared to use violence' but opposed deploying the Volunteers in a hopeless insurrection, according to his grandson Michael McDowell. 'Eoin MacNeill was open to armed struggle, 1916 gathering told,' *Irish Times*, 22 January 2016.
214. **unprovoked rebellion as a folly:** Tierney, *Eoin MacNeill*.
215. **remote and lacked a telephone:** Mulvagh and Purcell, *Eoin MacNeill*.
215. **Bulmer Hobson, had discovered evidence:** Hobson, *Ireland Yesterday and Tomorrow*, recalls learning of the plans on Holy Thursday 20 April and alerting MacNeill that night.
215. **MacNeill confronted the conspirators:** Roused from his bed early on Friday 21 April, Patrick Pearse admitted subterfuge. 'Yes, you were deceived, but it was necessary.' Ryan, *The Rising*.
215. **kidnapped Hobson:** Lured to a house in Phibsborough, north Dublin, on Friday 21 April, his hosts drew guns and forbade him to leave. He was released on Monday 24 April, once the rising was underway. Hobson, *Ireland Yesterday and Tomorrow*.
215. **cover for mobilisation:** Pearse had publicly announced the manoeuvres weeks earlier, conveying the impression of a routine repeat of Volunteer manoeuvres held on Easter Sunday 1915.

215. **according to his father, the Pope:** Tierney, *Eoin MacNeill*.
216. **'All hands to quarters:** Spindler, *The Mystery of the Casement Ship*.
216. **muffled explosion:** Bayly, *Pull Together!*, recalls watching the scene from the veranda of his house that overlooked the harbour. 'Suddenly the *Aud* stopped, hoisted two German naval ensigns, and lowered her boats ... then an explosion occurred in the *Aud*, and she went to the bottom.'
216. **saved the gramophone!':** Spindler, *The Mystery of the Casement Ship*: 'He swung himself down with the agility of a monkey and plumped into the boat like a sack. But the gramophone ... fell into the water and was seen no more.' Clayton, *Aud*, identifies the stoker as Friedrich Schmitz.
216. **fate of the mongrel Hector:** Unmentioned in Spindler's 1921 memoir, the 1965 edition has a brief, grim reference: 'The first engineer had mercifully despatched the dog.'
216. **seafloor of sand and shingle:** Cecil Albany Chard, a Royal Navy diver, recalled the operation in *Don't Forget The Diver*, Harrap, 1957, cited in Clayton, *Aud*.
217. **walk to the station and the 10.30 a.m. train:** O'Sullivan, *District Inspector John A. Kearney*.
217. **Several times he slipped in the mud:** Reid, *The Lives of Roger Casement*.
217. **Kearney ... took pity:** O'Sullivan, *District Inspector John A. Kearney*.
217. **hosts a pocket watch:** Kearney appreciated the gesture but fearing official reprimand he discreetly returned the watch to Casement's solicitor. O'Sullivan, *District Inspector John A. Kearney*.
217. **his oak walking stick:** Casement's trial notes state he gave 'an oaken alpen stock with iron point bought in Berlin' to Sergeant Hearn. NLI, MS 10764.
217. **on my account they were there,':** O'Sullivan, *District Inspector John A. Kearney*.
217. ***Post* presses. 'A rumour:** 'Landing Arms in Kerry', *The Kerry Evening Post*, 22 April 1916.
218. **six constables were waiting:** Philipps, *Broken Archangel*.
218. **Sir Matthew Nathan:** Before Ireland he had served as governor in Sierra Leone, the Gold Coast, Hong Kong and Natal and was chair of the Board of Inland Revenue. *Dictionary of Irish Biography*.
218. **lunatic traitor Casement:** Ó Broin, *Dublin Castle*, quotes a letter from Nathan to Birrell on Saturday 22 April: 'A telegram from the [RIC] County Inspector received this morning said that it is believed he is Sir Roger Casement. I shall probably know whether he is or not that lunatic traitor before I send off this.'
219. **'I see no indication of a rising,':** Nathan letter to Birrell, cited in Ó Broin, *Dublin Castle*.
219. **with an archaeologist friend:** Robert Macalister, professor of Celtic archaeology at UCD.

219. **genuine comrades:** Colm O Lochlainn, Seán Fitzgibbon, Michael O'Rahilly ('the' O'Rahilly).
220. **home of a friend in Rathgar:** *Séamus O'Kelly.*
220. **bicycles lay in the garden:** Tierney, *Eoin MacNeill.*
220. **Plunkett devoted talents ... outwitting his friends.':** Hobson, *Ireland Yesterday and Tomorrow.*
220. **British would probably *welcome*:** MacNeill memo written around February 1916: 'If the government knew that a revolt was about to take place, it would allow the revolt to take the place.' Cited in Michael Laffan, 'Countermand and Imprisonment, 1916–17', in Mulvagh and Purcell (eds), *Eoin MacNeill: The Pen and the Sword.*
220. **'grossly deceived:** Of all the plotters who misled him, MacNeill singled out Plunkett. 'I think the chief arranger of these details was Joseph Plunkett. Plunkett revelled in plotting and planning, and nothing in the arrangement was too minute for him.' Quoted in Tierney, *Eoin MacNeill.*
221. **frantic messages and meetings:** O Brolchain, *16 Lives: Joseph Plunkett.*
221. **Arbour Hill ... roughly handled:** Casement's trial notes refer to a sergeant-major, Frederick Whittaker, shouting at him 'as if I were a dog' and pulling at his clothes to search him. NLI, 10764.
221. **his birth, 51 years earlier:** Born 1 September 1864, at Doyle's Cottage, Lawson Terrace, Sandycove, less than a mile from Kingstown (now Dun Laoghaire) harbour.
221. **RMS *Ulster* ... bearing 223 mail bags:** RMS *Ulster* journals, 1860–1920, NLI, 2854–2886.
221. **steward ... gifted the prisoner cigarettes:** Hyde, *Famous Trials.*
221. **'Is that you, BT?':** This version of the call is the one Thomson recounted in *The Scene Changes. Odd People* gives slightly different dialogue.
222. **gathering at Rathgar Road:** Tierney, *Eoin MacNeill.*
222. **Ireland's bestselling newspapers:** Mark O'Brien, *The Sunday Independent 1905–84*, Dublin City University research repository.
222. **duty editor, Fred Cogley:** Cogley statement to Eoin MacNeill's court martial, 16 May 1916.
223. **'NO PARADES!' it declared:** *Sunday Independent* cutting, Kerry County Museum exhibition.

CHAPTER SEVENTEEN: EASTER SUNDAY: THIS FESTERING SORE

224. **Euston station at 6.10 a.m.:** Philipps, *Broken Archangel.*
224. **families coming to London for parks:** 'St George's Day Easter', *The Times*, 24 April 1916.

224. **chocolate eggs, hot cross buns:** *London Daily News*, 21 April 1916.
224. **roses sprouted from caps:** 'St George's Day', *Newcastle Daily Journal and Courant*, 24 April 1916.
225. **women doing men's jobs . . . smoking:** 'London Letter', *Bristol Times and Mirror*, 22 April 1916.
225. **10 o'clock he was summoned:** Inspector Joseph Sandercock written statement, 23 April 1916, TNA, HO 144/1636/311643/3A.
226. **cannibals and pirates in the South Seas:** Thomson, *South Sea Yarns*, 1894.
226. **Some enemies Hall could respect:** Hall and Rintelen became such good friends after the war that the Dark Invader attended the wedding of Hall's daughter. James, *The Eyes of the Navy*.
226. **a fireplace, armchair:** Descriptions taken from Sir Harold Scott, *Scotland Yard*, Penguin, 1957, and George Dilnot, *Scotland Yard: The Methods and Organisation of the Metropolitan Police*, Percival Marshall, 1915.
226. **oak-framed roll of honour:** 'Legion of the redeemed', *Liverpool Echo*, 25 May 1916. The article inferred magnanimity from Thomson's décor. 'A noble commentary on the scrupulous impartiality of British police methods and the undeviating fairness of British justice.'
226. **Major Frank Hall . . . MI5:** An Ulster unionist, Hall helped to land arms for the Ulster Volunteer Force in April 1914 before joining military intelligence. His codename, Q, was later used by Ian Fleming in his James Bond novels. Dudgeon, *Roger Casement: The Black Diaries*.
226. **'Tall and thin, and rather cadaverous:** Thomson, *The Scene Changes*.
227. **Casement sat in the armchair:** There are several sources for the interrogation: a typed transcript at TNA based on notes taken by a clerk who was not always present; books and articles by Basil Thomson; recollections by Casement, including statements to his lawyers.
227. **'waiting for you, Sir Roger,' said Blinker:** Mitchell, *16 Lives: Roger Casement*.
227. **'Do you realise, sir,' Blinker interjected:** Judge Sir Thomas Artemus Jones, *Without My Wig*, Brython Press, 1944. Jones was part of Casement's legal team.
227. **'Yes, I do. I have committed:** Jones, *Without My Wig*.
227. **across as histrionic, theatrical:** Thomson, *The Scene Changes*: 'He was very vivacious and at times histrionic . . . I thought he was an idealist, not a self-seeker, but extraordinarily vain.' Thomson, *Odd People*: 'Casement struck me as one of those men who are born with a strong strain of the feminine in their character. He was greedy for approbation and he had the quick intuition of a woman as to the effect he was making on the people around him.'
228. **To encourage the prisoner's flow the clerk:** Thomson, *The Scene Changes*: 'When he was alone with us he became more communicative.'

228. **clerk was for a time dismissed:** According to Hyde, *Famous Trials*, the young clerk was impressed by Casement's refusal to betray his friends, and as he passed the prisoner he tapped him and whispered: 'Greater love hath no man than this.'

228. **had come not to lead but to *stop* the rising:** Thomson, *Odd People*: 'He returned again to his object in coming to Ireland. It was to stop, not to lead, a rising which could only fail with the paltry aid that the Germans had sent. He wanted to prevent "the boys" from throwing away their lives.'

228. **Let me send a message:** Thomson, *The Scene Changes*: 'He was very insistent that the news of his capture should be published, as it would prevent bloodshed.'

229. **'No, better let this festering sore come to a head':** Casement recollection of Hall statement, NLI, 10764. In a separate statement, NLI, 13088, he gave a slightly different wording: 'It is better a festering sore like this should be cut out.' In a note to the Home Office on 18 July 1916, Thomson denied Hall made the statement and said they did not announce Casement's arrest lest it be 'useful to the Germans'. TNA, HO 144/1637/311643/176. In *The Scene Changes*, Thomson said Hall thought that publicising the arrest might incite bloodshed.

229. **'Hall . . . act as he saw fit:** O'Halpin, *British Intelligence in Ireland*. Andrews, *Secret Service*, gives a similar verdict: 'Hall refused, possibly in the hope that the rising would go ahead and force the government to respond with the repression he thought necessary.'

229. **not a hair of his head':** Interrogation transcript, TNA, KV 2/8.

229. **'What's that?' James Connolly roared:** Caulfield, *The Easter Rebellion*.

230. **dimly lit passageways:** William Brennan-Whitmore, *Dublin Burning: The Easter Rising from Behind the Barricades*, Gill and Macmillan, 2013. First published 1996.

230. **'We've another saviour now:** Caulfield, *The Easter Rebellion*.

230. **Some rebels vowed to shoot MacNeill:** Constance Markievicz, the Anglo-Irish aristocrat and ICA leader better known Countess Markievicz, was among them. Townshend, *Easter 1916*.

230. **plan for action outside Dublin had always been shaky:** In the absence of surviving written plans it is difficult to judge the planning, but historians such as Desmond Ryan think there was limited capacity outside the capital: 'Volunteers in the provinces were weak in transport, in control of communications, in numbers, in resolution, above all in arms.' Ryan, *The Rising*.

231. **Tom Clarke favoured striking . . . outvoted:** Le Roux, *Tom Clarke*.

231. **Sprays of Easter lilies adorned the white linen:** Caulfield, *The Easter Rebellion*.

231. **aide to give her a pistol:** The aide, Michael Collins, also gave Gifford £20 lest she needed to bribe her way out of trouble. Gifford statement to Irish Bureau of Military History, 1 June 1949.
232. **9 p.m. he wrote a letter to Grace:** O Brolchain, *16 Lives: Joseph Plunkett*.
232. **arrested tonight,' Lord Wimborne declared:** Caulfield, *The Easter Rebellion*.
232. **Sir Ivor Churchill Guest:** Born 1873, served as an army officer in the Boer War before becoming an MP, then a peer and from February 1915 was lord lieutenant of Ireland.
232. **Nathan, had kept him on a tight leash:** Ó Broin, *Dublin Castle*.
233. **'On what charge? To hold them:** Caulfield, *The Easter Rebellion*.
233. **Army commanders cited:** Major-General Lovick Friend, the army's commander-in-chief in Ireland, had left for England so two staff officers, Colonel H. V. Cowan and Major Owen Lewis, stood in for him at this meeting.
233. **pre-dawn round-ups – later in the week:** Ó Broin, *Dublin Castle*.
233. **inmate registered as Mr C.R.:** Note at the end of interrogation transcript, TNA, KV 2/8.

CHAPTER EIGHTEEN: EASTER MONDAY: LEFT TURN, CHARGE

235. **Volunteer also hovered:** William Brennan-Whitmore, who described the scene in *Dublin Burning*.
235. **Plunkett smiled and waved her aside:** Brennan-Whitmore, *Dublin Burning*.
235. **covered the bandage with a silk scarf:** O Brolchain, *16 Lives: Joseph Plunkett*.
236. **Only a fraction of the Volunteers were turning up:** Townshend, *Easter 1916*, depicts near chaos: 'Units assembled in fragments, individuals set off on random paths, capricious orders and counter-orders were issued by a baggy collection of commanders. Most had little idea what was happening.'
236. **'We are going out to be slaughtered,':** Le Roux, *Patrick Pearse*.
237. **pot-belly, bandy legs and disorderly moustache:** Good, *Inside the GPO*.
237. **'Ludendorff,' a voice whispered:** Good, *Inside the GPO*.
237. **'Come home, Pat:** Tim Pat Coogan, *1916: The Easter Rising*, Phoenix, 2005.
237. **A group of urchins jeered:** Caulfield, *The Easter Rebellion*.
237. **British officers lounging outside the Metropole:** Brennan-Whitmore, *Dublin Burning*.

237. **Two Volunteers linked arms around Plunkett:** Michael Collins and Brennan-Whitmore.
238. **distillation of nationalist doctrine:** Townshend, *Easter 1916*.
238. **'The response was chilling,' a witness later wrote:** Stephen MacKenna, *Memories of the Dead*, Powell Press, 1917, a pamphlet published under the name Martin Daly. NLI, A17853.
239. **storming of the Bastille:** Redmond-Howard, *Six Days of the Irish Republic*.
240. **cheers greeted its appearance,':** Caulfield, *The Easter Rebellion*.
240. **Other rebel units had mixed success:** Townshend, *Easter 1916*.
240. **detachment of about 30 rebels:** ICA unit led by Sean Connolly, no relation to James.
241. **bolt from Mount Olympus:** Dangerfield, *The Damnable Question*: 'Captain Hall, even if he had wished to speak, was obliged for security reasons to remain silent. And so the Birrell administration was thrown to the wolves.'
241. **'I want to tell you . . .':** interrogation transcript for Monday 24 April 1916, TNA, KV 2/8.
241. **Daniel Bailey was singing like a canary:** Captured a day after Casement, Bailey told the RIC about the voyage from Germany and plans for a rising but withheld, or did not know, important details.
242. **Thomson. 'There is no secret about it:** interrogation transcript, TNA, KV 2/8.
242. **issued at 10.25 p.m.:** 'Capture of Sir Roger Casement', *The London Daily News and Leader*. Report included time of the Admiralty press bureau statement.
242. **It started with Noblett's:** Plunkett-Dillon, *All in the Blood*.
242. **Turkish delight, glacier mints:** Caulfield, *The Easter Rebellion*.
243. **Sean O'Casey observed:** O'Casey, *Autobiographies*.
243. **someone had stolen her stolen tea:** Ryan, *The Rising*.
243. **clasping a rosary, to implore:** Redmond-Howard, *Six Days of the Irish Republic*.
244. **'Shitehawks! Lousers! Bowsies!':** Good, *Inside the GPO*.
244. **'1st day of the republic':** *Memoirs of Desmond FitzGerald*, edited by Fergus FitzGerald and others, Routledge, 1968.
244. **garrison to more than 200 defenders:** *Memoirs of Desmond FitzGerald*, citing an estimate by Patrick Pearse. Other estimates suggest the figure was closer to 400.
244. **waxworks . . . capture of George V:** Caulfield, *The Easter Rebellion*.
244. **great things,' one comrade later wrote:** Brennan-Whitmore, *Dublin Burning*.
244. **'My children will have to accept it:** McCoole, *Easter Widows*.

245. **colloquial usage ... the Irish Republican Army, or IRA:** Townshend, *Easter 1916*.
245. **spotted a fellow poet, Desmond FitzGerald:** *Memoirs of Desmond FitzGerald*.
245. **a beautiful shot,' his sister Geraldine:** Plunkett-Dillon, *All in the Blood*.
245. **Plunkett ... transferred the Finn:** Kerrigan, *The Scrap*.
245. **'more courage in his little finger':** James Connolly's son, Roddy, quoted in O Brolchain, *16 Lives: Joseph Plunkett*: 'I had never seen Joe Plunkett and there he was gorgeously apparelled in his uniform with a long sword and a silk scarf ... I thought he was out of place, lying on a mattress in the middle of a revolution. I didn't think he was much of a leader ... My father said, and I remember his remark, I think it was very striking, "That's Joe Plunkett and he has more courage in his little finger than all the other leaders combined."'
246. **Desmond FitzGerald recalled.** '**Plunkett:** *Memoirs of Desmond FitzGerald*.
246. **'We have no machine-guns.':** Good, *Inside the GPO*.

CHAPTER NINETEEN: EASTER WEEK: DON'T BE AFRAID

247. **eclipsed other war news:** Such as a Zeppelin raid on England's east coast, a Turkish attack near the Suez Canal and continued fighting at Verdun.
248. **William Patrick Germain:** Census records list him as an 'apartment housekeeper' who was married with two sons, who in 1916 would have been aged 10 and 15.
248. **Pearse issued a communiqué:** He read this out at the GPO and his handwritten manuscript was printed to become the first and only edition of *Irish War News* (Vol. 1, No. 1), a rebel pamphlet. Pearse also projected assurance in a letter to his mother on 26 April: 'We have plenty of the best food, all our meals being as good as if served in a hotel ... the men have fought with wonderful courage and gaiety.' Piaras Mac Lochlainn, *Last Words: Letters and Statements of the Leaders Executed After the Rising at Easter 1916*, Stationery Office, 1990.
249. **swills of brandy at the viceregal lodge:** Townshend, *Easter 1916*, quotes Wimborne's private secretary: 'his Ex simply swilled brandy the whole time' and used 'the most melodramatically grandiloquent language ... "It is His Excellency's command."' Original source: Lady Cynthia Asquith, *Diaries 1915–1918*, London, 1968.
249. **total troop level to 4,650 men:** Caulfield, *The Easter Rebellion*.
249. **Redmond-Howard, a young writer:** Nephew and biographer of the Irish Parliamentary Party leader John Redmond, and author of *Six Days of the Irish Republic*.
249. **'Since I saw you yesterday:** Interrogation transcript, TNA, KV 2/8.

250. **US secret service had raided a German:** Agents seized documents that Wolf von Igel, a German diplomat, kept in his Wall Street office, which lacked diplomatic immunity. The trove included letters and telegrams related to plans for the Irish rising. One alluded to a consideration – later discarded by the Germans – to send two ships with weapons. It seems the Americans took several weeks to relay this material to Reginald Hall. Devoy, *Recollections of an Irish Rebel*.

250. **'Have you got some trunks at 50 Ebury Street?':** Interrogation transcript, TNA, KV 2/8.

251. **in a storage depot:** W. J. Allison, a Farringdon Road shipping agent, held several trunks, a canvas bag and a deck chair belonging to Casement. Scotland Yard took charge of them on 27 April 1916. TNA, MEPO 3/2415.

251. **box of visiting cards, a trinket box:** TNA, MEPO 3/2415.

251. **four diaries:** Authenticity is discussed in a note on the forgery thesis.

252. **nothing in them,' Casement replied:** Interrogation transcript, National Archive.

252. **Thomson gave conflicting accounts:** His memoirs and newspaper articles contradicted each other over how and when Scotland Yard obtained the diaries but there is corroboration that William Germain delivered the trunks on 25 April 1916: a note by Superintendent Patrick Quinn dated 22 June 1916 and a police property list dated 28 July 1916, both cited in Dudgeon, *Roger Casement: The Black Diaries*.

253. **'Break them open.':** Interrogation transcript, TNA, KV 2/8.

253. **shot forthwith?' asked one MP:** Noel Pemberton Billing, an independent. 'Outbreak in Dublin', *The Times*, 26 April 1916, cites 'loud laughter and cheers' after the question was put to Asquith, who replied: 'I do not think that is a question that ought to be put to me at present.'

253. **Fred Dietrichsen ... pier at Kingstown:** Bríona Nic Dhiarmada, *The 1916 Irish Rebellion*, University of Notre Dame, 2016, and Dublin's GPO Museum.

254. **'bonjour mademoiselle!':** Unclear if in jest or if some soldiers still thought they were in France.

254. **spotted his own Beatrice:** Seán Enright, *Easter Rising 1916: The Trials*, Merrion Press, 2013.

254. **whistle from every angle:** Details of battle and aftermath from Caulfield, Howard-Redmond, Kerrigan, Yeates.

254. **'Dear Dad, thank you for choc:** 'Easter 1916: A British soldier's family reunion and death in Dublin', article by James Moran, *The Irish Times*, 6 April 2015.

255. **Casement ... using his spectacles:** Reid, *The Lives of Roger Casement*.

255. **guards sat in the cell, staring at him:** Hyde, *Famous Trials*.

255. **thoughts became a page of hell,':** Casement note to his lawyers, NLI, MS 10,764.
255. **French village of Hulluch:** BBC, 'Battle of Hulluch: Gassing of the Irish in 1916', 27 April 2016.
255. **placards that week: 'Irishmen! Heavy uproar:** BBC, 'Battle of Hulluch'.
256. **a chaplain wrote:** Father William 'Willie' Doyle. Royal Dublin Fusiliers Association, 'The Tragedy of Hulluch, April 1916', based on seminar hosted by Dublin City Council.
256. **4th day of the republic,' Plunkett wrote:** O Brolchain, *16 Lives: Joseph Plunkett*.
256. **speaking quietly to defenders:** Good, *Inside the GPO*.
257. **sighting of smoke in Dublin Bay:** *Memoirs of Desmond FitzGerald*.
257. **each garrison ... Improvised armoured trucks:** Townshend, *Easter 1916*.
257. **pounding Liberty Hall:** *The Irish Times Book of the 1916 Rising*, 2006, edited by Shane Hegarty and Fintan O'Toole, Gill & Macmillan, 2006.
257. **'When we are all wiped out ...':** Ryan, *The Rising*.
258. **Sean Francis Foster, killed in his pram:** GPO museum.
258. **'ought all to be shot,':** James Stephens, *The Insurrection in Dublin*, Scepter Books, 1965. First published 1916.
258. **in some quarters, grudging respect:** Stephens, *The Insurrection in Dublin*: 'Almost a feeling of gratitude towards the Volunteers because they are holding out for a little while, for had they been beaten the first or second day the city would have been humiliated to the soul.'
258. **eccentric appearance,' one rebel recalled:** Good, *Inside the GPO*.
258. **one witness called 'a gigantic waterfall of fire':** Caulfield, *The Easter Rebellion*.
258. **air seemed to be vibrating.':** Mary Louisa Hamilton Norway, *The Sinn Féin Rebellion as I Saw It*, Smith, Elder & Co., 1916.
258. **since Moscow,' Joe declared:** Ryan, *The Rising*, and Good, *Inside the GPO*. Since 1812 several capitals had in fact burned, including Washington DC, 1814, Paris, 1870, and Belgrade, 1914.
259. **'barbaric splendour:** Dick Humphreys, 'Easter Week in the GPO', NLI, MS 78,825.
259. **protest. 'No! We'll stay with the men!:** Good, *Inside the GPO*.
259. **indefatigable secretary Winifred Carney:** An imperturbable presence who ignored shelling and stayed with her chief to the end, click-clacking messages and proclamations on her typewriter.
259. **launched into 'A Soldier's Song':** Caulfield, *The Easter Rebellion*.
260. **'On! On! Don't be afraid:** O Brolchain, *16 Lives: Joseph Plunkett*.
260. **toppled over Connolly's stretcher:** Kerrigan, *The Scrap*.
260. **cared for, a wounded British soldier:** Dragged to safety by Joe Plunkett's younger brother, George, he groaned through the night. Pearse tried to soothe him. Kerrigan, *The Scrap*.

260. **decided to surrender:** Good, *Inside the GPO.*
260. **Plunkett wrote a letter to Grace Gifford:** O Brolchain, *16 Lives: Joseph Plunkett.*
260. **stood alone in the middle of Moore Street:** Good, *Inside the GPO.*

CHAPTER TWENTY: INTO THE DARK

262. **jeers and insults ... chamberpots:** Coogan, *1916: The Easter Rising.* Also Seán MacEntee, *Episode at Easter*, Gill and Son, 1966, which describes the scene when the prisoners were marched from Richmond barracks towards Kilmainham jail: 'A mob was gathered. It was composed almost entirely of women, soldiers' wives and dependents ... this rabble hooted, jeered and cursed us in insensate rage, and tried in their fury to get at us through the files of our guards.'
262. **exhortations to ... 'bayonet the bastards':** Caulfield, *The Easter Rebellion.*
262. **en route to prison camps:** By 3 May 1916 there were over 500 prisoners in Knutsford and almost 300 at Stafford. Within weeks more than a thousand others would follow across the Irish Sea to camps in England. Later many were transferred to Frongoch in Wales. Townshend, *Easter 1916.*
263. **editorial in the unionist *Irish Times*:** 1 May 1916.
263. **84 rebels, 144 soldiers:** Eunan O'Halpin and Daithí Ó Corráin, *The Dead of the Irish Revolution*, Yale University Press, 2020.
263. ***Punch* magazine drolly put it:** 3 May 1916.
263. **a tide in the affairs of men:** William Shakespeare, *Julius Caesar.*
263. **cardinal rule about 'covering up all tracks':** Hall, *A Clear Case of Genius.*
263. **pending official inquiry:** Chaired by Lord Charles Hardinge, it began hearings on 18 May 1916 and published its report six weeks later, on 26 June. It faulted Birrell's administration for tolerating armed militias before the rising and identified gaps in Dublin Castle's intelligence system. There was no mention of Reginald Hall or naval intelligence.
264. **reproached with having killed him secretly':** Thomson, *The Scene Changes.*
264. **lodging house and a storage:** 55 Ebury Street and Farringdon Road shipping agent W. J. Allison.
264. **Wilde's court case:** Convicted for gross indecency in 1895 and served two years' hard labour.
264. **many were teenagers:** Casement's diaries cite encounters with 16- and 17-year-olds but most were slightly older. Dudgeon, *Roger Casement: The Black Diaries*: 'In an era, and in countries, in which there was no age of consent for homosexual acts, as all were illicit or illegal, his behaviour was

unremarkable. Like Oscar Wilde, his interest was frequently angled toward youths. Yet nobody today in Dublin would even dare say that Wilde should still have been jailed for his sexual acts. The diarist-as-paedophile accusation, with all the echoes that has in contemporary Ireland, is being raised by those who cry forgery. They must be held responsible if Casement's reputation is needlessly sullied as a result.'

264. **imbalance of a privileged European:** Dudgeon, *Roger Casement: The Black Diaries*, says Casement groomed partners but was no predator: 'He did not exploit people and was no "sexual coloniser" or "sex tourist". The partners Casement described were largely urbanised and usually eager, consenting men and boys of many races.'

265. **Shakespeare, as ever, put it well:** 'Tremble, thou wretch': William Shakespeare, *King Lear*.

265. **copying and photographing:** Scotland Yard memo dated 5 May 1916 states 24 pages of extracts were typed and submitted to the director of public prosecutions. More extracts were copied and photographed in the following weeks. TNA, DPP 1/46.

265. **wished he were back in Egypt:** Sir George Arthur, *General Sir John Maxwell*, John Murray, 1932, includes an epilogue by Maxwell's daughter, Philae Clifford Carver, who was with him during his stint in Ireland. 'A most ungrateful task, which he heartily hated . . . the happiest part of his life was in Egypt, where he spent nearly 30 years of his military life and where he was both loved and understood.' After retiring from the army he became head of the Egyptian Exploration Society.

265. **vapour of charred wood:** O'Casey, *Autobiographies*.

265. **'no treason whispered – even whispered:** Kerrigan, *The Scrap*.

266. **slab of a nose – source of his nickname Conky:** Townshend, *Easter 1916*.

266. **freshly dug 28 ft × 9 ft pit at Arbour:** Le Roux, *Patrick H. Pearse*.

266. **shootings of civilians:** Most notoriously, three executed at Portobello barracks and 13 killed at North King Street.

266. **dispirited letters:** Arthur, *General Sir John Maxwell*: 'The censored letters of prisoners marked the barometer; at first they wrote in a dejected spirit; as if fully conscious of their own shame and the misery of others.'

266. **first courts martial:** Enright, *Easter Rising 1916: The Trials*: 'Although Maxwell adopted the formal language and proformas of trial under DORA [Defence of the Realm Act], the evidence suggests that the prisoners were tried under a trial regime of Maxwell's creation.' (Enright is a UK circuit court judge and legal historian.)

266. **'My comrades and I believe:** Kathleen Clarke and Helen Litton, *Revolutionary Woman: My Fight for Ireland's Freedom*, O'Brien Press, 1991.

267. **to be a widow – a pregnant widow:** Foy, *Tom Clarke*. The pregnancy ended in miscarriage.
267. **'I don't know how I am to live:** Clarke and Litton, *Revolutionary Woman*.
267. **still remember how the key sounded:** Clarke and Litton, *Revolutionary Woman*.
267. **pulled from a torpor:** Gifford witness statement, Irish Bureau of Military History. 'It is a sort of telepathy . . . [Joe's] thoughts were so powerful that I was simply pulled out of the bed.'
267. **dress of check fabric, a hat:** O'Neill, *Grace Gifford Plunkett and Irish Freedom*.
268. **He eyed her. 'Must you?':** Plunkett-Dillon, *All in the Blood*.
268. **owner noticed the stifled sob:** Mr Stoker, the jeweller, quoted in *Lloyd's Weekly News*, 7 May 1916, NLI, Grace Plunkett papers.
268. **evidence Grace was indeed pregnant:** Weeks after Joe's execution Gifford had a miscarriage, according to Plunkett-Dillon, *All in the Blood*: 'When I went into her bedroom I saw a large white chamberpot full of blood and a foetus. She said nothing and I said nothing.'
268. **flickering candles illuminated dark shapes:** O Brolchain, *16 Lives: Joseph Plunkett*.
269. **Maxwell . . . memo to Downing Street:** O Brolchain, *16 Lives*, and Dudley Edwards, *The Seven*.
270. **She was tongue-tied:** Gifford witness statement, Irish Bureau of Military History.
270. **He gave a priest his spectacles:** Father Sebastian. Mac Lochlainn, *Last Words*.
270. **utterly calm, the priest later recalled:** Father Augustine, quoted in article by Mary Purcell in *The Belvederian*, 1966, cited in Mac Lochlainn, *Last Words*.
270. **Sherwood Foresters . . . formed the firing squad:** Enright, *Easter Rising 1916: The Trials*.

CHAPTER TWENTY-ONE: THE OTHER THING

271. **ancient bolts and chains:** *A Pictorial and Descriptive Guide to London and Its Environs*, Ward, Lock & Co., 1916.
271. **swallowing crooked nails:** A. E. King, Welsh Guards corporal, in tape-recorded interview with Roger Sawyer, 20 February 1972. Transcript held at Public Record Office of Northern Ireland (PRONI).
272. **George Gavan Duffy:** Son of the nationalist politician Sir Charles Gavan Duffy. Qualified as a solicitor in London in 1907. After the Casement trial he moved to Ireland, helped to negotiate the Anglo-Irish treaty and served in the Free State government before becoming a judge.

272. **Elizabeth and Gertrude Bannister:** Casement lived with the Bannister family in Liverpool for three years as a teenager and remained close with both cousins, especially 'Gee'. The sisters were taking an Easter break near Lowestoft on 25 April 1916 when German ships bombed the town – an attempt to divert British attention and aid Ireland's rebellion. Upon hearing of Casement's arrest they hastened to London but were stonewalled in trying to see him until around 11 May. Bannister wrote a 51-page account of visiting Casement at the Tower and Brixton Prison and lobbying for clemency, in a manuscript held at the NLI, MS 7946. Her account forms a chapter titled 'The last days of Roger Casement' in *Dublin 1916, A Compendium on the Easter Rising*, edited by Roger McHugh, Arlington, 1966.
272. **gladdening news: Robert Monteith:** Bannister, NLI, MS 7946.
272. **Back in Zossen ... hoisted an Irish tricolour:** Keogh, *With Casement's Irish Brigade*.
272. **gap-toothed blond man:** The acting consul-general in Philadelphia reported an offer from 'a man named Adler Christensen to give evidence against Casement and if necessary to proceed to England'. TNA, FO 95/776.
273. **a trust in his keeping,' a biographer noted:** Reid, *The Lives of Roger Casement*.
273. **exception to the rule,' he told a visitor:** Jones, *Without My Wig*.
273. **angry mob gathered outside:** Edie Stopford, a niece of Alice Stopford Green, was 'aghast to find a seething and angry mob' outside Casement's hearing at Bow Street. León Ó Broin, *Protestant Nationalists in Revolutionary Ireland: The Stopford Connection*, Gill and Macmillan, 1985.
273. **'nerves vibrant as violin strings:** 'Contrasts in two prisoners', *Daily Express*, 16 May 1916.
274. **Royal Commission into the Irish rebellion:** Hearings held in the same venue where Casement testified in May 1914, Chapter 1.
274. **Hall asked Ben Allen to stay behind:** Allen two-page statement, made to a commissioner of oaths during a visit to Ireland, dated 19 August 1960, NLI, 13542.
274. **victim of perversions':** Allen statement included in William Maloney papers, NLI, MS 5588.
275. **done it,' an English author concluded:** MacColl, *Roger Casement*.
276. **Madame Tussauds, workers:** Tussaud ad in *The People*, 28 May 1916, and *Hampstead and St John's Wood Advertiser*, 'Sir Roger Casement at Madame Tussaud's', 1 June 1916.
276. **'prime minister should know ... quicklime:** Maxwell letter to Maurice Bonham-Carter, Asquith's principal private secretary, 26 May 1916, cited in Townshend, *Easter 1916*.

277. **a captain, apparently insane:** John Bowen-Colthurst was court-martialled and found guilty but insane and committed to an asylum for the criminally insane.
277. **Francis Sheehy Skeffington:** A prominent iconoclast who championed women's rights and was attempting to stop looting when arrested by British troops.
277. **denunciation in the House of Commons by John Dillon:** *Hansard*, 11 May 1916.
277. **blood seep from a closed door:** *Seventy Years Young: Memories of Elizabeth, Countess of Fingal*, Lilliput, 1991. First published 1937.
277. **detected 'sudden unfriendliness:** RIC report, 15 May 1916. Cited in Townshend, *Easter 1916*.
278. **bells tolled for Joe Plunkett ... Carmelite:** 'Requiem for Joseph Plunkett', *Irish Independent*, 9 June 1916, plus *The Freeman's Journal* and other newspapers on the same day.
278. **Yeats ... began sketching notes:** John Wilson Foster, 'Yeats and the Easter Rising', *Canadian Journal of Irish Studies*, June 1985.
278. **'are impossible people':** Maxwell to Bonham-Carter, 7 June 1916, cited in Townshend, *Easter 1916*.
279. **'Oh, Roddie! To think:** John Morgan, a member of Casement's defence team, witnessed part of the conversation and relayed it in a letter to George Gavan Duffy on 11 June 1916.
279. **rid him of the lice:** MacColl, *Roger Casement*.
279. **the other thing, Roddie?':** John Morgan letter to George Gavan Duffy.
280. **female American journalist:** Mary Boyle O'Reilly, a foreign correspondent who wrote for *Harper's* magazine and the *Boston Globe*.
280. **government prosecutor gave the defence:** Travers Humphreys, later knighted, passed the extracts to Artemus Jones. Hyde, *Famous Trials*.
280. **Antrim burned the contents:** After Casement's arrest, Francis Joseph Bigger opened a trunk that Casement had left in his safekeeping and discovered and destroyed sexually explicit writings, his nephew, Joseph Warwick Bigger, revealed decades later. Dudgeon, *Roger Casement: The Black Diaries*.

CHAPTER TWENTY-TWO: TRIAL

281. **rose festival scented London:** 'The Rose Maidens', *The Globe*, 21 June 1916.
281. **Battle of Jutland:** The biggest naval engagement of the war from 31 May to 1 June cost the Royal Navy 14 ships and 6,000 men but left it in control of the North Sea.
281. **Even Lord Kitchener:** HMS *Hampshire* sank off the Orkney Islands on 5 June 1916.

282. **British ambassador in Washington:** Cecil Spring-Rice.
282. **American military capacity:** The US army's struggle to contain and catch Pancho Villa's cross-border raiders had deepened British scepticism.
282. **sought Isaacs' advice:** Hall, *A Clear Case of Genius*.
283. **prison-issue blue foolscap:** Hyde, *Famous Trials*.
283. **George Bernard Shaw had drafted:** The playwright thought Casement should stage not a legal defence but a defiant oration and wrote a draft to 'thunder down the ages', *Beatrice Webb's Diaries 1912–24*, cited in McDowell, *Alice Stopford Green*.
284. **believed the rebels were hooligans:** *The Last Serjeant: The Memoirs of Serjeant A. M. Sullivan, QC*, MacDonald, 1952, called the rising 'a murderous riot'.
284. **apex of human civilisation:** *The Last Serjeant* invokes the 'golden mist', 'sacred tradition', 'great men' and 'ancient rites' of Middle Temple, London's legal quarter.
284. **rubbish them as unworthy:** 15 July 1916 Gavan Duffy letter to Gertrude Bannister laid out the policy: 'No such diary has the remotest connection with the case on which I am engaged and these rumours are simply spread about from the lowest and most malicious motives, a proceeding which is beneath contempt and which it would be preposterous to expect me to notice.' NLI, MS 10,763/16/39.
285. **ransacked the Clan's treasury:** Devoy sent $5,000 raised from the sale of his late brother's estate in New Mexico. Devoy, *Recollections of an Irish Rebel*.
285. **Irish tricolours were sprouting:** Gifford Czira, *The Years Flew By*: 'We introduced the flag to New York by flying it at the top of a Fifth Avenue bus and it was quite startling to see that the police already recognised it as, at every intersection of the streets, they stood to attention to salute.'
285. **tricolour badges on Long Island:** Monteith Lynch, *The Mystery Man of Banna Strand*.
285. **Music halls were lauding the rebels:** Gifford Czira, *The Years Flew By*.
285. **Gavan Duffy sounded an upbeat note:** Letter to Richard Morten, Hyde, *Famous Trials*.
286. **rudest man in England:** Enright, *Easter Rising 1916: The Trials*.
286. **his extraordinary success', noted a biography:** *Oxford Dictionary of National Biography*.
286. **Smith revealed to his guests:** Sir Travers Humphreys, *Criminal Days*, Hodder & Stoughton, 1946.
287. **a new dock to render the defendant fully visible:** Hyde, *Famous Trials*.
287. **intellectual cast of his features,' wrote one observer:** Artemus Jones.
287. **figure in Elizabethan ruffs:** Edith Shackleton of *The Daily Sketch*, cited in Redmond-Howard, *Six Days of the Irish Republic*.

288. **usher rose and with an affected air of weariness:** Hyde, *Famous Trials*.
288. **impudent replies to judges:** Two examples from the *Oxford Dictionary of National Biography*:
'Mr Smith, having listened to your case, I am no wiser.' 'Possibly not, m'lud, but much better informed.'
'What do you suppose I am on the bench for, Mr Smith?' 'It is not for me, your honour, to attempt to fathom the inscrutable workings of providence.'
288. **Smith joined the coalition:** Appointed solicitor-general in May 1915 and succeeded Edward Carson as attorney-general in October 1915.
289. **insider trading:** The 1912 Marconi scandal almost ousted as Isaacs as attorney-general.
289. **very grave one,' Smith began:** Hyde, *Famous Trials*, includes a verbatim record of the trial based on official shorthand writers' notes.
290. **'subtle and restrained invective':** Hyde, *Famous Trials*.
290. **exotica of their accents:** Routinely referred to as 'Kerry peasants', with Mary Gorman described as a 'colleen' whose brogue baffled lawyers. Extracts in Kerry county museum exhibition.
291. **'life upon a comma:** Casement letter to Richard Morten, 28 July 1916. NLI, 31,724(5).
292. **Sullivan looked for the clock, it was gone:** Sullivan, *The Last Serjeant*.
292. **Isaacs about a 'diary' found:** Some scholars consider the exchange innocuous but Inglis, *Roger Casement*, and Frank Callanan, *Between Treason and Blood Sacrifice: The Trials of Roger Casement* (essay in *Roger Casement in Irish and World History*, editor Mary Daly, Royal Irish Academy, 2005), think the judge and prosecutor staged it.
293. **The jury – a bank clerk, a baker:** Hyde, *Famous Trials*.
293. **the prisoner in the face:** Article by Smith's son, Frederick, 2nd Earl of Birkenhead, 'Roger Casement's Trial for High Treason', *Aberdeen Press and Journal*, 15 November 1934.
294. **and sauntered out:** An action censured by his otherwise sympathetic biographer, John Campbell, *F. E. Smith: First Earl of Birkenhead*, Pimlico, 1991: 'This graceless insult to a defeated antagonist whose courage he would in other circumstances have admired . . . was coarse, it was crude, it was callous, and it was sadly characteristic of F.E. in one of those recurrent fits of boorishness.'
294. **'deep-set eyes resembled an Italian's:** Smith's wife, Margaret Furneaux Smith, the future Lady Birkenhead, quoted in MacColl, *Roger Casement*.
295. **askew, adding a rakish air to Horridge's:** MacColl, *Roger Casement*.
295. **He bowed and smiled:** Hyde, *Famous Trials*.

CHAPTER TWENTY-THREE: ERASED

296. **waited at a long table in a long room:** Bannister, NLI, MS 7946.
296. **warder stood vigil:** McDowell, *Alice Stopford Green*, depicts the visiting room: 'Three warders, a distance about the length of a good sized room, every word called out … it is just a desolation except for his gentle dignity.'
297. **condemned Wilde to Pentonville:** The writer started and finished his jail term at Pentonville but spent time at other prisons, including Reading, subject of his poem 'The Ballad of Reading Gaol'.
297. **Buckingham Palace announced:** Announced on 30 June 1916 and published in the *London Gazette*, 4 July 1916.
297. **'glorious figure in my life':** Bannister letter to Casement's sister, Nina, 27 November 1916, NLI.
298. **acting headmistress:** Queen Anne's private school, Caversham, terminated her 17 years of service with a £40 pay-off. NLI, 13075/1.
298. **Walter Page, the US ambassador:** A journalist and publisher who encouraged Woodrow Wilson to run for the White House and was posted as ambassador to Britain in 1913. Page's extreme anglophilia, and frustration with US neutrality, strained his relations with Wilson.
298. **humorous,' noted Margot Asquith:** Diary entry 20 February 1915, *Margot Asquith's Great War Diary*.
298. **never saw a finer lot of men:** 'Gently bred, high-minded, physically fit, intellectually cultivated, patriotic.' Burton Jesse Hendrick, *The Life and Letters of Walter H. Page*, Doubleday, 1922.
299. **encomium in a letter to Wilson in 1918:** Hendrick, *Walter H. Page*.
299. **secrets and joint enterprises:** For example in 1915 they devised a plan to use the French navy to intercept a US ship bringing cotton to Germany. Beesly, *Room 40*, and Hendrick, *Walter H. Page*.
299. **'unspeakably filthy character':** Charles Callan Tansill, *America and the Fight for Irish Freedom, 1866–1922: An Old Story Based upon New Data*, Devin-Adair, 1957, citing Page letter in Casement file, Woodrow Wilson papers, Library of Congress.
299. **Atlantic, under marine guard:** Captain Colpoys Cleland Walcott was entrusted with photographic copies and sailed from Liverpool, bound for New York, with a guard of four marines on 17 July 1916. Released Irish state papers, 30 December 2024, 2022/25/865.
299. **atrocities in Congo:** Denis Gwynn, *The Life and Death of Roger Casement*, Cape, 1930.
300. **Joe Tumulty, the president's private secretary:** Proud of his Irish roots but above all a pragmatist who sought to shield Wilson from any Irish-American

electoral backlash, according to John Blum, *Joe Tumulty and the Wilson Era*, Houghton Mifflin, 1951.

300. **the president to a journalist:** Franz Krebs, a German-American, interviewed Casement in Berlin in April 1915 and with Albert Dawson, a cinematographer, filmed a short, silent clip of Casement at his desk. It was shown in US cinemas in June 1916 and is viewable on YouTube.

300. **Tammany Hall advocates:** Notably Judge Daniel Cohalan, who opposed Wilson's nomination at the Democratic convention in 1912. Tansill, *America and the Fight for Irish Freedom*.

300. **artist John Lavery sketched:** the result was a monumental oil painting measuring 10 ft × 6 ft. As a goodwill gesture, in 1951 the British government placed it on long-term loan to the Irish authorities, who displayed it at Dublin's legal temple, King's Inns, where it remains today.

301. **F. E. Smith refused to issue:** Justified decision in his book *Famous Trials of History*, Hutchinson, 1926. 'It would have been easy to have consented but that would have been a negation of my duty.'

301. **during the trial she buttonholed:** Bannister, NLI, MS 7946.

301. **ministers favoured commuting:** Among them Lord Lansdowne and Edward Grey. Jenkins, *Asquith*.

301. **prime minister had hinted:** Jenkins, *Asquith*. 'Asquith himself would have preferred a reprieve based on medical evidence but in the absence of this did not feel it right to treat Roger Casement more leniently than his supposed followers had been treated by Maxwell.'

301. **was 'mentally abnormal':** Report by the Harley Street doctors R. Percy Smith and Maurice Craig, dated 10 July 1916, analysed Casement's 1911 diaries: 'They contain definite evidence of sexual perversion of a very advanced type ... there appears to be no evidence of delusion or general intellectual defect ... [but] the writer must be regarded undoubtedly as a mentally abnormal individual. We cannot say that the condition amounted to certifiable insanity.' TNA, HO 144/1636/311643/40.

301. **Ernley then wrote two memos:** Both on 15 July; one circulated to cabinet on 17 July, the other on 18 July. TNA, HO/144/1636/53.

302. **tried to *avert* the rising:** Eva Gore-Booth and other supporters used the account of Fr Frank Ryan, the priest in whom Casement had confided in Tralee, to show his mindset upon landing in Ireland.

302. **to Norway to interview:** Inspector Sandercock questioned staff from the Grand Hotel, where Casement and Adler Christensen stayed in October 1914. Several alleged they had seen or heard evidence of homosexual activity. A receptionist, Gustav Adolph Olsen, claimed he had entered Casement's room and saw the pair 'half naked and in a suggestive position'. The claims were not used in court or at cabinet. TNA, HO 144/1637/311643/140.

302. **extracts to the Bishop of Durham:** Hyde, *Famous Trials*, cites no source. Ramsay, *'Blinker' Hall, Spymaster*, identifies Hall's royal fixer, Lord Richard Herschell, as the probable intermediary.
303. **Harris alone with a diary:** Letters between Harris and the Home Office just before and after the 19 July visit, TNA, HO 144/1636/311643/49.
303. **life 'poisoned by disease':** Hyde, *Famous Trials*, quotes from Harris's unpublished autobiography: 'I came upon two or three facts known only to Casement and myself, and then my hopes were shattered, for I realised that the wretched thing was genuine ... the diary was more than a record, it was the unfolding of a life which for years had been poisoned by disease.'
303. **President Wilson wrote:** Tansill, *America and the Fight for Irish Freedom*, and Blum, *Joe Tumulty*.
303. **Henry Massingham:** When the editor of the *Nation* reported his findings to Casement's support committee, Charlotte Shaw called it a 'crushing blow. We were rather knocked to pieces ... the thing entirely killed any English sympathy there might have been for Casement'. Inglis, *Roger Casement*.
303. **Shaw ... hardly any newspaper:** One exception was the *Manchester Guardian*.
303. **Ireland was strangely unmoved:** Reid, *The Lives of Roger Casement*, and Redmond-Howard, *Six Days of the Republic*. However, authorities did receive pleas from some members of the public, such as a JP from County Meath: 'If Roger Casement is hanged, England will get no more of my sons and I have nine.' Cited in Dudgeon, *Roger Casement: The Black Diaries*, and NLI, 13088.
304. **'What will you do, Gee:** Bannister, NLI, MS 7946.
304. **last letter to Richard Morten:** NLI, MA 31,724(5).
305. **Cardinal Francis Bourne ... apology:** Denis Gwynn, 'Roger Casement's Last Weeks', *Studies*, Vol. 54, No. 213, Spring 1965.
305. **Sympathetic prison chaplains:** James McCarroll, Thomas Carey and Edward Murnane.
305. **baptised a Catholic:** Discreetly arranged by his mother in Rhyl, Wales, on 5 August 1868.
305. **worried about Robert Monteith:** Casement 25 July 1916 letter to his sister Nina: 'The only person alive, if he is alive – who knows the whole of my coming and why I came, with what aim and hope, is Monteith. I hope he is alive.'
305. **New York ... massive explosion:** Ramsay, *'Blinker' Hall, Spymaster*, and FBI history website, 'Black Tom 1916 Bombing'. https://www.fbi.gov/history/famous-cases/black-tom-1916-bombing.
306. **said the Negro Fellowship League:** Quoted in Inglis, *Roger Casement*.

306. **'Ireland and Mexico:** Page memo about the lunch quoted in Hendrick, *Walter H. Page*.
307. **'Excellent,' said Asquith:** The references to Casement's diaries come from Thomson, *The Scene Changes*, which cites a briefing on the lunch by Edward Bell, US embassy intelligence officer.
307. **'*Sursum corda*:** Reid, *The Lives of Roger Casement*.
307. **contrition was said to be intense:** Fr Thomas Carey letter to Sidney Parry, Gwynn, *The Life and Death of Roger Casement*.
307. **An inmate watching the scene:** Archibald Fenner Brockway, a pacifist jailed for resisting conscription, went on to become a Labour MP and crusader against colonialism.
307. **Ellis ... study a condemned man's physique:** John Ellis, *Diary of a Hangman*, True Crime, 1996.
307. **bag of equivalent weight:** 'Casement's Last Hours', *Daily Express*, 3 August 1916.
308. **modern method was a trapdoor:** Steve Fielding, *Hanged at Pentonville*, History Press, 2008, and interview with author, March 2024.
308. **a hasty, secret copy:** Father James McCarroll made the copy in the condemned cell after Casement's execution and in 1946 shared a copy with the author Herbert Mackey.
308. **own execution,' one guest:** Henry Nevinson, *Last Changes, Last Chances*, Mayflower, 1928.
309. **gathered on Caledonian Road:** 'Execution of Casement', *The Times*, 4 August 1916.
309. **'He ain't got long now.':** 'Casement Hanged', *The Northern Whig*, 4 August 1916.
309. **shielding eyes from the sun:** *Daily Mirror* photograph captioned 'Crowd waiting to hear the tolling of the bell', 4 August 1916.
309. **prison doctor, somewhat nervously:** Hyde, *Famous Trials*.
309. **Ellis ... my unhappy lot to execute.':** Ellis, *Diary of a Hangman*.
310. **Last words: 'Into thy hands:** Press Association report endorsed by Mac Lochlainn, *Last Words*. Other versions say his last words were 'I die for my country'.

CHAPTER TWENTY-FOUR: GOD IS NOT AN ENGLISHMAN

311. **clemency petition ... Bernard Shaw:** Hyde, *Famous Trials*.
311. **laments in South America:** Reid, *Roger Casement*.
311. ***Times* ... the 'inspired innuendos:** A fuller quote: 'We cannot help protesting against certain other attempts which have been made to use the press for the purpose of raising issues which are utterly damaging to Casement's characters but which have no connexion whatever with the

charges on which he was tried. These issues should either have been raised in a public or straightforward manner, or they should have been left severely alone ... if there was ever any virtue in the pomp and circumstance of a great state trial, it can only be weakened by inspired innuendoes which, whatever their substance, are now irrelevant, improper and un-English.' 4 August 1916.

312. **Autopsy ... 'unmistakeable evidence':** Dr Percy Mander, Pentonville's medical officer, also found that the vertebrae and spinal cord were completely severed, indicating instantaneous death. TNA, HO 144/1637/311643/141.

312. **Belfast bank clerk as the 'Millar':** Joseph Millar Gordon. Dudgeon, *Roger Casement: The Black Diaries*.

312. **ministers received rifles from the wreck of the *Aud*:** Clayton, *Aud*.

312. **Scotland Yard's private museum ... sword:** Scott, *Scotland Yard*.

313. **tramped aboard the SS *Adriatic*:** Monteith, *Casement's Last Adventure*.

313. **lived with a hermit, posed as a farmer:** Monteith, *Casement's Last Adventure*.

313. **Dantean conditions of ... 'firemen':** Larson, *Dead Wake*.

313. **caught the crosstown trolley:** Monteith, *Casement's Last Adventure*.

313. **A small girl nodded, but looked fearfully:** Monteith Lynch, *The Mystery Man of Banna Strand*.

314. **seismic result in a rural by-election:** Foster, *Modern Ireland*.

314. **stiff speaker and awkward campaigner:** 'Count Plunkett, MP', *Daily Express*, 6 February 1917: 'A rather colourless and unimpressive candidate.'

314. **'My place henceforward,' the papal count:** 'Count Plunkett Wins N. Roscommon', *Irish Independent*, 6 February 1917.

314. **feverish anxiety,' said the *Evening Herald*:** 'Plunkett In: Sensational result in North Roscommon', 5 February 1917.

315. **praying not only for but *to*:** Townshend, *Easter 1916*.

315. **released from internment camps:** Foster, *Modern Ireland*: Their return home in late 1916 had an 'electrifying effect' and started 'a hesitant revival of separatist activity'.

315. **historian wrote, had 'burst the limits:** Townshend, *Easter 1916*.

316. **Hall's agony of suspense:** Hall, *A Clear Case of Genius*.

316. **In January, Room 40 had intercepted:** Tuchman, *The Zimmermann Telegram*.

316. **Britain was running out of men and money:** Norman Stone, *World War One: A Short History*, Penguin, 2007: 'British credit, by the end of 1916, had nearly been exhausted.'

316. **'I lived in a kind of nightmare,':** Hall, *A Clear Case of Genius*.

316. **celebrated with champagne:** Hall, *A Clear Case of Genius*. American dollars and ships gave an immediate boost to the Allies but it took many

months for the US to train, equip and send significant troop numbers to France.

316. **gaze returned to Ireland … a bumbler:** O'Halpin, *British Intelligence in Ireland*: 'Reginald Hall wielded a great deal of power. He did not wield it wisely where Ireland was concerned.'

317. **rumours and gossip:** O'Halpin, *British Intelligence in Ireland*: 'Despite the vagueness and evident unreliability of such reports, Captain Hall appeared to heed them rather than the more prosaic account of affairs provided by the Irish authorities, who month after month found no trace of German intrigue in Ireland.'

317. **arrest Sinn Féin leaders:** Andrew, *Secret Service*: 'That and the conscription threat backfired.'

317. **Admiralty in-fighting and … diary business:** James, *The Eyes of the Navy*.

317. **staged a farewell concert:** Beesly, *Room 40*.

318. *They call me Blinker Hall, Damn their eyes*: Hoy, *40 O.B.*

319. **'a bellyful of fire:** O'Beirne Ranelagh, *The IRB*, citing Albert Sylvester, George's principal private secretary.

319. **the first colony – foundation stone of empire:** Jane Ohlmeyer, *Making Empire: Ireland, Imperialism and the Early Modern World*, OUP, 2023.

319. **reconstructed Irish Republican Brotherhood:** O'Beirne Ranelagh, *The IRB*.

319. **'nothing ever gave me greater delight':** Interview with the *Boston Post*, 18 January 1918.

319. **Collins to view the notorious diaries:** Collins and a colleague, Eamonn Duggan, viewed the volumes at the House of Lords on 6 February 1922. Duggan said Collins recognised Casement's handwriting. NLI, MS 17,601/6/1.

320. **Parades in Kerry marched:** The tradition started on the first anniversary of his execution in August 1917 when a crowd with drums and tricolours trekked to the spot where Casement was arrested, and heard a eulogy by Thomas Ashe. 'The English gaolers can bury his body – but his soul lives. He has escaped, and is now where no one can reach him. He lives in Irish hearts a hero.'

321. **Nevil Macready:** Album of *Irish Times* photographs shows Macready on the deck of HMS *Dragon*.

321. **he loathed Ireland:** Nevil Macready, *Annals of an Active Life*, Hutchinson, 1924.

321. **reporter felt awed:** *Ulster Herald* report cited in the *Irish Times*, 'A look at Britain's military commanders in Ireland up to the end of War of Independence', 11 December 2022.

321. **grey warships:** Macready, *Annals of an Active Life*: 'As the lights of Howth sank in the distance the curtain fell on the Irish drama in which British troops had played their part for 750 years.'

EPILOGUE

323. **the 'Zinoviev letter':** Purportedly written by Grigori Zinoviev, president of the Comintern, and almost certainly forged, it depicted the Labour government as soft on Bolshevism and was leaked to the *Daily Mail* on the eve of the October 1924 election – one of the era's greatest political scandals. Elements of the intelligence services and Conservative party were involved, with Hall's role 'instrumental', according to the *Oxford Dictionary of National Biography*.
323. **faltered in politics:** As the party's principal agent, Hall was blamed for electoral defeat in 1923 and lost his seat. He returned to parliament as the member for Eastbourne in 1925 'but made little impact' and retired from politics in 1929. *Oxford Dictionary of National Biography*.
323. **Thomson ... ousted from Scotland Yard:** Dismissed in October 1921 after a dispute with Lloyd George's government. Eunan O'Halpin, 'Sir Warren Fisher and the Coalition, 1919–1922', *The Historical Journal*, Vol. 24, No. 4, 1981. Before departing, Thomson was said to have 'filched' documents and is believed to be the source that gave copies of Casement's diaries to Peter Singleton-Gates. Dudgeon, *Roger Casement: The Black Diaries*.
323. **Thelma de Lava:** Thomson was arrested in Hyde Park on 12 December 1925 and convicted of gross indecency on 5 January 1926. He continued a prolific writing career and died in 1939.
324. **Admiralty vetoed Hall's request:** He abandoned his memoir project in 1933 and much of the draft was destroyed. Of 30 envisaged chapters, seven were completed and survived, forming the basis of *A Clear Case of Genius*, edited by Vickers and first published in 2017.
324. **'If you're the undertaker, my man:** Beesly, *Room 40*.
324. **remembered, and celebrated:** obituaries hailed his contribution to victory in the First World War and did not mention his role in leaking Casement's diaries. Biographies and most histories of Room 40 also paint positive portraits of Hall.
324. **cold earth of Pentonville's:** Paul Keating, an Irish diplomat at the London embassy, detailed the exhumation in a 4 March 1965 memo to the Department of Foreign Affairs in Dublin.
325. **rifle volleys and clarion bugles:** 'Casement's Last Salute', *The Cork Examiner*, 2 March 1965.

325. **facilitated Casement's sanctification:** W. B. Yeats accepted and promoted the forgery theory in two poems in the 1930s, including *Roger Casement*, which has the lines:
Afraid they might be beaten
Before the bench of Time,
They turned a trick by forgery
And blackened his good name.

A perjurer stood ready
To prove their forgery true;
They gave it out to all the world,
And that is something new;

325. **Kerry ... atone for the county's shame:** Despite periodic attempts at exculpation, such as an April 1966 *Kerryman* article, 'Ardfert is Defended', outsiders still lob accusations of betrayal. One example: during a 1975 Gaelic football match Cork fans left early because they were losing. A Kerry supporter shouted: 'Leaving early, can't take ye'r beating!' Back came the riposte: 'What do ye mean "leaving"? Ye bastards, ye left Casement on Banna Strand!' Cited in 'How the Rising and Casement Fell Victim to Murphy's Law in Kerry', *The Irish Examiner*, 15 April 2006.

325. **inspire independence movements:** 'It seemed to point out exactly how a subject nation should feel,' Jawaharlal Nehru, cited in Mitchell, *16 Lives: Roger Casement*.

327. **'memory in motion':** Kevin Grant, 'Roger Casement: gay Irish martyr or victim of British forgery?' *Guardian*, 28 September 2016.

327. **1934 Hollywood screenplay:** Julius Klein, a German-American writer who met Casement in Berlin, wrote the 29-page draft and pitched it to Universal Studios. It dropped the project after opposition from the British and Irish governments. Roger Sawyer, 'Casement by Hollywood', *The Sunday Press*, 25 March 1984. Casement's papers at PRONI include a copy of the screenplay.

327. **T. E. Lawrence ... penning a biography:** Reid, *The Lives of Roger Casement*.

327. **bronze statue:** Sculpted by Mark Richards, it exudes defiance and overlooks a popular bathing spot.

328. **Patrick Casement ... takes visitors:** Author visit to Magherintemple, July 2024.